Surburg's Works

Vol I
Luther/Reformation - Messianic Prophecy

Edited by
Herman J. Otten

LUTHERAN NEWS, INC., New Haven, Missouri

Surburg's Works

Library of Congress Card
Lutheran News, Inc.
684 Luther Lane
New Haven, MO 63068
Published 2017
Printed in the United States of America
IngramSpark, TN
ISBN #978-0-9864232-4-6

Table of Contents

Messianic Prophecy

Acknowledgements

Many thanks to Naomi Finck, who transferred all of these works of Dr. Raymond Surburg from the original articles, which first appeared in *Christian News*, and to the secretaries at the Missourian Publishers in Washington, Missouri, particularly Cathy Keller, who first set the type for the more than 170 articles Dr. Surburg sent to *Christian News,* and to Luke Otten, Managing Editor of *Christian News*, who made the arrangements for this printing.

Foreword

I had the privilege of taking numerous classes taught by Dr. Surburg. Therefore my comments are based on knowing Dr. Surburg during these seminary years.

Dr. Surburg was **brilliant.** He had two earned doctorates. He had numerous Master Degrees. He was fluent in multiple languages. When I knew him in his late 70's, he challenged himself to learn a language a month. He had a photographic memory. He could quote from memory the publisher's name, the year the book was published, and the page number of the book he was quoting.

Dr. Surburg was **faithful.** Faithful to God's Word and faithful to the Lutheran Confessions. He once stated that if being a fundamentalist meant believing in the inspiration of Scripture, then he was a fundamentalist. Of course, anybody who knew Dr. Surburg knew that he was anything but a fundamentalist. He stands in stark contrast to those who take a less than stellar stand on the inspiration of Scripture.

Dr. Surburg was **humble.** He always stated that he was not a scholar. If you read his writings, very seldom does he ever quote himself. I remember asking him that question one time in class, and he said he did not consider himself to be a scholar. This from a man who had two earned Doctorates and numerous Master Degrees.

Dr. Surburg wrote not just for pastors, but he also wrote for laymen; and he wrote in a style laymen can understand. Read through Dr. Surburg's writing: *The Summary of the Lutheran Hermeneutical Principles.* Any layman will realize why this is such an important Lutheran teaching. Laymen must not simply rely on their pastors. Laymen need to know how to defend their faith, too! We must educate our laymen, so that they, too, take a strong stand on God's Word.

Rev. Otten is once again to be commended for publishing the writings of Dr. Surburg. Rev. Otten's publishing of Dr. Kurt Marquart, and Dr. Surburg's writings are no doubt his greatest contributions to the Church. As you read Dr. Surburg's writings you will see the **brilliance,** the **faithfulness** and the **humble heart** of a faithful Confessor of Christ.

Rev. Ray R. Ohlendorf
Taylorsville, North Carolina
Christmas Day, 2016

Preface

This series of volumes on the writings of Raymond Surburg end with a tribute and reports at his death in 2001 which appeared in *Christian News*. Volume V concludes with the sermon preached at Surburg's funeral by Walter Maier III in the chapel of Concordia Theological Seminary, Ft. Wayne, Indiana.

Surburg's Works has letters Raymond Surburg sent to *Christian News* (*CN*) followed by the more than 170 articles this seminary professor mailed to *CN* for publication. The words on the cover with Surburg's photo are from a banner in his office which read "Raymond, I have called you by your name; you are Mine." They are taken from Isaiah 43:1, the text Dr. Walter Maier used for Surburg's funeral (Vol. V, p. 1864). More Surburg letters are interspersed with articles throughout the series. He regularly read not only books, but magazines and newspapers to keep informed. *Christian News* has a long history of reproducing articles by liberals with a response from a Christian theologian and scholar such as Raymond Surburg.

The future seminary professor met his wife when he was serving as a vicar at Saint Stephen's Lutheran Church, Bronx, New York, in 1931. When Surburg was the pastor of Bethlehem Lutheran Church in Brooklyn, New York, 1941-1954, the editor's father was a member of a calling committee at Messiah Lutheran in Manhattan which later merged with St. Matthew Lutheran. It's charter is dated 1664. It is often reported to be the oldest Lutheran Church in America. Dad Otten, who had painted in the homes of many pastors and professors, was impressed with Surburg's knowledge, scholarship, and books. He voted to have Surburg serve as pastor at Messiah-St. Matthew. The young scholarly Brooklyn pastor may have been too much of a confessional Lutheran for the majority, which, according to the editor's father, did not vote for Surburg.

The young Bronx and Brooklyn pastor did graduate work at Fordham University in the Bronx and Columbia University in Manhattan. The *CN* editor's home was not far from Fordham and like Surburg, he also studied on subway rides to Columbia University's graduate school. After Surburg's years in the Bronx and Brooklyn, the editor's father continued to appreciate the work of Raymond Surburg and Henry Koch, who had taught at Concordia College, Bronxville, New York.

Practical Helps for Pastors
There are sections on the Bible, Lutheranism, the Church Year and Music, Apologetics, Messianic Prophecy and Doctrine.

Surburg began his life's work as a pastor and then became a professor of future pastors. These volumes are loaded with vital helpful information for pastors preparing sermons, lectures, and Bible classes. Questions at the end of each article help make Surburg writings easy to use for

Bible class study.

October 31, 2017 marks the 500th Anniversary of the Reformation. These volumes with the writings of Raymond Surburg are a call to now go **"Back to the Bible, Luther and Old Missouri."** The Christian faith began in the Garden of Eden when man first believed that God would send a Messiah, Jesus Christ, to redeem man from sin (Genesis 3:15 and 4:1). Surburg recognized that Genesis 4:1 is properly translated as Martin Luther did: "Ich habe den Mann, den Herrn" and as William Beck's An American Translation did: "She said, 'I have gotten a man, the Lord.'" Surburg was a member of the revision committee of Beck's AAT. He shared Luther's and Beck's position on direct rectilinear Messianic prophecy. Surburg was also a member of The Lutheran Church-Missouri Synod's Commission on Theology and Church Relations (CTCR). He agreed with the writer of Hebrew's 2:9 and Luther that Psalms 8:4-6 refers to Jesus Christ. Now the LCMS's CTCR and the ESV promoted through CPH in most LCMS churches disagrees with Luther and says Psalm 8 does not refer to Jesus Christ.

Luther emphasized that Adam was the first Christian.

The Christian faith did not gradually evolve down through the centuries. It was directly revealed by God to man in the pages of Holy Scripture. True Lutheranism is nothing more nor less than Bible Christianity. In many of his articles Surburg shows that such theologians of "Old Missouri" as C.F.W. Walther, Francis Pieper, Theodore Laetsch, Paul E. Kretzmann, Walter Maier, Theodore Engelder, Ludwig Fuerbringer and George Stoeckhardt were faithful to the Bible, Martin Luther and the Lutheran Confessions. The theologians of "Old Missouri" did not affirm the inerrancy of the Bible in all matters and strongly oppose evolution because they were following "American Fundamentalism." Such heroes of American Fundamentalists as Charles Hodge and Benjamin Warfield, unlike the theologians of "Old Missouri," wavered on the inerrancy of the Bible and evolution. "Old Missouri" recognized that the Bible itself teaches it was inerrant in all matters and that God created man and the universe in six natural days as the Bible teaches.

Missouri's Battle for the Bible in the 1970's

Raymond Surburg began sending articles to *Christian News* at the time of the LCMS's great "Battle For the Bible" in the 1970's. He recommended the editor's *Baal or God*, published in 1965. This book showed why the position of the liberals was anti-scriptural. It defended the Mosaic authority of the Pentateuch, the unity of Isaiah, direct Messianic prophecy, the inerrancy of the Bible, the virgin birth, deity and physical resurrection of Jesus Christ.

Other publications were hesitating to take a stand against the liberal professors at Concordia Seminary who were denying the inerrancy of the Bible and promoting historical criticism of the Bible and evolution. Surburg came to the defense of the position of such recent graduates of Concordia Seminary, St. Louis, as Kurt Marquart and Herman Otten, who were challenging their liberal professors and defending "Old Missouri."

The LCMS momentarily won the "battle" in the 1970s. In 1973 at its convention in New Orleans the LCMS adopted Resolution 3-09. This long resolution declared that the theological position of those who formed Seminex in 1974 was false doctrine not to be tolerated within the LCMS.

Unfortunately, the officials of the LCMS did not follow through on 3-09 by disciplining the liberals. They were allowed to remain within the LCMS.

While the honest liberals left the LCMS, the majority of liberals remained. John Tietjen, President of Concordia Seminary and then Seminex, wrote in his *Memoirs in Exile – Confessional Hope and Institutional Conflict*, published by Fortress Press of the Evangelical Lutheran Church in America in 1990: "I am convinced that 40 percent of those in the Missouri Synod compromised their integrity rather than pay the price of following through on the principles to which they were committed. We at Seminex were continually tempted to back away from our convictions to ensure the financial support from our friends" (283-4).

Seminaries Today

Since the death of Raymond Surburg, professors at Concordia Seminary, St. Louis and elsewhere in the LCMS have promoted the destructive anti-scriptural notions of higher critics of the Bible even more than those who formed Seminex. The LCMS bureaucracy now wants peace at any price. It has been silent about what is really going on theologically in the LCMS. Most pastors are keeping the laymen ignorant. Few professors have the courage of Raymond Surburg to speak up.

Luther - Reformation

Current Lutheran Beliefs and Misbeliefs According to "A Study of Generations"

Christian News, February 19, 1973
(Reprinted from *The Springfielder*)

IN THE LAST TEN years, a number of sociological studies dealing with Lutherans have appeared in the United States. In 1968 R. Stark and C. Y. Glock issued *American Piety: the Nature of Religious Commitment*. The next year J. K. Hadden published *The Gathering Storm in the Churches*. In 1970 Walter Theophil Janzow made a study of the Lutheran Church-Missouri Synod's beliefs and practice, entitling his study, *Secularization in An Orthodox Denomination* (Available from the publisher, University Microfilms, Ann Arbor, Michigan). In the same year, Dr. Lawrence L. Kersten published *The Lutheran Ethic: The Impact of Religion on Laymen and Clergy*. Kersten's research was focused on the distinct characteristics of the religious ideology of four Lutheran denominations in southern Michigan. In Kersten's study the following branches of Lutheranism were involved: The Wisconsin Evangelical Lutheran Synod (WELS), the Lutheran Church-Missouri Synod (LCMS), the American Lutheran Church (ALC), and the Lutheran Church in America (LCA).

Dr. Kersten showed that Lutheranism has an ethic, developed by Martin Luther and the theologians that followed Luther, whose views are represented in the ecumenical creeds and in the Lutheran Confessions as given in the *Book of Concord* of 1580. The Michigan investigation

9

showed that a distinctly Lutheran orientation toward God, man, life, and religion was found to exist, especially when compared with Roman Catholicism, other forms of Protestantism and Judaism.

In 1972 a more ambitious type of religious research appeared, called *A Study of Generations*. It was sponsored and paid for by the Lutheran Brotherhood and published by Augsburg. This volume is based on over seven million pieces of data from 4,745 persons out of 316 congregations of the Lutheran Church in America, the American Lutheran Church and the Lutheran Church-Missouri Synod. It gives a religious profile of six million confirmed Lutherans belonging to 15,000 congregations.

The authors and collaborators of this nearly half-million dollar project are four social scientists, headed by Dr. Merton P. Strommen, president of Youth Research Center, Minneapolis, Minnesota, an educational psychologist, counselor and Lutheran clergyman. Assisting were the Rev. Milo L. Brekke, and Ralph Underwager, also members of the Youth Research Center, and Lutheran clergyman. Rev. Brekke is a doctoral candidate in educational psychology and Dr. Underwager has a doctorate in clinical psychology. The fourth member was Dr. Arthur L. Johnson, a professor of sociology at the University of Minnesota, and an active lay church leader. Time has said about this book ". . . seems assured of becoming a classic." Dr. George Elford, Research Director of the National Catholic Educational Association claims that *A Study of Generations* is "the best piece of religious research ever done." Dr. James E. Dittes of Yale University wrote in the Foreword: "Lutherans can be assured that their portrait has been drawn here sensibly and responsibly by a skilled team. The first thorough denominational portrait has set high standards for others to follow."

The authors wrote: "The task of assembling the information could be compared with the task of fitting together 7,000,000 pieces of massive jigsaw puzzle with the box cover picture missing. To minimize the subjective influence of the research team in assembling the data, empirical methods were used which would allow the data to organize themselves" (p. 286). Most of the 7,000,000 answers are said to have grouped themselves around 78 descriptive dimensions, which formed 14 factors.

Compared with the Glock research the controls employed by the four-man research team factored out many of the things that made the study of Glock deficient in that it had glaring over simplifications and generalities. Thus Glock equated prejudice and anti-Semitism with "orthodox" or conservative theology.

The publishers of *A Study of Generations* claim that it is the most complete study ever made of the personal beliefs, values, attitudes and behavior of a major religious group in the United States. The Lutherans who participated were between the ages of 15 and 65. There is in this book a storehouse of information for today's church leaders. This penetrating book transcends the usual measurement of a church's vitality-statistics, that usually give the assets, income, geographic location, membership and activities of individual or collective churches. Because of the sufficient magnitude of the research here for the first time revealed the diversity and general posture of what church members of three major Lutheran Church bodies value, believe and do.

A Study of Generations emphasis was in part a control to check age and educational differences against 740 items on the interviews. The four major generations are 15-29, 30-39, 40-49, 50-65. However, the subgenerations of youth: 15-18, 19-23, 24-29 were also significant to the study. Much of the study of youth verifies concepts developed by Erik Erkson's study of life cycles and especially his works on Luther and Ghandi.

This massive study gives answers to questions relating to the clergy-laity gap, outlines the tension factors between generations, sets forth the prejudices, behavior patterns, biblical knowledge, educational influence, mission concepts, social involvements, peer orientation, concepts about law and order and many other data.

The book was organized into four sections. Section I has three chapters. Chapter 1 gives the reason for the research study, while chapter 2 presents a general overview of the social characteristics of Lutherans, showing among other things the erroneous character of a number of Lutheran myths held till now. Chapter 3 deals with methodology and contains what might be termed a layman's introduction to statistics and sociological research. Section II has chapters 4-9. Chapter 4 states the beliefs and opinions with action in the manner of Simon's *Value and Teaching.* Chapter 5 deals with the heart of Lutheran piety. Chapter 6 is called: "Law-oriented Lutherans." Chapters 7 and 8 are closely related to the previous two chapters, dealing with mission and ministry and Lutheran life styles. Section III embraces the last three chapters of the volume. Chapter 10 shows how there is tension between the generations. Chapter 11 is entitled: "Slices of Diversity," and Chapter 12 gives a summary of the study. Section IV has three appendices, the first of which describes how the study was conducted. A bibliography and an index increase the utility of the volume.

It is impossible adequately to summarize the many interesting data supplied by Strommen and his associates. The reader is urged to buy, or somehow secure *A Study of Generations,* study and analyze the 400 pages of this sociological study of American Lutheranism. It constitutes a mine of information relative to Lutheranism at the end of the sixth decade and beginning of the seventh decade of the twentieth century.

In this article the focus of attention will be on the beliefs and misbeliefs of American Lutherans. The *Study* asserts that "the massive and decisive struggle in the last quarter of the twentieth century is going to be about beliefs, in every area of human activity the decisive questions are narrowing down to issues of belief" (p. 101).

A Study of Generations endeavors to answer questions like these: What is a Lutheran? What do Lutherans believe about God?, about Jesus Christ? Do Lutherans know what it means to be saved?

Do they understand and feel the Gospel? What is their understanding of justification by faith alone? What is the relationship between belief and prejudice?

The report of Strommen and his colleagues points out that such factors as age, occupation, level of education, sex or financial status determine a Lutheran's attitude toward belief and behavior. Most Lutherans are reported as accepting a transcendental view of life as their basic orientation. What a Lutheran values and believes will determine his behavior in the community and in the church.

The report claims that in general, most Lutherans choose a God-directed life over the self-directed life, the supernatural over the natural, dualism over monism. There are, however, a considerable number of Lutherans who by contrast emphasize the value of self-development. "Persons preoccupied with values of self-development place a high priority upon pleasure, personal freedom, physical appearance, achievement, and recognition, preferring the natural over the supernatural. They adopt a world view and life style that can become inimical to the purposes of the church. About one out of four rejects transcendental values in favor of the values of self-development" (p. 287). That means that 25% of Lutheranism is completely out of step with historic Lutheranism.

A Study of Generations further claims that "for most Lutherans faith in Jesus Christ is at the heart of what they value and believe. For them Christianity is to believe and know Christ; in that sense they believe and know the Gospel. This life orientation emerges as one of the most distinctive characteristics of a Lutheran" (p. 287). However, only 66% of Lutherans hold this position, thus indicating a radical departure from historic Lutheranism on the part 34% of today's Lutherans. Three out of every ten Lutherans doubt the divinity of Jesus Christ. Four out of ten Lutherans are not certain about the existence of God!

According to the interpretation of the four researchers most Lutherans would consider themselves conservatives in their theology and have accepted the historic doctrines of Lutheranism as set forth in the confessional writings of the *Book of Concord*. The Biblical accounts of the birth, death and resurrection of Christ are firmly held by most Lutherans. Other doctrines according to the report generally subscribed to by Lutherans are: the Bible as God's Word, the law of God as a guide and judge of men's lives; Christ's death as the atonement for sin. They believe in the gifts of the Spirit, Baptism, and the real presence in the Holy Communion, the Second Coming of Christ, the value of intercessory prayer.

Present Neglect of Important Doctrines

Some Biblical teachings, stressed by Lutheranism in the past, are now being neglected. According to the *Study* they are: the doctrines of eternal life, providence, and sanctification (p. 288). Some Lutherans classify themselves as fundamentalists while others claim they are liberals. While the term "fundamentalism" occurs repeatedly in the report, it is never defined.

Lutherans and Biblical Miracles

The Strommen Report shows that there are wide variations on many beliefs and attitudes to Christian behavior. About 33% of Lutherans do not believe in Biblical miracles as described in the Bible. The creation of the world by fiat command, the deliverance of Israel by the miracle of the parting of the waters of the Red Sea, the miracles of Elisha and Elijah, the incarnation of God as man, the resurrection of Christ, the ascension and second return could all be involved. 82% of the members of the LCMS believe the miracles the way they are said to have happened in the Bible, as compared with 69% in the ALC, and 61% in the LCA.

Lutherans and the Hereafter
Three of every ten Lutherans do not believe in a life after death. For these individuals the grave is the end of man's existence. This also means no heaven or hell.

Lutherans and Other Religions
Seven out of ten Lutherans believe that all religions lead to the same God, while four out of ten agree that all religions are equally important to God. These Lutherans are either ignorant or do not believe the claim of Christ: "I am the way the truth and the life, no man cometh unto the father but by me" (John 14;6) or the declaration of Peter: "And there is salvation in no one else, for there is no other name under heaven given among men by which we must be saved" (Acts 4:12, RSV).

Some Lutherans do not appear to be very consistent in their thinking. Thus according to the report "Three out of four Lutherans say all religions lead to the same *God,* yet three out of four Lutherans, and some of them must be the same people, say belief in Jesus Christ is absolutely necessary for salvation. Half of the respondents reject the statement that all religions are equally important before God, but only 13% agree that being ignorant of Jesus prevents salvation. Something very curious is going on (p. 169)." One solution to this discrepancy is that the preaching and religious instruction in the three major Lutheran Church bodies is defective or that opposing points of view on fundamental doctrines are being set forth in the pulpit and in the printed material to which Lutherans are exposed in their instructional programs. *The Gap of Generations* in commenting on this strange situation, says:

> The most we can say is that most Lutherans appear to say belief in Jesus is necessary FOR ME and the Christian faith is right and true FOR ME . They appear to reject statements implying the same for the other person. What this means for the traditional model of mission is not clear. It seems to imply that the mission sermon appealing for support for the salvation of the heathen is politely turned off by most Lutherans (p. 172).

Lutherans and Missions
In the past Lutheran Churches, like other Christian Churches took the missionary command of Christ seriously, namely, "to make disciples of all nations" (Matt. 28:20). Lutheran churches, both in Europe and America, were convinced that people needed to become converted in order to be saved Christians. The Lutheran Churches have sponsored and supported mission endeavors on the six continents and on many islands

found in the various oceans of the world. The report published by Augsburg Publishing House states that Lutherans are confused about the mission of the church. While they believe faith in Christ is a necessity for them, this is not the case for other people, who can reach God through the religion they have chosen. The authors of the report say about this type of thinking: "This may be called relativism or synergism. Whatever it is called, Lutherans are not likely to respond enthusiastically to the rallying cry, 'Evangelize the world!'" (p. 172).

The report took cognizance of the beliefs and attitudes of members of the Lutheran Church in America, The American Lutheran Church, and The Lutheran Church-Missouri Synod. The data furnished indicate that more lay members of the LCMS "tend toward a stronger conservative or even fundamentalist stance than do laymen in the ALC and LCA" (p. 269).

20% of the LCMS laity believe that if people of other countries are ignorant of Christ, that they cannot be saved. The same position is held by 10% of the members of the ALC and 8% of the LCA (Item 422).

Lutherans and the Devil

The devil is described in Holy Writ as the demonic personality that tempted Eve in Eden, that caused David to number the people, who tempted Jesus in the wilderness and who is active tempting and seducing people to sin. Luther and the Lutheran Confessions believe in Satan's reality and in his activities. Associated with the devil's existence is the corollary doctrine of evil angels who according to the New Testament on occasion took bodily possession of human beings. According to the report 75% of the members of the Missouri Synod believe in the Devil's reality, while only 50% of the ALC, and 33% of the LCA.

The Relationship Between Justification and Sanctification

Historic Lutheranism has emphasized the necessity of the correct relationship between justification and sanctification, Luther taught that justification occurred the moment a person believed that Jesus Christ had paid for his sins by His vicarious and substitutionary death upon the cross. This faith was created in the individual's heart by the Holy Spirit through the means of grace, either by the Word or the Sacraments. The moment a person's sins are forgiven he is declared righteous and he becomes a member of God's family. Salvation is 100% a gift of God, the forgiven sinner cannot contribute anything toward his justification and salvation. The report shows how serious misconceptions exist on this important matter in American Lutheranism. 33% of the members of the ALC indicate that loving your neighbor and doing good to others are absolutely necessary for salvation. More members of the LCMS (20%) definitely reject these assertions than do people affiliated with the ALC or LCA.

Lutherans and the Sacraments

Ninety-five percent of Lutherans state that faith, prayer, and Baptism are important to them. Only 5% claim that they are of little importance or of no importance. 54% state that Baptism is very important to them. However, only 28% "strongly agree" that in the Holy Communion we are given the true Body and Blood of Jesus for the forgiveness of sins.

Virgin Birth of Christ

Two Gospel passages set forth the truth that Mary became pregnant because the Holy Spirit brought about this condition in her womb. According to the report only 40% of Lutherans agreed with the statement: "Jesus was conceived by the Holy Spirit and born of the Virgin Mary" (p. 379). Historic Lutheranism has held to and confessed its belief in the deity of Christ, who is depicted in the New Testament as possessing the attributes of omniscience, omnipresence, and omnipotence. 56% of Lutherans reject Christ's omnipresence. According to John 1:3, Colossians 1:16 and Hebrews 1:2, Christ is set forth as the Creator of all that exists. Yet 54% of Lutherans who are supposed to draw their doctrines and beliefs solely from the Holy Scriptures, deny that Jesus Christ created everything.

A vital part of Christian doctrine is the correct understanding of the nature and purpose of Christ's death. One of the statements to which responses were requested was: "Jesus died for sinners. As a substitute, he suffered the just penalty due to us for sins in order to satisfy the wrath of God and to save guilty men from hell" (p. 379). Only 37% would strongly agree with this statement. Only 24% would assert about those people who deny the substitutionary death of Christ or disbelieve the Pauline statement about the nature of Christ's atoning death that they are not true Christians.

The Nature of the Scriptures

Historically Lutherans have recognized only one source for doctrine and ethical directives, the Holy Scriptures. That "the Bible is the Word of God, and that God inspired men to report verbally what he said. The Bible in the original text contained no errors," only 24% were willing to accept it in 1970.

The Method of Salvation

Two of the "solas" of the Lutheran Reformation were *sola gratia* and *sola fide*. Salvation is a gift of God and it is God's grace which prompted Him to create faith in people's hearts in Christ crucified. 59% believe that the main emphasis of the Gospel is on God's rules for right living (Scale 15, item 17, p. 369). 50% said: "God is satisfied if a person lives the best life he can" (p. 369). Half of the nearly 5,000 Lutherans interviewed hold that "God is satisfied if a person lives the best life he can." That at birth a person is neither good nor bad is the conviction of one-half of Lutheranism, a stance which conflicts with the Scripture on original sin and the statements in the Lutheran Confessions that subscribe to the doctrine of original sin. 44% believe that "Salvation depends upon being sincere in whatever you believe" (p. 369). 31% contend that "If I believe in God and do right, I will get to Heaven" (p. 369).

Lutherans and the Charismatic Movement

One of the great problems affecting Protestant and Lutheran Churches has been the charismatic movement in the last decade (1960 onward). Speaking with tongues and miraculous healing were practices and beliefs limited to the holiness churches and Pentecostal churches. Congregations have been divided, pastors have been expelled from some churches, others have resigned and formed their own churches. Some pastors are speaking about "Luthercostals," others are employing the term "Lutheran charisciples." On page 119 the *Strommen Report* informs us:

> The charismatic movement has had an impact on Lutheranism. Six percent are sure they have had an experience of speaking in tongues and 12% think they have. This compares with 12% who were willing to say that anyone who did not believe speaking in tongues should be practiced today was not a true Christian. An additional 15% agree that speaking in tongues should be practiced but aren't willing to say that a person who disagrees isn't a true Christian (Scale 44, Item 79). A significant minority of Lutherans are either involved in the charismatic movement or fairly receptive to it.

From other sources, we learn that Lutherans adopting the charismatic theology have shown a willingness to worship and cooperate with Roman Catholic, Reformed churches and even theological liberals. This of course condones erroneous teachings rejected by the Lutheran Confessions. The doctrine of baptism held by Pentecostals is not the understanding of this sacrament in the Confessions. Neo-Pentecostals do not hold that the Holy Spirit operates solely through the means of grace.

Indifference to doctrine and ignorance of Bible teaching could be the reason why two out of three Lutherans are ready for the merger of all Lutherans in one Lutheran Church in America, a dream that has been vigorously promoted for a number of years by leaders in all Lutheran denominations, except the Wisconsin Evangelical Lutheran Synod.

Again the writer asserts that *A Study of Generations* contains a wealth of information and only certain aspects of this study have been set forth. Since Lutheranism, however, has a definite ethic, it would not be out of place to call attention to some conclusions that can be made about the current Lutheran scene. The heart of Lutheranism can be succinctly stated in the four solas: *sola Scriptura, sola gratia, sola fide, solus Christus.*

For many Lutherans the Bible is not the Word of God and *the* source for obtaining a correct world view, but they allow philosophy, human reason or the current feelings and beliefs to determine their *Weltanschauung*. Millions of Lutherans are as bad off as the heathen, because like the latter they do not know the plan of salvation. Since for a significant minority Christ is not God, he cannot be a Savior. Many Lutherans deny the need for a Savior and believe in salvation by works. Again for at least one-fourth of Lutheranism this life constitutes man's existence.

Beliefs, attitudes and practices are determined by what people are taught or what they adopt from their secular reading and contacts with non-Lutherans. Indications are that the Lutheran religious press and many Lutheran seminaries have been partly responsible for many of the misbeliefs and doctrinal errors found in Lutheranism today.

Questions

1. J. K. Hadden published ____.
2. Lawrence L. Kersten published ____.
3. Who sponsored and paid for *A Study of Generations?* ____
4. The publishers of *A Study of Generations* claimed ____.
5. 25% of Lutheranism is completely out of step with ____.
6. Three out of every ten Lutherans doubt ____.
7. Four out of ten Lutherans are not certain about ____.
8. About 33% of Lutherans do not believe in Biblical ____.
9. Three out of every ten Lutherans do not believe in life after ____.
10. Seven out of ten Lutherans believe that all religions ____.
11. Only 13% agree that being ignorant about Jesus prevents ____.
12. Lutherans are confused about the ____ of the church.
13. According to the report, ____% of the members of the Missouri Synod believe in the Devil's reality, while only ___% of the members of the ALC, and ____% of the LCA.
14. Only 28% "strongly agree" that "in the Holy Communion we are given ____."
15. According to the report, how many Lutherans accept the virgin birth of Christ? ____
16. Only 54% of Lutherans deny that Jesus Christ ____.
17. What does the majority of Lutherans believe about the vicarious satisfaction of Jesus Christ? ____
18. How many Lutherans accept the inerrancy of the Bible? ____
19. What do half of the Lutherans believe about original sin? ____
20. How many Lutherans are involved in the charismatic movement? ____
21. The heart of Lutheranism can be succinctly stated in the four ____.
22. Millions of Lutherans are as bad off as the ____, because like the latter they do not know ____.
23. The Lutheran ___ and many Lutheran seminaries have been partly responsible for ____.

The "Identity Crisis" In American Lutheranism and The Lutheran Church-Missouri Synod

Christian News, July 26, 1976

Between 1970 and 1972 two sociological studies dealing with the beliefs and practices of Lutheranism in America have appeared and what they contain ought to cause many members of the Lutheran Church — Missouri Synod to think seriously about the status of American Lutheranism and what the relationship of our synod to it is. Professor Kersten of Eastern Michigan University published a sociological study entitled, *The Lutheran Ethic — The Impact of Religion on Laymen and Clergy.* Kersten's research was focused on the distinctive characteristics of the religious ideology of four Lutheran denominations in southern Michigan, in Kersten's study the following branches of Lutheranism were involved: The Wisconsin Evangelical/Lutheran Synod (WELS), the Lutheran Church—Missouri Synod (LCMS), the American Lutheran Church (ALC), and the Lutheran Church in America (LCA). The Kersten report showed that Lutheranism has an ethic, developed by Martin Luther and the theologians who followed Luther, whose views are represented in the ecumenical creeds (the Apostles Creed, the Nicene Creed, and the Athanasian Creed) and in the Lutheran Confessions as found in the *Book of Concord* of 1580. The Michigan investigation showed that a distinctly Lutheran orientation toward God, man, life and religion was found to exist, especially when compared with Roman Catholicism, the various Protestant denominations and Judaism.

In chapter 9 (pp. 204-222) Kersten presents the findings of his study. The difference among Lutherans that once characterized earlier twentieth century Lutheranism still exists. Dr. Kersten concludes: "In addition to large scale disagreements on basic Christian beliefs, Lutherans show differences on such fundamentals as the role, nature, purpose, and function of the institution of religion" (p. 204).

The reader is encouraged to secure Dr. Kersten's book and to read it carefully. All of his conclusions cannot be presented in this brief article. According to Kersten's study on the matter of ecumenical involvement, 81 per cent of the LCA clergy would like to see all Lutherans merged into one body; 70 percent of the ALC and 46 per cent of the LCMS would favor merger; 60 percent of the LCA clergy consider "all American Protestant religions as equally good." Liberal Lutherans also favor joining other Protestants in church work.

The Detroit Study indicates that in Lutheranism there is a trend away from supernaturalism to a religion dominated by a humanistic orientation toward life (p. 208). Ninety percent of the ALC clergy do not consider the Bible entirely true; only five percent in the ALC accepts the complete truthfulness and reliability of the Scriptures. More than 75 percent of the LCA clergy do not accept the Virgin Birth as a necessary doctrine.

Nearly 33 percent of the LCA clergy do not believe that faith in Jesus is necessary for salvation. Nearly half of the ministers of the LCA, ALC and LCMS hold that correct conduct is more important than religious beliefs. Concerning this doctrinal change reflected in the Detroit Study, Kersten concludes: "Thus, the theological modernism which affected most other Protestant bodies early in this century apparently now has permeated Lutheranism. The fact that the trends are stronger among the clergy, usually the defenders of the faith, is very significant for the future of Lutheranism (p. 208)."

Although at present the Lutheran Church (LCMS) is still strongly conservative, the younger clergy show trends that reflect a liberal and humanistic attitude toward religion and ethics. Dr. Kersten predicts (p. 211) that within twenty years there will be a merger of the LCMS Church with the liberal churches of Lutheranism. This was written before the New Orleans and Anaheim Conventions of the LCMS which has endeavored to reverse and stop the liberalistic trend that had been taking over as a result of a theological and teacher education at the LCMS' terminal schools and a number of junior colleges.

It is Kersten's contention that as a result of the growth of theological liberalism, the Lutheran Churches in America may face some very serious problems in the years ahead. As Modernism takes over, traditional forms of religious commitment are being surrendered. Attending church, working for missions, participation in evangelistic efforts and becoming involved in religious programs of education will be considered unimportant. As a result of this diminishing interest in these matters, the financial support of the church and its program will suffer seriously.

In 1972 a much more ambitious type of religious research appeared, called *A Study of Generations.* It was sponsored and paid for by the Lutheran Brotherhood and published by Augsburg Publishing House of Minneapolis. This volume claims to be based on over seven million pieces of data from 4,745 persons out of 316 congregations of the LCA, the ALC, and the LCMS. It claims to give a religious profile of six million confirmed Lutherans belonging to 15,000 congregations.

If it were possible for Luther to arise from his grave today, he would be surprised and shocked as to what the beliefs and practices of millions of Lutherans are who are now called after his name. Again the reader is encouraged to secure this 411 page volume and examine the evidence for himself and see firsthand what the situation in American Lutheranism as it is reflected in this definitive study, hailed by many as the best of all the sociological studies on religion which have been thus far produced. J. K. Luoma, a Roman Catholic scholar, in volume 16 of *The New Catholic Encyclopedia* (1975), which endeavors to update articles appearing in the 15 volumes of the *New Catholic Encyclopedia,* has given his evaluation of current Lutheranism based on *The Study of Generations.* In writing about the Lutheranism in America, Luoma made this assertion:

Thus, *The Study of Generations* seems to underline what James A. Scherer has called the "identity crisis" in contemporary Lutheranism, i.e. the total linkage of Lutheranism with certain formulations of ritual observances. Paradoxically, the study indicates that Lutheranism is most identifiably so, at least in the mind of many of its adherents, precisely at the point where the reformers said there should be greatest liberty. If real unity is to characterize Lutheranism, **it is obvious that its members must be brought to a clearer understanding of their own confessions, especially the principle of justification by grace** (p. 265 of Vol. 16).

Traditionally Lutheranism has held the four solas, **sola Scriptura, sola gratia, sola fide and solus Christus.** Only the Scriptures are the source and norm for doctrine and practice. It is only by the grace of God that man can be saved. It is only through saving faith in Christ's atoning death that men can be declared righteous in God's sight. Christ is the only Savior, faith in his atoning blood, shed for the sins of the world, is the only God-acceptable means and way of salvation.

The Study of Generations focuses on beliefs and practices of American Lutherans. The Study asserts that "the massive and decisive struggle in the last quarter of the twentieth century is going to be about beliefs. In every area of human activity the decisive questions are narrowing down to issues of belief" (p. 101).

The report claims that in general most Lutherans choose a God-directed life over the self-directed life, the supernatural over the natural, dualism over monism. There are, however, a considerable number of Lutherans who by contrast emphasize the value of self-development. Thus the report asserts:

> Persons preoccupied with values of self-development place a high priority upon pleasure, personal freedom, physical appearance, achievement, and recognition, preferring, the natural over the supernatural. They adopt a world view and life style that can become inimical to the purposes of the church. About one out of four rejects transcended values in favor of the values of self-development (p. 287).

This means that 25% of Lutheranism is completely out of step with historic Lutheranism and Biblical teaching.

A Study of Generations further claims that "for most Lutherans faith in Jesus Christ is at the heart of the way they value and believe and know Christ; in that sense they believe and know the Gospel. The life orientation emerges as one of the most distinctive characteristics of a Lutheran" (p. 287).

However, only 66% of Lutherans hold this position, thus indicating a radical departure from historic Lutheranism on the part of 34% of today's Lutherans. That certainly cannot be said to be an insignificant and unimportant number. *The Study* shows that one out of every three Lutherans doubt the divinity of Jesus Christ. Four out of ten Lutherans are not certain about the existence of God.

The statistics and findings of the report are shocking in what they reveal. Thus seven out of ten Lutherans believe that all religions lead to the same God. What does this do to Christ's claim: "I am the way and the truth and the life, no man cometh unto the father but by me" (John 14:6). Or the declaration of Peter: "Neither is there salvation in any other or

20

any other name under heaven by which man can be saved" (Acts 4:12).

Some Lutherans do not appear to be very consistent in their thinking. Thus according to the report: "Three out of four Lutherans say all religions lead to the same, yet three out of four Lutherans, and some of them must be the same people, say belief in Christ is absolutely necessary for salvation. Half of the respondents reject the statement that all religions are equally important before God, but only 13% agree that being ignorant of Jesus prevents salvation. Something very curious is going on" (p. 169).

Lutherans have always supported missionary endeavors, in harmony with Christ's Great Commission (Matt. 28:20). The report published by Augsburg states that Lutherans are confused about the mission of the church. About this the report asserts: "This may be called relativism or synergism. Whatever it is called, Lutherans are not likely to respond enthusiastically to the rally cry, 'Evangelize the world!'"

The Bible and the Lutheran Confessions teach the existence of the Devil and of evil angels. Jesus was tempted by the Devil and the New Testament depicts Satan as seducing people to sin. According to the report, 75% of the members of the LCMS, 50% of the ALC and 33% of the LCA only believe in the Devil's reality.

Both the *Kersten Report* and the *Study of Generations* show that the evaluation of Luoma is correct when he wrote: "If real unity is to characterize Lutheranism, it is obvious that its members must be brought to a clearer understanding of their own confessions, especially the principle of justification by grace." (p. 265).

Historic Lutheranism, following Paul and Luther, held that man cannot save himself. Furthermore, man can contribute nothing toward his salvation; the believer's salvation is due purely to the grace of God. Yet the Kersten Study shows some disconcerting evidence in this matter. Thus 60% in the LCA hold that people are saved by keeping the Ten Commandments, 59% hold this in the ALC, and 54% in the LCMS and 46% in the WELS. Only 22% in the LCA believe that man plays, no part in his salvation, 33% in the ALC, 73% in the LCMS, and 93% in WELS. Concerning this, Dr. Kersten wrote:

> The response to the question on the Ten Commandments reveals definite problems between the clergy and the laity in interpreting the Lutheran concepts of salvation. More than half of the laymen think that people are saved by keeping the Ten Commandments. In contrast the clergy show great unanimity in holding Justification by faith apart from the keeping of the Law (pp. 157-158).

According to *A Study of Generations,* 59% of those who responded to the questionnaire stated that "the main emphasis of the Gospel is on God's rule for right living" (p. 369). Nearly 60% of Lutheranism does not understand the true difference between Law and Gospel. According to the Bible the Gospel tells men and women what God has done for their salvation; salvation is bestowed 100% as the gift of God. By keeping the Law perfectly all His existence in thought, word and deed   and by suffering the punishment of mankind's sins, Jesus has reconciled man to God.

Questions

1. Kersten's study showed that in Lutheranism there is a trend away from ____.
2. Younger clergy show a trend toward ____.
3. *A Study of Generations* was paid for by ____ and published by ____.
4. Traditionally Lutheranism has held the four ____.
5. *The Study* showed that one out of three Lutherans doubt ____.
6. Four out of ten Lutherans are not certain about the ____.
7. Seven out of ten Lutherans believe that all religions lead ____.
8. The studies show that Lutherans must be brought to a clearer understanding of ____.
9. More than half of the Lutheran laymen believe that people are saved by ____.
10. Nearly 60% of Lutheranism does not understand ____.

The Interpretation of The Bible

The Relationship of Luther, The Lutheran Confessions and The Lutheran Church-Missouri Synod to the Historical-Grammatical Method

Christian News, May 9, 1977

The existence of many different denominations and sects, although all purport to base their theological tenets on the Bible, has been a source of great perplexity to Christian and non-Christian students of the religious life of the past and present. While a number of reasons have been advanced for this situation, one of the underlying causes has been correctly stated by Burrows when he wrote: "Wrong methods of interpretation and use have prevented Christians hitherto from arriving at any unity in their understanding of the Scriptures."[1]

There is no error of the human mind which has not claimed support for itself in some Scripture passage. Polygamy, slavery, racial discrimination, and a host of abnormal and absurd religious developments have all used the Bible as a basis for their contention.[2] The conclusions which religionists have deduced from Holy Writ have determined the manner in which they have handled Scripture.[3] Even such anti-Christian cults as Christian Science, Mormonism, Spiritualism, and Millennial Darwinism adduce Scriptural warrant for their religious systems.

It goes beyond question that the Bible was not given to have multifarious and variegated meanings or to cause confusion in the minds of its readers.[4] As sane men, the writers of the Scriptures must have had a single, definite, and clear-cut meaning in mind at the time they penned their books. It is, therefore, unreasonable to assume that a Biblical writer did not understand his own words and meant them to be construed in a double sense. Thus it can be asserted, on the basis of the Bible self-testimony concerning its perspicuity that there can be but one system of related and interdependent revelation in God's Word.[5] Although Calvinism, Arminianism, Romanism, Lutheranism, and various forms of Millennialism build their respective theological systems on the Scriptures, they certainly cannot all be correct in the doctrines in which they differ and in which they sometimes are even diametrically opposed to each other. These widely divergent and contradictory systems of dogmatical formulations emphasize the fallibility even of sincere men when handling the Bible and clearly show that there is no unity on the principles underlying sound interpretation. The assertion of Christian Preus is true when he wrote: "The urgent need of Protestantism is agreement, not so much in polity or practice, nor even in the doctrine, but in principles of interpretation."[6]

The divisions and polarization which currently characterize the Lutheran Church-Missouri Synod are not merely caused by a clash in personalities, but are primarily one of interpretation, resulting in different understanding of the Bible.[7] Much in the last years has been written about the historical-critical method, a method not employed in the history of orthodox Lutheranism, nor in the exegetical history of the Lutheran Church—Missouri Synod, as may be seen from official synodical doctrinal resolutions. In this essay the historical-grammatical method and its presuppositions will be set forth and it will be shown that this interpretative methodology,[8] employed by Luther and the authors of the Lutheran Confessions as embodied in the *Book of Concord*, is the one followed in our Synod in contradistinction from the historical-critical method, whose usage has divided the Synod.

The presuppositions of the historical-grammatical method were a part of the hermeneutics of the Lutheran Confessions and the hermeneutics of the Lutheran Church-Missouri Synod since its inception in 1847.

The majority of books that give the history of hermeneutics do not have a special section treating of the historical-grammatical method. The Christian Church has been interpreting the Bible for over 1900 years. In the course of that history various schools of interpretation have appeared upon the scene, which have differed significantly from each other and consequently resulted in different understandings and promulgations of what the Bible taught on specific subjects and doctrines.[9]

Early in the postapostolic period allegory entered the church as a method of Scriptural interpretation.[10] Fourfold meaning for each passage was predicted in the Early Church and after Augustine's time allegorism controlled the interpretation of the Bible.[11] In addition the authority of the Church became supreme requiring of all Church people to accept the interpretations of the magisterium of the Church of Rome.[12] Without the aid of tradition, Roman Catholic doctrines could often not be seen by any stretch of the imagination as Biblically based. In addition, the Vulgate of Jerome became the definitive text, which determined the doctrines and morals of people, and as such were to be taught in the Church.[13] Furthermore, the Roman Catholic Church had adopted a number of Apocrypha as additional deutero-canonical books.[14] There were of course some exceptions. The School of Antioch emphasized the literal and historical interpretation, but this school was a part of the Eastern branch of Christendom.[15] In Paris there was the school of the Victorines which took a position against that of the basic hermeneutical position of the Western Church of their day.[16] Nicholas of Lyra also sponsored hermeneutical views that later on influenced Luther.[17]

However, it was in the sixteenth century that a hermeneutical revolution was sponsored mainly by Martin Luther, a movement that changed the course of church history and led to the breakup of the unity of Western Christianity.[18] The Protestant Reformation would have been impossible apart from an hermeneutical revolt. The sole authority of the Church was challenged when Luther found and advocated his Sola Scriptura principle, namely, that the Word of God and only the Word of God establishes doctrine.[19] Luther advocated the stance: "The Scriptures are not under the Church but the Church is under the Bible." Furthermore, Luther realized that permitting the Scriptures to have four possible different meanings made of the Bible a waxen nose, which could be given any shape desired.[20] Luther, Calvin and other Protestant reformers reject the allegorical method and insisted that a Bible passage has one intended sense.[21] With the abandonment of the allegorical system and the principle that the Church alone has the right to determine the meaning of the Scriptures, a new era began in theology and in the history of the Church. The Protestant movement cost the Church of Rome the loss of millions of adherents and resulted in the development of a different system of hermeneutics from that which had obtained for over a thousand years in Western Christianity and as well in the history and hermeneutical practice as employed in Eastern Orthodox Churches, of which the see of Constantinople was the head.

Luther, we may say, was a proponent in essence of the historical-grammatical method. The historical-grammatical method was refined and improved after the sixteenth century. Professor Terry lived most of his life before the twentieth century, a century which saw a more complex development of the historical-critical method than the critical method in use in Terry's lifetime, which existed in less developed form in his day, because of form criticism, as propounded by Gunkel and then adopted in 1919 by Dibelius and Bultmann in the *New Testament Studies*, or redaction criticism developed especially since 1945, argued that of all interpretative methods to appear on the stage of church history, from apostolic times till the end of the nineteenth century, the historical-grammatical was the best. Thus he wrote:

In distinction from the above-mentioned methods of interpretation, we may name the Grammatico-Historical as the method which most fully commends itself to the judgment and conscience of Christian scholars. Its fundamental principles is to gather from the Scriptures themselves the precise meaning which the writers intended to convey. It applies to the sacred books the same principles, the same grammatical process and exercise of common sense and reason, which we apply to other books. The grammatico-historical exegete, furnished with suitable qualifications, intellectual, educational, and moral, will accomplish the claims of the Bible without prejudice or adverse prepossession, and, with no ambition to prove him true or false, will investigate the language and import of each book with fearless independence. He will master the language and import of the writer, and particular dialect which he used and his peculiar style and manner of expression. He will inquire into the circumstances under which he wrote, the manner and customs of his age, and the purpose or object which he had in view. He has a right to assume that no sensible author will be knowingly inconsistent with himself, or seek to bewilder and mislead his readers.[22]

Luther and the Reformers insisted that the Scriptures should be studied in the original languages, Hebrew[23] and Aramaic (Ezra and Daniel) and Greek in the New Testament. The Northern Renaissance contributed to the hermeneutics developed and employed by Luther, Calvin, Zwingli, John Knox and other reformers. Erasmus published the first Greek New

Testament in modern times in 1516. By Luther's time the entire Bible in its original languages was available, for a Hebrew Old Testament had been printed by 1494. Some of Luther's basic principles were the following: 1) The Scriptures are a unique book because the Holy Spirit was their author. In *The Table Talk* he is reported as saying: "We ought not to criticize the Scriptures, or judge the Scriptures by our mere reason, but diligently, with prayer, meditate upon them and seek their meaning (On God's Word, IV)."[24] Because the Bible was inspired Luther contended: "The Bible should be regarded with wholly different eyes from those which we view other productions (On God's Word, IX)."[25] 2) The authority principle of Luther — Ramm states as follows: "The Bible is the supreme and final authority in theological authority. Its teaching cannot be countermanded nor qualified nor substantiated to ecclesiastical authorities whether of persons or documents."[25a] The literal principle was promoted, defended and employed by Luther.[26] The Scholastics had developed their hermeneutics into two divisions: literal and spiritual. The latter was divided into the allegorical, anagogical, and topological, Luther contended for the primacy of the literal. Dean Farrar quoted Luther as holding: "The literal sense of Scripture alone is the whole essence of faith and of Christian theology."[27] C.A. Briggs cited Luther as writing: "Every word should be allowed to stand in its natural meaning and that should not be abandoned unless faith forces us to it."[28]

The literal meaning was to be based on no translation like Vulgate but upon the original languages of the Bible. Luther gave the following advice: "While a preacher may preach Christ with edification though he may be unable to read the Scriptures in the originals, he cannot expound or maintain their teaching against the heretics without this indispensable knowledge."[29] It is generally acknowledged that Luther played an important role in sponsoring the revival of Hebrew and Greek studies.

Luther sponsored what Ramm called "the historical and grammatical principle." This principle is inseparable from the literal principle. Luther claimed that the interpreter must give attention to grammar. In addition, the exegete must know about the historical background of a Biblical book or any portion of it; have a knowledge of the times, circumstances and the conditions of the author of the book which are necessary for correct interpretation.[30] Connected with the historical-grammatical method is the law of the context.

Luther took the stance that the ordinary Biblical reader could understand the true meaning of the Scriptures because they were intended by the Holy Spirit to be understood. The Wittenberg Reformer held that the average believer could understand the Bible because it is a clear book. Protestantism holds to the perspicuity of the Scriptures. Luther associated the clarity of Scriptures with the general priesthood of all believers. Therefore, the Bible was not the private domain of the Church, but the property of all believers.[31]

Inasmuch as the Bible was a book sufficiently clear by all to be understood, the Christian was under no obligation to accept the interpretations of the Church, if they contradicted the Scriptures.

Since the Bible was given by inspiration of the Holy Spirit, it was in a unique class as compared with all other books in the world. The Bible is in a class by itself. Scripture interprets Scripture.[32] When obscurities or dark passages were found in the sixty-six canonical books, the Roman Catholic interpreter is referred to the Church for its understanding of the verse or verses; Luther, on the other hand, shuts the interpreter up to the confines of the Bible itself. Before and at Luther's time much of Biblical exposition was a study of patristics and a study of the so-called catenae, collections of statements from the Church Fathers on a given passage.[33] In his controversy with Dr. Eck, Luther complained: "I ask for Scriptures and Eck offers me the Fathers. I ask for the sun, and he shows me his lantern. I ask: 'Where is your Scripture proof?' and he adduces Ambrose and Cyril. . . With all due respect to the Fathers, I prefer the authority of the Scriptures."[34]

Luther believed in the organic, theological unity of the Bible. The analogy of faith became for Luther and the other authors of the Lutheran Confessions an important hermeneutical principle. "All relevant material on a given subject was to be collected together so that the pattern of divine revelation concerning that subject would be apparent."[35]

For Luther the end of all interpretation was to find Christ and help individuals come to faith in Jesus Christ as their personal Savior from all sin and prepare men, women and children someday to be with Christ in the everlasting blissful habitations. Christ's coming was foretold already in the Garden of Eden immediately after Eve and Adam had eaten of the forbidden tree (Gen. 3:15). For Luther the entire Bible was a Christian book.[36] In the Old Testament there were many prophecies about the Messiah, which were fulfilled in Jesus of Nazareth, whom the Jews crucified, but whom God had raised from the dead on the third day.[37]

Luther held to the verbal and plenary inspiration of the Bible. "Critical scholars claim that Luther took a very free view of the Bible and did not hesitate to reject assertions that were not to his liking. These same scholars contend that Luther did not hesitate to reject or question Scriptural statements that did not affect a Christological interpretation of the Word of God. However, it is necessary to distinguish between views in Biblical criticism and a hermeneutical principle. That Luther held to the verbal inspiration of the Bible, Ramm claims, is crystal clear and for Luther this was a hermeneutical principle."[38]

The proper distinction between Law and Gospel was another hermeneutical rule followed especially by Luther as compared with other Protestant reformers.[39] According to Luther the heresy of the Galatians, adding something to the Gospel as necessary for salvation, was the root heresy of the Roman Catholic Church in Luther's time.[40] Ramm has described the parallel between the situation in Paul's day and in Luther's time as follows:

The Galatians had been taught to (i) be circumcised the seal of the Old Testament Covenant and (ii) to believe in Christ-the center of the New Covenant, and they would be saved. The Catholic Church taught that (i) to do religious works, and (ii) believe that Christ would save

27

them. Justification by faith alone not only repudiated the Judaizers of the Gospel, but the Roman Catholic system of salvation (p. 56, 57).[41]

Law and Gospel must be properly distinguished; any fusion between Law and Gospel was erroneous. Here the difference between Lutheranism, Roman Catholicism and the Reformed churches was pronounced. Either the Law/Gospel was made a new Law or there was the complete repudiation of the Law (anti-nomianism). This is a problem to this day. Law stated what God demanded of man and threatened condemnation for failure to live up to it; while the Gospel announced the good news of what God through the vicarious death of Christ had done for man and that forgiveness of sins was available without money or price. Gospel and Social Gospel are really contradictory terms.

Calvin and Luther essentially agreed on their hermeneutical principles. Like Luther, Calvin ruled out the allegorical method of interpretation.[42] Calvin termed the allegorical method Satanic because by its use men were led away from the true meaning of God's Word. "Scripture interprets Scripture" was a basic rule of interpretation.[43] Involved in its application were a number of interpretative procedures. For one thing it meant literalism in exegesis with a repudiation of the Medieval system of the four-fold sense of the Bible. It further involved the listening to what the text said, not reading something into the text in order to support some preconceived doctrinal idea. His insistence on "Scripture interprets Scripture" led Calvin to make much of grammatical exegesis, philological work, and the necessity of observing the context, and also comparing topics in the Bible which dealt with each other. Ramm claims that Calvin rejected with most, Catholic principles of interpretation, but refused to support any exegesis of orthodox doctrine if it was not solidly found in the text.[44]

The Hermeneutical Principles of the Lutheran Confessions

Luther and Melanchthon authored five of the six Symbols found in the *Book of Concord*. The hermeneutical principles outlined as Luther's are also found as the principles of interpretation that determined the exposition of the Scripture on which the doctrinal positions are based not only in Luther's two Catechisms, the *Augsburg Confession* and the *Apology* of the *Augsburg Confession*s and the Smalcald Articles but also the longest of the symbols, the *Formula of Concord*. Since 1580 Lutheranism in Europe had a variegated history. The age of orthodoxy, the age of pietism, the era of rationalism, the period of Kantian influence on Lutheran theology in the eighteenth century, idealism and Hegelianism in the nineteenth century, evolutionism, existentialism, process philosophy of the twentieth have witnessed different attitudes regarding the Lutheran Confessions and the hermeneutics underlying the interpretation of its doctrines. Nearly 400 years have elapsed since the adoption of the *Book of Concord* and during those four hundred years the pendulum has swung from a complete acceptance of their teaching to the position that these writings are interesting as documents in a history that has constantly changed, moved by the worldview that happened to have won the favor of men at a given time in world history.[45]

For the founders of The Evangelical Synod of Missouri, Ohio and other States who accepted the six confessional writings that comprise the *Book of Concord*, the Bible was the **norma normans** and the Lutheran symbols the **norma normata**.[46] This was the position of the organizers of the Synod in 1847 in Chicago. Missouri's founding fathers were violently opposed to all forms of rationalism, which is and was a component of the historical-critical method as generally defined and practiced by its advocates.[47]

The attitude of the interpreter toward the nature of Holy Scriptures will materially influence his principles of Biblical interpretation. Bohlmann asserted concerning this matter: "If the Scriptures are regarded as some sort of esoteric language, the interpreter is likely to follow some rather bizarre interpretative techniques. If he sees the Scriptures merely as the word of men written at different times and in different languages, he will adopt only such interpretative techniques as are common to the exposition of any piece of literature. If, on the other hand, he sees the Scriptures as God's own word, his interpretative techniques will reflect this unique factor."[48]

The Lutheran Confessions have no article on the doctrine of the Scriptures, because belief in the divine inspiration, infallibility, and authority of the Bible was the common property of Roman Catholicism, Calvinism and Lutheranism.[49] Since church confessions are primarily concerned with controverted issues, there was no need to set forth an article on the nature of the Holy Scriptures. Fagerberg states: "Als die BK (Bekenntnisschriften) verfasst wurden, war die Auctoritat des Bibelwortes in keiner Weise ein Problem, sondern wurde auf beiden Seiten der konfessionellen Grenzlinie anerkannt."[50]

Because the Holy Scriptures were inspired by the Holy Spirit, divine authorship and divine authority were concepts not to be separated in the Lutheran Confessions. The divine authorship is the basic reason according to the Confessions for their reliability.[51] In the *Large Catechism* Luther wrote "that God does not lie" (IV 57) and "God's Word does not err" (IV 57). Therefore Luther urges: "Believe the Scriptures. They will not lie to you (LC V 76)." *The Formula* rejects errancy as a false opinion because "in this way it would be taught that God, who is eternal Truth, contradicts himself" (SD XI 35). The preface to the *Book of Concord* describes the Scriptures as the "pure, infallible, and unalterable Word of God."[52]

As far as the confessors were concerned the Holy Scripture is Christocentric, that its contents from beginning to end deal with justification of the sinner for Christ's sake through faith.[53] Thus *Apology* states: "The promise of Christ . . . either when it promises forgiveness of sins, justification, and eternal life" (AP IV 5). The belief that the O.T. testifies to Christ results in the confessional writers treating many texts Christologically.[54]

The Holy Scriptures, Old and New Testaments, God's Word to us about Christ is clear and understandable (gemeinverstandlich). The Scriptures are perspicuous for the authors of the Lutheran symbols.[55] The Holy Scriptures are portrayed in the Confessions as literary documents; although God is the primary author He yet employed human writers and this fact has implications for Biblical interpretation. How are the Holy Scriptures, God's clear Word about Jesus Christ to us, to be interpreted? The Confessions give basically one answer: through the grammatical-historical method. To enthusiasts of every stripe "who boast that they possess the Spirit without and before the Word and who therefore judge, interpret, and twist the Scriptures or spoken Word according to their pleasure" (SA-III VIII 3), the Lutheran Symbols assert that God's message does not lie behind or above or apart from the Word but in the Word.[56]

The basic principle of interpretation for the authors of the Confessions was: "Derive the meaning from the text." This hermeneutical principle is patent especially in the *Apology's* arguments of the exegesis of the *Roman Confutation*. The Romanists were criticized because of a selective use of texts, for twisting and distorting the Scriptures to achieve their own purposes and goals. Melanchthon criticized the Roman exegetes for slovenly, careless, illogical and sometimes dishonest interpretation. Sometimes they omitted a word and the central thought as well. They garbled the text, putting passages out of context. A study of the actual exegesis of the Confessions will reveal that its authors took very seriously the principle of deriving the meaning from the text of Scriptures. The appeal through the symbols is: what does Paul say? Where does the Scripture say this?

The Confessions were greatly concerned for many aspects of grammatical exegesis. They allude to the importance of word study and usage.[57] Attention is given to words like "justification," "faith," "Gospel," "repentance" and other key theological terms.[58] Particular attention is oft given to a single word in a passage. Melanchthon carefully explains the force of the word "judge" in I Cor. 11:32 (Ap. XII 163). Much weight is attached to such particles as "Alone," "Freely," "Not of works," "It is a gift," in passages dealing with justification. In Apol. IV 312 Melanchthon stresses the distinction between the words, "faith," and "hope." In the LC III 113 Luther appeals to the original text: In the Greek this petition reads, "Deliver or keep us from the Evil One, or the Wicked One." There are a number of passages in the Confessions where the literary context and historical setting are stressed.[59]

Another major rule of the hermeneutics practiced by the authors of the Lutheran Symbols was: "Seek the native sense of the text."[60] According to Farrar the insistence of the Lutheran Reformation that every passage of Holy Scripture has but one simple sense was a major breakthrough in the history of Biblical interpretation. Nowhere in the Confessions is the appeal to the native sense more evident than in the Reformer's interpretation of the Lord's Supper, especially in the understanding of the words of institution. In the *Large Catechism* Luther said: "Here we shall take our stand and see who dares to instruct Christ and alter what he has spoken. . . For as we have it from the lips of Christ, so it is; he cannot lie or deceive" (v 13f).

Still another principle of interpretation employed by Luther, Melanchthon and the authors of the *Formula of Concord* is: "Let Scripture interpret itself."[61] The classic formulation **Scriptura Sacra sui ipsius interpres** is evident in Luther's writings as early as 1519. This same principle is sometimes called "the analogy of faith."[62] This was a principle that was used by a number of scholars before Luther's time. In a general way, the principle that an interpreter uses the writings of a given author to explain statements in a book is a principle of general literature. That Scripture interprets Scripture is associated with the clarity of Scripture and with the fact that God is the author of all the books of the Bible and that the Scriptures were authored by God suggests that the principle **Scriptura Sacra sui ipsius interpres** is simply an extension of the general hermeneutical principle of grammatical interpretation that any passage must be considered and explained in terms of its context. For any Bible passage the context is ultimately the entire Scripture.[63] That the "context" of Scripture can give a true explanation of any passage rests on the fact of its divine authorship, by virtue of which Scripture is held to be in agreement with itself. [64]In harmony with this is the principle that passages dealing with the same matter (parallelismus realis) can be employed to explain or corroborate each other. In accordance with this hermeneutical rule, the Reformers expounded Old Testament passages in the light of the New, the New Testament being the clearer portion of Holy Writ.[65]

This principle that Scripture interprets itself is also employed to explain passages where the meaning is obscure or difficult of comprehension. This principle is utilized, for example, in connection with the understanding of the Law:

> Whenever law and works are mentioned, we must know that Christ, the mediator, should not be excluded. He is the end of the law (Rom. 10:4), and he himself says, "Apart from me you can do nothing" (John 15:5). By this rule as we have said earlier, all passages on works can be interpreted (p. 372).[66]

From the principle that Scripture interprets itself the Lutheran Symbol writers believed it was legitimate to use deductions, inferences, or analogies based on Scripture.[67] Articles VII and VIII of the *Formula of Concord*, dealing with the Lord's Supper and the Person of Christ use this principle a number of times.[68] There are also occurrences of its employment in other confessional writings.

An important principle, although some claim it is a presupposition, is the Law-Gospel distinction. Thus the *Formula of Concord* has the following famous statement:

> The distinction between Law and Gospel is an especially brilliant light which serves the purpose that the Word of God may be rightly divided and the writings of the holy prophets and apostles may be explained and understood correctly (eigentlich erklart und verstanden). FC SD V 1.[69]

31

Again:

The article of justification is of special service for the clear, correct understanding of the entire Holy Scriptures, and alone shows the way to the unspeakable treasure and right knowledge of Christ, and alone opens the door of the entire Bible (AP. IV 2 German).[70]

The Lutheran Confessions never arbitrarily force the doctrine of justification on a passage where it is not found, for that would be eisegesis. But this principle cannot be used to deny doctrines of Scripture that the theologians call non-fundamental. The hard facts of Scripture which are clearly enunciated are to be accepted.

Hermeneutics and the Lutheran Church—Missouri Synod

The founding fathers of our synod were well versed in Luther and the Lutheran Confessions.[71] The writings of Johann Gerhard and Martin Chemnitz were also known. In Martin Chemnitz' Examination of the Council of Trent, Part I as translated by Fred Kramer, contains a chapter entitled, "Concerning the Interpretation of Scripture."[72] The same interpretative principles will be found that are found in Luther and Melanchthon. Dr. C.F.W. Walther, an avid student of Luther and the Lutheran Confessions, enunciated the basic Lutheran principles in his treatise: "The Lutheran Church, the True Visible Church of God," in theses XIII-XXI set forth basic hermeneutical principles that agree with those hermeneutical rules followed in the Lutheran symbols.[73] When the synod was a hundred years old, two volumes were published, known as *The Abiding Word*, two volumes of essays showing the stance of the synod regarding its doctrine and practices.[74] In Volume I there is an article on "Biblical Interpretation."[75]

A reading of this article by Mennicke will show that he repeats the most important principles of interpretation that were used by Luther, Chemnitz, Gerhard and those in the history of Lutheranism that were true to the exegesis of the Lutheran Confessions. Dr. Arndt's short article in the *Lutheran Cyclopedia* (1954) follows the same interpretative principles.[76] Dr. L. Fuerbringer's *Theological Hermeneutics*, used probably by over a thousand or more of Synod's clergy was faithful to Luther, the Lutheran Confessions and other Lutheran fathers in the hermeneutical principles advocated.[77]

In the fall of 1966 The Commission on Theology and Church Relations produced a study document, "A Stance toward Biblical Studies"[78] which express views that were departures from a hermeneutics that had been the official position of the Synod and were in disagreement with *The Statement of Scripture*, originally adopted by the San Francisco Convention.[79] It prompted the concept that the Biblical interpreter could question statements of Scripture and if these interpretations did not violate the Law-Gospel dichotomy that they were permissible. The Gospel reduction view is clearly permitted in this study document.[80]

Another item that caused eyebrows to be raised was the attempt to describe what is basically the technique of the historical-grammatical method and called it the historical-critical method. The steps of what the

Stance Document called the historical-critical method are as follows:

1. Establishing the text.
2. Ascertaining the literary form.
3. Determining the historical situation.
4. Apprehending the meaning which the words had for the original author and his readers.
5. Understanding a passage in the light of the total contact and the background of which it emerged.[81]

That is precisely what Terry would tell the reader in his *Biblical Hermeneutics*[82] or Michelsen, in his *Interpreting the Bible* as constituting the historical-grammatical method.[83] That that is all that is involved in the historical-critical method is not according to the facts as can easily be demonstrated.

The committee that prepared the *Stance Document* was inspired and influenced by *Biblical Authority for Today*, a volume edited by Alan Richardson and W. Schweitzer.[84] It contains the World Council of Churches' symposium on "The Biblical Authority for the Churches' Social and Political Message." A reading of the various articles in this symposium of essays contributed from parts of Protestantism and Greek Orthodoxy contains many statements not in harmony with a sound Biblical hermeneutics.

The "moderates" in the Lutheran Church-Missouri Synod have been utilizing *The Stance Document* to justify some of their erroneous theological positions. *The Stance Document* was the product of the Commission on Theology and Church Relations during the time when this commission was dominated by professors and persons who now are affiliated with Evangelical Lutherans in Mission (ELIM) or AELC, whose chairman. Dr. Richard Jungkuntz, became the first chairman of the Board of Control of Seminex.

The Commission on Theology and Church Relations

(CTCR), under the chairmanship of Dr. Ralph Bohlmann has made a study of the historical-critical method and has clearly shown the historical-critical method as it is customarily understood and described is completely incompatible with the theological hermeneutics used in the Bible and the hermeneutical principles followed by the Lutheran Confessions.[85] The August 11, 1974 *Lutheran Witness Reporter* edition included a reprint of this document, under the title "A Comparative Study of Varying Contemporary Approaches to Biblical Interpretation." Dr. J.A.O. Preus devoted a number of issues of the *Lutheran Witness* in treating the ideas rejected and defended in this CTCR document. In the column, called "With One Voice," the Synodical President by means of the catechetical method, dealt with an exposition, interpretation and justification of the stance taken by the CTCR, in which the correct Lutheran position was clearly and unequivocally enunciated.[86]

The Lutheran Church-Missouri Synod was opposed to negative higher criticism from the very beginning of its existence as an American Lutheran church body. *Lehre und Wehre*, the first theological journal of

Concordia Seminary St. Louis, in issue after issue, warned its readers against the rationalism and anti-supernaturalism which controlled the interpretation of the Bible of those who had adopted the higher-critical methodology in Europe and America.[87] For a little better than a hundred years the theological teachers at the terminal schools and also at the junior colleges of The Lutheran Church-Missouri Synod employed the historical-grammatical method in their interpretations of the Holy Scriptures. However, in the fifth and sixth decades of the twentieth century there were instructors and professors at Concordia Seminary, St. Louis, Concordia Teachers College River Forest and at Valparaiso University, who began to use the historical critical method and began to indoctrinate their students with views which were contrary to the historical position of the Lutheran Church and of the Synod which had hired them to teach the isagogics, hermeneutics and exegesis which were reflected in hundreds of synodical essays as well as in the theological literature of the synod, in its doctrinal textbooks, as represented by Pieper, Mueller, Koehler, Graebner, Engelder, Arndt, Maier, Sr. and a host of others. In the fifties there came into being a group of scholars and pastors whom one might call the "young Turks," a group who was determined to take Missouri down another road from that on which she had been traveling. Between 1957-1977 there developed with the Lutheran Church-Missouri Synod a hermeneutical civil war, which is a development which needs a separate treatment and will not be covered in this essay.

Footnotes

1. Millar Burrows, *An Outline of Biblical Theology* (Philadelphia: Westminster Press, 1940, p. 51.
2. W. R. Harper, *Religion and the Higher Life* (Chicago: University of Chicago Press, 1904), p. 51.
3. John Edgar McFayden, *The Interest of the Bible* (New York: Hodder & Stoughton, 1922), pp. 18-19.
4. Theodore Graebner, "Faith and Reason," in E.C. Fendt, editor, *What Lutherans Are Thinking* (Columbus: The Wartburg Press, 1947), p. 337.
5. Francis Pieper, *Christliche Dogmatik* (St. Louis: Concordia Publishing House, 1942), I, pp. 338-389.
6. Christian Preus, "The Contemporary Relevance of von Hofmann's Hermeneutical Principles," Interpretation. 4:321, July 1950.
7. Richard R. Caemmerer, "The New Hermeneutic and Preaching," *Concordia Theological Monthly*, 37:99-110, Feb. 1966.; and Edgar Krentz, Hermeneutics and the Teacher of Theology, *Concordia Theological Monthly*, 42:265-282, May, 1971; Edgar Krentz, *The Historical-Critical Method,* Philadelphia: Fortress Press, 1975); *Various Essays in Aspects of Biblical Hermeneutics* (St. Louis: Concordia Publishing House, 1966 *Concordia Theological Monthly,* Occasional Papers No. 1); John Warwick Montgomery, *Crisis in Lutheranism Theology* (Grand Rapids: Baker Book House, 1907). Contains essays by Dr. Montgomery; Vol. II (1967) contains essays by Sasse, R. Preus, Bohlmann, Spitz, Sr. and others dealing with hermeneutics; Manfred Roensch, "A Critical Investigation of the So-called Historical-Critical Method in the Interpretation of Holy Scripture," *The Springfielder*, 28:32-42,

Spring, 1964; Walter A. Maier, *Form-Criticism Reexamined* (St. Louis: Concordia Publishing House, 1973). 46 pp.; Raymond F. Surburg, *How Dependable Is the Bible?* (New York and Philadelphia: J.B. Lippencott Company, 1972), pp. 18-91.

8. Milton S. Terry, *Biblical Hermeneutics* (New York and Cincinnati: Eaton & Mains, 1890), p 70.

9. Cf. Bernard Ramm, *Protestant Biblical Interpretation* (Grand Rapids: 3rd revised edition; Baker Book House, 1970). Chapter 2 deals will the different schools of interpretation that have appeared in the last two thousand years of church history.

10. L. Berkhof, *Principles of Biblical Interpretation* (Grand Rapids: Baker Book House, 1950), p 27.

11. A. Berkeley Mickelsen, *Interpreting the Bible* (Grand Rapids: William B. Eerdmans Publishing Company, 1963), p. 35.

12. *Rome and the Study of Scriptures* (St. Meinrad: Indiana: Grail Publications, 1958; Sixth Edition; Newly revised and enlarged), p. 19.

13. **Ibid.**, p. 92.

14. Michelsen, **op. cit.**, p. 33.

15. **Ibid.**

16. Ramm, **op. cit.** p 51.

17. Elmer C. Kiessling, "Lyra, Nicholaus de (1270-1340)," Vergilius Ferm, editor. *An Encyclopedia of Religion* (New York: The Philosophical Library, 1945), p. 459. Eric Brauer, editor. *The Westminster Dictionary of Church History* (Philadelphia: The Westminster Press. 1971), pp. 62-603.

18. Raymond F. Surburg, "The Significance of Luther's Hermeneutics for the Protestant Reformation," *Concordia Theological Monthly*, 24:241-261, April, 1953.

19. Ramm, **op. cit.**, pp. 55, 58.

20. E. C. Blackman, *Biblical Interpretation* (London: Independent Press, 1957), pp. 119-124.

21. Ramm, **op. cit.**, p.p. 54, 58.

22. Terry, **op. cit.**, p. 174.

23. Cf. W. H. Koenig, "Luther as a Student of Hebrew," *Concordia Theological Monthly*, 24:845-853, November, 1953; Cf. the many statements from *Luther's Works* cited by Ewald M. Plass, *What Luther Says, An Anthology* (St. Louis: Concordia Publishing House, 1959), II, pp. 727-732, statements which emphasis the importance of studying the Bible in Hebrew and Greek.

24. As cited by Ramm, **op. cit.**, p. 53.

25. **Ibid.**, p. 53. 25a. **Ibid.**

26. **Ibid.**

27. Frederick W. Farrar, *History of Interpretation* (London: Macmillan and Co., 1886), p. 327.

28. C.A. Briggs, *History of the Study of Theology* (New York: Charles Scribners and Sons, 1916), II, p. 107.

29. *Weimar Edition of Luther's Writings*, vol. 8, p. 236.

30. *Weimar Edition of Luther's Writings*, 6, p. 509; Vol. ii, p. 434.

31. St. Louis Edition of the *Works of Martin Luther*, V, pp. 334ff.; XVIII, pp. 1681ff.; John Theodore Mueller, *Christian Dogmatics* (St. Louis: Concordia Publishing House, 1955), pp 139-141.

32. Weimar Edition, 14, p. 556.

33. Berkhof, **op. cit.**, p. 24.

34. Farrar, **op. cit.**, II, p. 327.

35. Ramm, **op. cit.**, p 56.

36. Luther, "How Christians Should Regard Moses," 1525, Weimar Edition, 24, p. 11.

37. Reinhold Seeberg, *Lehrbuch der Dogmengeschichte, vierte Band, erste Abteilung. Die Lehre Luthers*, IV, i (Leipiig), p. 414.

38. Ramm, **op. cit.**, p. 58.

39. *Weimar Edition of Luther's Writings*, vol. 9, pp. 80-86.

40. Ramm, **op. cit.**, pp. 56-57.

41. **Ibid.**

42. **Ibid.**, p. 58.

43. St. Louis Edition of *Luther's Works*, vol. 9, p. 1362.

44. Ramm, **op. cit.**, p. 58.

45. Cf. E. L. Lueker, "Lutheran Confessions," E. L. Lueker, editor, *Lutheran Cyclopedia* (St. Louis: Concordia Publishing House, 1954), pp. 630-035; L. W. Spitz, "Lutheran Theology after 1580," *Lutheran Cyclopedia*, **op. cit.**, pp. 638-641.

46. *Handbook of the Lutheran Church—Missouri Synod* (St. Louis, 1975), p. 15.

47. Cf. "Emigration Regulations of the Saxon Pilgrims," as given in *Lutheran Cyclopedia*, **op. cit.**, pp. 606-607.

48. Ralph A. Bohlmann, *Principles of Biblical Interpretation in the Lutheran Confessions* (St. Louis: Concordia Publishing House, 1968), p. 23.

49. F. E. Mayer, *The Religious Bodies in America* (St. Louis: Concordia Publishing House, 1961), p. 144; Fred Kramer, "Sacra Scriptura and Verbum Dei in the Lutheran Confessions," *Concordia Theological Monthly*, 28:81-95, February, 1955.

50. Holstem Fagerberg, *Die Theologie der Lutherischen Bekennisschiften* (Gottingen: Vandenhoek and Ruprecht, IMS), p. 14.

51. *Concordia Triglotta, The Symbolical Books of the Lutheran Church*, German-Latin-English (St. Louis: Concordia Publishing House, 1921), p. 851.

52. **Ibid.**, p. 776.

53. Bohlmann, **op. cit.**, p. 55.

54. **Ibid.**,

55. **Ibid.**, pp. 83-84.

56. **Ibid.**, pp. 84-86.

57. **Ibid.**, pp. 85-86.

58. **Ibid.**, pp. 87-88.

59. **Ibid.**, p. 88.

60. **Ibid.**, p. 89.

61. **Ibid.**, chapter 6, pp. 99-109.

82. Louis Fuerbringer, *Theologische Hermeneutik* (St. Louis: Concordia Publishing House, 1812). p. 16.

63. Bohlmann, **op. cit.**, p. 60.

64. Fuerbringer, **op. cit.**, p. 15.

65. A reading of the various confessional writings will make this evident.

66. *Apology* IV, 372 as cited by Bohlmann, **op. cit.** p. 103.

67. Bohlmann, **op. cit.**, p. 101.

68. **Ibid.**, p. 105.

69. Die Bekenntniischriften der evangelisch - Lutherischen Kirche. Herausgegeben im Gedenkjahr der Augsburgischen Konfession 1930. 2. Verbesserte Auflage (Gottingen: Vandenhoek & Ruprecht, 1952), p. 151.

70. F. Bente, *Concordia Triglotta*, **op. cit.**, p. 121.

71. Cf. "Walther, Carl Ferdinand Wilhelm." *Concordia Cyclopedia,* **op. cit.**, p. 1117.

72. Martin Chemnitz, *Examination of the Council of Trent*, Part I. Translation by Fred Kramer (St. Louis: Concordia Publishing House, 1971), pp. 207-221.

73. William Dallmann, W.H.T. Dau and Th. Engelder with a Foreword by F. Pfoten-hauer, *Walther and the Church* (St. Louis: Concordia Publishing House, 1938), pp 122-127.

74. Theodore Laetsch, editor, *The Abiding Word* (St. Louis, Concordia Publishing House, 1947). 2 volumes.

75. Victor E. Mennicke, "Bible Interpretation," Theodore Laetsch, editor, *The Abiding Word* (St. Louis: Concordia Publishing House, 1947), II, pp. 35-S8.

76. William Arndt, "Hermeneutics," *Lutheran Cyclopedia*, **op. cit.**, pp. 463-464.

77. L. Fuerbringer, Theologische Hermeneutik (St. Louis: Concordia Publishing House, 1912), 24 pp.; This was issued in English as *Theological Hermeneutics* (St. Louis: Concordia Publishing House, 1924), 24 pp.

78. *A Lutheran Stance Toward Contemporary Biblical Studies*. Report of the Commission on Theology and Church Relations. St. Louis: The Lutheran Church-Missouri Synod, 1966. 10 pages.

79. "A Statement on Scripture" originally adopted by the Synodical Conference in 1958, and adopted as doctrinal statement by The Lutheran Church-Missouri Synod in 1959 at the San Francisco Convention. Published in *The Lutheran Witness*. February 24,1959. pp. 8-9.

80. Cf. Raymond F. Surburg, *An Evaluation of A Lutheran Stance toward Contemporary Biblical Studies,*' p. 4f., a faculty Study Paper delivered October, 1966 at Concordia Theological Seminary, Springfield, Ill. Available from the Seminary Library.

81. *Report of the Commission on Theology and Church Relations—A Lutheran Stance Toward Contemporary Biblical Studies* (St. Louis: The Lutheran Church-Missouri Synod, 1966), p. 9.

82. Milton S. Terry, *Biblical Hermeneutics*, op. cit., p. 70.

83. A. Berkeley Mickelsen, *Interpreting the Bible* (Grand Rapids: Wm. B. Eerdmans Publishing Company, 1963), p. 35.

84. Alan Richardson and Wolfgang Schweitzer, *Biblical Authority for Today* (Philadelphia: The Westminster Press, 1951), 347 pp.

85. *A Comparative Study of Varying Contemporary Approaches to Biblical Interpretation - A report of the Commission on Theology and Church Relations*, The Lutheran Church—Missouri Synod, March, 1973, 19 pp.

86. J.A.O. Preus, "With One Voice," The *Lutheran Witness*, August 25.1974, pp. 18, 26; October 6, 1974, pp. 9, 28.

87. *Lehre und Wehre, Theologisches und Kirschlich-Zeltgeschischt-Liches Monatsblatt*. Redigiert von C.F.W. Walther (Druckerei der Evang. —Luth. Synode von Missouri, Ohio, v.a. St., 1855 ff). Altogether 75 volumes were published between 1855-1929.

Questions

1. What has been a source of great perplexity to Christian and non-Christian students? ____
2. Did the LCMS follow the Historical-Grammatical or Historical-Critical Method? ____
3. According to Luther, only the Word of God establishes ____.

37

4. Luther and the Reformers insisted that the Scriptura should be studied in ____.
5. Erasmus published the first ____.
6. Scripture interprets ____.
7. Luther held to the ____ and ____ interpretation of Scripture.
8. Law and Gospel must be ____.
9. Rome's root heresy in Luther's time was ____.
10. For the founders of the LCMS the Bible is ____ and the Lutheran symbols ____.
11. Why do the Lutheran Confessions have no articles on the doctrine of Scripture? ____
12. Luther wrote that "God's Word does not ____."
13. The preface to the *Book of Concord* describes the Scriptures as ____.
14. What is the "analogy of faith?" ____
15. What led the LCMS's the *Stance Document* to justify some of their erroneous view? ____
17. The LCMS's *Lehre und Wehre* in issue after issue warned ____.
18. What kind of "war" developed in the LCMS between 1957-1977? ____

The 450th Anniversary of the *Apology*
With Special Reference to the History of Its Central Article: Justification

Christian News, February 8 and 16, 1981

This year the Lutheran Church throughout the world will, or at least should, commemorate the 450th anniversary of the writing and publication of the *Apology of the Augsburg Confession*. This confession is the second in order of time of the symbolical writings of the Lutheran Church. It is intended to be, as its name indicates, a justification of the *Augsburg Confession*, especially with reference to the attempted Roman theologians' attempt to repudiate the *Augsburg Confession*.[1]

The Occasion for Its Writings

A few days after the presentation of the *Augsburg Confession* Charles V. and the diet ordered a refutation of the Augustana to be prepared and also to be read before the assembly of princes. Twenty scholars drew up the Roman Confutatio, among them were Eck, Faber, Cochlaeus, Wimpina. Instruction to the Roman theologians was to prepare a confutation written in moderate language. However, with such champions of Rome arrayed against the Lutherans, compromise was out of the question. Five times they produced a refutation but it was unsatisfactory for Charles V. Finally, a sixth revision was accepted and read on August 3, 1530 as Responsio Augustanae, or, as the Lutherans afterwards called it, "Confutatio Pontifica," read in the same hall that had heard the *Augsburg Confession*.[2]

One Lutheran writer described the *Confutation*, a very lengthy and bitter document, as follows:

It allowed the majority of the doctrinal articles, some unconditionally, articles 14 and 18 if rightly interpreted, 2, 4, 5, 6, 7, 10, and 11 with certain limitations, art. 12 and 15 as regards the first part, while the second was rejected. Arts. 20 and 21, and the articles concerning abuses, were unqualifiedly rejected and the abuses cited therein declared to be proper ecclesiastical usages.[3]

No copy of the *Confutation* was given to the Evangelicals. Its publication was prohibited. The first Latin edition appeared in 1573 and the first German edition in 1608.

The Emperor declared the *Roman Confutation* to be his faith and simultaneously demanded that the Evangelicals accept it; the subject was closed and adherence by the princes was demanded. The inability of the Evangelicals to accept the *Confutation* led to a new series of attempts to adjust the difficulty. Two committees, one of 14, and the other of 6 members, attempted to pacify the Evangelicals. Out of these meetings came the result, that the Romish party accepted most of the articles, but demanded submission to the authority of the Church.[4]

On September 22, 1530 the decree of the diet in matters dealing with religion was read. The Evangelicals were given until April 15, 1531, to comply with the decree. While the evangelical party was considering complying no publications were permitted to be issued. The Evangelicals expected this action and had taken measures to respond to it. They protested and handed Charles V a copy of the *Apology* of the *Augsburg Confession*. The Emperor was about to accept the *Apology* but then was dissuaded from receiving it by his brother Ferdinand.

The copy of the *Apology* handed the emperor was based on notes which Brueck had made at the public reading of the Roman Confutatio. The days between September 22 and April 15 were dark days. "In these dark days the timid Melanchthon as well as others almost wrecked the Lutheran cause by their concessions, and Luther, from the Coburg, and the laymen had to bolster them up."[5] After some time Melanchthon was able to secure a copy of the *Roman Confutation* and revised the *Apology* accordingly. Although the Emperor had forbidden the printing of the Lutheran confession without his consent, seven editions of the Augustana appeared, some even during the days the Reichstag was held.

This situation forced · Melanchthon to publish the Augustana and its *Apology* in the spring of 1531. He called this the first edition even though it was a revision; a second edition appeared in September, again altered. A free German edition of the *Apology*, made by Justus Jonas, appeared in October, 1531. The German Estates in 1532, at a convent in Schweinfurt officially accepted the *Apology* as "an apology and exposition of the Confession" along with the Confession and formerly signed the *Augsburg Confession*, the *Apology* at Smalcald in 1537, and by this action declared them as the Confessions of the Lutheran Church.[6]

The Polemical Character of the *Apology*

The tone between the Augustana and the *Apology* is not the same. The *Apology* was designed to answer the attacks of the *Roman Confutation*, and this helps to explain its strongly polemical character. Now that there was no possibility of reconciliation with the Roman Church, Melanchthon "has entirely laid aside the mildness which he formerly exercised toward the opponents."

The Concordia Cyclopedia calls attention to the fact that Melanchthon made many changes in the *Augsburg Confession* which though they did not alter the sense, caused Elector John Frederick to criticize these changes as a bit of arrogance on Melanchthon's part. However, real changes were made by Melanchthon on article X in 1540.[7] The following may be said to specifically characterize the *Apology*: The aim of this document was to (1) reject the assertion that the *Roman Confutation* had shown the errors of the Augustana; (2) to show that the significant difference between the Roman document and that of the Lutherans was to be found in their respective understanding of law and grace, sin and justification. The doctrine of justification by faith was considered by the Evangelicals as the central doctrine of the Bible; (3) Additional doctrines which needed further exposition were treated, namely the doctrine of the Church, the number of sacraments, the mass, the invocation of saints,

40

celibacy and others. Historically speaking, it should be noted that the *Augsburg Confession* contains an exposition by its writer in the *Apology*, a rather unique feature.[8]

While Luther's two catechisms were intended for the laity, the *Apology* is meant particularly for theologians. Gieschen has in his characterization among other things asserted this:

> The *Apology* is theological writing at its best. Motivated by a deep love for the Gospel, Melanchthon put all his great talents as a scholar and teacher into the production of this epoch-making work. While the thought-patterns and mode of argumentation are frequently tinged with the scholasticism from which the Reformers came, the *Apology* amazes us by the vast amount of theological, historical, and linguistic learning it displays. The writings of the Church Fathers, the great teachers of the medieval church, the decrees of popes and councils, all move through it in colorful procession; Hebrew and Greek are familiar friends; philosophy and logic also make their contributions.[9]

But what especially will impress the evangelical reader of the *Apology* is Melanchthon's comprehensive knowledge of the Scriptures as well as the insight Luther's coworker had into the meaning of the Biblical text. Gieschen also praises the "biblical emphasis, moreover, is evangelical rather than legalistic; in all its exegesis, argument, and polemics, it is the Gospel with which it is concerned."[10]

Contents of the *Apology*

The Augustana contains 28 articles, of which the *Roman Confutation* had approved eighteen, eight of them without, and ten with reservations. The articles entirely accepted were: I, III, VIII, IX, XVI, XVII, IXIII and XIX. In the *Apology* they are given little consideration. Articles accepted but with reservations were: II, IV, V, VI, X, XI, XII, XIII, XIV, and XV. These are handled more or less thoroughly and their treatment was determined by the name of the Roman objections. The *Roman Confutation* had rejected part of article VII all of XX, and XXL The second part of the Augustana, articles XXII to XXVIII were repudiated. In the discussion of justification articles IV, V, VI, and XX are dealt with simultaneously; in addition to this there is also a separate article on XX.[11]

The following topics are treated more at length: Original Sin (II), Justification (IV, V, VI, and XX), the Church (VII and VIII). Penitence (XII), Human traditions (XV), the Invocations or Saints (XXI), the Marriage of Priests (XXIII), the Mass (XXIV), and Monastic Vows (XXVII).

The Doctrine of Justification by Faith

The doctrine of justification by faith constitutes about one third of the *Apology*. This doctrine is most prominent among all doctrines held by the Lutheran Church. According to Luther it "was the doctrine of a standing or falling church." Church historians agree that it was the turning point of the Reformation. This is a doctrine that Luther discovered after a number of years of struggle. One 19th century writer claimed that "it was the experience of its necessity and efficacy made Luther what he was, and

41

equipped him for his work and power."[12] Luther in his consolatory writing of 1533, addressed to certain Leipzigers, who were exiled because they confessed the doctrine of justification by faith and not by works, stated:

Under the circumstances you should certainly be glad that you have come out of a city and a country in which people are bidden to deny and to persecute the Word of grace and the forgiveness of sins and the doctrine that we are justified and saved only through Christ, without any merit on our part. For this is the chief article from which all other doctrines have flowed.[13]

The Reformer also claimed: "If this article remains pure, the Christian Church remains pure; but if not, it is impossible to resist any error or fanatical spirit."[14] The other articles of the church must remain pure if they are consistent with this article when it is pure, and if they are consistent with each other.

The doctrine of justification is the principle or fundamental article of the Christian faith, not that it originates others, but that it regulates and controls them. Justification by faith apart from works is a doctrine interwoven with all important topics of systematic theology. Justification reaches back to the Doctrine of the Triune God, the Doctrine of Man, the Doctrine of Christ. Further it is the heart of Pneumatology and reaches forward to the Doctrine of the Church.[15]

For a clear and correct understanding of the doctrine of justification a sound doctrinal comprehension of the nature of God, predestination, the Person and Work of Christ, especially the atonement, the operation of the Holy Spirit, the Church, the Means of Grace, and her Ministry are required.[16]

The Lutheran Confessions contain many references to the doctrine of justification. The subject index of the *Concordia Triglotta* lists over ninety references in the different Lutheran Confessions to the doctrine of justification.[17] Article IV of the Augustana has set forth the doctrine of justification this way:

It is also taught among us that we cannot obtain forgiveness of sin and righteousness before God by our own merits, works, or satisfactions but that we receive forgiveness of sin and become righteous before God by grace, for Christ's sake, through faith, when we believe that Christ suffered for us and that for his sake our sin is forgiven and righteousness and eternal life are given to us. For God will reward and reckon this faith as righteousness, as Paul says in Romans 3:21-26 and 4:5.[18]

Articles IV, V, VI and XX of the *Roman Confutation* condemned the Lutheran teaching that the sinner receives forgiveness of sins purely for Christ's sake, without in any way doing anything meritorious to receive Christ's forgiveness. It is especially in the *Apology* that the doctrine of justification received a great deal of attention. In the Augustana Article IV is the central doctrine and when the Roman Catholic scholars attacked this in the *Confutation* they were assaulting the Citadel of the Christian faith. According to Bouman "the prior articles lead up to it, and those that follow it either express the consequences of justification for the faith and life of the church, or further explain the article."[19] Of the 28 articles in the *Augsburg Confession*, more than half are explicitly related to the doctrine of justification of the nearly 190 pages of the *Apology*, the explicit treatment of justification takes up over 60 pages; in nearly every other article, the doctrine of justification is also the obvious concern. Luther, the author of the Smalcald Articles, has devoted two articles to justification (SA II, 1; III, xiii); in fact, this doctrine was Luther's concern in all that he wrote about. The *Formula of Concord* has the entire third article devoted to it; there are also other discussions of this central teaching in other articles. The great frequency with which justification is discussed, explained and defended led Bouman to declare: "In short, the Lutheran Confessions are from beginning to end an exposition of this doctrine and a confession of it before men and God." The observation of Herbert Bouman is worth giving at this time:

A serious student of the symbols is overwhelmed by the subject on nearly every page he meets the **cantus firmus** of justification as the ever-recurring theme which, though developed in a hundred fascinating variations, always remains plainly recognizable as the same theme.[20]

It was the contention of the Lutheran Confessions that the doctrine of justification is the chief doctrine of Holy Writ. This means that while the teaching of justification is set forth in its clearest and most comprehensive way in the New Testament, especially in the writings of St. Paul, it is also a doctrine clearly taught in the Old Testament. Thus Melanchthon in the *Apology* (Art. IV, 2f.) declared:

It is the chief topic of Christian doctrine, which understood aright illumines and applies and amplifies the honor of Christ, is of special service for the clear, correct understanding of the entire Holy Scriptures, alone shows the way to the unspeakable treasure and right knowledge of Christ, and brings the necessary and most abundant consolation to devour conscience.

Melanchthon expressed amazement that his opponents were "unmoved by the many passages in the Scriptures that clearly attribute justification to faith and specifically deny it to works." Bible passages are employed profusely throughout Melanchthon's presentation of justification. Thus he cited verses from Paul, John, Acts, Psalms, Habakkuk and Isaiah to show that the statement that "faith justifies" is found in both testaments of the Bible. Fagerberg has correctly noted: "The promise grounds itself upon that, which God in Holy Scripture has promised. Since the promise is repeated throughout Holy Writ, it is not necessary to look for specific promised word; it is much more present there, where God promises, to lift upon oppressed and sorrowing consciences."[21]

Justification by faith is not only a New Testament doctrine, but also taught in the Old Testament. When Melanchthon quoted passages from the Old Testament, he was merely following St. Paul and many New Testament writers who claimed that the Gospel was known during Old Testament times and that Abraham and David were justified by faith which was imputed to them.

The Doctrine of Justification between 1546 and 1577

After Luther's death the storm broke out over the Evangelical Lutheran churches. The Emperor conquered South Germany and most of North Germany. At the Augsburg Interim, 1548, the doctrine of justification was given up, and seven sacraments and transubstantiation were recognized by the majority of Protestant princes. Melanchthon opposed the Augsburg Interim but soon became afraid and yielded in the Leipzig Interim, 1548, at which the doctrine of justification was compromised; the clergy were pledged to obey the pope, agreed to the reintroduction of Roman ceremonies at Baptism, confirmation, extreme unction. In the three decades following Luther's death numerous controversies broke out among the Lutherans, caused by Interim aberrations of Melanchthon's pupils and the extremism of Flacius and others. The following were the major controversies to wrack the churches: Adiaphoristic, 1548; Osiandrian, 1550; Majoristic, 1551; Synergistic, 1555; Antinomistic, 1556; Flacian, 1560; Crypto-Calvinistic, 1571.

Osiander in 1550 declared that God does not declare the sinner just, that God does not impute Christ's obedience and righteousness to the sinner, but has Christ Himself dwell in the sinner for his justification. God does not act as judge but as physician. The assurance of justification rests upon a pseudomystical union of Christ and not on the objective work of Christ. The atonement is not the ground for justification. Osiander also taught that Christ is man's righteousness only according to His divine nature. The Italian Francesco Stancaro opposed this error by claiming that only according to Christ's human nature is He our Righteousness.[21a]

Article III of The *Formula of Concord* is directed against both of these errorists and declared that "the entire Christ according to both natures, alone by His obedience, which as God and man He rendered the Father even to death, merited for us the forgiveness of sins and eternal life, as it is written in Rom. 5:19." The *Formula of Concord* also holds that mankind's salvation is founded upon the imputation of Christ's righteousness; that faith alone is the instrument by which sinners lay hold of Christ; that this faith is not an intellectual act, but assent and trust; that justification is not making righteous but a declaring of the forgiveness of our sins, and a treating of men as if they were righteous, that men are firmly to rest in our undoubting assurance of salvation.

On the basis of Eph. 2:8; Rom. 1:17; 3:24; Gal. 3:11, *The Formula of Concord* retained with care the exclusive particles used by Paul, "without works," "without merit," "not of works," "of grace," all which taken together means "we are justified and saved alone by faith in Christ." The article on justification also stresses that even though contrition precedes justification and good works do not belong to the doctrine of justification, yet no justifying faith can exist when there is the wicked intention to sin coexisting, but after man is justified by faith, then a true genuine faith will work by love (Gal. 5: 6), and so good works always follow justifying faith, and are found with justifying faith, if it is true and living; for justifying faith is never alone, but always has with it love and hope.

Mayer pointed out that the Lutheran emphasis upon justification by faith led to two charges made against the Lutherans. The fact that such great emphasis was placed upon justification **apart from works** led to the accusation that Lutheranism has given up the dynamics of Lutheran piety.[21b] The Lutheran Confessions make a sharp distinction between justification and sanctification (this point was made against the Romanists as well as against Osiander). However, Mayer responds: "This, however, is only a logical distinction, not a chronological differentiation; a distinction, not a separation; the one an act in the heart of God and the other an act in the heart of man; the one the complete and present victory over every foe, the other the continuous battle between the Christian and his enemies; the one as the 'already,' the other as the 'not yet'."[21c] The Lutheran Confessions stress the sola gratia (grace alone), but at the same time they emphasize the necessity for the believer to express his Spirit-given faith by good works. The theologians expressed this in the epigram: **"Sola fides justificat, et tamen numguam est sola"** (Faith alone justifies, but faith is never alone).

The second charge that the **sola fide** (faith alone) was conducive to look at faith as static and intellectual is not supported from the Lutheran Confessions. Thus both Luther and Melanchthon in various confessional writings prepared by them depict faith as living and vital (Cf. Ap. IV, 64: A.C. XX, 27-40; Small Cat., Baptism, quest. 4).

The *Formula of Concord* was forced to take up the problem of the proper relationship of faith and works. Some Lutheran theologians to ward off a charge of antinomianism argued that "good works are necessary to salvation." In answering this erroneous view the Formula declared that the mingling of man's works into the article on redemption would result in despair and to a false security relative to man's eternal salvation. Further, good works must be performed for other reasons. Good works should be performed because this is the will of God, they are the fruits of the Holy Spirit, they are a constant exercise of faith and a testimony to the world.

The Doctrine of Justification during the Period of Classical Lutheran Orthodoxy

During the period of orthodoxy (ca. 1580-1715) "no other article of faith was given such a thorough treatment as the locus on justification," asserts Robert Preus,[22] an authority on the theology of the period of orthodoxy. In fact R. Preus wrote:

> Not only did dogmaticians like Chemnitz and Gerhard, and Calov devote hundreds of pages in their dogmatics to the doctrine, but immense monographs were written on the theme (H. Hoepfner) and vast commentaries were written primarily to present the article of justification in all its depth and breadth (Gerhard, Seb. Schmidt, Calov, Balduin, Brochmand).[23]

Preus claims that the orthodox Lutheran theologians were greatly dependent on Luther in their presentation of the doctrine of justification. From Chemnitz to Hollaz "there was a total lack of originality in developing the doctrine of justification—that is, if we consider any advance from the presentation of Luther necessary."[24] However, with Chemnitz systemization begins to take shape and by the times of Gerhard and Quenstedt the doctrine of justification is set forth according to a neat outline, which was structured like this: the meaning of justification, the subject of justification (man) the author of justification (God), the meritorious cause (Christ's work), the means, the organon leptikon, the nature of justification and etc. One of the characteristics of the language used by the Lutheran orthodox scholars was the use of scholastic terminology, "a technical language which was thoroughly known and used by Roman Catholic, Reformed and Lutheran theologians alike. Scholastic terminology served as a medium of scholarly communication in those days, like the Latin language, and the Lutherans were compelled to employ it in the interest of inter-confessional dialogue."[25] However, the Lutheran theologians only used a minimum of scholastic terminology and adhered to the language of Luther and Melanchthon is their presentations of justification. They especially stressed the forensic or legal character of justification.

Just as for Luther, so for the theologians of orthodoxy, justification was the doctrine of "the standing or falling church" (the articulus stantis et cadentis ecclesiae). The Lutheran theologians of the 17th century regarded it the central article of the Bible, because for them justification was the summation of Christ's work, it was the heart of the Gospel. Preus points out that Chemnitz began his study of justification with the discussion of Law and Gospel and of the grace of God. Gerhard placed his lengthy treatment of the work of Christ under the locus of justification.[26] The theologians of orthodoxy considered justification not merely a Pauline teaching because a correct understanding of justification embraced the whole Gospel message. To truly appreciate the biblical doctrine of justification it was necessary to distinguish correctly between Law and Gospel and also have a true understanding of the obedience of Christ according to both natures.

Thus Calov wrote: "Everything which we teach, witness and urge against pope, devil and the whole world in this life is centered and set forth in this article."[27] Chemnitz also was convinced of the importance of justification, as may be seen from the following assertion:

This teaching is the most important in our Christian doctrine. For anxious and frightened minds which struggle under sin and the wrath of God seek this one gate through which they might have a God who is pacified and propitiated.[28] (Preus translation)

The doctrine of justification was one which was very practical for Chemnitz, that this is so may be seen from the following quotation:

This locus contains the sum of the Gospel. For it indicates the benefit which we derive from Christ, and offers immovable consolation to pious souls; it teaches which are the proper ways of worshipping God, what it means truly to call upon Him; and sets the Church of God apart from other peoples, Jews, Mohammedans, and Pelagians, that is, from all who imagine that a man is righteous by the Law or by outward discipline and who bid us doubt concerning the remission of sins.[29] (Preus translation)

Like Luther, Chemnitz insisted on the importance of keeping this doctrine pure:

> This article is in a sense the stronghold and the high fortress of all the doctrine and of the entire Christian religion; if it is obscured or adulterated or set aside, the purity of doctrine in other articles of faith cannot possibly be maintained. But if this article is kept pure, all idolatry, superstitions, and whatever corruptions there are in other articles of faith tumble down of their own weight.[30] (Preus rendering).

From the quotations just given it is apparent that Lutheran orthodoxy did not simply consider justification an image of the earliest Christian tradition, one image among a number employed to delineate God's deed in Christ. On the contrary, for the Lutherans of orthodoxy justification was the result of Christ's redemptive work on behalf of fallen mankind.

The Roman Catholic Doctrine of Justification

At this juncture it will be well to set forth the Roman Catholic doctrine on justification against which Luther, Melanchthon and the scholars of Lutheran orthodoxy rebelled. The controversy between Lutherans and the Roman Church concerned the nature of justification. The Roman Church denies that men are justified before God only through faith in the merit of Christ. Thus the Council of Trent, Sess. VI, canon 11,12 declared:

> If anyone says that men are justified, either by the sole imputation of the justice of Christ or by the sole remission of sins, to the exclusion of the grace and charity which is poured forth in their hearts by the Holy Ghost and is inherent in them; or even that the grace whereby we are justified is only the favor of God: let him be accursed.
>
> If any one saith that justifying faith is nothing else but confidence in the divine mercy, which remits sins for Christ's sake, or that this confidence alone is that whereby we are justified; let him be accursed.[31]

The Roman Catholic doctrine of justification denies that the justification of the sinner is a **judicial** act, in which God declares the sinner just by imputing to him the righteousness of Christ, which he has apprehended by faith. The *Apology* teaches the forensic concept of justification. Thus Melanchthon wrote:

> "Moreover, in this passage (Rom. 5:1) to justify signifies, according to forensic usage, to acquit a guilty one and to declare him righteous but on account of the righteousness of another, namely, of Christ, which righteousness of another is communicated unto us by faith. Therefore, since in this passage our righteousness is the imputation of another, we must speak here concerning the righteousness otherwise than in philosophy or in a civil court we seek after the righteousness of one's own work" (Art. III, 185).

The *Concordia Cyclopedia* describes the Roman Catholic doctrine as involving the following teaching:

> The unmerited grace of God touches the sinner's heart, and calls upon

47

him to repentance and faith. The sinner may, of his own power, accept or reject this grace. If he accepts it and turns to God, he receives through Baptism, full forgiveness of his past sins. That forgiveness is the one part of justification. The other part consists in this, that the sinner, by the renewal of his inner nature, is himself transformed into an intrinsically just man. As a just man he is able to do good and perfect works, which fulfill the demands of God's Law, render satisfaction for sin, and merit rewards of God, including eternal life (p. 823).[32]

Thus Session VI, Canon 32 of the Council of Trent has put it this way:

"If any one saith that the justified, by the good works which he performs through the grace of God and the merits of Jesus Christ, whose living members he is, does not truly merit increase of grace, eternal life, and the attainment of that eternal life — if so be, however, that he depart in grace — and also an increase in glory"— let him be accursed.[33]

Again the Council of Trent decided:

Life eternal is to be proposed to those working well unto the end and hoping in God, both as a grace promised to the sons of God through Jesus Christ and as a reward which is, according to the promise of God Himself, to be faithfully rendered to their good works and merits (chapter 16, Sees, VI).[34]

The Council of Trent took place between 1545-1563, a number of years after the *Apology* was published. Martin Chemnitz (1522-1580) responded with his *Examen Concilii Tridentini* (*Examination of the Council of Trent*), a massive work for four volumes directed mainly against the Roman Catholic scholar Bellarmine.

The great concern of the period of Lutheran orthodoxy was to define the nature of justification. As a typical definition of justification, R. Preus adduced the definition of Johann Mentzer (1658-1734) who in his *Exegesis Augustanae Confessionis* (*The Exegesis of the Augustana Confession*) wrote:

Justification is an act of God the Father, Son and Holy Spirit, an act which forgives the sinner all his sins, imputes to him the righteousness of Christ and receives him into everlasting life. It is an act of pure grace, love and mercy, performed because of the most holy obedience which our Mediator Christ rendered to the entire divine Law and because of the full satisfaction He made. The sinner is justified who through the ministry of the Gospel truly believes that Christ is the Redeemer of the whole world, and he is justified by grace without his own work or merits.[35] (Preus translation)

Mentzer's definition shows that justification is totally monergistic, that man can do nothing toward his justification. The forensic or legal aspect is also a part of this definition. Man deserves to be condemned but because of Christ's atoning work it is imputed to the guilty, moved solely by the mercy and love of the Triune God. During the latter part of the 16th century justification, as both Mentzer and Chemnitz show, involves: (1) the forgiveness or non-imputation of sins: and (2) the-imputation and gift of Christ's righteousness. For both of these Lutheran theologians the work of Christ was the heart and center of the doctrine of justification. They treated justification under the heading of the work of Christ.[36]

The forensic nature of justification R. Preus correctly contends was not merely a Lutheran teaching, for a study of Schrenk's articles in *Theologisches Worterbuch zum Neuen Testament* shows that **dikaioo** and its cognates are never used to teach infused grace.[37] The word **dikaioo** is never employed to designate a qualitative change in man, but a judicial act of God. Chemnitz argued that the whole New Testament is replete with forensic terminology. Romans 3, 5 and 8 show the judicial character of **dikaioo**, as may be seen from such neutral passages as Luke 7:29; 10:29; 16:15; 7:35; 1 Tim. 3:16. Since forgiveness of sins is interchangeable with justification, Chemnitz also argues that forgiveness is also a forensic term. In the New Testament justification is contrasted with "condemnation" (cf. Rom. 5:18; 8:33,34; John 5:24). In many Old Testament passages the forensic concept may be seen, such are: Gen. 44:16 (cf LXX), 2 Sam.15: 4; Is. 43:9; Ps. 51:4; Deut. 25:1; Prov. 17:15; Is. 5:23. Other Old Testament verses would be Ps. 19:9; 143:2; Dan. 8:14; Job 13:18; 34:5; 33:9-12, 32; 32:2.

Justification of Ungodly not Forgiven without Payment

It might appear that the Lutheran understanding teaches that God capriciously forgives the ungodly their sins. When God forgives, He is just, because payment had to be made for mankind's sins. The demands of the divine justice were met because Jesus by his victorious life and his sacrificial death payed the penalty which the Law demanded of its violators. Jesus made satisfaction and payed the price of punishment required by the Law. On the basis of Christ's atoning work, God now imputes to man the righteousness which Christ earned. Luther asserted that God does not justify until satisfaction has been rendered for sins to the law. God thus does not justify out of fickelness or carelessness or mistakenness. Chemnitz expressed it this way:

> This foreign righteousness is such that the parent of guilt and the complete obedience to the Law satisfied divine wrath. And the result is that there can be a propitiation for the sins of the whole world. To this righteousness the sinner, terrified and condemned by the voice of the Law, flees with true faith. He desires, implores and seizes this righteousness. To this righteousness he surrenders himself. This righteousness he sets against the judgment of God and the accusation of the Law. And by virtue of this righteousness and its being imputed to him he is justified, that is, absolved from the sweeping sentence of condemnation, and he receives the decree of life eternal.[38]

In Roman Catholic theology Christ's death is a remote meritorious cause, but in Lutheran, Christ's death is the very form of justification. What Christ did for mankind and Christ's imputed righteousness to the ungodly are the heart of justification, and therefore the heart of the Gospel.

The imputation of an alien righteousness was completely unacceptable to Roman theology. From the perspective of Rome such a kind of justification was merely relational and not ontological. Without a basis for justification in man, Rome argued that there simply could not be a righteous imputation to the sinner. In answer to the Roman charge Chemnitz argued that there was a real basis for justification; it was to be found in Christ, who had made satisfaction for sins.

Satisfaction had to be made for mankind's sins, and it was Christ the Mediator, who obeyed the Law of God and took away the sins of the world.[39] Sins which are in man are transferred to Christ who was sinless. In turn Christ's righteousness imputed to sinners. Calov wrote that justification means "that he who is justified was not previously righteous, but becomes (fieri) righteous."[40] This justification does not take place in a future life, but right now. Of the repentant publican it is asserted that he went to his house justified.

In the opinion of Lutheran orthodoxy the greatness of our justification, of the forgiveness of sins, and the imputation of Christ's righteousness to us cannot be overemphasized. Quenstedt held the same views as Luther on the greatness of justification and on the truth and validity of God's imputation.[41]

Thus Luther said: "This imputation is not a thing of no consequence, but is greater than the whole world, yea, than all the holy angels. Reason cannot see all this, for reason disregards the Word of God; but we (I say) thank God that we have such a Savior who is able to pass us by and reckon our sin as nothing."[42]

Important Aspects of Justification by Faith

Lutheran Orthodoxy according to R. Preus wrote considerably on the doctrine of justification. However, certain points are stressed especially. They are: The order of salvation; the nature of justifying faith; justification by faith and the activity of faith.

1. The Order of Justification

Relative to the so-called **ordo salutis** (order of salvation) there has been a difference among Protestant theologians since the days of the Reformation. According to Chemnitz the order used by God in preparing the sinner for justification is: first contrition; the sinners must experience the terrors of conscience when he is told of the wrath of God for sin. Preus claims that "this point is stressed by all the orthodox Lutherans as it was by Luther and Melanchthon."[43] But then, says Chemnitz, to this must be added faith. By faith man approaches God; faith asks, desires, seeks seizes and receives forgiveness of sins. The simple **ordo** (Order) is organized around preaching of Law and Gospel and the effects produced by these two distinctive words of God. Contrast this with the doctrine of Rome which taught that man merits God's grace and forgiveness (Meritum congrui) and the grace freely given (Gratia gratis data) by means of which the free will in man is moved, who then by his own natural powers inclines himself toward justification. The Lutherans, following Scripture held that faith apprehends the merits of Christ, not merely that it opens the way for hope and charity. Contrition and faith represent the only order that gives all glory to God and offers sinners lasting comfort and peace of conscience.

2. The Nature of Faith

Orthodox Lutheran writers maintained that faith was not mere assent to doctrine, a knowledge of facts, or the conviction that certain teachings were true. R. Preus claims that for theologians like Martin Chemnitz, Jesper Brochmand and Abraham Calov faith "involves the whole man, the sinner crushed by God's Law, and all his faculties."[44] These men held that it is the troubled and desperate sinner who believes. For these men faith was the sinner's personal trust in Christ. Further they held that faith is essentially trust and confidence and that it was linked up with the forgiveness of sins. Faith looks away from itself to the treasure God has and does offer in Christ. The object of faith is the work of Christ. According to orthodox Lutheranism faith is in the unseen; the unempirical, the absurd, namely, in forgiveness of sins, grace and eternal life.

3. Justification by Faith (per Fidem)

Historic Lutheranism has been influenced by the views of Luther and Chemnitz on justifying faith. Faith justifies in that its grasps, desires and accepts "in the promise of Christ with all His merits and in Christ also the mercy of God who forgives sins." To illustrate this R. Preus cites Chemnitz:

> On our part in this faith alone which justifies us and effects (Influit) our justification. Whatever merely embraces apprehends to itself the promises of grace, the forgiveness of sins and the merit of Christ does so without any admixture of works. And only that on the part of man which enters into the picture when we consider God justifying him can be said to justify. Thus we are said to be justified by faith exclusively without the deeds of the Law (Rom. 3:28; Eph. 2:8, 9). True, faith is never alone, never all by itself and isolated from good works, and yet faith alone apprehends the merit of Christ, and we are justified by means of faith alone.[45]

The Lutheran dogmaticians were careful to state that faith only justified because of its object, Christ, and did not justify because it accepted and received its object, but Chemnitz averred that "the whole justifying power of faith depends on the thing apprehended."[46] Forgiveness of sins is solely due to Christ (propter Christum) and this emphasis gives the believer the assurance that he can be certain of salvation.

Ragner Bring wrongly claims that Protestant Scholasticism separated sanctification from justification. Thus he wrote: "In Protestant Scholasticism theologians tried to escape 'justification by works' by stressing the doctrine of imputation. But this involved viewing Sanctification as a separate event, a necessary addition to justification."[47] In order to effect this separation Orthodoxy supposedly invented the one element. Roman Catholic theologians of the 16th and 17th centuries charged that Lutherans separated faith and good works, justification and sanctification. Chemnitz and his contemporaries spent much effort to show the falsity of Rome's claims. Chemnitz refuted it in the **Examen**, and here is one of the relevant passages as given and rendered by Robert Preus:

The Lutheran Church has always taught the renewal must and does follow reconciliation, and in such a manner that the Holy Spirit comes with the remission of sins, and He begins renewal in us. Therefore the Holy Spirit initiates sanctification and renewal in those who have been reconciled because of Christ the Mediator . . . Thus in no sense do we teach that justifying faith is all alone, that is, that it is a mere persuasion which is without repentance and with no good works springing from it. Such faith without works is barren and dead. We insist that it is not true and living faith at all which does not work by love (Gal. 5:6).[48]

As R. Preus has stated it: "True faith apprehends Christ; at the same time true faith is not without works (Jas. 2) and works through love (Gal. 5)."

Luther appears to have been embarrassed by James, who taught that Abraham was justified by faith and works. Preus states about orthodox theologians: "Rather they accept its canonicity unquestioningly and use it in enunciating their doctrine of justification."[49] Jesper Brochmand wrote a commentary of James and endeavored to show that Lutheranism accepted James teachings on all points. The point that James makes is that true faith expresses itself in good works. There is no true faith which is not active through love (Matt. 17:17-18; James 2:14-15ff.).

The Doctrine of Justification after the
Age of Orthodoxy The Age of Pietism

It is necessary to distinguish between orthodox, or the maintenance of pure doctrine, and orthodoxism, which denotes a mere outward and mechanical adherence to transmitted doctrines and forms. The latter often fails to distinguish between essential and accidental things and frequently degenerates into an ossified and perfunctory observance of the religious rites and a zeal not according to real knowledge and true Christian love.

Pietism was a reaction movement of the later 17th and early 18th centuries against the prevailing orthodoxism.[50] When men become convinced that a certain position, to which they take exception, presents an extreme, they are apt to go to the opposite extreme in combating the alleged error. This act explains, at least in part, why we have the phenomena of Pietism in the Church.

The origin of Pietism is to be found in three causes. The first is the reaction against the externalization in the church membership. The second is the extreme position taken by some teachers of the Church, according to which they did not hesitate to make use even of the subtleties in their exposition of Scriptural truths. The third is to be found in the conditions following the conclusion of the Thirty Year's War, especially in the general demoralization among the great mass of the people.[51] After Grossgebauer of Rostock had pointed out some of these unfortunate conditions, Spener (1635-1705) took up the matter in earnest. His great natural ability made him a natural leader in the movement. Before Pietism took over men like Arndt, Herberger and Nicolai endeavored to combine full ortho-doxy with spiritual life. In his *Pia Desideria,* Spener set forth six propos-als for the improvement of Christianity.[52] They were at first accepted by the orthodox Lutheran scholars. However, when the Pietists put their proposals in force with a vengeance, there was a reaction by other Lutherans who called the former "a sect." The orthodox universities of Leipzig and Wittenberg excluded them, forcing August Francke to found the University of Halle.

While Pietism claimed to be concerned with practical matters rather than theological, there developed points on controversy about the doc-trines of regeneration, justification, church and millennium. Klotsche stated concerning this issue:

> The orthodox affirmed that regeneration is an act of God, taking place in baptism, the effect of which must last throughout the entire life. For baptism is a never failing fountain of power and encourage-ment for the daily conflict with sin and of consolation and strength for daily renewal of the spiritual life. The Pietists identified awaken-ing or conversion with regeneration which only begins in baptism and in subsequent life is to be consummated or "sealed" by actual experi-ence or subjective feeling of God's grace. Hence they regarded con-frontation as a renewal, on the part of God and man of the baptismal covenant.[53]

Pietists also confused justification and sanctification. Contrary to the orthodox and Biblical position the Pietists taught that only a living faith that gives evidence of a pious life and active Christianity attains justifi-cation.[54] This means that the Pietistic striving for sanctification caused them to misunderstand the objective character of justification which oc-curs outside man.[55]

The author of the article on "Pietism" in the *Lutheran Cyclopedia* ob-served:

> In combating this situation a reformed leaven was added to the Lutheran mass, so that the final result was an emotionalism which deprecated the power of the means of grace as such and stressed spir-itual experience as being more important.[56]

Grossgebauer believed that justification had been emphasized at the expense of sanctification, so that the fruits of faith had suffered as the result of a dead formalism. One of the errors resulting from the separa-tion of piety from the means of grace, from a misunderstanding of ortho-doxy, was its erroneous teachings on the concepts of spirit and letter, spirit and flesh, resulting in the mixture of justification and sanctifica-tion. Another serious result of Pietism was that because of its teachings of Scripture, the amount of rationalizing the Bible grew, until it opened the way for rationalism.

The Age of Rationalism or The Enlightenment

It is always a dangerous thing when religion loses its balance, when the emphasis on the fundamental doctrines of the Bible is reduced in favor of quarrels about side issues and insignificant details. While it is important that not one revealed truth be surrendered, at the same time one must keep in mind the relative importance of its teachings, not making issue of matters which are not so regarded in the Scriptures, for else we are in danger of frustrating the Gospel.

In the first quarter of the eighteenth century many people became weary of strife and of theological controversy about insignificant details. The result was they turned to natural religion or discarded revealed religion altogether. They claimed that they would surrender superstition and instead have according to the dictates of their reasons. Some men advocating this new position, kept a belief in God, or in a supreme being. They were called deists.[57] They endeavored to form a system of religion whereby they could evaluate the various creeds and the supernatural religion of Protestantism. As their chief problem of study the deists made the historical connection between natural religion and revelation. England, as well as Voltaire and Rousseau in France were the exponents of this movement. Some deists departed so far from any form of religion are to become atheists and pantheists. That justification by faith without the deeds of the law was unacceptable to deism therefore does not surprise.

Deism was closely related to rationalism and materialism and partly identical with it. But rationalism in its full development rejected all adherence to a supernatural being. It wanted reason to rule in all domains, in law, architecture art poetry and in religion.[58] It became known as the Age of "Aufklarung" or "Illumination." From England, to France to Germany rationalism spread. Rationalistic theologians tried to correct the doctrines of Holy Writ according to the thought of contemporary times and logically criticized the teaching of Biblical orthodoxy. There was no room for such doctrines as reconciliation or original sin, which are the basis of justification.

Kant and Justification by Faith

Rationalism in a refined form is found in Immanuel Kant's *Religion innerhalb der Grenzen der blossen Vernunft, 1793* (trans. Theodore M. Greene and Hoyt H. Hudson, *Religion Within the Limits of Reason Alone*, (New York: Harper Torchbook, 1960). Kant distinguished between rationalism and naturalism (radical deism) in that he did not deny revelation.[59] Kant claimed that the most important facet of religious experience is the change of character by means of which "the radical evil" in a person is overcome and the good is brought to emerge. This change is effected through punishment and repentance. Kant said that the church, Christianity can furnish the impulse which leads to such salvation. The teaching of the Bible ought to be interpreted according those moral ideas which alone are universal and are consistent with the religion of reason. While Kant broke with the eudaemonism of the Enlightenment by placing the absolute ethical demand before happiness, he nevertheless "retained its Pelagian doctrine of salvation and its moralistic doctrine of salvation and its moralistic concept of religion. The deistic emphasis of God, virtue, and immortality had a form place in his theory."[60]

The foremost dogmatician of rationalism was Julius Wegschneider. In 1815 he published his *Institutiones theologiae Christianae* (Institutes of Christian Theology). In it he either rejected or reinterpreted the basic doctrines of Scriptures.[61] The supernatural was repudiated. Miracles were out as was anything savoring of the supernatural. Conversion was conceived of in a Pelagian sense. The resurrection was merely the resuscitation of a person who really was not dead, but merely appeared so. He did not accept the atonement, holding that the ascension was a fairy tale. Original sin was rejected and repentance was depicted as man's own work. Justification as set forth in the Bible was unacceptable. Lindberg summarized the stance of Kant and the moralists:

> By justification they meant that what is offered here on earth to make us well pleasing to God is credited to our account in advance so that we are now considered as possessing it ... However, it all takes place in our own subjective consciousness.[62]

The only valid truth remaining of old Lutheran doctrine was the fact that God does not scrutinize our separate acts but only our state of mind and for this reason grants men favor.

Theological Development of the Nineteenth Century

The Nineteenth century saw a revival of Orthodoxy but Pietism and Rationalism were also existing simultaneously. William Pauck has pointed out that in the history of Protestantism the doctrine of justification was developed either on the basis of the "orthodox" teaching of divine justifying grace (forensic justification) or as a reaction to it.[63] He wrote: "In liberal Protestantism it lost all significance, partly in connection with the dissolution of the traditional Christology and partly under the influence of the evolutionary interpretation of religious experience."[64]

Two Competing theologies in Lutheranism in the 19th and 20th Centuries

While Confessional Lutheranism suffered as a result of the coming of Pietism and Rationalism, it must be emphasized that the Old Lutheranism was not dead, as may be seen from the protest of Claus Harms (d. 1855) with his Ninety-Five Thesis.[65] However, Rationalism did not die either. Thus two streams of theological development can be traced in Lutheran lands of Europe in the nineteenth and twentieth centuries the conservative and the liberalistic. Wherever liberalism prevailed the doctrine of justification was reinterpreted or denied.

At the departure of Luther from the Diet of Augsburg he announced the view that all who held to the *Augsburg Confession*, whether openly or secretly were brothers of the faith. This same stance was taken by C.F.W. Walther, and was also held by such theologians as Krauth, Jacobs, Schmauck, and others. The true subscriber to the *Augsburg Confession* indicated that he has the Lutheran attitude toward the great fundamentals, sola Scriptura, sola gratia, sola fide and solus Christus. He that conscientiously studies the Augustana will find himself in agreement with the other Lutheran Confessions. In early American

Lutheranism church conferences and synods did not emphasize confessional loyalty and the confessions were omitted in constitutions. H.H. Muhlenberg (1711-1787) tried to induce Lutherans to subscribe to the *Augsburg Confession* and other symbols. Unfortunately after Muhlenberg's death there was a movement away from confessionalism, brought about by rationalistic influence.[66]

The movement known as "American Lutheranism" was a nineteenth century development in American Lutheranism that decried the Lutheran Confessions. This anti-confessional movement was fathered by S.S. Schmucker, B. Kurtz, S. Sprecher, and other leaders of the General Synod about the middle of the nineteenth century. As a movement it has been characterized as "essentially Calvinistic Methodistic Puritanic, indifferentistic, and unionistic, hence anything but truly Lutheran; denied and assailed every doctrine distinctive of Lutheranism... attacked what was most sacred to Luther and most prominent in the Lutheran Confessions."[67] This was sponsored by B. Kurt in the *Observer*, by Weyl in *Luth. Hirtenstimme*, and later by the *American Lutheran* (1865). These men attacked those who insisted on subscription to the Lutheran Confessions as "Symbolists" and portrayed the latter as "extremist of the most dangerous sort." "Although they had no use for the *Augsburg Confession*, they planned to unite all Lutherans in America on the basis of a definite Platform."[68] This movement contributed to the disruption the General Synod in 1866. Hereafter the General Synod became more conservative, heading a more confessional foundation.[69]

The first American Synod to insist on a strict confessionalism was the Tennessee Synod. In the last three decades of the nineteenth century an awakening of confessionalism swept the Lutheran Church in America, in consequence of the determined stand taken by such men as Walther, Wynecken, and others who sounded the tocsin of true Lutheranism in the United States. Whereas before this awakening a large part of the Lutheran Church along the Eastern seaboard had become rationalistic, a new wave of confessionalism swept over the church bodies formerly indifferent to it. This meant that the doctrine of justification by faith received the attention it should.

The Lutheran Situation in Germany and
The Scandinavian Countries in the Nineteenth Century

The first half of the nineteenth century saw a revival of religion throughout Germany. But before taking up that revival, something should be said about negative forms of religiosity which sprang up. Friedrich Daniel Schleiermacher (1768-1834) exercised a great influence at the end of the eighteenth and also during the first three decades of the nineteenth. He became the founder of modern protestant theology.[70] His chief work was: *Christlicher Glaube, nach den Grundsaetzen der evangelischen Kirche im Zusammenhalt dargestellt* (1821-22). This dogmatic showed him to be a rationalist and pantheist. Although Schleiermacher attacked rationalism he did not teach Biblical Christianity. Religion for him was a feeling of dependence upon God, who is the highest Causality, manifesting Himself in His attributes of omnipotence, eternity, omnipresence, and omniscience.

Justification according to Schleiermacher is identical with the living union with Christ. The negative element in justification is the forgiveness of sins; the positive is the adoption of believers as the children of God. He repudiated the doctrine of the imputation of Christ's merit. A powerful consciousness of God is infused in man, which God considers perfect, although here in time it is imperfect.[71]

John Tobias Beck (1804-1878)

Beck was an opponent of the critico-historical method as developed by Strauss and Baur; he emphasized the need for a return to the Bible and Biblical truth. His theologizing, unfortunately, swerved from Lutheran orthodoxy. He rejected the Lutheran position that the Confessions were a correct exposition of Biblical doctrines. The latter were only important as historical documents because they performed a purpose in bygone history. Beck claimed that the ethical or moral is the first and essential mark of the Christian. He adopted different formal and material principles for his theological system. In the doctrine of justification his emphasis was placed upon the psychological, seeing the saving hand of love rather than the majestic pronouncement of the Judge; faith was understood as the active ethical grasp of Christ. This was a dynamic gift which produced personal righteousness, for Beck made the foundation for justification. He rejected the view that justification was a momentary forensic act, but taught that justification is a process that continues throughout life. Beck resembled Osiander in he believed righteousness essentially dwelt in man.[72]

Influential during the first half of the nineteenth century was George Wilhelm Hegel, German philosopher, who was the main exponent of Absolute Idealism in modern philosophy. Hegel taught that all that exists is the result, ultimately, of the development of one absolute thought or idea, or, expressed in terms of religion, the world, mankind and everything in it, is only the self-manifestation of God.[73] While the claim was made that this philosophical speculation was in harmony with Biblical theology and that it was a reconciling of religion and philosophy, it represented a complete rejection of historic Biblical Christianity.[74] At best it set forth pantheism. In this system of thought there was no room for a concrete historical Christ. The doctrine of justification was impossible to bring into any relationship with idealism.

The nineteenth century saw a revival of religion throughout Germany. Lutheran confessional theology was found in a more conservative form in what is known as the "theology of Repristination," as well in a more liberal form, known as the "Erlangen Theology."[75]

Ernst Wilhelm Hengstenberg (1802-1869) found in the Lutheran Confessions the clearest exposition of the teachings of the Bible.[76] By his work in the Old Testament he became the staunchest defender of it against rationalism and the higher criticism that was being developed by other Lutherans. In 1827 Hengstenberg founded the **Evangelische Kirchen-**

zeitung, a most influential organ against erroristic teaching. He edited this organ for forty-two years. He was slandered and defamed because of his Biblical stand and because of his attacks upon error. However, he refused to leave "the Union," which harbored nationalists. In his last years Hengstenberg unfortunately adopted Romanizing views on Justification. Hengstenberg, appealing to Luke 7:36ff, claimed that justification was a gradual process.[77]

The Erlangen School tried to combine Lutheran theology with the new learning, and also differentiated between Reformation theology and post-Reformation theology. This school held that confessional theology was not to remain static but was to be dynamic. Outstanding scholars of the Erlangen school were: J.C.K. von Hofmann (d. 1877), F.H.R. von Frank (d, 1894), G. Thomasius Cd. 1875) and men from various universities like Theodosius Harnack (d. 1891), J.H. Kurtz (d. 1890), F. Delitzsch (d. 1890), F.A. Kahnis (d. 1888), E. Luthardt (d. 1904), G. Plitt (d. 1880), G. von Zeschwitz (d. 1886), Th. Zahn (d. 1933), L.H. Ihmels (d. 1933). The Erlangen School fought rationalism in its old crass form. Its organ of communication was **Zeitschrift fuer Protestantismus und Kirche**. This theological school claimed to defend conservative confessional Lutheranism, but it is sad to say, its members left the Lutheran base. It repudiated the Lutheran principle of **sola Scriptura** as the only source of theology and substituted the believing **ego**, the Christian consciousness and thus followed Schleiermacher. The Erlangen School insisted upon the right to develop the doctrine of the confessions along the lines of "a scientific theology."

Johann Christian Konrad von Hofmann (1810-1877) one of the leading theologians of the Erlangen School whose hermeneutics is at present being advocated in certain Lutheran circles, was a theologian whose theologizing is not in harmony with the Lutheran Confessions. His writings are replete with theological errors. Christianity, according to Hofmann, is the communion of God and man as mediated by the Christ in us. Hofmann followed Schleiermacher and developed his theology from his own religious consciousness. He taught that Christ did only suffer and die on our behalf but not in our stead. He reproached the Lutheran Symbols for teaching the juridical character of justification. His erroneous doctrine of reconciliation denied whole areas of Christian doctrine.

Footnotes

1. E.H. Klotsche, *Christian Symbolics* (Burlington, Iowa: The Lutheran Literary Board, 1929), p. 143. J.L. Neve, *Introduction to the Symbolical Books of the Lutheran Church* (Columbus, The Lutheran Book Concern, 1926), p. 398.

2. Cf. James W. Richard, *The Confessional History of the Lutheran Church* (Philadelphia: Lutheran Publication Society, 1909), pp. 26-268.

3. "The *Apology* of the *Augsburg Confession*," Henry Eyster Jacobs and John A.W. Haas, editors, *The Lutheran Cyclopedia* (New York: Charles Scribners's Sons, 1899), p. 19.

4. F. Bente, *Historical Introduction to the Symbolical Books of the Evangelical Lutheran Church* (St. Louis: Concordia Publishing House, 1921), pp. 40-41.

5. "*Augsburg Confession* and Its *Apology*," L. Fuerbringer, Th. Engelder, P.E. Kretz-mann, Editors-in Chief, *The Concordia Cyclopedia* (St. Louis: Concordia Publishing House, 1927), p. 47.
6. **Ibid.**
7. **Ibid.**
8. J.L. Neve, *Churches and Sects of Christendom* (Burlington, Iowa: Lutheran Literary Board, 1940), p. 184.
9. Gerhard Gieschen, '*Apology* of the *Augsburg Confession*,' Julius Bodensieck, *The Encyclopedia of the Lutheran Church* (Minneapolis: Augsburg Publishing House, 1965), I, p. 96.
10. **Ibid.**
11. **Ibid.**
12. H. G.H., "Justification," in Jacobs and Haas, *The Lutheran Cyclopedia*, **op, cit.**, p. 256.
13. The Weimar edition of Luther, 38, 113.
14. **Ibid.**, 31:255; also quoted FC SOL Dec. III, 6, Tappert, 1cf2 **op. cit.**, D. 540.
15. Reverend Franklin Weidner, Pneumatology of *The Doctrine of the Work of The Holy Spirit* (Chicago: Wartburg Press, 1915).
16. Francis Pieper, *Christian Dogmatics* (St. Louis: Concordia Publishing House), II, p. 514.
17. *Concordia Triglotta, Libri symbolici Ecclesiae Lutheranae, Germanice-Latine-Ger-manice* (St. Louis: Concordia Publishing House, 1921), p. 1266.
18. Theodore G. Tappert et. al., *The Book of Concord* (Philadelphia Fortress Press, 1959), p. 30.
19. Ralph A. Bohlmann, *Principles of Biblical Interpretation* (St. Louis: Concordia Publishing House, 1968), pp. 73-74.
20. Herbert J. A. Bouman, "Some Thoughts on the Theological Presuppositions for a Lutheran Approach to the Scriptures," in *Aspects of Biblical Hermeneutics: Con-fessional Principles and Practical Applications*, Occasional Papers No. 1 of *Con-cordia Theological Monthly* (St. Louis: Concordia Publishing House, 1966), p. 16.
21. Die Theologie der lutherischen Bekenntnischriften von 1529-bis 1537, trans. Ger-hard Klose (Gottingen: Vandenhoeck & Ruprecht, 1965), p. 98.
21a. Klotsche, **op. cit.**, pp. 145-148; Erwin J. Lueker, *Lutheran Cyclopedia* (St. Louis: Concordia Publishing House, 1954), p. 633.
21b. F.E. Mayer, *Lutheran Bodies In America* (St. Louis: Concordia Publishing House, 1956), pp. 156-157.
21c. **Ibid.**
22. Robert O. Preus, "The Doctrine of Justification in the Theology of Lutheran Or-thodoxy," *The Springfielder*, Spring, 1956, p. 24.
23. **Ibid.**, p. 24.
24. **Ibid.**, p. 25.
25. **Ibid.**
26. **Ibid.**
27. Abraham Calov, *Synopsis Controversiarum* (Wittenberg: 1653), p. 18.
28. Martin Chemnitz, *Examen Concilii Tridentini* (Bertini, 1861), p. 146.
29. Martin Chemnitz, *Loci Theologi*, 163 ed. II, p. 215.
30. **Ibid.**, II, p. 200. 823
32. "Merit of Works," *The Concordia Cyclopedia*, **op. cit.**, 823.
31. Quoted from J. Waterworth, *Canons and Decrees of the Council of Trent* (Chicago:

Christian Symbolic Pub I. Society).

33. Waterworth, **op. cit.**
34. **Ibid.**
35. B. Mentzer, *Exegesis Augustanae Confessions. Pera Latina,* (Frankurti, 1669), I. p. 60. Translation by Preus.
36. Preus, "The Doctrine of Justification, etc." **op. cit.**, p. 28.
37. **Ibid.**, p. 29.
38. Martin Chemnitz, *Loci Theologici II*, p. 234.
39. Quenstedt, *Systema*, P. III, C. 7, P. 1, Th. 13 (III, p. 522) as cited by Preus, p. 19.
40. Abraham Calov, *Socinismus Profligatus*, p. 735.
41. Quenstedt, *Systema*, P. III, C. 7, P. 1, H. 19 (III, p. 525).
42. Weimar edition of *Luther's Works*, 30, pp. 97-98.
43. Preus, **op. cit.**, p. 32.
44. **Ibid.**, p. 33.
45. Martin Chemnitz, *Systema*, P. III, C. I, S. 1, Th. 11 (III, p. 519).
46. **Ibid.**
47. Ragner Bring, "Justification," *The Encyclopedia of the Lutheran Church*, **op. cit.**, p. 1193.
48. Chemnitz, *Examen*, **op. cit.**, p. 188.
49. Preus, **op. cit.**, p. 37.
50. "Pietism," *The Lutheran Cyclopedia*, **op. cit.**, p. 818.
51. Kenneth Scott Latourette, *History of Christianity* (New York: Harper & Brothers, 1953), pp. 894-897.
52. E .H. Klotsche, *The History of Christian Doctrine* (Burlington, Iowa: The Lutheran Literary Board, 1945), p. 283.
53. **Ibid.**, pp. 283-284.
54. Cf. Pietism, Jacob and Hass, *The Lutheran Cyclopedia*, **op. cit.**, p. 381.
55. "Pietism," Lueker, *Lutheran Encyclopedia* (1954), pp. 818-819.
56. **Ibid.**
57. Otto W. Heick, *A. History of Christian Thought* (Philadelphia: Fortress Press, 1966), II, pp. 97-104.
58. Klotsche, **op. cit.**, p. 299.
59. Bengt Hagglund, *History of Theology*. Translated by Gene J. Lund (St. Louis: Concordia Publishing House, 1968), pp. 349-350.
60. **Ibid.**, p. 350.
61. **Ibid.**
62. C. E. Lindbergh, *Christian Dogmatics*. The Swedish Edition translated into English by Rev. C. E. Hoffsten (Augustana, IL: Augustans Book Concern, 1928), p. 340.
63. Wilhelm Pauck, "Justification," Vergilius Ferm, *The Encyclopedia of Religion* (New York: The Philosophical Library, 1945), p. 410.
64. **Ibid.**
65. A.G. Voight, "Harms, Claus," Jacob and Haas, **op. cit.**, p. 214.
66. "Muhlenberg, Heinrich Melchior," Lueker, *Concordia Cyclopedia*, **op. cit.**, p. 721.
67. "American Lutheranism," **Ibid.**, p. 28.
68. "General Synod of the Evangelical Lutheran Church in the United States of America," *Lutheran Cyclopedia*, **op. cit.**, p. 406.
69. **Ibid.**, pp. 404, 406.
70. Hagglund, **op. cit.**, pp. 353-359.
71. Lindberg, **op. cit.**, p. 340.

72. "Beck, Johann Tobias (1804-78)," *Lutheran Cyclopedia* (1954), **op. cit.**, pp. 99-100.
73. Lindberg, **op. cit.**, p. 340-341.
74. Hagglund, **op. cit.**, pp. 360-362.
75. Lewis W. Spitz, "Lutheran Theology after 1560," *Lutheran Cyclopedia*, **op. cit.**, p. 639.
76. Klotsche, **op. cit.**, p. 323.
77. Pieper, *Christian Dogmatics*, **op. cit.**, II, p. 537.
78. Hagglund, **op. cit.**, pp. 368-370.

Questions
1. What was the *Roman Confutation*? ____
2. The Evangelicals considered the doctrine of ____ the central doctrine of the Bible.
3. The Augustana contains ____ articles.
4. What constitutes one third of the *Apology*? ____
5. The *Roman Confutation* condemned ____.
6. Is the doctrine of justification taught in the Old Testament? ____
7. What was given up at the Augsburg Interim? ____
8. Justifying faith is never alone but always has with it ____.
9. The Council of Trent condemned the doctrine of ____.
10. When did the Council of Trent take place? ____
11. The word **dikaioo** is never employed to ____.
12. What was completely unacceptable to Roman Catholic theology? ____
13. Faith is essentially ____.
14. True faith is never ____.
15. What point does James make? ____
16. What kind of movement was pietism? ____
17. Who founded the University of Halle? ____
18. Pietism opened the way for ____.
19. Quarrels about insignificant and side issues may ____.
20. Who were the proponents of deism? ____
21. Rationalistic theologians tried to ____.
22. Immanuel Kant claimed that ____.
23. What happened where liberalism prevailed? ____
24. Who agreed with what Luther said about the *Augsburg Confession*? ____
25. The anti-confessional movement was fathered by ____.
26. Who sounded the doctrine of true Lutheranism in the United States? ____
27. Who became the father of modern Protestant theology? ____
28. Schleiermacher repudiated the doctrine of ____.
29. What did John Tobian Beck teach about justification? ____
30. The German Philosopher Hegel taught? ____
31. Hengstenberg founded ____.
32. The Erlangen school insisted on the right to ____.
33. What did Hofmann maintain? ____

Luther's Attitude Toward Scripture and Basic Hermeneutical Principles

Christian News, October 18, 1982

Frederick C. Grant, *In An Introduction to New Testament Thought* stated that the Scriptures testify about themselves as follows:

> Everywhere it is taken for granted that what is written in scripture is the work of divine inspiration, and is therefore trustworthy, infallible, and inerrant. The scripture must be "fulfilled" (Luke 22:37). What was written for our instruction (Rom. 15:4; I Cor. 10:11); what is described or related in the Old Testament is unquestionably true. No New Testament writer would dream of questioning a statement contained in the Old Testament, though the exact manner or mode of its inspiration is nowhere stated explicitly.[1]

This is the judgment of a critical scholar who does not believe himself bound by Scriptural teaching. But he does accurately enunciate the position of the Scriptures concerning their inerrancy and infallibility.

Emil Brunner claims that the doctrine of verbal inspiration was a doctrine that was known before New Testament times: "The doctrine of verbal inspiration was already known to pre-Christian Judaism . . . and was probably also taken over by Paul and the rest of the apostles."[2] Brunner argues that the doctrine of verbal inspiration was of no great consequence throughout the medieval period because of the use of allegorical interpretation allowed by the scholastics, but that the doctrine was revived in the days of the Reformation.[3]

Luther found the Gospel message of free and full salvation in Christ the heart of the Bible. Luther's triumphant rejoicing in the Gospel message of grace influenced his whole use of the Bible. The God who spoke (Deus Locutus) is the God who is still speaking in the Bible (Deus loquens), and what He there utters is not primarily and essentially not law, but Gospel. In the Scriptures Christ was all in all.[4]

Reinhold Seeberg, in his *Lehrbuch der Dogmengeschichte*, summarized Luther's position as follows:

> The thought of the absolute authority of Scripture finds its culmination in Luther . . . in the inspiration of the Bible. To him the words of Scripture are the real words of God, for the Holy Spirit has comprehended His wisdom and mystery in the Word and revealed it in Scripture, for which reason he (Luther) distinguishes the "manifest external Word" (W. 36,501). The veracious God speaks in Scripture and therefore we must believingly accept what is written in it (W 40 2, 593). What St. Paul says, the Holy Spirit says, and so whatever opposes the Word of Paul opposes the Holy Spirit (W 10.2,139f.). According to God's will, the Apostles were to be infallible teachers (Di, 12). They possess authority as do the prophets (**ibid.**, 100). In addition, they received the Holy Ghost so that their words are the words of God (W 40.1, 173f.). As men, they are subject to sin and error, just as Peter

was at Antioch, but then the Holy Spirit corrects their failings (W 40,1, 195f.). He moves them to speak the truth, even when they commit grammatical errors. . . For this reason Scripture is the Word of God and not the word of man (W5, 184; 8, 597). What is more: God is the Author of the Gospel (W 8, 584) and the Holy Spirit Himself is the writer of Genesis (W 44, 532). Scripture, therefore is the very Word of the Holy Spirit (W 7, 638; 46, 545; 47, 133).[5]

Seeberg in his *Dogmengeschichte* claims that Luther took over the medieval theory of inspiration "and treats Luther's position fairly in that he disclaims that the great Reformer espoused 'mechanical inspiration.'"[6] To depict Luther as a person who was a forerunner of the historical critical method simply is not factual.

Dr. Pieper in this *Christian Dogmatics* repudiated the assertion that there was a difference between Luther and later Lutherans on the doctrine of inspiration:

The alleged difference between Luther and the Lutheran dogmaticians is pure fabrication. The real difference between Luther and the dogmaticians is that the dogmaticians weakly stammer and re-echo what Luther had taught much more strongly about Scripture from Scripture. Quenstedt, for example, writes concerning Holy Scripture as the inspired Word of God: "The canonical Holy Scriptures in the original text are the infallible truth and are free from every error; in other words, in the canonical sacred Scriptures there is found no lie, no falsity, no error, not even in the least, whether in subject matter or expressions, but in all things and in all details that are handed down in them, they are most certainly true, whether they pertain to doctrines or morals, to history or chronology, to topography or nomenclature. No ignorance, no thoughtlessness, no forgetfulness, no lapse of memory. No ignorance can and dare be ascribed to the amenuenses of the Holy Ghost in their penning the Sacred Writings" (Systema I, 112). This statement of Quenstedt has been called a "horrible assertion." But everything that Quenstedt says about Scripture is said by Luther, including the details mentioned by Quenstedt, only Luther states these things with incomparably greater force. To demonstrate this, we shall record here, first, what Luther says regarding the entire Scripture, and, then, what Luther says on the details concerning which it is claimed that he plainly differed from the dogmaticians.[7]

In this section of his *Christian Dogmatics* Dr. Pieper argues against those who claim that Luther had a different doctrine of inspiration and inerrancy than that held by the Lutheran Confessions and the dogmaticians of the seventeenth century.

Dr. Pieper quotes from the St. Louis edition of *Luther's Works* 38 follows: "So, then, the entire Scriptures are assigned to the Holy Ghost" (1890); "The Holy Scriptures did not grow on earth" (St. 1:VII 2095). "The Holy Scriptures have been spoken by the Holy Ghost (St. L., III: 1895); Scripture is 'the book of the Holy Ghost' (St. L., IX: 1775. Scripture is God's Epistle addressed to men" (St. L., I: 1055).[8]

Dr. Pieper claims that there are hundreds of similar passages in

Luther's writings. Other passages in the St. Louis edition supporting Pieper's position would be:

No other doctrine should be proclaimed in the Church than the pure Word of God, that is, the Holy Scriptures (St. L. IX:87).

In the Book of the Holy Ghost, that is. Holy Scripture, we must seek and find Christ, not only in the promise (Gospel), but also in the law (St. L. IX: 1775).

It is our unbelief and corrupt carnal mind which does not allow us to perceive and consider that God speaks to us in Scripture or that Scripture is the Word of God (St. L. IX: 1800).

In Scriptures you are reading not the word of man, but the Word of the most exalted God, who desires to have disciples that diligently observe and note what he says (St. L. IX: 1818).[9]

Today a great deal is made about the human side of the Scriptures. The emphasis on the humanity of Scriptures is supposed to be a great accomplishment of the historical critical method. Luther was aware of the human side of Scripture, but only in the sense that God employed human writers to record his word. Luther criticized those people who claim that the Scriptures in their entirety are not God's Word because human writers were used. In remarking on I Peter 3:15 Luther said:

But if they take exception and say: You preach that one should not hold to man's doctrine and yet Peter and Paul and even Christ were men — when you hear people of this stamp who are so blinded and hardened as to deny that which Christ and the apostles spoke and wrote in God's Word, or doubt it, then be silent, speak no more with them and let them go (St. L. IX: 1238).

Luther maintained that the so-called human parts of the Bible must be identified as the Word of God. The Reformer believed that the Holy Spirit inspired David to state what was in his heart. Thus he wrote: "I believe that the Holy Ghost Himself wanted to take the trouble to compile a short Bible and book of illustrations for all Christendom and all saints" (St. L. XIV:21).

Luther regarded the so-called trivial things (levicula) in the Bible as inspired by the Holy Spirit. Thus the Reformer asserted:

God takes pleasure in describing such lowly things to show and testify that He does not despise or abhor the household, nor wants to be far away from it and from a pious husband, his wife, and children (St. L. II:537ff).

The story of Judah and Tamar, which Luther calls an atrocious tale, is also attributed to the Holy Ghost:

The Holy Spirit is wonderfully diligent in narrating this shameful adulterous story . . . What has induced the most pure mouth of the Holy Spirit to condescend to such low, despised, yes, and even unchaste and filthy things and damnable . . . to teach a lesson to the Church and congregation of God? (St. L. II:120ff).

Concerning the Mosaic creation Luther asserted:

If you cannot understand how it could have been done in six days then accord the Holy Ghost the honor that he is more learned than you are. When you read the words of Holy Scripture, you must realize that God is speaking them (St. L. 111:21).

Regarding the differences found in the Four Evangelists Luther wrote:

The Holy Spirit arranged it so that no evangelist agrees with the other in using the same words (St. L. 19:1104).

Concerning the chronology of Scripture, Luther held that whenever the chronological data disagreed with the Bible, the secular writers were to be corrected by the Scriptures:

I make use of secular writers in such a way that I am not compelled to contradict Scripture. For I believe that in the Scriptures the God of truth speaks, but in the histories good people display, according to their ability, their diligence and fidelity (but only as men), or at least that their (The Scriptures) copyists have perhaps erred (St. L. XIV: 1481).

Luther held that the autographs only were inerrant. He realized that there were copyist mistakes in the transmitted manuscripts. He assumed a copyist mistake had been made in Acts. 13:19f, a discrepancy that later texts verified. Luther believed that there was a contradiction between Numbers 14:22 and I Cor. 10:9 (WA 64:66), a problem rectified by recent translations.

The Authority of Scripture

Luther held that the Church has no right to teach anything contrary to God's Word, or to promulgate teachings independently of it.

Every Christian knows that the Church cannot decree or regulate anything independently of the Bible. He who, nevertheless, does so belongs to the nominal church only, as Christ says in Jn. 10:27, 'My sheep hear my voice.' They do not hear the voice of the stranger but flee him. . . Something is not God's Word because the Church says it, but the Church is where the word of God is spoken. . . Therefore, things that are ordained without the word of God are not ordinations of the Church, but of Satan's synagogue which goes under the name of the Church (WA, 8:49).

Every believer has the obligation and right to evaluate and judge teachers and doctrines in the light of the Scriptures:

Bishops, Pope, the learned . . . have the right to teach; but the sheep (the believers) are to judge whether they are teaching what Christ says, or what a stranger says (WA, 11:409).

On the basis of this principle, Luther wrote:

We should . . . let the Scripture rule and master us, and we should not be masters ourselves according to our mad heads, setting ourselves above Scriptures (WA, 47:367).

On the question whether or not the Scripture contradicted itself Luther asserted: "that Scripture does not contradict itself nor any one article of faith, even though to our mind a contradiction and inconsistency may exist" (WA, 34:11:385).

Because of this truth Luther was convinced that the Bible was to be explained in an "harmonistic way." The Bible must never be interpreted in a manner that one passage contradicts another, for "the Bible agrees with itself everywhere" (St. L. 3:18). "It is impossible that Scripture would contradict itself" (St L. 9:356).

Luther's Christocentric Principles and Its Relationship to the Total Scripture.

That Luther is supposed to have taken a liberal attitude to the Scripture is often the claim of those opposed to verbal and plenary inspiration.[10] Thus Luther is quoted as saying: "If our opponents urge Scripture, we urge Christ against Scripture" (WA 39, 1:47). This assertion of Luther has been cited as evidence that one can use Christ for not accepting clear statements of Scripture. Only that which "Christum treibt" is supposed to be binding on the consciences of men. However, an examination of the context of this passage will show that this is an erroneous interpretation. Luther's discussion concerns the doctrine of justification by grace, which was not accepted by the Romanists. The latter appealed to Scriptural passages as: "Thou shall keep the commandments" (Dt. 8:6), "Thou shall love the Lord thy God" (Mt 22:37), "This do, and thou shall live" (Luke 10:28). When the Roman Catholics used these passages to support the necessity of good works, Luther claimed that against such misusage he would "urge Christ against the Scripture." In speaking about "urging Christ against (such misuse of) Scripture" Luther wrote: "Scripture is to be understood as testifying for Christ, not against Him; it must therefore be considered as referring to Him, or not to be considered true Scripture" (WA, 39:147). In affirming that Scripture is God's Word insofar as it impels towards Christ, he is laying down a principle of interpretation, not of selection. There is no part of Scripture which does not impel toward Christ. "The whole Scripture exists for the Son" (WA Tr 5, 5585).

When Luther asserted that he would quote Christ against the Scripture, he was saying, that if there were individuals who would take certain words and employ them in a way that would place them in conflict with his actual teachings (as the Romanists did do with the quoted passages), they are not the true Scripture, even though they are taken from the Bible.

Luther is depicted as taking a liberal attitude toward the Bible, because of certain remarks made by him concerning Biblical books that Ancient Church classified as Antilegomena, Luther was following the Ancient Church which had doubts relative to the canonicity of certain books. Francis Pieper said concerning this matter:

> Even the weakest mind can see without much reflection how foolish it is to conclude from an adverse verdict of Luther on a book which he did not regard as canonical that he held liberal views on the inspiration of those books which he regarded as canonical, just the opposite ought to be concluded.[11]

Those who want to have Luther appear as exhibiting a liberal attitude to Biblical studies have also cited W. Link's Annotations to the Five Books of Moses, where Luther says that "some hay, straw, and stubble slipped in at times (into the writings) of these good and faithful teachers"

(St. L. 14:150). Dr. Pieper responded to this interpretation as follows:

It is utterly impossible to refer Luther's words to the Biblical authors, that is, to the Prophets insofar as they wrote the Bible of the Old Testament. Luther is rather speaking of those periods in the lives of the prophets when they were not moved as infallible organs of the Holy Spirit to write the Holy Scriptures, but when outside the state of (this kind of) inspiration they, just like other people, made the Scriptures of the Old Testament the object of their study and, in doing this, entered in a book the good thoughts the Holy Spirit awakened in them during this study. To this study and this writing which took place when they were not inspired to write the Holy Scriptures, refer Luther's words: Though some hay, straw, and wood (stubble) slipped in at times, etc. What Luther teaches is that the Prophets of the Old Testament did not always infallibly speak and write God's Word, but only at times, temporarily, namely, when inspired by the Holy Ghost. Read his remarks on Gen. 44:18: "The Holy Ghost did not always touch the hearts of the prophets."[12]

Luther's Hermeneutics

Not every person can understand the Scriptures according to Luther. Regarding this requirement the Reformer asserted:

No human being sees one iota of Scripture unless he has the Spirit of God. All men have a darkened heart, so that even if they knew how to tell and set forth all that the Bible contains, yet they are unable to feel and know how it...For the Spirit is needed for the understanding of the Bible as a whole and its every part (WA, 18:609).

The Holy Bible wants to be dealt with fear and humility, and one can get into its meaning better by studying it with pious prayer than with keenness of intellect. It is therefore impossible for those who rely on their bare ingenuity (nudo ingenio) and rush into the Bible with dirty feet, like pigs, as though Scripture were a sort of human knowledge, not to harm themselves and others, whom they instruct. So utterly they fail to understand it (WA, 1:507).

Luther insisted that a passage be studied in the light of its context:

It will not do to tear a statement out of its context and then urge it (drauf pochen, use it as a strong proof). One might consider the meaning of the entire text, the relation of its thoughts to one another (wie er an einander haengt (WA, 18:69).

Scripture must interpret Scripture, passages that treat of the same subject or ideas must be used to explain one another:

The Bible wants to interpret itself by comparison of passages from everywhere ... And the safest of all ways to search for the meaning of Scripture is to strive for it by comparison of the passages (WA, 14:556).

However, Luther warns against placing passages together for purposes of elucidation that do not belong together:

It is not enough to cite a different passage without the slightest regard to whether it proves the same point or something else. No mistake is more easily and commonly made in dealing with the Bible than bringing together Scripture passages that are different, as though they were identical (WA, 18:728).

Luther and the other Reformers believed that the Bible was clear and plain and that any converted believer could understand the Scriptures as far as his spiritual needs were concerned. Against the papacy he stated:

No clearer book has been written than the Holy Bible...It is a horrible...crime against Scripture and all Christendom to say that the Bible is dark and not so clear that everybody may understand it in order to teach and prove his faith (WA, 8:236).

Luther was opposed to the allegorical method, a methodology that had been in vogue for over a thousand years in the history of the Church.

Luther and the Literal Sense

In commenting on Isaiah 36:6 Luther wrote:

The Christian reader should devote his first effort to searching what is called the literal sense. It alone is the entire substance of faith and Christian theology; it holds its own in tribulation and temptation and gains victory over the gates of hell and triumphs to the praise and glory of God. But allegory is often uncertain and unreliable and very unsafe as a prop of faith, since it frequently depends upon human conjecture and opinion. If anyone leans on it, he is leaning on the reed of Egypt (WA, 14:560).

Luther insisted that the Scriptures be interpreted in their literal sense because they had been given by God:

The Holy Spirit is the plainest writer and speaker in heaven and on earth. His words can therefore have no more than one sense, and it is the most obvious sense. This we call the literal or natural sense...It is...surer and safer to abide by the words in their simple sense (WA, 23:92).

Luther was strongly opposed to those who departed from the literal meaning of the text. When the text should be understood in a literal manner, the Reformer believed it was wrong to deal with it figuratively:

It is the manner of all who evade arguments by means of figurative language, arrogantly holding the text itself in contempt and having for their aim merely to pick out a certain term and twisting and crucifying it on the cross of their own opinion, with utter disregard of the circumstances, of the preceding and following context, and of the intent and purpose of the writer (WA, 18:713).

Luther insisted:

Whoever is so bold as to give the words of Scripture a meaning that differs from the sense that their simple sound confers is obliged to prove his explanation from the text before him or from the article of faith (WA, 23:92).

Neither a conclusion or a figure of speech should be admitted in any place of the Bible, unless evident contextual circumstances or the absurdity of anything obviously militating against an article of faith

68

requires it. On the contrary, we must everywhere adhere to the simple, pure and natural meaning of the words. This accords with the rules of grammar and the usage of speech which God has given men (WA, 18:700).

Luther opposed Zwingli on the interpretation of the words of institution. Zwingli rejected the real   presence of Christ in the Lord's Supper and consequently the fact that the recipient also received the body and blood of Christ for the forgiveness of sins. Luther was completely against Zwingli's **alloeosis**. Accepting Zwingli's interpretation would result in uncertainty and obscuring the teaching of Christ. Luther warned his readers against this faulty method of interpretation:

> Beware, beware, I say, of that alloeosis. It is the devil's mask; for from it is born such a Christ, according to whom I would not wish to be a Christian (WA, 26:319).

Luther was aware of the fact that the Scriptures do employ figurative language. The Reformer knew that there were parables and types in the Bible, but he also believed that when these literary forms were employed that they could be recognized. The normal rule is to follow the literal meaning of the text.

> If everyone is allowed to invent conclusions and figures of speech according to his own whim, nothing could be determined and proved to a certainty concerning an article of faith...We must avoid as the most deadly poison all figurative language that the Bible itself does not force us to find in a passage (WA, 18:700f).

Refusing to abide by the plain and literal meaning to the Bible was a problem in Luther's time just as it is in the 20th century. Barth, Brunner, Bultmann have resorted to methods that reject the clear and literal meaning of the Scriptural text. Form criticism and Bultmannian demythologizing resort to questioning the literal character of text that give no indications that they are parabolic or symbolical.

Luther warns against doing violence to the plain meaning of the Bible:

> No violence should be done to the words of God...; but as far as possible we should retain them in their simplest meaning and take them in their grammatical and literal sense, unless an obvious circumstance plainly forbids it (WA, 6:509).

> We must not commit sacrilege against the word of God and without warrant of any express passage of Scripture give a word a meaning that differs from its natural sense (WA, 11:434).[13]

The Attributes of Scripture

For the Reformer of Wittenberg Scriptures were not only authoritative and normative but they also contained a causative authority, that is, they were powerful, creating and sustaining faith and engendering works, the evidence of a justifying faith. "In other words," wrote Dr. J. T. Mueller, "Luther regarded the divine Word of Scripture as the efficacious means of grace, by which the Holy Spirit works faith in men and keeps them in the true faith to the end. In many respects this causative authority of the Bible is central in Luther's theological thought and reformatory work.

Against his Romanist and enthusiastic opponents he consistently defends the divine Word as both the normative and the causative authority of the Christian faith and life."[14]

Luther taught that "faith cometh by learning and preaching by the Word of God" (Rom. 10:17); "The words that I speak unto you are spirit and life" (John 6:36); "The Gospel is the power of God unto salvation" (Romans 1:16). This did not mean that Luther ascribed a magical power to the Word of God, but the Word of God became the means through which the Holy Spirit operated. Luther was aware of the problem of why some believed and others did not. This is a problem which he did not endeavor to solve, considering it a mystery that would be answered in heaven (Rom. 11:33-36; I Cor. 13:9-12). The Wittenberg Reformer did not formulate the doctrine of the efficacy of the Word as it was done during the age of orthodoxy. And yet what the later Lutheran dogmaticians formulated as the attributes of Holy Writ are found scattered through Luther's writings.[15]

In contradistinction to Rome, Luther stressed the **sola Scriptura** as the only source of authority. "Back to the divine World" however, did not mean the return to the Bible as a divine set of rules, a legal code, but to the living and dynamic Word of God, by means of which the Holy Spirit accomplishes His saving work in men. Seeberg wrote that Luther believed that "the Word was the sole authority of the Christian Church and that this Word interpret itself, and that it becomes such an authority because of the inward testimony of the Holy Spirit."[16] The name Spirit who inspired the objective Word causes the individual believer to have subjective certainty about the doctrines of the Holy Scripture. Luther wrote very clearly: "The Holy Spirit must address us through the Word of God."[17] Again he asserted; "The content of Scripture is true and certain per se, but we perceive this fact only inasmuch as by its objective operation we experience it subjectively."[18]

Luther insisted on the operation of the Holy Spirit through the Word, in Scripture and the Sacraments. The Holy Spirit was not to be separated from the Word, a position he took against enthusiasm and spiritualism. Seeberg quoted the following passages from Luther:

"Since God has now permitted His Holy Gospel to go forth, He deals with us in two ways; first outwardly, and second, inwardly. Outwardly He deals with us through the oral Word, that is, the proclaimed Word, which Luther emphasized since the Roman Catholic Church had practically ceased preaching the Gospel, or the Gospel and through visible signs, as Baptism and the Lord's Supper. Inwardly He deals with us through the Holy Spirit and faith ... but always in such a way and in this order that the outward means must precede the inward means. So, then, God has willed that He will not give to anyone the inward gifts (of the Spirit and faith) except through the outwardmeans."[19]

In describing Luther's teaching on the causative authority of Scripture Seeberg wrote:

The indissoluble connection of Word and Spirit proves itself also by this that the Spirit grants to anyone nothing else and nothing more than that which the Word, heard by him says. He goes further than the Word goes. The Holy Spirit therefore does not enlarge the area of revelation, but puts into the hearts of men only what the words declare.[20]

In his explanation of the Third Article Luther taught that the Holy Spirit has called us by the Gospel; it was not by man's strength and reason that he became a Christian.

The Perspicuity of Scriptures

Over against Rome and the enthusiasts Luther reaffirmed the clarity of the Scriptures. In an exposition of Psalm 37 Luther stated:

> If anyone of them (the papists) should trouble you and say; "You must have the interpretations of the Fathers since Scripture is obscure," then reply; "It is not true! There is no clearer book upon earth than the Holy Bible, which in comparison to all other books is like the sun in its relation to all other lights. They say such things only because they want to lead us away from Scripture and elevate themselves to the place of masters over us, in order that we might believe their sermons based upon their own dreams ... It is indeed true, some passages in Scripture are obscure, but in these you find nothing but what is found elsewhere in clear and plain passages. ... Do not permit yourselves to be led out of and away from Scripture, no matter how hard they (the papists) may try; for if you get away from Scripture, you are lost; then they will mislead you as they please. But if you stay in the Bible, you have won the victory...Be absolutely certain that there is nothing else than the same clear sun behind it. So if you find an obscure passage in Scripture, do not be alarmed, for certainly the same truth is set forth in it which in another place is taught plainly. If you cannot understand the obscure, then adhere to the clear."[21]

Luther believed that the Scriptures were clear in a threefold way. To quote J. T. Mueller:

> A comparison of Luther's expressions on the perspicuity of Scripture shows that he speaks of clarity of the Bible in a threefold way, namely, its grammatical clarity, its spiritual clarity and its essential clarity.[22]

By the grammatical perspicuity is meant that any reader could understand the words and expressions in the Scriptures because they are clear in conforming to the normal usage of language. By spiritual perspicuity is meant that the Scriptures are clear to those who believe in Christ Jesus. Luther wrote; "Take Christ out of the Bible, then what more will you find in it?" (St. L. XVIII; 168ff). The essential perspicuity relates to an understanding of the mysteries of faith, discussed by Paul in I Cor. 13:9-12.

The Sufficiency of the Scriptures

"In Christian teaching we must not declare anything which the Holy Scripture does not teach" (St. L. XIX:593). Again: "The apostles proved all their teaching from Scripture. So we too must exercise ourselves in it that it is to us the norm of all things" (St. L. IX:915). This shows that Luther held the Bible sufficient to establish all teachings and that the laity could judge the clergy's teachings and lives by the Bible's clear and authoritative doctrines and precepts. The Scriptures were all sufficient for salvation.

During the hectic times of the early sixteenth century, when Luther was grappling with the theological questions of his time, he wrote these words to George Spalatin:

In the first place, it is most certain that one cannot enter into the Scriptures by study or skill alone. Therefore, you should begin by praying that, if it pleases the Lord to accomplish something through you for His glory, and not for your own glory or that of any other man, he may grant you a true understanding of His words. For there is no master of the Scripture other than Him who is the author. Hence it is written, "They shall be taught by God."[23]

Footnotes

1. Frederick C. Grant, *An Introduction to New Testament Thought* (New York: Abingdon Press, 1950), p. 75.
2. Emit Brunner, *Die Christliche Lehre von Gott* (Zurich: Zwingli Verlag, 1946), pp. 113-114.
3. **Ibid.**, p. 114.
4. J. Theodore Mueller, "Luther and The Bible," in John F. Walvoord, editor, *Inspiration and Interpretation* (Grand Rapids: Wm. B. Eerdmans Publishing Co., 1957), p. 93.
5. Reinhold Seeberg, *Lehrbuck der Dogmengeschichte*, vierter Band, erste Abteilung, *Die Lehre Luthers*, IV, i (Leipzig, 1933), IV, 1, p. 414f. The symbol "Di" in Seeberg's Dogmengeschichte stands for: *Die Disputationen, Dr. M. Luther*, ed. Drews, 1896, cf. p. 55.
6. **Ibid.**
7. Francis Pieper, *Christian Dogmatics* (St. Louis: Concordia Publishing House, 1950), 1, pp. 277-278.
8. **Ibid.**, p. 278.
9. **Ibid.**, pp. 276ff.
10. Cf. Warren Quanbeck, "The Bible," in Robert Bertram, editor. *Theology in the Life of The Church* (Philadelphia: Fortress Press, 1963), pp. 22-23.: Ralph W. Doermann, "Luther's Principles of Biblical Interpretation," in Fred W. Meuser and Stanlet D. Schneider, editors. *Interpreting Luther's Legacy* (Minneapolis: Augsburg Publishing House, 1969), pp. 18-20.
11. Pieper, *Christian Dogmatics*, I, p. 292.
12. **Ibid.**, p. 288.
13. These quotations are taken from Uuras Saarnivaara, *Hath God Said?* (Minneapolis: Osterhus Publishing House, Inc. 1957), pp. 12-57.
14. Mueller, "Luther and the Bible," **op. cit.**, p. 107.
15. **Ibid.**, p. 108.
16. Seeberg, **op. cit.**, p. 411.
17. *Spiritus Sanctus muss uns ansprechen Verbo Dei*, W 29,580, Seeberg, **op. cit.**, p. 411.

18. Seeberg, **op. cit.**, p. 411.

19. W 18,136: 33, 189ff: Seeberg, **op. cit.**, p. 381f.

20. **Ibid.**, p. 331.

21. St. L. V:334ff. Cf. John Theodore Mueller, *Christian Dogmatics* (St. Louis: Concordia Publishing House, 1955), pp. 139-141.

22. Mueller, "Luther and the Bible," **op. cit.**, p. 111.

23. Theodore Tappert, *Luther: Letters of Spiritual Counsel* (Philadelphia: The Westminster Press, 1955), p. 112.

Questions

1. What does Emil Brunner say about the doctrine of verbal inspiration? ____

2. Luther maintained that in the Scripture Christ was ____.

3. Was Luther the forerunner of the historical critical method? ____

4. Everything Quenstedt said about Scripture is said by ____.

5. What did Luther say about a six-day creation ____.

6. Did Luther recognize that copyists make mistakes? ____

7. Luther said that Scripture does not ____ itself.

8. Scripture must interpret ____.

9. What did Luther say about the literal sense? ____

10. Zwingly rejected ____.

11. Did Luther ignore the efficacy of the Word of God? ____

12. Does man become a Christian by his strength and reason? ____

13. What did Luther say about the perspicuity of Scripture? ____

A Comparison of the Lives, Writings, Philosophies and Influence of the Two Germans Whose Anniversaries the DDR Is Commemorating in 1983

Christian News, October 24, 1983

In 1983 Die Deutsche Demokratische Republik (DDR), known to Americans and West Europeans as East Germany or the Eastern Zone of Germany, is celebrating the anniversaries of two persons once born in the eastern part of Germany, namely, one who was born nearly five hundred years ago and the other who died a century ago. The two Germans so honored by the DDR are Martin Luther and Karl Marx. Marx's centennial was observed on May 5, 1983 (born 1818) and Martin Luther's five hundreth birthday to be commemorated on November 10th. This year's visitors to the DDR found notices and official proclamations of these two anniversaries. Of the two Germans, Marx's life, activities and writings are of special importance for the DDR, because it is Marx's philosophy of life which has been put into practice and determines the DDR's economic theory. Luther's views and activities are being integrated with the communistic view of life and he is depicted as a forerunner of that social revolution that changed the way of life for people living in Russia, Poland, East Germany, Bulgaria, Albania and other satellite countries.

Luther, whose religious views were diametrically opposite to those of Marx, is being used for propaganda purposes and also as a means of drawing many Protestants and Lutherans to the Luther sites and thereby to bring into the DDR much needed American and West German coinage. Taking statements from Luther's correspondence and writing out of their context, the Wittenberg Reformer is made to support the peace movement against the placement of new nuclear weapons in Western Europe as well as supporting the Marxist view of life. Slogans of Marx are found all over the DDR, setting forth various aspects of his socialistic theory. Opposite this writer's hotel in Erfurt, just across the main railroad station, were these placards, saying: "The teachings of Karl Marx are true because they work." Still another stated: "The never-to-be broken friendship with the Soviet Union - is the foundation for true progress." The person from the West coming out of West Germany and listening to what he has been told by people in the DDR will know that Marxism's claims of a better and happier life are not true. The standard of living is much lower than that in Western Europe not to mention the great restrictions on travel, religion and opportunities for work. It should also be noted, there is no wall between West Germany and East Germany to keep people from leaving so that they might seek the paradise of the communistic countries. But there is a wall around West Berlin and between communistic countries and free Europe to prevent their inhabitants from leaving the countries controlled by the Soviet Union.

The pictures of Karl Marx and Luther are found side by side in a number of stores and places. The writer saw them in stores in Erfurt and Leipzig. The DDR is hailing both men this year for their contributions in the past centuries of Germany and especially to that part of Germany now occupied by Soviets and German communists, called now "The New Germany." Luther is being depicted as the great rebel who revolted against the tyranny of the Pope and the Roman Catholic Church. Luther is now seen as the harbinger of that revolution that reached its zenith in the Russian revolution sparked and undergirded by Marx's revolutionary writings. In this way, Luther and Marx are placed side by side and hailed as heroes of the New Germany.

A Comparison of the Early Lives and Education Luther and Karl Marx

Both Luther and Marx were born in Germany, in that part now known as DDR. Shortly after their birth became members of God's kingdom. Luther was born in Eisleben, November 10, 1483 and Karl Marx saw the Light of day in Treves, in the Prussian Rhineland, May 5, 1818. Luther's father was a miner, who later acquired some wealth and standing and who came to occupy an important position in the town council. Karl Marx was of Jewish descent, the second son of seven children of Hirschel Marx, who changed his name to Heinrich, after his conversion (1824) to Christianity, specifically to Lutheranism. Marx's ancestors for a number of generations had been Jewish rabbis. Heinrich Marx had all the children baptized in the Lutheran faith. Heinrich was a small town lawyer and his son Karl had all the advantages of an intellectual background that was considerably broadened by access to the library of, and frequent conversations with, the cultivated Baron von Westphalen, whose daughter Marx later married.

Luther was baptized as a Roman Catholic on November 11, 1483 on St. Martin's Day. The parents of Luther and Marx were men of importance in their centuries. Luther's father Hans was a spokesman for the people in the town council and a highly respected citizen. In the last century Marx's father was a lawyer and public official.

Both Luther and Marx were given the best education that their respective centuries offered. At seven, Luther entered the Latin school at Mansfeld; later attended the school of Common Brethren at Magdeburg. After that he continued his education in Eisenach, where he sang in the choir of St. Georg Church. In 1501, at age 17, he matriculated in the University of Erfurt.

As Karl Marx grew up, he pursued an academic career. He studied history, philosophy and law at the universities of Bonn and Berlin and in 1841 earned the doctorate at the University of Jena. Luther had earned a doctorate in 1512.

Luther and Marx's Later Lives Further Compared

Martin's parents had high expectations for their son.[4] It was their hope that Martin might become a lawyer. Perhaps he might marry well

75

and take care of them in their old age. However, instead of becoming a lawyer, Luther, to the surprise of everybody entered the Monastery House at Erfurt, and became a member of the strict Augustinian order. In 1505, while a student at Erfurt's University where he was studying logic and philosophy, the Black Plague was raging in Germany and Europe and often cast a spell over the happenings of Luther's life. His best friend died of the plague. While Marx gave up the belief in religion and concentrated altogether on the concerns of this world, Luther's thinking was primarily otherworldly. Luther was troubled about the uncertainty of life itself. Luther's sins disturbed him and when caught in a severe thunderstorm in Stotterheim, not far from Erfurt, he cried out: "St. Anne, help me! and I will become a monk." He kept his promise and entered the Augustinian monastery.

Marx's Political Life Beginning with 1842

While living in Berlin, Marx came under the influence of Hegel, the great proponent of idealism, who had a great effect upon theology in the first half of the nineteenth century.[5] In 1842 Marx became the editor of the *Rheinishe Zeitung*, a paper of liberal tendencies. In Berlin, he studied social political thought and joined the left-wing Hegelians.[6] Hegel's law of the dialectic became a principle for Marx, employed by him for analyzing history and the development of society. Hegel contended that the idea was real, a stance Marx rejected and claimed that only matter was real. Thus Marx turned Hegel's philosophical position upside down. When Marx's paper was suppressed, he went to Paris and continued his life as a journalist. In Paris he formed a friendship with Friedrich Engels, where he also organized a German's Working Men's Association. In 1847 Marx and Engels proposed a program known as the Communist Manifesto, which practically became the creed of the socialistic revolutionaries.

When Marx went to Paris, he took with him as his bride, Jenny von Westphalen, daughter of a Prussian aristocrat and government official. In Paris, Marx also edited the radical Deutsche-Franzoesische Yahrbuecher and also the magazine Forwaerts. Marx's political thinking developed markedly as he associated with socialists Pierre Joseph Proudhon and the Saint Simonians.

In 1848 Marx returned to Germany and revived Zeitung but the latter's revolutionary character led to his banishment from Germany in 1849; today, by a strange quirk of history, Marx is held up as a German hero for 16 million Germans in the DDR, where the writer was told by a knowledgeable person that only about five percent of the people believe these slogans, plastered on the wall of buildings, eulogizing Marx and his economic and political views.

Expelled from Belgium because of his revolutionary views and the Manifesto, Marx went briefly to Paris and then back to Germany to participate in revolutionary movements there. In Koln or Cologne, Marx revived the paper *Rheinische Zeitung*, which lasted a year before being suppressed. He was acquitted of a charge to incite to treason, but was expelled from the Rhineland. Later he was also banished from Paris, whereupon he went to London and lived there with his family, often existing in poverty and often depended on the generosity of Engels. Marx was convinced that he was right. He was intolerant of criticism and contradiction and was considered arrogant and conceited by many. Although often in ill health, he spent much time in the British Museum reading constantly and passionately all the literature in his fields of interest in order to develop his political and economic theories.

Luther's Career from 1517 to 1541

The nailing of 95 theses for debate on the Schlosskirche of Wittenberg unleashed a stream, whose development Luther did not dream was possible.[7] The main point of these theses was that God's forgiveness is given freely to all who are sorry for their sins. Within a short time the 95 theses were printed and distributed throughout the Holy Roman Empire and what Luther had intended to be an academic debate became the harbinger of a new church eventually. Through them the teachings of the Gospel were unleashed. The rediscovered New Testament teachings were like a new "word" in the air. What Brokering wrote is true: "Luther's proclamation through Christ influenced both church life and daily lives of people. Students walked across nations to hear him lecture. Church councils planned strategies to quiet the young monk."[8]

Luther was summoned to give an account of his teachings in Heidelberg, than in Augsburg. The climax of his defense of his theological position occurred on April 21, 1521 at the Diet of Worms, where before Charles V and the might of the Holy Roman Empire, Luther refused to recant. Prince Frederick saw Luther's dangerous position and rescued him by having him kidnapped and kept at the Wartburg Castle, where in a short time he translated the New Testament into German from Erasmus' Greek New Testament and printed in September, 1522. Luther's German New Testament created a new German language in that the Reformer created a new language out of the many different dialects that were found in Germany in which earlier German translations had existed. It became a mighty instrument for helping spread Luther's evangelical teachings throughout Germany and beyond.

In the meantime disorder had broken out at Wittenberg and Luther returned in 1522 and in eight days restored order. Between 1522 and 1546 Luther led a very active life. During a 24 year period Luther preached a great deal, wrote much and helped lay the foundations for the Evangelical Lutheran Church. With the excommunication of Luther at the end of 1521 and with the burning of the papal bull of excommunication the future course of the life of Luther was determined. Weekly he preached in both the city and castle churches. His two catechisms were written to counteract the ignorance of priests and people relative to the basics of the Christian religion. Although Luther was not present at Augsburg when the Confession written by Melanchthon, was presented, he still directed matters from the Coburg.

Luther was interested in the congregation's participation in the public services and wrote hymns for congregational singing. Luther is credited with making possible the first Lutheran hymnal. He rewrote the order of service. In 1525 Luther married Catherine from Borah, a nun, and thus may be said to be the "father of the evangelical parsonage." He raised a family of six children, living in the Augustinian monastery which became the Luther House. The Reformer was a strong advocate for Christians to live the common life as Christians. He emphasized the importance of home life, of the dignity of labor, of good and honest politics, and the necessity of education for both sexes.

Luther was limited in his travels because he had been placed under the ban of Empire by Charles V and had to be circumspect as to where he travelled and went, lest some Roman Catholic fanatic would undertake to kill him.

In 1545 Luther travelled to Eisleben, where he was born, and though not well, in the company of two of his sons he went to settle a dispute between two counts. He was also there to organize another school in that city. As the monasteries began to empty out, Luther organized schools for children. Luther is often referred to as the "father of modern public education." While in Eisleben Luther suddenly took sick and died on February 18, 1546

Marx and Luther as Writers and Authors Marx as Author

Karl Marx wielded the pen with considerable vigor.[9] Besides his editorials and articles in various newspapers, he published *The Holy Family* (1845), *The German Ideology* (with Engels), *The Poverty of Philosophy* (1847). *The Communist Manifesto* (with Engels, 1848), *Critique of Political Economy* (1859), *Du Kapital* vol. 1 (1867), *Du Kapital*, volumes 2 and 3 (with Engels as editor, 1885-95), and his contributions to *The German Yearbook* (1944). As a writer and author Marx was a propagandist, a pamphleteer, a revolutionary, an organizer of labor movements, a scholar of unusual breath and depth; some would even say he was a genius. In his writings he surveyed practically the whole field of political economy, and from its midst ferreting out ideas and evidence which would favor his philosophical system.

Luther as Writer and Author

Luther, who lived three centuries before Marx, also wielded a mighty pen, beginning with 1512.[10] The standard Weimar Edition, begun in 1883 has reached 110 volumes by now and is still not complete. Thus Luther wrote much more than Karl Marx. A partial translation of Weimar's *Luther Works* is now available in the 55 volume American edition, the joint effort of the Muhlenberg-Fortress Press and Concordia Publishing House. Luther was able to use effectively the printing press with its movable type in the spread of his teachings and views. The writings of Luther were varied. He published pamphlets, sermons, apologetical treatises, commentaries, books of instructions as his two catechisms, hymns, a confessional writing, The Smalcald Articles (now numbered among the Confessional writings of Lutheranism). Plass has listed in an appendix of his three volume opus, *What Luther Says*, a list of 193 different writings, large and small.

The chronological study of the writings of Luther has made it possible for Luther scholars to trace the development of Luther's thought, especially in his chief writings. The earliest writings, "the so-called early lectures," began with the first lectures on the Psalms (1512-1513), the lectures on Paul's Letter to the Romans (1515-16), and on the Letter of Paul to the Galatians (1516), and on the Letter to the Hebrews (1517), and the second series on the Psalms (1519-21). Sometime between 1512 and 1521 Luther had what is known as "the tower experience," which according to Luther occurred in the "black Monastery." In 1523 Luther reworked the Galatians Commentary and a longer version of Galatians appeared in 1535.

Early in his writing career, in 1520, there appeared a trilogy of writings that was very influential. They were: *The Babylonian Captivity*, *To the Christian Nobility*, and *On Christian Liberty*. Pelikan claimed that "the first of these refutes three basic assumptions of the medieval Church: the supremacy of the spiritual over the secular arm, the absolute right of the Pope to interpret the Holy Scriptures, and the exclusive authority of the Pope to convoke a council. Closely associated with these assumptions is the sacramentalism and sacerdotalism of the Roman Church. This is subjected to serious scrutiny in the essay the Babylonian Captivity. And against the entire authoritarian structure of the Church, Luther's treatise on Christian liberty asserted the freedom of the Christian from any heteronomous authority, but his bondage through the lordship of Christ to serve all men."[11]

On the *Bondage of the Human Will* of 1525, written against Erasmus, is one of the most difficult of Luther's writings, and in some scholar's opinion his most profound work. In it Luther argued that the freedom of the Christian man was not to be construed to prove man's freedom in his relation to God, not man, but God is the directing agent in the divine human relationship. God alone does the choosing, and not man.

Between 1535 and 1545 Luther worked on his *Genesis Commentary*, which contains some of his best theological work combined with sections of deep devotion and much practical pastoral counsel. There are few theological problems left untouched in it. It was Luther's last great work. An important writing of 1539 was Luther's essay on The Council of Churches, a work of profound historical scholarship, written to overthrow the historical claims of the papacy. Pelikan said about it: "The treatise is also revelatory of Luther's thought on the nature of the Church, a problem to which he devoted the entire section. Here is the clearest and most systematic between the visible and invisible Church."[12]

A Comparison of the Life Philosophies of Marx and Luther

Marx was a monist. *Dictionary of Philosophical Terms* has defined monism as: "A theory which would explain the world as the manifestation of the principle, whether this be spiritual or material. It is opposed to Dualism and Pluralism. Idealism, Materialism, Naturalism are monistic theories."[13]

Marx was a pure materialist. Materialism is a philosophical doctrine which interprets all nature and experience in terms of matter in motion. It is bound up with a sensational theory of knowledge and interprets sensation in terms of nerve-process, its ethics are apt to be hedonistic; and the idea of God either as Creator or Substitute is foreign to its system.[14]

Luther did not limit reality to one kind of thing; no, he was a dualist. The Reformer believed in mind and matter. In anthropology Luther believed that man was a dual being, having a body and a soul. This was clearly stated by him in the explanation of the First Article of the Creed; "I believe that God has made me and all creatures and has given me body and soul."

Metaphysics of Marx and Luther

Metaphysics is the inquiry into the ultimate nature of Being. It seeks to discover what lies within or behind Nature, to penetrate the world of appearances, and to seize a principle or principles which shall explain human experiences on all its sides. Many different philosophical systems have given different answers to the question of the ultimate nature of things.[15] Positivism, e.g. which denies the possibility of metaphysical knowledge, naturalism, materialism, agnosticism and atheism are unmetaphysical. The only materials for the recognition of a theory of the world accepted by those just mentioned are such as are given through observation and experiments upon phenomena, whether physical or psychological. This view has been termed "scientific," and that in the strict sense of the word, but positivism, materialism, agnosticism and atheism are philosophies inasmuch as they attempt to explain the whole world of Nature and man by the light of one or two principles.[16]

Luther, like the scholastic philosophy of his day, believed in metaphysics. Cosmological dualism was espoused by Lutheranism the world there are to be found both spirit and matter. God as the great Absolute Spirit existed prior to all things.

Marx and Theism

Theism is the doctrine of God which teaches that God is the intelligent personal Creator of the world and its present Sustainer. Originally theism was opposed merely to atheism and agnosticism, but now it is so defined by certain philosophers to exclude Deism and pantheism. According to Theism, God is not merely the All, nor is He merely a remote Creator existing out of immediate relation to His creation, nor has He need of a world order in order to be real, as some idealistic theories of the Absolute teacher. God is self-conscious, personal, and self-contained.

Theism has been and still is totally unacceptable to Marxism or Dialectical Materialism.[17] Marxism is opposed to the idea of the existence of God and all conclusions which the Bible states that follow from God's existence, creation, of the world and of all living creature together with its being sustained by the Creator are rejected by Marxism. On this issue Marx and Luther are diametrically opposed to each other.

The Economic and Political Views of Karl Marx

Hegel believed that all life is a process of social change. Everything for which Hegel contended is related to something else and every movement automatically produces his opposite, and from the inevitable conflict between opposites emerges the final synthesis. Marx accepted Hegel's principle of the dialectic with one exception. Marx substituted material conditions for "ideas" By materialism Marx meant that the basic element in society was economic. He rejected the Hegelian notion that "ideas" changed society, and instead Marx proposed that man's society determines their lives by creating certain ideas by which they then live. Marx claimed that all history could be understood as a history of class struggle.[19] The history of mankind reveals that men have consisted either of masters and slaves, the exploiters and the exploited, the patrician and capitalist and the proletariat. For the founder of dialectical materialism it is the substructure of economics which has and does determine the superstructure of ideology, politics, culture, and society. The structure of the modern world reflects the domination of bourgeoisie capitalistic world. Marx concluded that the working classes were exploited by the capitalistic class, and the dignity of the common people was turned into a negotiable commodity which could be sold or bought. The historical development of history would develop a class consciousness, which would further develop into violent revolution and eventually produce a socialistic society whose end development would be a classless society in which each person's needs would automatically be taken care of. It was Marx's contention that the catalyst in this progressive social movement would be the class struggle. When this occurrs then real history will begin.

Marx's dialectical materialism was a powerful force in destroying religion, as well as other foundations and pillars of society.[20] State, church, law, morality, the home and government became "bourgeois" mentality and served as instruments for its subjugation of the masses. Religion was an opium of the people to help in their subjugation to the capitalistic class. Nothing in the world was absolute or permanent. Marxism made all things to look transient and relative.

However, it should be noted that once Marxism became the philosophy of a government committed to communism, the ideal of relativity is abandoned. The alterability and changeability of the communistic system is not subject to change this only holds true of systems that disagree or oppose communism.

Luther's Views of Society and Government

Luther taught that the Triune God had created the world, who made man in his own image and held him responsible for his action, instituted the orders of creation, namely, the church, the home and the state. According to the Bible these three institutions were established by God; no man or state, therefore, has the right to question the validity of their existence or remove them from man's societal structure. Christ taught, "I will establish my church and the fortresses of hell shall not prevail against it." In the Decalogue God gave parents authority over their children. The New Testament in the Table of Duties stressed the same truth. The parents have the right to train their children in the fear of God. The state has not been placed over the parents as far as the education of their children is concerned. Paul taught that government was a divine institution, establishing for the curbing of evil doers and for the maintenance of peace and order. Both the Old and New Testaments clearly have set forth the orders of creation. The Church was established by God as the place where the doctrine of salvation was to be taught and where God's children were to be instructed in the living of God-pleasing lives, loving God above all things and their neighbor as themselves. Church, home and state were the true pillars of society, they are the foundation of a society that had the possibility of prospering and being blessed.

On all major issues Marx and Luther were diametrically opposed to each other. Luther, if he lived today and followed his philosophical orientation, would vehemently oppose Marx. Marx, while he lived, certainly rejected Luther's philosophy and way of life.

The Influence of Marx and Luther

It has been claimed by a number of scholars that Marx's influence in philosophy and economics has been prodigious. Since 1917, beginning with the Russian revolution, Marx's views were incorporated by various communistic countries: The Soviet Union, China, all Eastern European countries, Albania, Cuba, countries of Central America, Vietnam, and also in some of the countries of the free world. Sad to say so-called Christian theologians have been influenced by Marxist views and ideology. Millions of people have been and are being forcibly subjected to Marxism and are being made to subscribe to it, even though they totally disagree with it. Karl Marx is the darling of the advocates of socialism and communism. The writer of the article on Marxism in the *American Encyclopedia* wrote:

> Marx's political creed exerted a long-range and powerful influence on subsequent generations, and his social philosophy and program of action for the rising proletariat inspired a great mass movement. At death some theories were still uncoordinated, and certain contradictions were left unreconciled. These uncoordinated theories and unreconciled contradictions became the source of dissension among followers and critics.[21]

Luther's Influence

Luther's work as theologian, hymnologist, professor, preacher, writer, controversialist and translator, was of such colossal magnitude that, had it been the united work of a dozen eminent men, it would have made them all forever illustrious in the history of great men of the world. This writer agrees with Gruber when he wrote many years ago: "He was one of those few over towering personalities that have turned history into totally different channels and forever afterwards dominate the thought of nations. Himself largely the composite product of the century that also produced the Revival of Learning, through the religious Reformation

Luther saved that intellectual movement from ending in utter worldliness and infidelity."[22]

Through the Renaissance (the Christian aspect of it) and through the Reformation Luther ended the Medieval Age and ushered in the Modern Age. Luther's life and ideas changed the course of history and influenced millions for a better life in church and state. Charles Jacobs made this evaluation of Luther and his influence: "He has left behind a record of achievement that has made him the best loved and the best hated, the most revered and the most denounced character in Christian history since the death of Paul."[23]

Footnotes

1. Cf. Henry Koch, "A Revisit to the Land of Luther," *The Christian News*, September 19, 1983, pp. 7,9.
2. For the life of Luther, cf. R. H. Bainton, *Here I Stand – A Life of Martin Luther* (Nashville: Abingdon-Cokesbury Press, 1950); Heinrich Boehmer, *Luther in the Light of Modern Research* (New York: MacVeigh, 1848); E. M. Plass, *This is Luther* (St. Louis: Concordia Publishing House, 1948); E. G. Schwiebert, *Luther and His Times* (St. Louis: Concordia Publishing House, 1950).
3. Marx-Engels, *Selected Works* (Moscow, 935); K. Loeiwth, Von Hegel zu Nietsche (Zurich, 1940); Sidney Hokk, *Toward the Understanding Karl Marx* (New York, 19330; Sidney Hook, *From Hegel to Marx* (New York, 1935).
4. Cf. Heinrich Boehmer, *Der junge Luther* (Gotha: Flamberg, 1925).
5. "Karl Marx," *Encyclopedia Americana* (1979, ed., 18,344).
6. For a good summary of the life of Marx. Cf. "Marx, Karl," *Encyclopedia Americana*, 1979 ed., 18, 344-345; "Marx Karl," *New Catholic Encyclopedia*, 9, 334-335; L.S.F. Lewis Feuer, "Marx, Karl," *The New Encyclopedia Britannica*, 15th ed., 11, 549-553.
7. For Luther's Life from 1517 to 1546, cf. E. G. Schwiebert, "Luther Martin," *Lutheran Cyclopedia* (St. Louis: Concordia Publishing House, 1975), pp. 483-485.
8. H. B. Brokering, "Celebrating a 500th Birthday," *Lutheran Brotherhood Bond*, 1983, pp. 4-5.
9. "Marx, Karl," *Encyclopedia Americana*, 18, 334.
10. For a listing of enumeration of Luther's major writings, cf. Appendix B of Ewald Plass, What Luther Says (St. Louis: Concordia Publishing House, 1959), III, pp. 1588-1624; P. E. Kretzmann, *Die Hauptschriften Luthers in chronologischer Reinhenfolge* (St. Louis: Concordia Publishing House, no date), 32 pp.
11. Jarislov Pelikan, "Luther, Chief Writings of," *Lutheran Cyclopedia* (St. Louis: Concordia Publishing House, 1954 edition), p. 597.
12. **Ibid.**, pp. 597-598.
13. Arthur Butler, *A Dictionary of Philosophical Terms* (London: George Routledte & Sons, no date), p. 66.
14. **Ibid.**, 60.
15. **Ibid.**, pp. 63-64.
16. **Ibid.**, pp. 80-81.
17. Edward D. Ramsdall, "Theism," Vergilius Ferm, *An Encyclopedia of Religion* (New York the Philosophical Library, 1945), p. 774.
18. Cf. Robert V. Daniel, "Marxism," *Encyclopedia Americana*, vol. 18, pp. 345-346;

Siegfried Marck, "Dialectical materialism," Vergilius Ferm, ed., *A History of Philosophical Systems* (New York: The Philosophical Library, 1950), pp. 306-314.

19. "Marx, Karl," in Jerald C. Brauer, *The Westminster Dictionary of Church History* (Philadelphia: Westminster Press, 1971), pp. 531-532.
20. **Ibid.**, p. 532.
21. "Marx, Karl," *Encyclopedia Americana*, **op. cit.**, p. 345.
22. L. Franklin Gruber, "Luther, Prince of Translators," in O.M. Norlie, *The Translated Bible*, 1534-1934 (Philadelphia: The United Lutheran Publication House, 1934), p. 113.
23. Charles Michael Jacobs, "The Life of Luther," *In the Translated Bible*, **op. cit.**, p. 18.

Questions

1. What were the two anniversaries Communist East Germany commemorated in 1983? ____
2. Luther's religious views were ___ those of Marx.
3. The "Wall" was built to ____.
4. What did the writer see in East Germany? ____
5. Karl Marx was of ____ descent.
6. Marx's ancestors for generations had been ____.
7. Heinrich Marx had all of his children ____.
8. Luther matriculated in the University of ____.
9. Marx earned his doctorate at ____.
10. Marx gave up his belief in ____.
11. Luther's thinking was primarily ____.
12. Marx came under the influence of ____.
13. In Paris Marx formed a friendship with ____.
14. ____ became the creed of the socialistic revolutionaries.
15. The climax of Luther's defense of his theological position came in ____.
16. Luther's German New Testament created ____.
17. Luther may be said to be "the father of ____."
18. Luther emphasized the importance of "___ life."
19. What did Luther argue in his the *Bondage of the Human Will?* ____
20. What was Luther's last great work? ____
21. Marx was a pure ____.
22. ____ is unacceptable to Marx.
23. Marx's dialectical materialism was a powerful force in destroying ____.
24. Marxism made all things to look ____.
25. Luther would have vehemently opposed ____.
26. Have any Christian theologians been influenced by Marx? ____
27. Luther ushered in the ____.

Reformation, 1985
Did Luther Cheat When He Inserted "Alone" in His Translation of Romans 3:28?

Christian News, November 11, 1985

The doctrine of justification by faith apart from works has been called the doctrine of "the standing or falling church." The Lutheran Confessions cite Romans 3:28 no less than seven times. It is referred to in the *Apology*, the Smalcald Articles and in *The Formula of Concord*.[1] It may be said about Romans 3:28 that it explains what is involved in "believing in Jesus Christ (John 3:16; Acts 4:12)." Luther's rendering of Romans 3:28 in the original German read: "So halten wyrs nu das der mensch gerechtfertigt werde on zu tun der werk des gesetzes alleyn durch de glauben." A recent German Luther translation reads: "So halten wir es nun, dass der Mensch gerecht werde ohne des Gesetzes Werke, allein durch den Glauben."[2] That would be Luther's translation of the Vulgate text of Romans 3:28: "Arbitramus hominem justificari ex fide absque operibus."[3] In English this would read: "So we hold that a man is justified without the deeds of the law, alone by faith."

On September 12, 1530, Luther addressed a letter to his friend Wencelaus Link of Nuerenberg relative to an inquiry directed to him. In this letter, Luther formulated his thoughts on translating. Link turned the letter over to the Nuerenberg printer Johann Petreus, together with his own brief introduction, dated September 15, 1530. In this letter, Luther answered two questions: the matter of justification by works and the matter of intercessory prayer by the saints.[4] Both issues had again come up for discussion during the summer at Augsburg, notably in Melanchthon's encounter with John Eck on the matter of *sola fide*.[5]

Luther's rendering of *sola fide* involved a direct discussion of a principle of translation. Luther admits that at times it is necessary for the translator to depart from the literal meaning of the words of the original in order to clarify in the new language their actual sense and that a careful translation will sometimes, therefore, convey a meaning different from the one conventionally held. Luther's much criticized translation of Romans 3:28 is defended by the Wittenberg Reformer as being linguistically and theologically just and necessary. By way of illustration and in buttressing this claim Luther also touched on the problem of relinquishing the letter and rendering the sense of Matthew 12:34; 26:8 and the angelic salutation to Mary in Luke 1:18.[6]

Parenthetically it should be noted here that Luther was a forerunner or precursor of what is today known as "the dynamic equivalence" theory of Bible translation, as opposed to the "correspondence" theory of translation.[7] Nida has described these two opposing philosophies of Bible translation as "Form-emphasizing translation the 'old way' of translating which sought to establish" techniques for moving from one set of surface structures to another, with the least possible interference or distortion." In contrast, the content-emphasizing translation-the "new" recognizes that:

> Instead of going directly from one set of surface structures to another, the competent translator actually goes through a seemingly roundabout process or analysis, transfer, and restructuring. That is to say, the translator first analyzes the message of the **source** language into its simplest and structurally clearest forms, transfers it at this level (here is where we said that paraphrase comes into the picture), and then restructures it to the level in the **receptor** language which is most appropriate for the audience which he intends to reach.[8]

It would be instructive to make a study of Luther's German translation to see to what extent he practiced and used the "dynamic equivalence" approach in his translational activity.

Luther's Response to His Critics
That He Tampered With the Text

Luther was attacked by his enemies for making changes in the New Testament text. They claimed that Luther modified or even changed the text. People ignorant of Greek and Hebrew brought accusations against the Reformer. Luther's response was: "Those who have never even been able to speak properly, to say nothing of translating have all become my masters and I must be the pupil of them all."[9]

This writer heard a Reformation sermon a few years back in which the speaker claimed that Luther had "cheated" when he inserted the word "alone" in Romans 3:28. Emser, a contemporary and an opponent of Luther, issued a New Testament in German which has been said to be a plagiarism.[9]

Duke George, "the Bearded" of Saxony (1471-1531) issued a translation which was actually Emser's New Testament. Emser took Luther's German New Testament nearly word for word, removed Luther's introduction and explanations and inserted his own and sold it under his own name. Emser attacked Luther's translation of Romans 3:28, contending that the word "alone" was not in the Pauline text to this criticism, Luther gave the following reply: "Here in Romans 3(28), I know very well that the word **solum** is not in the Greek or Latin text; the papists did not have to teach me that. It is a fact that these four letters with sola are not there. And these blockheads state them like cows at a new gate."[10] The reason the Papists did not need to tell Luther this is, that they fail to realize that it is implied in the text and must be given in the translation, if the latter is to express the sense with due clearness and force. Luther stated that it was his objective to speak German and not Latin or Greek.[11] It is characteristic of German when two things are spoken of, the one of which is denied and the other affirmed, that it employs the word "solum", "alone," with the word not, or none. Where the Latin and Greek would say: "The farmer brings corn and money", the German says: "The father brings corn only and no money."

Greek says: "I have now no money, but corn only." German says: "I

86

have now no money, but corn only." Greek says: "I have eaten, but not drunken." German says: "I have eaten only, but not drunken." Although these expressions in Latin and Greek do not do it, the German does and it is the manner of German to add alone. Although a person may assert "The farmer brings corn only, and no money." Which would be corrected in German, yet the words no money express the idea not so fully and so clearly as when a person says. "The farmer brings corn only, and no money." The word "only" helps the word no, so much that the whole becomes a full and clear expression. It is not for us to ask the teller of the Latin language how to speak German, as these Papists do also. Rather it is necessary when translating to consult the mother in the home, the children on the street, the common man in the market place and to look at their mouths to see how they speak, and render our translation accordingly. When this is done, the common reader will see that we are speaking their German.

Luther claimed that if he had to give an account of every choice of words and ideas in his German translation, it would take him years to do so. Translation, the Reformer contended, is an art requiring much labor and weariness. Luther said be experienced all these, of which his detractors and opponents know nothing, because they have never been involved in the translation of a testament of Holy Writ.

To his opponents Luther suggested that if they do not like his translation that they should leave it alone, because it is not their work. If any correction is to be done, it will be done by him. Where Luther does not make changes and corrections, others should desist from tampering with his translation efforts.

Luther asserted that he acted in good conscience when he rendered Erasmus' Greek New Testament into German. He declared: "I have observed the utmost faithfulness and exercised the severest diligence and never have given away to improper thought."[12] Luther claimed that he did not make a single cent (German: farthing) and reaped no profit whatever from his translation.[13] He only had God's honor in view as God knows. His goal in putting the Greek testament into German was to serve the Christian people and to promote the honor of Him, from Whom he had been the recipient of so much good. That he was able to achieve his translation was due to the grace and mercy of God. Even if the Papists see fit to abuse him, Luther declared that Christian people will truly appreciate his translation efforts, as will the Lord Jesus Christ Himself. Luther stated that he would feel himself compensated if one solitary Christian person recognized him as a faithful laborer. He would grieve if his opponents praised him but despite their criticism of him, he knew that he was a teacher of theology who possessed as much competence as they had.

Further Luther claimed that he did not translate with undue freedom.[14] In company with his assistants he aimed with great care to retain the letter wherever this was possible. He preferred rather to have the German give way than depart from the literal sense. Despite what the Papists claimed, Luther noted, not every person can serve as a translator.

No, said the Reformer, "it requires a truly pious, faithful, God-fearing, learned, experienced and practical Christian and Christian heart." False Christians or false teachers should not be allowed to translate Scripturest.[15]

Additional Reasons for the Addition of "Alone" in Romans 3:28

Luther also explained that there were other reasons besides the German idiom that prompted him to insert "allein" in his rendering of Romans 3:28.[16] In defense of his translation he claimed that the text and meaning of Paul demanded this insertion. Asserted Luther:

He is dealing in this passage with the main point of Christian doctrine, viz. that we are justified by faith in Christ, without any works of the law, though it is God's law and His Word, do not help us to righteousness. He cites Abraham as an example and says that he justified so entirely without works, that even the highest work, which had then been newly commanded by God, before and above all other works, namely circumcision, did not help him to righteousness, but he was justified by faith, without circumcision without any works at all.[17]

Luther further wrote in his "On Translating: An Open Letter" about Abraham and the manner he was justified:

So he says in Chapter IV: "If Abraham was justified by works, he may glory, but not before God." But when works are so completely cut away the meaning of it must be that faith alone justifies, and who would speak plainly and clearly about this cutting away of all works, must say, "Faith alone justifies us, and not work." The matter itself, and not the nature of the language only, compels this translation.[18]

The opponents of Luther's "alone," "solum," or "allein" translation claimed it had an offensive sound and that further, it gave the impression that Christians did not need to be active in good works. To this criticism and objection Luther responded as follows:

"Dear Sir, what are we to say? Is it not much more offensive that St. Paul does not say 'faith alone,' but makes it even plainer and goes to the very limit and says 'Without works of the law?' In Galatians 1, also, and in many other places, he says 'Not by the works of the law.' A gloss (i.e. an interpretation distorting the meaning) might be found for the words 'faith alone' but the words 'without the works of the law' are so plain and offensive and scandalous that they cannot be helped out by any gloss. How much rather might people learn not to do any good works, when they hear the preaching about works put in such plain, strong words: 'No works'! If it is not offensive when one preaches 'without works,' 'no works,' 'not by works,' why should it be offensive when one preaches 'by faith alone'?"[19]

The Reformer argues further as he rejected the "offense objection," by saying:

And what is still more of an offense, St. Paul does not reject simple, common works, but "the works of the law." From that it would be quite possible for someone to take offense and say that the law is condemned and accursed before God, and we ought to do nothing but evil, as the people in Romans III, "Let us do evil that good may come." This is the very thing that a spirit of discord began to in our time. Dear fellow, St. Paul and we wanted to give this offense, and we preach so strongly against works and insist on faith alone, for no other reason than that people may be offered and stumble and fall. In order that they may learn to know that they do not become righteous by good works, but only by Christ's death and resurrection.[20]

L. Franklin Gruber, a former Luther scholar, contended that Luther's translation of the Bible is noted for its simplicity of expression and for its faithfulness to the idiom of the original Hebrew and Greek.[21] Gruber believed that it was not Luther's goal to give the world an academically literal translation of the original languages, as it was to give a real interpretation of the meaning and spirit of the inspired writings. Concerning Romans 3:23 with its "alleyn durch de glawben" he wrote:

This is a very free rendering, and has been criticized because the word "alleyn" could not be used in a literal translation, even as it does not appear in the somewhat free rendering in our own Revised Version, in which the translation is as follows: "We reckon therefore that a man is justified by faith apart from the works of the Law." But while it is true that the word "alone" would not have a place in a very literal translation, it is also true that it is undoubtedly just what Paul meant to convey, as a comparison of this passage with his many statements on faith and justification elsewhere will prove. The remarkable thing about Luther's translation in this and many other passages is therefore the fact that he seemed to have such a spiritual insight into truth conveyed by the original text as to enable him to express the unmistakable meaning in the mind of the inspired writer.[22]

Roman Catholic Translation of Romans 3:28

The Rheims-Douay Version of 1582-1610, made from the Latin Vulgate text, rendered Romans 3:28 like this: "For we account a man to be justified by faith, without the works of the law."[23] This translation is clear in stating that a person is not justified by the works of the law, but solely by faith. However, Dr. Challoner and Dr. H. J. Ganss published a version of the Rheims-Douay with notes, in which they endeavored to support the Roman Catholic doctrine of infused grace. On Romans 3:28 this version has the following:

By faith. The faith, to which the apostle here attributes man's justification, is not a **presumptuous** assurance of our being justified; but a form and lively belief of all that God has revealed or promised. Heb. 11. A faith working through charity in Jesus Christ, Gal. 5:6. In short, a faith takes in hope, love, repentance, and the use of sacraments. And the **works** which he excludes are only the works of the law; that is, such as are done by the law of nature, or that of Moses, antecedent to the faith of Christ but by means no means, such as follow faith, and proceed from it.[24]

The annotations of the Challoner-Ganss version are asserting some-

89

thing about "faith" and "works" which are not found in the text nor the text of Romans 3:28. These explanations are a good example of reading something into the words of Romans 3:28 which in hermeneutics is known as eisegesis, instead of exegesis, that is, selling only forth what the text teaches and not what one wished the text to say to support a theological system.

There are a number of Roman Catholic translations that render Romans 3:28 correctly and do not try to influence the reader's understanding by notes which read infused grace into the text. Thus the Knox *Holy Bible. A Translation from the Latin Vulgate in the Light of the Hebrew and Greek Originals*, rendered Romans 3:28 as follows: "No, the principle: which depends upon faith, our contention is, that a man is justified by faith apart from the observance of the law."[25] *The Jerusalem Bible, Reader's Edition* (without footnotes) translated Romans 3:28: "On the contrary, it is the law of faith, since as we see it, a man is justified by faith and not by doing something the Law tells him to do."[26] *The Confraternity Version of the Bible* (1970) has rendered Romans 3:28 on this wise: "For we hold that a man is justified apart from the observance of the law." Francis Spencer V.P. in his New Testament translated from the original Greek, translated Romans 3:28: "For we argue that a man is justified by faith apart from legal observances."[27]

The Ancient Versions and Romans 3:28

The Peshitta in the Syriac reads: "Methra 'inan dabehaimanutha hu mezdak barnosho welo bahabde de nemoshe."[28] In English: "Therefore we conclude that by faith is a man justified and not by works of the law." The Coptic (Sahidic and Thebaic) Version has this for Romans 3:28: "Enjo gar emmos alla je promc patmaio hen tpistis enwesh enehbewe empnomos."[29] Literally: "For we say that a man will be justified in the faith without the works of the law." The Vulgate has rendered Romans 3:28: "Arbitramus enim justificari hominem sine operibus legis."[30] Translation: "We hold namely, that a man is justified by faith without the works of the law." All these versions place salvation by faith in contrast to salvation by works.

Different European Translations Agree in Placing
Salvation by Works in Opposition to Salvation by Faith

An examination of a number of European translations will show that faith versus works is the contrast St. Paul depicted in his Romans' Letter.

An Italian Version:

Noi adunque conchiudiamos che' nomo giustificato per fede senza le opere della legge. Translation:

"Therefore we conclude that a man is justified by faith without the deeds of the law."[31]

A Spanish Version:

"Concluimos, pues, que el hombre es justoficado por fe sin las obras de la ley." Translation: "We conclude that a man is justified by faith without the works of the law."[32]

The Good News for Modern Man in Spanish has this rendering for Romans 3:28: "Hemos, comprobado, entonces, que Dios pone en la debida relacion con el al hombre que tiene fe, sin tomar en cuenta si la hecho o no lo que la ley mand."[33] Translation: "For we hold that a person is put right with God only through faith, and not by doing what the Law demands."

A French Version:

In Louis Segond's **La Sainte Bible** Romans 3:28 was rendered as follows: "Car nous pensons qui l'homme est justify par loi foi, sansles oevres de la foi."[34] Translation: "but we hold that a man is justified by faith without the words of the law."

A Dutch Version:

"Wij besluiten dan dat de mensch door het geloof gerechvaardigt wordt, zonder de werken der Wet."[35]

Translation: "We conclude then that a man becomes justified through faith, without the words of the law."

A Danish Version:

"Vi mener nemlig, at et Menneske bliverretfer diggjort ved Tro, uden Lovgeniger."[36] Translation.

"We hold namely that a man becomes justified by faith without works."

A Swedish Version:

So halle wi nu det, all menniskan warder raetfaerdig af trone, utan lagsens gerningar.[37] Translation: Thus we hold that a man is justified by faith without the works of the law.

A Norwegian Version:

For wi holder for at mennesket blir retferdiggjort ved troen, uten lovgjerninger.[38] Translation: "For we hold that a man becomes justified by faith, without the works of the law."

The Salkinson-Ginsburg Hebrew New Testament:

Ki kayosher chatzun lemor be emunah yitzdak ish mibbalhadi hammahasim asher 'al pi hattorah.[39]

Translation: "As the truth (or right we hold that a man is justified by faith without the deeds or the law."

Translations that Approach the Intent of Luther's "Alone"

The New Testament In Modern English by Helen Barrett Montgomery comes close to doing the same things Luther did in his translation of Romans 3:28. Here is her rendering "For we conclude that a man is justified by faith, **altogether** apart from the deeds or the law."[40] (boldface supplied). James Moffatt, *The Bible: A New Translation* adds a word which the Greek does not have but correctly gave the sense of Romans 3:28, which Moffatt rendered: "We hold that a man is justified by faith, apart from deeds of the Law **altogether**." (Bold face supplied).[41] *The New English Bible* rendered Romans 3:28: "For our argument is that a man is justified by faith **quite** apart from success in keeping the law."[42] (Bold face supplied).

The best translation of Romans 3:28 is that rendering which gave the verb "dikaioo" as declare righteous. *The New World Translation* of the

Jehovah Witnesses does this, when this version has for Romans 3:28: "For we reckon that a man is declared righteous by faith apart from works of law."[43]

Weymouth has this correct rendering for this Pauline verse: "For we see that a man is accounted righteous by faith apart from the fulfillment of the law."[44]

Footnotes

1. Theodore Tappert, *The Book of Concord* (Philadelphia: Fortress Press, 1959), pp. 117.73; 165.382; 292.4; 474.10; 541.12; 543.27; 547.43.
2. Martin Luther, *Neuses Testament und Psalmen* (Stuttgart: Wuertembergishe Bibelanstalt, 1973), p. 234.
3. Augustinus Merk, *Novum Testamentum Graece et Latine* (Romae: Sumptibus Pontifici Instituti Biblice, 1951), p. 517.
4. *Works of Martin Luther*, Translated with Introduction and Notes (Philadelphia: A. J. Holman Company and Castle press, 1931), pp. 10-27.
5. Michel Reu, *The Augsburg Confession* (Chicago: Wartburg Press, 1930), pp. 18ff.
6. Cf. *Sendbrief vom Dolmetchem (An Open Letter on Translation)*. This is a writing penned by Luther on the Coburg. Found in Weimar editor of *Luther's Works*, 30 II in the Erlangen Edition of *Luther's Works* 65 and in the St. Louis Edition (the Revidiert Walsh edition). In this essay the Holman Edition of *Luther's Works* will be referred to.
7. Cf. Eugene H. Glassman, *The Translation Debate* (Downers Grove: InterVarsity Press, 1981), pp. 47-68.
8. Eugene Nida, *Language Structure and Translation*, pp. 79-80.
9. *Martin Luther: An Open Letter on Translating*, Holman, *Luther's Works*, VI, footnote, p. 12.
10. **Ibid.**, p. 15.
11. **Ibid.**
12. **Ibid.**, p. 18.
13. **Ibid.**
14. **Ibid.**, p. 19.
15. **Ibid.**
16. **Ibid.**, p. 20.
17. **Ibid.**
18. **Ibid.**, pp. 20-21.
19. **Ibid.**, p. 21
20. L. Franklin Gruber, "Luther, Prince of Translators" in *The Translated Bible* (Philadelphia: The United Lutheran Publication House, 1934), p. 109.
21. **Ibid.**, pp. 109-110.
22. *The New Testament of Our Lord and Savior Jesus Christ*. With Annotations and Reference by Dr. Challoner and Dr. H. J. Gans (New York: The C. Wildermann Co., 1905), pp. 374-375.
23. **Ibid.**, p. 375.
24. **Ibid.**, pp. 374-375.
25. Published by Sheed & Ward, New York, 1956, New Testament, p. 151.
26. *The Jerusalem Bible. The Reader's Edition* (New York: Doubleday & Company, 1966), New Testament, p. 130.
27. Francis Aloysius Spencer, O.P., *The New Testament of Our Lord and Savior Jesus Christ*. Translated into English from the Greek (New York: The Macmillan Company, 1937), p.419.

28. *The Syriac New Testament According to the Peshito Version* (New York James Pott & Co., no date), p. 321.

29. G. Horner, *The Coptic Version of the New Testament in the Southern Dialect Otherwise Called Sahidic and Thebaic* (Osnabueck: Otto Zeller. Reprint of the edition of 1911-1924, 1969, p. 34; translation on page 35.

30. *Biblica Sacra Juxta Vulgatam Clementinam* (Romae-Tornaci-Parisiis: Typis Scoietatis S. Joannis Evang., Desclee et Socii, 1956), Novum Testamentum, p. 165.

31. *II Nuovo Testamento Del Nostro Signore E. Salvatore Tradotte in Lingua Italiana Da Govanni Diodati* (New York American Bible Society, 19330, p. 382.

32. *La Santa Biblia Antiguio Y Nuevo Testament, Antigua Version De Casiodoro De Reina* (1568) 1960 Revision (San Hose; Sociedades Biblicos en America Latina, 1960), p. 1041.

33. *Dios LLega Al Hombre, El Neuvo Testamento* (San Juan: Sociedades Biblicas in America Latina, 1966), p. 337

34. Louis Segond, *La Sainte Bible Qiu Comprend L'Ancien et Le Noveau Testament.* Traduits Sur Les Textes Originaux Hebreu Et grec (Paris: 20 Rue De Tournon, 1911), Noveau Testament, pp. 116.

35. *Bijbel Dat Is De Gansche Heilige Schrift Vervattende Al De Kanonieke Boeken Des Ouden En Nieuwen Testaments* (London: The British and Foreign Bible Society, 1921), Nieuwee Testament, p. 201.

36. *Det Nye Testamente* (Koebenhavn: Det Danke Bibelselskab, 1949), p. 288.

37. *Bibelen Eller Den Heliga Skrift, Innhaellande Gamla Och Nya Testamentets Canoniska Boecker* (New York: American Bible Society, 1900), p. 978.

38. *Bibelen Eller Den Hellige Skrift. Det Gamle Og Det Nye Testamentes Kanoniske Boeker* (New Yorker: American Bible Society 1943), New Testament, p. 192.

39. *Ha Berith Ha Chdasha, The Salkinson-Gingsburg Hebrew New Testament* (New York: J. Freshman, 17 St. Mark, 1891), p. 303.

40. Helen Barrett Montgomery, *The New Testament in Modern English* (Philadelphia: The Judson Press, 1924), p. 406.

41. James Moffatt, *A New Translation of the Bible Containing Old and New Testaments* (New York: Harper & Brothers Publishers, 1922), New Testament, p. 190.

42. *The New English Bible with the Apocrypha* (Oxford and Cambridge: The University Presses, 1970. New Testament), p. 194.

43. *New World Translation of the Holy Scriptures*. Rendered from the Original Languages by New World Bible Translation Committee (New York: Watchtower Bible and Tract Society of New York, Inc., 1961).

44. Richard Frances Weymouth, *The New Testament in Modern Speech*. Newly Revised by James Alexander Robertson, Fifth Edition (Boston: The Pilgrim Press, 1943), p. 359.

Questions

1. The doctrine of justification by faith apart from works has been called ____.

2. Luther admits that at times it is necessary for a translator to depart from ____.

3. Luther was a forerunner of what today is known as ___ of Bible translation.

4. Luther said that translation is an art which requires much ____.

5. It is the manner of Germans to add ____.

6. How much money did Luther make from his translation? ____

7. What is the difference between exegesis and eisegesis? ____

93

Luther's Isagogical Views
As Expressed in His Prefaces to the Books of the Old Testament in His *German Bible* (1534)

Christian News, October 10, 1988

Biblical introduction (isagogics) deals with the questions of authorship, time of composition, the addresses, purpose of the book, its general contents, its integrity and canonicity. In his Prefaces to both the books of Old Testament and the New Testament, Luther frequently expressed his position on some of these topics, which have implications for the correct interpretation of a Biblical book.

In the past, a great deal has been made by scholars of the importance and value of Luther's Preface to the New Testament. Since in August 1984 the Protestant world did take cognizance of the 450th anniversary of the publication of Luther's *German Bible*, it will not be amiss to examine Luther's views as they pertain to introductory questions on books of the Old Testament. In another essay, the writer has examined Luther's hermeneutics as they were reflected in his *Old Testament Prefaces*. Concerning Luther's "Old Testament Prefaces" Charles Jacobs wrote a number of years ago:

> In most cases they were very brief and consisted of little more than summaries of contents, in a few instances they were more extensive, and discussed questions of authorship, and doctrine. Because of the importance of some of these prefaces, it has seemed wise to include all of them in this edition, with the exception of those to the Apocrypha, which are interesting, but not especially important.[1]

In the Holman edition of the *Works of Martin Luther*, all the Prefaces to the Old Testament are given in volume VI pp. 367-437, a total of 70 pages.[2] The text of the Holman edition was utilized by the American edition of *Luther's Writings*, Vol. 35, *Word and Sacrament*, and are found on pages 235-333.[2a] In the Holman edition, the longest of these Prefaces is the "Introduction to the Old Testament," occupying pages 367-382 (16 pages). The following books have no prefaces in the *German Bible*: Joshua, Judges, I and II Samuel, I and II Kings, I and II Chronicles, Ezra, Nehemiah, Esther, and Lamentations.

There are Prefaces for the following books: Job, the Psalter, the Three Books of Solomon, one each for Proverbs and Ecclesiastes. These are followed by a general "Introduction to the Prophets." There are Prefaces for Isaiah, Jeremiah Ezekiel (two of them) and Daniel (two of them). The Major Prophets have a Preface for each of the Minor Prophets, namely, Hosea, Joel, Amos, Obadiah, Johan, Micah, Nahum, Habakkuk, Zephaniah, Zechariah, Haggai and Malachi.

To understand and to appreciate Luther's isagogical stance on matters of introduction, it is imperative first to set forth his understanding of the relationship of the Old Testament to the New.

Know then, that the Old Testament is a book of laws which teaches what men are to do and not do, and gives besides, examples and stories of how these laws are kept or broken, just as the New Testament is a Gospel book, or book of grace, and teaches where one is to get the power to fulfill the law. But in the New Testament there are given along with the teaching about grace many other teachings that are laws and commandments for the ruling of the flesh, since in this life the spirit is not perfected and grace alone cannot rule.[3]

Luther continues to depict the relationship in this way:

Just so in the Old Testament there are besides the laws, certain promises and offers of grace, by which the holy fathers and prophets under the law, were kept under the law, like us under the faith of Christ. Nevertheless, just as the peculiar and chief teaching of the New Testament is the proclamation of grace and peace in Christ, through the forgiveness of sins; so the peculiar and chief teaching of the Old Testament is the teaching of laws, the showing of sin, and the furtherance of good. Know that this is what you have to expect in Old Testament.[4]

Luther and Mosaic Authorship

The Mosaic authorship of the Pentateuch is assumed throughout the "Preface on the Old Testament." Luther, of course lived two hundred years before the beginning of the rationalistic type of criticism which became the vogue in Germany, Holland, France and eventually in England. If modern historical criticism is correct,[5] then Luther would be hopelessly wrong and his views misleading. With the current forms of rationalistic literary criticism, tradition, form, redaction and structural criticisms, Luther would be completely out of step and his theological views as deduced from the five Books of Moses would be erroneous. The only use of Luther's Prefaces would be as a record to show how Luther and his contemporaries thought about Biblical introductory questions. Luther found in Genesis 3:15 a Gospel promise,[6] a passage in which the death of Christ is predicted, a view totally unacceptable to modern Old Testament scholarship.[7] In his "General Introduction to the Old Testament" Luther gave a short summary of each of the five books of the Pentateuch. In his remarks from Genesis, Luther claimed about Moses: "He (i.e. Moses) teaches in his first book how all creatures were made, and (and as the chief cause for his writing) where sin came, death, namely by Adam's fall, from the devil's wickedness.[8]

But in Genesis 3:15 Moses taught that by "the seed of the woman," namely, Christ, man would be saved from the curse to which he became subject because of violating God's law and sinning.[9] Luther claims that Christ was promised to Adam and Abraham. It was the conclusion of the Reformer about Genesis: "Thus from the beginning of the Scriptures, and throughout them all, faith is praised above all works and laws and merits. The first book of Moses, therefore, is made up almost entirely of illustrations of faith and unbelief, and the fruits that faith and unbelief bear, and is almost a Gospel book"[10] (p. 369). How different is this from Mowinkel's understanding of Genesis 3:15.[11]

Luther on Exodus

In Exodus Luther pointed out that God chose one nation and brought forth Moses to "enlighten the world again, by them and by the law to reveal sin anew. Thus he organizes this people with all kinds of laws and separates it from all other people, has then build a tabernacle and begins a form of worship and provides laws by which men can live."[12]

Luther on Leviticus

The main purpose of Moses' Third Book is the appointment of the priesthood, with statues and laws according to which the priests are to act in teaching the people. In Leviticus Luther claimed "we see that a priestly office is instituted only because of sin, to proclaim sin to the people and make atonement before God."[13] The work of the law is to deal with sin and the sinner. Critical scholars assign Leviticus 1-6 to the Priestly code and 17-27 to Ezekiel's Holiness code.[14]

Luther on Numbers

After the laws, moral, ceremonial, and political had been given, the priests and princes erected the tabernacle and instituted worship forms. After erection of the tabernacle then came the work for the Israelites to live and carry out Yahweh's disobedience and about the plagues which came upon the people. Luther observed that it is one thing for laws to be given, it is another matter for them to be obeyed. Observed Luther: "This book is a notable example of how there is nothing but hindrance, and nothing at all in making people righteous with laws, but as St. Paul says, laws cause only sin and wrath."[15]

Luther on Deuteronomy

In the fifth book of Moses, Luther claims that the Hebrew lawgiver repeated the whole law, with an account of all that happened and "explained anew everything that belongs either to the body or to the spiritual government of a people." Luther credited Moses with being the perfect lawgiver, who fulfilled his duties, but who was also available to explain when things went wrong and present the matter when things needed to be re-established. The Reformer claimed that Moses' fifth book actually contains nothing but faith toward God and love to one's neighbor, for all of God's law amount to that. In the light of this statement the Reformer claims that in chapters 1 to 20 Moses guards against everything which would destroy faith in God and in chapters 21-34 against everything that hinders love.[16] Modern Lutheran scholars assigned Deuteronomy to the seventh century B.C.

In his introductory Preface to the Old Testament Luther devoted better than ten pages (pp. 370-380) to the discussion of the various laws of the Pentateuch, to their significance and purpose, to the wrong way the Jews interpreted them, to the relationship of the Law to the Gospel, to the place of law in the plan of salvation.[17] Not only did God give the Jews religious laws, averred Luther, but he also provided them with instructions for planting and tilling and marrying and fighting and ruling chil-

dren, servants and households, buying and selling and borrowing and re-
paying and everything a person can do, either outwardly or inwardly.

Preface to the Book of Job (1524)

Luther in his "Preface to Job" is mainly concerned with the purpose
and meaning of this wisdom book. He wrote: "The book of Job deals with
the question, whether misfortune can come to the righteous from God.
Job stands fast, holds that God chastises even the righteous without reason, to his praise, as Christ says in John III, of the man born blind."[18]
Job's friends, Luther claims, held that God is just and does not punish
a righteous person. If God also punished a man, it means he has sinned.
However, Job in great sickness spoke too much against God and thus
sinned among his sufferings. Job insisted that he had not deserved his
offerings more than others.[19]

The value of the book of Job for the Christian is: God alone is righteous, more righteous, than any man. Observed Luther: "It is written for
our comfort, in order that we may know that God allows even His great
saints to stumble, especially in adversity."[20]

When Luther translated Job he had great difficulty with its Hebrew
and had this to say about its language: "The language of this book is more
lofty and splendid than that of any other book in all the Scriptures, and
if it were translated everywhere word for word (as the Jews and foolish
translators would have it done), and not for the most part, according to
the sense, no one would understand."[21]

The Book of Psalms

Luther held the Book of Psalms in high esteem. He gave it a good evaluation. In fact, he called it "the little Bible." He contrasts in his "Preface
on the Psalms" the book of Psalms with the saints books of his day and
asserted this in his comparison:

> For here we find not only what one or two saints have done, but
> what He has done who is the head of all saints, and what the saints
> still do — the attitude they took toward God, toward friends and en-
> emies, the way they conduct themselves in all dangers and suffering,
> all this, besides the divine and wholesome commandments of every
> kind that are contained there.[22]

Luther believed that the Psalter predicted the death and resurrection
of Christ so clearly "and so typifies His kingdom and the conditions and
nature of all Christendom that it might be called a little Bible."[23]

All that which is in the Bible is briefly found in the Psalter, so that
the latter amounts to an Enchiridion, or handbook of what saints should
know. Luther believed that in the Psalms the Holy Spirit "wanted to take
the trouble to compile a short Bible and example-book of all Christendom,
or of all saints. Thus, whoever would have almost an entire summary of
it, comprised of one book."[24]

According to Luther the Psalter is valuable because it tells not only of
the saints' works, but also records how they spoke with God and how they
prayed to Him.[25] Luther believed that the Psalter was valuable because

it tells not only of saints speaking in different life-situation, but it covers the entire gamut of man's emotional experiences. Because the saints speak to God and with God, the reformer opined: "Hence it comes that the Psalter is the book of all saints and everyone, in whatever case he is, finds in it psalms and words that fit his case and suit him exactly, as though they were put thus for his sake only, so that he could not put it better himself, or find better words or wish for better."[26] Modern critical scholarship has completely departed from Luther's views on the Psalter.[27]

The Writings of Solomon

In 1524 Luther wrote a Preface for three books, which bear the name of Solomon: namely, Proverbs, Ecclesiastes (in German: der Prediger) and Song of Solomon German (Hohelied).[28] In addition, Luther penned a separate Preface for both Proverbs and Ecclesiastes. If the student of Luther's writings also consults the Reformer's Lectures on Proverbs and the Song of Solomon, he will see that Luther really did not doubt the Solomonic authorship of the three books traditionally ascribed to him before the application of the historical-critical approach to these three books. Toward the end of his introductory Preface on Solomon's books Luther said: "Undoubtedly it (i.e. Proverbs) was for this purpose that it was written by King Solomon, as an example to all kings and Lords to take an interest in the young people."[29]

In his Preface to the Preacher of Solomon (Ecclesiastes) Luther wrote:

But this book was certainly not written or set down by King Solomon with his own hand; but what others heard from his lips was put together in this form by the scholars as they admit at the end when they say: "These words of the wise are as spears and nails fixed by the masters of the congregation and given from the shepherd." (Eccl. 12:11).[30]

Luther believed that certain persons selected by the kings and the people were appointed at the same time to fix and arrange this and other books, handed down by Solomon, so that everyone would have to make books as he pleased; for they lament in the same place that of books there is no need and forbid others to take up the work."[31] How different are the views of modern critical scholarship relative to Solomonic authorship of the wisdom books.[32]

The Purpose of Proverbs

In Luther's opinion Proverbs is a book especially useful for young people to study for "they need and must have teachers and rulers to exhort, warn, rebuke, and chastise them, hold them constantly to the fear of God and to His commandments, and to keep off the devil, the world; and the flesh. This, then, is what Solomon does diligently and richly, in this book, putting the doctrine into proverbs, so that it can be grasped the more easily and kept the more gladly."[33]

How elevated were Luther's views when compared with that of critical scholars. Because Proverbs was the Word of God, those who despise its proverbs are fools and all those who keep God's commandments "wise."

In a more detailed Preface of 1524 Luther wrote: "That which Solomon here calls wisdom is nothing else than the wisdom of God, which is taught in God's words and works."[34] "Besides, no proverbs have their origin anywhere else than in God's words and works since all human proposals are vain and deception and nothing comes out of them except what God will and does."[35]

The Preacher of Solomon (Ecclesiastes)
The Hebrew name for what in German was called "Der Prediger Salomonis," in English "Ecclesiastes," is **Koheleth**, averred Luther and is "one who speaks publicly in a congregation."[36]

The Purpose of "Der Prediger"
In his general "Preface on Books of Solomon" the Reformer enunciated the view that Ecclesiastes "was a book of comfort."[37] Said the Reformer about Kobeleth's purpose:
> "Now Solomon, in his first book, teaches obedience in the face of mad lust and curiosity, so in this book he teaches that men are to be patient and steadfast in obedience, in the face of unpleasantness and the temptation, and are constantly to do the duty of the hour with peace and Joy. What they cannot keep or alter, they are to let go, they will be well off."[38]

The Authorship of Ecclesiastes
Luther appears to ascribe the book to Solomon, but at the same time seems to imply that the composition of the Solomonic material was arranged by others. In the "Preface to the Preacher of Solomon" (1524) he wrote: "But this book was certainly not written or set down by the King Solomon with his own hand; but what others heard from his lips was put together in this form by the scholars, as they admit at the end, when they say: "These words of the wise are as spears and nail, fixed by masters of the congregation and given from one shepherd."[39] Again "this book, too, is put together by others out of sayings of Solomon, and the doctrine and sayings of some wise men are added at the end."[40]

These statements seem to imply that the book is substantially from Solomon, and this is a far cry from the view of historical-critical Old Testament scholars who ascribe the book to an anonymous author who lived in the third or even second century B. C.[41]

According to Luther this Solomonic book of Ecclesiastes should have the title: "Against the Free Will," because all the book tends to show that all men's counsels,[42] proposal undertakings are vain and fruitless and always have a different end from that which we want and expect.[43] Koheleth is not to be considered and understood in a pessimistic manner, the way some modern scholars have explained Ecclesiastes. Relative to one of the distinctive statements, often reappearing in its chapters, "all is vanity," Luther remarked:
> "Therefore you must understand this book to be abusing God's creatures when he says, "All is vanity and misery;" for God's creatures are

all good (Gen. 1 and II Timothy 4) and this book itself says that one shall be happy with one's wife and enjoy life, etc.[45] The proper attitude, averred Luther, was to be passive and let God alone do everything above and against our knowledge and counsel.

Luther on the Song of Songs (In German: das Hohelied)

Luther did not write a separate Preface for the Song of Songs, but has a brief statement about it is his "Preface to the Books of Solomon." (1524)[46]

The Authorship of the Song of Songs

Luther in his "Preface to Solomon's Books" and also in his "Exposition of Das Hohelied" ascribed the authorship of these poems to Solomon.[47] Modern Lutheran critical scholars have adopted the position of critical scholarship in general which has placed the Solomonic books late, in fact among the latest of the Old Testament canon.[48]

Contents and Purpose of the Song of Songs

Here Luther's views are somewhat unique. He claimed that it was a song of praise, in which Solomon praises God for obedience as a gift of God.[49] Here is Luther's understanding of the purpose of the Song of Songs: "For where God is not in the household and ruler, there is neither obedience nor peace in any station of life; but where there is obedience and good rule there God dwells and kisses and embraces His clear bride with His Word, which is the kiss of his lips."[50] L. Fuerbringer believes that Luther's explanation of the Song as referring and discussing good government does not really deal with the purpose of Luther's Hohelied.[51]

Luther's Preface to the Prophetical Books

Luther wrote nearly a nine-page introduction to the Major and Minor Prophets.[52] This is the only place in his prefaces where the Reformer quotes from those books the Jews classified as the Former Prophets. The latter comprise, according to the Jewish reckoning: Joshua, Judges, I and II Samuel, I and II Kings, for which Luther wrote no Prefaces. Luther complained that in his days there were people who despised the writing of the prophets, and by so doing were despising God's Word.[53] Christians, Luther claimed, should read and use the prophetical writings. The reason for this would be: First of all, they proclaim and bear witness to the kingdom of Christ, in which we now live, and in which all who are believers in Christ have heretofore lived and will live unto the end of the world.[54]

Luther held on the strength of I Peter 1:11-12 that the prophets revealed teachings which were especially intended for the New Testament era. The Old Testament prophets predicted that Christ should suffer and die and that Christians would be in Christ's kingdom.[55] From a study of the prophetic books two facts become clear: "By this we become aware of two things," averred Luther, "first that the great glory of Christ's kingdom is surely ours, will come hereafter and second, that it is preceded by crosses, shame, contempt and all kinds of sufferings for Christ's sake."[56]

The Prophets are of great value for they give many examples and experiences which illustrate the First Commandment: "You should love no other gods before me." Thus Luther wrote:

For they have prophesied of Christ's kingdom, all the rest is nothing but illustration of how God has so strictly and severely confirmed the First Commandment to read or hear the prophets is surely nothing else than to read and hear God's threats and comforts.[57] In his analysis of the contents of the prophetic books, Luther claimed that there was more of threatening than of promise.[58] The prophets especially cry out against idolatry. In his discussion of the prophetical books the Reformer drew illustrations from the Books of Judges and Kings, classified by the Jews in their Hebrew Bibles as constituting the former Prophets. Luther castigated specifically the idolatry and the practices of Jeroboam I, (931-911), who violated God's Word (Cf. Deuteronomy 12 relative to the place where Jehovah was to be worshipped and the manner of worshipping God by use of animals). The Israelites in the period beginning with Judges were frequently guilty of idolatry and idolatrous practices.[59] The application Luther made for himself was: "On the contrary, let everyone have a care to be sure that his own devotion and good intention."[60]

Luther's Preface to the Book of Isaiah

Luther's believed that the 66 chapters of Isaiah were written by the prophet Isaiah.[61] In the introduction he devoted the employment of the historico-grammatical method. It is necessary for a correct interpretation to know the history as well as to have a knowledge of the geography of the Near East of the eighth century.[62]

Luther on the Contents and Organization of Isaiah

After ascertaining the time and place of Isaiah's prophecies, Luther advised: "After this you must divide the prophet into these three parts. In the first he deals, like other prophets, with two subjects. First, he preaches to his people and rebukes their many sins, especially the manifold idolatry, which has got the upper hand among the people as godly preachers, now and at all times do and must do, keeps them in check with threats of punishment and promises of good."[63]

Secondly, said Luther, Isaiah disposes and prepares his readers for the Kingdom of Christ, of which he prophesies more clearly and more often than does any other prophet. In chapter 7:14 the prophet "describes the Mother of Christ, how she is to conceive and bear Him without injury to her virginity, and chapter 53 the Passion together with His Resurrection from the dead..."[64]

According to the Reformer Isaiah also proclaimed Christ's kingdom powerfully and in plain language, as though it had then come. In Luther's opinion: "This must have been a splendid, highly enlightened prophet. For all the prophets do the same thing; they teach and rebuke the people of their time, and they proclaim the coming and Kingdom of Christ and direct and point the people to Him, as the Savior of both of those who have gone before and after and of those who have gone more fully than another; among them as all, however, Isaiah does the most and is the fullest."[65]

Isaiah also has prophecies about Assyria and Babylonia. In Part II, Luther claimed, Isaiah deals with Sennacherib and his empire (Chs. 36-37). To Hezekiah the prophet announced that Jerusalem would not fall.[66]

In the third part, Isaiah deals with Babylonia, in which he predicts the Babylonian Captivity of the Jews and the destruction of Jerusalem by the Babylonian king. God's prophet also announced that it will be Cyrus who will free the Jews from captivity.[67] The views of critical scholars on Isaiah's authorship, unity and Messianic nature are the opposite of the Reformers.[68]

Luther's Preface to Jeremiah (1532)

In order to understand the Book of Jeremiah, whose unity Luther did not question as modern critical scholars do,[69] he claimed that the historical events of the prophet's time must be known and considered. "For his preaching has reference to the condition of the land at that time."[70]

During the first twenty years of Jeremiah's preaching the prophets sermons are almost entirely rebukes; the prophet Jeremiah complains about the vices and idolatry and the wickedness of the people.[71]

Prominent in Jeremiah's preaching was the announcement of the coming of the Babylonians and the destruction of Jerusalem. However, Jeremiah also foretold that God's anger would not last forever but that a remnant would return to the Promised Land. Luther noted especially the difficult task Yahweh had assigned to Jeremiah, who had a very difficult, trying and discouraging ministry.[72] Luther accepted the Jewish Talmudical tradition that Jeremiah was murdered in Egypt by the Jewish people who had taken him by force to Egypt.

Like Isaiah, Ezekiel, Daniel and a number of the Minor Prophets, Luther asserted, that Jeremiah has a few outstanding Messianic prophecies. Luther wrote relative to this matter: "In the third place, like all other prophets, he prophesied of Christ and His kingdom, especially in the twenty-third and thirty-first chapters, where he clearly prophesies of the person of Christ, of the New Testament and the end of the Old Testament."[73]

Luther recognized the present book of Jeremiah is not organized in a chronological order. Asserted the Wittenberg Reformer: "Upon the first subject indeed, there is often something in a later chapter which happened before that which is spoken of in an earlier chapter, and so it seems as though Jeremiah had not composed these books himself, but that parts of his utterances were taken and written into the book. Therefore, one must not care about the order, or be hindered by lack of it."[74]

The latter part of the Preface deals with the application of the messages for Jeremiah's and Luther's times.

Luther's Preface to Ezekiel

Luther wrote two Prefaces for Ezekiel, a brief one in 1532 and in 1545 one of the longest of any Biblical book composed for his *German Bible*.[75] The Reformer gave the historical circumstances of the 598 or 597 B. C. attack upon Jerusalem by Nebuchadnezzar II. When the people became restless and were sorry that they had listened to Jeremiah (chapter xxiv) and became impatient, God, so argued Luther, raised up the prophet Ezekiel to encourage the captives. Ezekiel supported Jeremiah's preaching, the climax of his preaching was the announcement that Jerusalem would be destroyed.[76] In chapter 25 Ezekiel deals with this matter.

After chapter 24 Ezekiel also prophesied the downfall of other countries of the Near Eastern world. Then in Ezekiel there follows four chapters on the spirit and kingdom of Christ, and after that on the tyrant in Christ's kingdom, Gog and Magog. At the end he rebuilds Jerusalem, encouraging the people to believe that they shall go home again; but in the Spirit he means the eternal city, the heavenly Jerusalem, of which the Apocalypse also speaks.[77]

Luther's Second Ezekiel Preface (1545)

This Preface was written a year before his death. Luther discusses chapter 1 and Ezekiel 40-48 in a very general way.[78] It's character is polemical, directed against the Jews, who he feels are unable to really understand the Old Testament, for according to Isaiah xxix, so Luther contends, the Jews are incapable of understanding the Scriptures, for "as Paul says in II Corinthians iii, that the veil of Moses remains over the Scripture, so long as they do not believe in Christ."[79]

The remarkable chariot vision Luther considered a revelation of the kingdom of Christ in faith here on earth, in all four quarters of the whole world, according to Psalm XIX, in omnem terram. For no one can be a prophet, as St. Peter testifies, "unless he have the spirit of Christ."[80] Luther's interpretation is rather unique and can be given a completely different interpretation.[81]

The Book of Ezekiel is used by Luther to contrast the Old versus the New Covenants. Jeremiah 31:31 is understood by Luther as it has been in the Epistle to the Hebrews, namely, as referring to Christ and His kingdom.[82] The Reformer rejects the Jewish belief of an ultimate return to Palestine to repossess it as in the days before the Babylonian Captivity. Wrote Luther: "There are to be no more two kingdoms, but one kingdom, under their King David, who is to come, and it shall be an everlasting kingdom in the same physical land."[83]

Luther faulted the Jews for not recognizing in Christ the King David prophesied by Hosea and others. The new covenant included all people who accepted the new covenant predicted by Jeremiah and Ezekiel.

Luther concluded the 1545 Ezekiel Preface with an interpretation of the Vision of the Temple described by Ezekiel in chapters 40-43. The Jews believed that a third Temple someday would be built in Palestine. But that was a mistake. The Reformer showed that Ezekiel was not speaking of a literal Temple, but was using the term symbolically. Thus the Reformer wrote:

These two things Ezekiel teaches us when he encourages the people

103

to expect the return from Babylon, but prophesies more about the new Israel and the kingdom of Christ. That is his vision of the chariot, and it is also the temple, in the last part of his book.[84]

The critical interpretation of Ezekiel is radically different from that of Luther.[85]

Luther's Preface on Daniel

The Holman Edition of *Luther's Works* has published in Vol. VI, the concluding part of a "Preface for the Book of Daniel," issued separately in 1530, with a dedication to John Frederick of Saxony (printed in Smith and Jacobs, *Luther's Correspondence*, II, 516ff.). The *American Edition of Luther's Works*, Vol. 35, has printed the entire Preface, pp. 294-316. The latter amounts to a commentary on Daniel. In the long form Luther explains chapter by chapter its contents and significant teachings.

Luther believed that Daniel was a prophet, a man of God who experienced the historical events in which he took part and that he was the recipient of the revelations about the Babylonian Empire, Medo-Persian Empire, Alexander the Great's rule and the reign of the Diadochi and the Roman Empire. For Luther the events of Daniel did not terminate with the reign of Antiochus Epiphanes. The Reformer believed that Daniel prophesied the coming of Christ, which was to occur in the time of the Roman Empire. The Reformer wrote:

> "For Daniel prophesied boldly and determines plainly that the coming of Christ and the beginning of His kingdom (that is, His baptism and preaching) is to happen five hundred and ten years after King Cyrus (Daniel ix), and empire of the Persians and Greeks is to be at an end, and the Roman Empire in force (Dan. iii, vii), that Christ therefore , must certainly come at the time of the Roman Empire, when it was in its best estate..."[86]

Daniel did not merely write his prophecies about the coming of future kingdoms, argued Luther, but they were given to encourage the righteous, make them happy and encourage their faith that their misery will have an end, as they are freed from sins, death, the devil and all evil, and be brought to heaven to Christ, in His blessed kingdom.[87]

Luther's views are diametrically opposed on the nature, purpose, contents and authorship of the Book of Daniel as those set forth by modern critical scholarship.[88]

Preface to Hosea

Hosea lived during the reign of Jeroboam II, and was a contemporary of Isaiah, Amos, and Micah and of them Hosea was the oldest.[89] He married a harlot-wife (chapter 1), but that Luther claimed, did not mean that Hosea was unchaste in words or deeds. The Reformer claimed that Hosea used the words "harlot" and "harlotry" in a spiritual sense, and asserted that Gomer was his real, honest wife, and with her he begot legitimate children; but the wife and children had to bear these shameful names as a sign and rebuke to the idolatrous nation which is full of spiritual adultery, that is, idolatry, as he himself says in the text, "The land runneth from the Lord after whoredom."[90] Luther seems to believe that Gomer was no harlot but had to bear this name as a sign against the whoring, idolatrous nation.[91]

Relative to the composition of Hosea, the Reformer believed that the 14 chapters comprising this prophetic book were not fully written, but that pieces and sayings out of his preaching were arranged and brought together.[92] Luther averred that because Hosea preached against the idolatry practiced by priest and people that he suffered death.[93] Luther further believed that Hosea preached about Christ and His Kingdom, as is shown especially by chapters ii, xiii, and xiv.[94]

Preface to Joel (1532)

The book of Joel does not state when the latter prophesied and preached. Luther accepted the view of the ancients, namely, that Joel was contemporary of Hosea and Amos.[95] The Wittenberg Reformer pictures Joel "as a kindly and gentle man and does not denounce and rebuke as do the other prophets, but beseeches and laments and would make people righteous with good, friendly word and protect them against harm and misfortune."[96] Unfortunately, the people did not believe Joel.

In setting forth the contents of this three-chapter book, he somewhat contradicts himself by stating that he prophesied the future punishment of Israel, that they are to be destroyed and carried away by the Assyrians.[97] The grasshoppers of 1:1-4 he identified with the Assyrians, whom he also calls caterpillars, grasshoppers, beetles and vermin. Joel 2:20 which reads "And him from the north will I drive far from you," he identified with Sennacherib who was defeated before Jerusalem.[98]

In the end of the second chapter and to the end of chapter 3, Luther believed Joel "prophesied of the Kingdom of Christ and of the Holy Ghost and speaks of the everlasting Jerusalem."[99] The calling of the nations to the Valley of Jehoshaphat was believed to refer to the general judgment of the nations at the Last Judgment by the Church Fathers, but Luther had a different interpretation. Luther gave this explanation: "As he calls the Christian Church the everlasting Jerusalem so he calls it also the Valley of Jehoshaphat, for the reason that all the world is summoned to the Christian Church by the Word, and there is judged and punished by preaching, since all of them are sinners before God."[100] By contrast modern critical scholarship dates Joel in the post exilic period.[101]

Preface to the Prophet Amos (1532)

According to Luther Amos indicates when he prophesied, namely, at the time of Hosea and Isaiah. Amos predicted the Assyrian captivity. In Luther's opinion no other writing prophet does so much denouncing and threatening as Amos of Tekoa.[102] It is only in chapter 9 that Amos foretells Christ and His kingdom and on that note the book closes.[103]

The phrase "for three and for four sins I when not forgive" is explained by Luther that "these three or four sins are only one sin, because against Damascus he names only the sin that" they have threshed. But he calls this sin "three and four" because they do not repent of sin or recognize it, but rather boast of it and rely upon it, as though it were a good deed, as the false saints always do."[104]

Amos is quoted twice in the New Testament. In Acts 7:42ff. where Stephen shows that the Jews did not keep God's Law from the time they left Egypt. The other quotation is from Amos 9:9f. where James quotes in Acts 15 the last chapter as proof for Christian liberty, namely, the Gentiles under the New Testament are not bound to keep the law of Moses.[105]

The Preface to Obadiah (1532)

While Obadiah does not state when he lived, Luther placed his prophesying at the time of the Babylonian Captivity. The prophet comforts his countrymen, announcing to them that they shall return to Zion.[106]

The prophecy of Obadiah is specifically directed against Edom and the Edomites who were filled with hatred and envy against the people of Israel and Judah. Not only Obadiah, but many other prophets in the Old Testament denounce the Edomites for their animosities.

The psalmist in Psalm 137 declared: "Remember the Edomites, O Lord, in the day of Jerusalem, who said, 'Down with it to its foundation.'"

The last part of his short prophecy, Obadiah prophesies about. Christ's kingdom, that it shall not be in Jerusalem only, but everywhere. Thus reasoned Luther: "For he mixes all the nations together, — Ephraim, Benjamin, Gilead, the Philistines, the Canaanites, Zarephath, — and this cannot be understood to refer to the temporal kingdom of Israel, for according to the law of Moses, these tribes and peoples had to be separated in the land."[107]

Preface to the Prophet Jonah (1526)

Luther rejected Jerome's idea that Jonah was the son of the widow at Zaraphath, near Sidon.[108] The Reformer was convinced that he was a prophet who lived during the reign of Jeroboam II and that his father was Amittai. Contemporaries of Jonah were Hosea, Amos and Joel and in Judah Uzziah ruled. Luther claimed that God did great things through Jonah, "for it was through his preaching that King Jeroboam was so fortunate and won back all that Hazael, King of Syria, had taken from the kingdom of Israel..."[109] Greater than his preaching in Israel, averred Luther, was Jonah's preaching in the Assyrian Empire. In Assyria Jonah accomplished successes by his preaching which the prophet could not achieve in Israel, through Jonah's success Luther believed:

It was as through God willed to demonstrate by him the word of Isaiah, "He that hath not heard shall hear it," as an illustration of the fact that they who have the Word richly despise it mightily, and they who cannot have it accept it gladly, Christ Himself says in Matthew xxi, "The kingdom of God shall be taken from you and given to the Gentiles, who bear its fruit. Modern Lutheran scholarship do not consider the Book of Jonah historical."[110]

Preface to the Prophet Micah (1532)

Luther placed Micah into the eighth century, saying he lived at Isaiah's time. In Chapter 4 Micah, so the Reformer held used the very words of Isaiah. Both Isaiah and Micah preached Christ.[111]

Micah rebuked the people for their idolatry and constantly referred to Christ and His Kingdom. The fact that Christ was to be born in Bethlehem was only foretold by Micah and Moresheth.

Micah prophecies consisted of denunciations of Judah's and Israel's sins. He preached and rebuked, and announced that even though Judah and Israel would go to pieces Christ will come and make it all good.[112]

Modern critical scholarship does not believe Micah in its entirety comes from the pen of Micah.[113]

Preface to the Prophet Nahum (1523)

Luther's views on Nahum are different from those generally held today by conservative Biblical scholarship.[114] Luther understood the three chapters of Nahum as being as prophecy of the destruction which the Assyrians were going to inflict upon Israel and Judah and that actually was fulfilled by Schalmanezer and Sennacherib, because of the people of God's great sins.[115] Only a remnant was preserved as Hezekiah and those like him experienced. Present day conservative scholars would hold that the main purpose of Nahum is to announce the downfall of the Assyrian empire and its capital Nineveh. The book was written around about 630. But Luther placed Nahum prior to Isaiah or no later than Isaiah's time.[116]

The name Nahum means "comfort," and Nahum was a "Comforter," because in his book he tells the Hebrew people that their enemies will be destroyed. Nineveh which had responded so nobly in Jonah's day had gone back to its own sinful ways and God announces to God's people that their enemies will be destroyed.[117]

At the end of chapter one, Nahum speaks, as Isaiah did (52:7) did of good preachers who proclaim peace and salvation on the mountains and asks Judah to rejoice. Although Luther claim that the prophecy could refer to Hezekiah, after Sennacherib's time, yet nevertheless, Luther claimed: "it is a general prophecy, and refers also to Christ, telling that the good tidings and the glad worship of God, taught and confirmed by God's Word, shall remain in Judah. Thus he is and is rightly called, a real Nahum."[118]

Preface to the Prophet Habakkuk

According to Luther the purpose of the prophecy of Habakkuk is "to strengthen and support the people and prevent them from despairing of the coming of Christ, however strangely things may go."[119] His further purpose is to keep faith in the promised Christ strong in the people's hearts.[120]

Habakkuk announces in his book the downfall of Judah, to be effected by the King of Babylon. But the Babylonians will not get much of it, because he too will be destroyed. Habakkuk lived before the Babylonian Captivity; possibly he was a contemporary of Jeremiah. The story that Habakkuk brought food to Daniel while in the lion's den is required by Luther.[121]

The Preface to Zephaniah

Luther believed that Zephaniah was a contemporary of Jeremiah and prophesied many of the same things as Jeremiah did during the reign of Josiah. Like Jeremiah Zephaniah predicted that Jerusalem and Judah would be carried into captivity because of their wicked lives.[122] Zephaniah did not mention King Nebuchadnezzar, who was to take the southern kingdom into final captivity in 587 B.C. Zephaniah not only prophesied against Judah and Jerusalem but also made dire prediction about the Philistines, Moabites, the Ethiopians and Assyrians. For Luther Zephaniah chapter 3 "prophesied gloriously and clearly of the happy and blessed kingdom of Christ, which shall be spread over all the world. Although he is a small prophet, he speaks more about Christ than many other great prophets, more than even Jeremiah."[123] Thus by this prophecy God gave comfort to the Jews that even though the Babylonian Captivity would occur, they were to receive grace when the promised Savior, Christ, with His glorious kingdom, would come. Luther's understanding of the Messianic nature of Zephaniah would not be accepted by modern critical scholarship's understanding of this seventh century prophet.[124]

Critical Scholarship has adopted views considerably different from those of Luther.[125]

The Preface to Zechariah

Unlike modern critical scholars Luther knows nothing of two or three different Zechariahs. All 14 chapters were considered by Luther to have been penned by Zechariah, who lived after the Babylonian Captivity.[126] Both Zechariah and Haggai were responsible, as Yahweh's prophets, for the building of the Second Temple. This is Luther's judgment about Zechariah: "Here is in truth one of the most comforting of the prophets, for he brings forward many lovely and comforting visions, and gives many kindly words, in order to encourage and strengthen the troubled and scattered people to set up the building and the government, in spite of the great and various resistance which they had endured. He does this down to the fifth chapter." [127]

In his preface to Zechariah Luther briefly sets forth the contents of this 14 chapter book. Luther was of the opinion that Zechariah in chapter five, under the vision of the letter and ephah, was predicting the coming of false prophets among the Jews would deny Christ.[128] In the sixth chapter the Reformer averred that Zechariah prophesies about the Gospel of Christ and the spiritual temple, to be built in all the world.[129]

Luther claimed that beginning with chapter 9 Zechariah is predicting events in connection with Alexander the Great's coming, who would defeat Tyre, Sidon and Philistia.[130] This would help open the whole world to the coming of the Gospel of Christ, and predicted Christ's triumphal entrance into Jerusalem.[131]

In chapters 12-14 Luther, accepting the New Testament's interpretations, finds a number of Messianic prophecies dealing with Maundy Thursday and Good Friday. Zechariah predicted, so Luther states, that Christ will be sold for thirty pieces of silver, for which cause He will leave

Jerusalem and the Jews in it will be destroyed because they are hardened in their error, and dispersed.[132] The result will be that the Gospel and the Kingdom of Christ will come to the Gentiles.

Christ as the Shepherd will be smitten and the sheep, the apostles scattered. First Christ must suffer but then He will enter His glory.[133]

Luther interpreted chapter 14 as speaking about the destruction of Jerusalem, and the Levitical priesthood together with its organization will be abolished.[134] There will be a new priesthood which will belong to other people even Egyptians and all Gentiles. With Chapter 14:14ff. the Levitical priesthood is abolished, and its vessels and festivals. It means the Old Testament is to be abolished and be taken away.[135]

Critical modern Lutheran scholarship has a completely different view about the unity and Messianic character of Zechariah.[136]

Preface to the Book of Haggai (1532)

Haggai began prophesying a few months before Zechariah did. Haggai was the first of the prophets after the Babylonian Captivity to prophecy. God used Haggai and Zechariah to encourage the people to rebuild the Temple which had been in ruling since 587 B.C. Luther believed that Haggai was predicted in Daniel 9:25, where it is written: "From the time when the command goeth out that Jerusalem shall be rebuilt, until the prince, Christ," there are seven weeks and two and sixty weeks etc. Although Cyrus the Great had issued a decree to rebuild the Temple, it was only when Yahweh's call through Haggai and Zechariah came, that the Temple was rebuilt, between 521-515 B.C.[137] In Chapter 1 God's prophet denounced the selfishness of the returned exiles and rebuked them for their indifference and lassitude. Because the people neglected God's House, he did not bless them.[138]

In chapter 2:7 Luther found a prophecy of Christ who would come as "a comfort of all nations." Wrote Luther "By which he indicates in a mystery that the kingdom of the Jews shall have an end, and the kingdoms of all the world be destroyed and become subject to Christ. This has happened before now and is constantly happening until the Last Day, when it will all be fulfilled."[139]

The Preface to the Prophet Malachi

Luther mentioned the fact that the Hebrews identified Malachi with Ezra, but Luther does not seem to accept this view. But the Reformer claimed that he was the last of the Old Testament prophets.[140]

For the Reformer Malachi was "a fine prophet" because his prophetic book contains prophecies about Christ the Lord. The saying about Christ and His Gospel are said by Luther to be "a pure offering in all the world."[141] In addition to God's grace being so beautifully proclaimed, Luther also said that Malaci prophesied the coming of John the Baptist, and Christ Himself pointed out in Matthew 11, calling John His angel and the Elijah of whom Malachi writes.[142]

After describing the Messianic kingdom prediction, the remainder of Luther's Preface to the last book of the Twelve Minor Prophets, he calls attention to the law assertions, in which the people are castigated for their social and religious sins. People failed to give the priests the tithe, the animals that were offered were blemished. The priests were no model to follow, because motivated by greed, they accepted these deficient animals. The priests were especially guilty because they were falsifiers of God's Word.[143]

Footnotes

1. *Works of Martin Luther, Translated with Introduction and Notes* (Philadelphia: A.J. Holman Company and The Castle Press; 1932), VI, p. 366. This work thereafter will be cited as Holman, VL.
2. **Ibid.**, pp. 367-437.
3. *D. Martin Luther Werke. Kritische Samtausgabe* (Weimar. 1883) Hereafter cited as Deutsche Bibel, 5, 3. The Weimar Edition will cited as WA.
4. **Ibid.**
5. Cf. Otto Kaiser, *Introduction to the Old Testament - A Presentation of Its Results and Problems* (Minneapolis: Augsburg Publishing House, 1975), pp. 33-114.
6. WA 42, p. 146; D. Martin Luther's *Saemmtliche Schriften*, 23 vols. in 25, ed. Johann G. Walsh, in modern German (St. Louis: Concordia Publishing House, 1880-1913), I, p. 240.
7. Holman, **op. cit.**, VI, pp. 368-369.
8. **Ibid.**, p. 369.
9. **Ibid.**
10. **Ibid.**
11. Sigmund Mowinkel, *He That Cometh - Translated by G.W. Anderson* (New York and Nashville: Abingdon Press, 1954), pp. II, 283.
12, Holman, **op. cit.**, VI, 369,
13. **Ibid.**
14. Horace D. Hummel, *The Word Becoming Flesh An Introduction to the Origin, Purpose, and Meaning of the Old Testament* (St Louis: Concordia Publishing House, 1979), pp. 79-114.
15. Holman, **op. cit.**, VI, p. 370.
16. **Ibid.**
17. **Ibid.**
18. **Ibid.**, p. 383.
19. **Ibid.**
20. **Ibid.**
21. **Ibid.**, p. 384.
22. **Ibid.**, p. 385.
23. **Ibid.**, p. 385.
24. **Ibid.**
25. **Ibid.**
26. **Ibid.**, p. 387.
27. Arthur Weiser, *The Psalms, A Commentary The Old Testament Library* (Philadelphia: The Westminster Press, Fourth Edition, 1962), pp. 19-101. Christopher F. Barth, *Introduction to the Psalms*. Translated by R.A. Wilson (New York: Charles Scribner's Sons, 1966), pp. 1-76.
28. *American Edition of Luther's Works*. Jaraslov Pelikan and Helmut T. Lehmann, gen. eds., (Philadelphia and St. Louis, 1955-1970), vol. 15, p. 495.
29. Holman, **op. cit.**, VI, p. 393.
30. **Ibid.**

31. **Ibid.**, p. 393.
32. Claus Westermann, *Handbook to the Old Testament*. Translated and edited by Robert H. Boyd (Minneapolis: Augsburg Publishing House, 1967), pp. 226-243.
33. Holman, **op. cit.**, VI, p. 393.
34. **Ibid.**, p. 392.
35. **Ibid.**, p. 392.
36. **Ibid.**, p. 393.
37. **Ibid.**
38. **Ibid.**
39. **Ibid.**, p. 394.
40. **Ibid.**
41. Arthur Weiser, *The Old Testament - Its Formation and Development* (New York: Association Press, 1961), pp. 309-310.
42. Holman, **op. cit.**, VI, p. 394.
43. **Ibid.**
44. Westermann, **op. cit.**, p. 246.
45. Holman, **op. cit.**, VI, p. 390.
46. **Ibid.**, p. 391.
47. **Ibid.**, p. 391.
48. Bernhard W. Anderson, *Understanding the Old Testament*, Third Edition (Englewood Cliffs, New Jersey: Prentice-Hall, Inc. 1970), p. 535.
49. Holman, **op. cit.**, VI, p. 391.
50. **Ibid.**
51. Louis Fuerbringer, *Introduction to the Old Testament* (St. Louis: Holy Cross Press. Reprint of the 1925 Concordia Publishing House 1925 edition) p. 67.
52. Holman, **op. cit.**, VI, pp. 395-403.
53. **Ibid.**, p. 395.
54. **Ibid.**
55. **Ibid.**, p. 396.
56. **Ibid.**, p. 396.
57. **Ibid.**
58. **Ibid.**, p. 398.
59. **Ibid.**
60. **Ibid.**, p. 402.
61. **Ibid.**, p. 403.
62. **Ibid.**, pp. 403-404.
63. **Ibid.**, p. 405.
64. **Ibid.**, p. 405.
65. **Ibid.**, p. 405.
66. **Ibid.**, p. 406.
67. **Ibid.**
68. Weiser, **op. cit.**, pp. 183-207.
69. Edward J. Young, *An Introduction to the Old Testament* (Grand Rapids: Wm. B. Eerdmans Publishing Company, 1964), p. 230. Westermann, **op. cit.**, pp. 162-167.
70. Holman, **op. cit.**, VI, p. 408.
71. **Ibid.**, p. 409.
72. **Ibid.**, pp. 409-410.
73. **Ibid.**, p. 409.
74. **Ibid.**, pp. 409-410.
75. **Ibid.**, pp. 411-412.
76. **Ibid.**, p. 141.
77. **Ibid.**, p. 412.

78. **Ibid.**, p, 412.
79. **Ibid.**, p. 412.
80. **Ibid.**, p. 413.
81. Walter S. Roehrs, *Concordia Self-Study Commentary - Old Testament Introduction, Notes and References* (St. Louis: Concordia Publishing House, 1979) pp. 537-538. W.R. Roehrs, "The Inaugural Vision of Ezekiel," *Concordia Theological Monthly*, pp. 721-739, October, 1948.
82. Holman, **op. cit.**, VI, p. 415.
83. **Ibid.**, p. 416.
84. **Ibid.**, pc 418.
85. Westermann, **op. cit.**, p. 262-264.
86. Holman, **op. cit.**, VI, p. 421.
87. **Ibid.**, p. 423.
88. Arthur Weiser, *The Old Testament - Its Formation and Development* (New York: Association Press, 1961), pp. 313-315.
89. Holman, **op. cit.**, VI, p. 423.
90. **Ibid.**, p. 424.
91. **Ibid.**, p. 425.
92. **Ibid.**, p. 424.
93. **Ibid.**, p. 424.
94. **Ibid.**
95. **Ibid.**, p. 425.
96. **Ibid.**
97. **Ibid.**
98. **Ibid.**, p. 426.
99. **Ibid.**, pp. 425-426.
100. **Ibid.**, p. 426.
101. Robert B. Laurin, *The Layman's Introduction to the Old Testament* (Valley Forge, PA: The Judson Press, 1979), pp. 142, 145.
102. Holman, **op. cit.**, VI, p. 426.
103. **Ibid.**, p. 427.
104. **Ibid.**, p. 427.
105. **Ibid.** 109. **Ibid.**
106. **Ibid.**
107. **Ibid.**, p. 428.
108. **Ibid.**, p. 429.
109. **Ibid.**
110. Gerhard von Rad, *Old Testament Theology* (New York: Harper & Row Publishers; 1965), II, p. 289.
111. Holman, **op. cit.**, VI, p. 430.
112. **Ibid.**, p. 430.
113. William Sanford La Sor, David Allan Hubbard and Frederic William Bush, *Old Testament Survey* (Grand Rapids: William E. Eerdmans Publishing Company, 1982), p. 359.
114. Holman, **op. cit.**, VI; p. 431.
115. **Ibid.**, p. 431.
116. **Ibid.**
117. **Ibid.**
118. **Ibid.**
119. **Ibid.**
120. **Ibid.**, pp. 431-432.
121. **Ibid.**, p. 432.

122. **Ibid.**, p. 432.
123. **Ibid.**, p. 433.
124. **Ibid.**, p. 433.
125. Cf. James H. Gailey, *Micah, Nahum, Habukkuk, Zephaniah, Haggai, Zechariah, Malachi. The Layman's Commentary.* Vol. 15 (Richmond: The John Knox Press, 1962), 1962; pp. 74-84.
126. Holman, **op. cit.**, VI, p. 435.
127. **Ibid.**, p. 435.
128. **Ibid.**
129. **Ibid.**
130. **Ibid.**
131. **Ibid.**, p. 436.
132. **Ibid.**
133. **Ibid.**, p. 436.
134. **Ibid.**
135. **Ibid.**
136. Claus Westermann, *Handbook to the Old Testament.* Translated and edited by Robert Boyd (Minneapolis: Augsburg Publishing House. 1967), pp. 200-205.
137. Holman, **op. cit.**, VI, p. 434.
138. **Ibid.**
139. **Ibid.**, p. 436.
140. **Ibid.**
141. **Ibid.**, p 436.
142. **Ibid.**
143. **Ibid.**, p. 437.

Questions

1. Isagogics deals with ____.
2. Where may Luther's prefaces to Old Testament books be found? ____
3. Luther found in Genesis 3:15 ____.
4. Luther credited Moses with being the ____.
5. Modern Lutheran scholars assign Deuteronomy to ____.
6. Luther observed that the Book of Job was written for ____.
7. Luther called the Book of Psalms the ____.
8. How elevated were Luther's views when compared with ____.
9. According to Luther, the 66 chapters of Isaiah were written by ____.
10. Whose views of Isaiah are opposite from Luther's views? ____
11. The real wife of Hosea was, according to Luther, ____.
12. Luther believed that Hosea preached about ____.
13. Modern Lutheran scholarship does not considered the book of Jonah ____.
14. Who foretold that Christ would be born in Bethlehem? ____
15. The name Nahum means ____.
16. Critical scholarship has adopted vies considerably different from ____.
17. Luther said that Zechariah predicted ____.

The Abandonment of the Four Solas of the Lutheran Reformation By Liberal Lutherans

Christian News, October 22, 1990

The Fort Wayne newspapers, *The Journal Gazette* and *The News Sentinel* every Saturday devote a page of their respective Saturday editions to the subject of religion. Both newspapers as a rule present religious issues under current debate in the churches. On September 1, 1990 *The News Sentinel* published an article entitled; "Worldwide religious harmony hampered by one way dogma."[1] The author was Clark Morphew, a Lutheran pastor and also a writer for the *St. Paul* (Minnesota) *Pioneer Press*. The present writer does not know whether this caption was supplied by the religious editor of the Fort Wayne paper or whether this eye-catching caption was furnished by the Reverend Morphew. About half of the article represented the views of a Hindu scholar named Anantanand Rambachan, who asserted: "The way Christianity is formulated, that Jesus is the unique and universal savior and there is no salvation through no other, is often the greatest barrier to respect for other religions."[2] The last statement appears to be that of Morphew.

If the Reverend Morphew did not supply the title for his article, there are yet indications in this article that he appears to agree with Rambachan that insisting on Jesus as the world's only savior is detrimental to fostering harmony among the religions of the world. Morphew is a pastor of ELCA and in his article he has expressed views that are not in harmony with the Word of God nor are they in line with the beliefs of Lutheranism as expressed in its confessional writings in the *Book of Concord*.

Morphew's Justification for
Cooperation with Non-Christian Religions

Morphew argues that inasmuch as America is represented by so many different faiths and cultures from Asia, Africa, Central America and other geographical areas, that all these divergent religions and cultures cannot be brought together, if Christianity makes exclusivist claims. If harmonious relations are to be maintained and fostered, it will not be permissible that Christianity be considered superior to them. Morphew believes that it will be the task of the ecumenical movement, which for the last forty years has unsuccessfully endeavored to bring together the major denominations of Christendom, to tackle this task of also bringing about harmony among the great religions of the world. Morphew bemoans the fact that liberals and conservatives so far have been unable or unwilling to come together and forget their doctrinal differences. Thus he wrote: "Liberals ridicule conservatives. Conservatives warn their young to avoid liberals. Put the two sides in the same room to discuss a hot issue, and they'll be shaking fists at each other within an hour."[3]

How Can A True Lutheran Approve of Liberalism

Morphew as a Lutheran should certainly know that liberalism has rejected or reinterpreted every fundamental doctrine of the Christian faith. Bernard Ramm, in his *Protestant Biblical Interpretation* has shown in chapter 2 of that book, which treats the various hermeneutical schools to appear in the last two thousand years, how liberalism has adopted six major principles which completely change the true character of Biblical Christianity.[4] Liberalism rejects the Bible's claims to be the very Word of God, has repudiated the deity of Jesus Christ, has played down the seriousness of sin, denied the transcendence of God, made unnecessary the vicarious and substitutionary atonement of Christ, has made rejected the doctrine of justification by Christ and promoted the view that there is no real immortality, no resurrection of the body, guaranteed Christians by virtue of Christ's physical and bodily resurrection from the dead. That Lutherans and other Christians under no circumstance could be bed fellows with Bible denying and Christ-dishonoring liberalism, Morphew does not seem to grasp. Conservative are castigated for not getting along with theological liberals![5]

Universalism Advocated by Morphew

Thus Morphew wrote: "And now we want the ecumenical movement to bring Buddhists, Moslems, Hindus and Christians together in some kind of dialogue or discussion." The St. Paul ELCA pastor claims that to do this requires "profound answers."[6] To his delight he went to Northfield, Minnesota where he found this being attempted at St. Olaf College.

St. Olaf and the Promotion of Pagan Non-Christian Religions

St. Olaf College, Northfield, Minnesota was once an orthodox Lutheran institution of higher learning, promoting true confessional Lutheranism, but now helping to promote better relations with pagan religions, with such faiths as Islam, Buddhism, Hinduism and anti-Trinitarian Judaism. The board of regents through its administration has hired as professor of the regular faculty a Hindu scholar by the name of Rambachan, who has the assignment to involve students in an interreligious dialogue, in which they are asked to accept Rambachan's Hindu encounter with God as a "legitimate spiritual path."

The Fallacious Assumption of Religious Ecumenism

The assumption of the ecumenical approach to other non-Christian religions is that there are many divergent paths to God, that there are many roads that lead to heaven. There is not just one way to God, the claim made by Christianity, one based on numerous statements of the New Testament. The ecumenical approach to other non-Christian religions according to Morphew is to help foster better understanding of other cultures and other religions. When people understand other religions by personal observation and experience, a worldwide understanding of others is fostered and sympathy rather than hatred created toward other faiths different from Christianity.[7]

The Old Testament Forbids Sympathy Toward and Participation in Pagan Religions

The Revelation of God in the Old Testament did not advocate the study and practice of the religions of Israel's neighbors in the Near Eastern world.[8] From the very beginning of Biblical history the true god, called Yahweh Elohim (the LORD God) was known and worshipped. Yahweh Elohim was known and worshipped by Adam and Eve; He appeared to Noah and his sons, appeared to the people after the Flood. Yahweh had dealings with Abraham, Isaac and Jacob. Yahweh gave commands to Moses and Aaron and to the children of Israel. YAHWEH Elohim appeared to Joshua and the Judges, like Gideon. He inspired David and Solomon, the writer of Job and all the authors of the books of the Old Testament. Over 2,000 times the phrase occurs, namely "the Word of the Lord came" in relationship to the many prophets active in Biblical times. Yahweh Elohim was known by many different names during Old Testament times, such as El Shaddai, El Olam, El Hai, the Fear, the Holy One of Israel, the King, the Rock and other names. On Mt. Sinai Yahweh commanded Israel "You shall have no other gods before me." (Ex 20:3). Yahweh means the "self-Existant One," The "Eternal One."[10] Israel's God is described as the Creator and preserver of all things in the universe.[11] The Old Testament Scriptures give a large number of attributes to God, which only can apply to Deity in its fullest sense, namely, such as omnipresence, omniscience, omnipotence. Adjectives like holy, just, righteous, merciful and gracious, indivisible, good, loving, beneficent, truthful and other attributes, in their full meaning, only hold true of God.[12]

The children of Israel were warned by God through Moses, Joshua and the prophets that they were to avoid the gods of Canaan. The entire fertility cult, with its worship of sex and its gods Baal, El, Ashtart, Ashtoreth, Mot and other deities were to be avoided, yes, even wiped out. A survey of Israel's history reveals the sad fact that from the wilderness stay till the end of both the Northern and Southern kingdoms, it was the worship of foreign Gods which spelt destruction and captivity for both kingdoms.[13] An analysis of Israel's religious history reveals the fact that over twenty Gods of twelve different nations were worshipped by united Israel and then by the Northern Kingdom (939-722 B.C.) and the Southern Kingdom (930-587 B.C.). Isaiah, chapters 40-48, contain some of the sharpest denunciations of idolatry in the Old Testament.[14]

The New Testament and Foreign Religions

Surely, just as there was no room for the worship of other Gods than Yahweh and no allowance made for consideration of the good points of Baalism, or of the Egyptian, Babylonian or Assyrian pantheons, so that the Jews might better understand their cultures, so also the New Testament takes the same stance with regard to the Triune God and the importance of accepting Jesus Christ, Son of God and also Son of Man, who was born for man's eternal salvation. The Greek and Roman gods of the first Christian century were not recognized nor worshipped by the Jews and Christians. Many passages in the Old Testament had predicted the coming of the Messiah to redeem mankind from their sins.[15] The deity of the Messiah had been foretold in Jeremiah (23:5-6) and in Isaiah 9:6-7). Jesus of Nazareth,a descendant of the Davidic house, fulfilled the many Messianic prophecies of the Old Testament.[16] This is the claim Jesus made, also supported by the inspired writers of the New Testament.[17]

No Salvation Apart from Christ

The "one-way" dogma said to hinder world-wide religious harmony is the New Testaments teaching, namely that apart from Christ there is no salvation. No person with a modicum of intelligence can read the Gospel of John and not be impressed with the frequency of assertions that state that Christ is the world's only Savior and he who rejects Jesus Christ will be lost forever. Without Christ there is no salvation. Jesus declared in unmistakable terms: "I am the way, and the truth, and the life; no one comes to the father, but through me" (John 14:6). The prologue of John's Gospel declares: "In the beginning was the Word, and the Word was with God, and the Word was God. He was in the beginning with God. All things were made by Him, and without Him nothing was made that was made, in Him was the life, and the life was the light of men. And the light shines in the darkness and the darkness comprehends it not" (1:1-5).[18]

The darkness of which John wrote includes all religions and religionists that subscribe to Muhammedanism, Buddhism, Confucianism, Jainism, Zoroastianism, Taoism, Hinduism and Judaism.

In John 3:16 John wrote: "God so loved the world that he gave his only-begotten Son, that whosoever trusts in him should not perish, but have eternal life."[19] For God did not send his Son into the world to condemn the world, but that the world through him might be saved." Later, at the end of Chapter 3 John wrote: "The Father loves the Son and has committed all things into his hands. Whoever believes in the Son hath eternal life, but he who disobeys the Son shall not see life, but the wrath of God abides upon him."[19] The great theme of John's Gospel is the conflict between belief and unbelief as demonstrated by many Jews in Jesus' time. Read chapter 20:31 as to the purpose of John's Gospel. In connection with the healing of the man at the Pool of Bethesda Jesus said: "For as the Father raises the dead and gives life to them even so the Son gives life to whom he will. For the Father judges no one, but has committed all judgment to the Son, **that all should honor the Son just as they honor the Father. He who does not honor the Son does not honor the Father who sent Him."[20] (Bold Face per authors)**

The Watershed Issues of the First Century A.D.

To accept Jesus as God's Son and the Redeemer of the World or not to, constituted the great religious issue of Judaism between A.D. 26-30, while Christ set forth his message. He was rejected and condemned to death by the Jewish Sanhedrin who then delivered Him to Pontius Pilate and accused Him of being a rival to Caesar,[21] for which the death penalty was demanded.[22] The Roman governor exceeded to their demands and Jesus of Nazareth was crucified and died in April 7, 30 A.D.[23] On the third day after His crucifixion Jesus arose from the dead and showed Himself alive on at least ten different occasions, once to as many as five hundred people.[24] Forty-three days after His death Jesus left this earth after having given His disciples the commission to make disciples of nations (Matthew 28:20; Acts 1:8).

When Peter and John endeavored to carry out the great commission in Jerusalem, they were persecuted by the Jewish leaders who put them in jail and beat them.[25] To them Peter made this declaration of the importance of Christ: "Nor is there salvation in any other, for there is no other name under heaven given among men by which we must be saved (Acts 4:12).

The Success of the Christian Gospel

The Book of Acts records the fact that on the day of Pentecost three thousand Jews and proselytes accepted Christ as the promised Messiah and Savior of the world and were baptized in his name.[26] Sometime later, the Jerusalem Jewish congregation increased to five thousand souls; yea, there were even priests among the new converts.[27] Because of the activity of the first Christians they were persecuted. When Stephen was stoned to death, because he preached Christ, the Christians extended their missionary activity all over Palestine.[28] Paul on his missionary travels preached the Gospel to Jews first,[29] although his specific assignment was to convert the Gentiles. Many Jews resisted Paul and rejected Christ as promised Messiah as Paul himself had done before his conversion on the Damascene road.[30] That there were Jewish Christians in the Roman Empire is shown by the fact that one of the epistles of the New Testament, namely, *The Epistle to the Hebrews* was addressed to Jewish Christians who were being challenged by their compatriots to rethink their commitment to Christ and His teachings. The author of Hebrews showed the Christian Jews that in every respect Christ and His teachings were superior to anything that Judaism could offer.[31] Christ was greater than the angels, greater than Moses and Joshua, Christ's priesthood was superior to that of Aaron and the cult of the Old Testament was no longer necessary for Christ made one sacrifice by which, once and for all, all sins had been atoned. Jesus was the fulfillment of all the things the Old Testament said that Messiah was to achieve.[32] The great truth about Jesus was that He's "the same yesterday, today and forever" (Hebrew 13:8). Because of Christ's atoning sacrifice, Jewish Christians were urged "to lay aside every weight and the sin which so easily ensnares us and let us run with endurance the race that is set before us, looking to Jesus the author and finisher of our faith, who for the joy that was set before him endured the cross, despising the shame, and has sat down at the right hand of God" (Hebrew 12:1-2).[33]

The prophecy of Jeremiah 23:5-6: "See, the days are coming, says the LORD, when I will raise up to David a righteous Branch, and he shall reign as king, deal wisely, and execute judgment and righteousness in the land, in his days Judah will be saved, and Israel dwell securely and this is His name whereby He shall be called: THE LORD OUR RIGHT-

EOUSNESS."[34] Here the Messiah is identified with Yahweh. This prediction was fulfilled in Jesus, who declared "I and the Father are one." With the death and resurrection of Jesus the old Israel had ceased and the new spiritual Israel, the Israel of God, came into existence (Galatians 6:16).

The Significance of Jerusalem's Fall in A.D. 70

The great break between the old Judaism and the true continuation of the old faith in Christ and his teaching became final in A.D. 70. Henceforth the old Judaism grew into the type of religion as eventually was found in the Talmud. The Jews who refused to recognize Christ as the promised Messiah became a law-oriented religion. The difference between Talmudic Judaism and Christianity was great. In Judaism men and women endeavored to achieve their salvation by autosoterism, while in Christianity men were justified by faith, because that Christ's righteousness was applied to them. To teach Jews that they can be saved apart from Christ is totally opposed to the teachings of Christ and His inspired apostles.

Revealed Religion Versus Unrevealed Religions

Religion is either a matter of divine revelation or religion is the creation of man's thinking or philosophizing about the great issues of human existence.[35] According to the Old Testament it was Yahweh Elohim who appeared to Adam and Eve, to Cain and Abel, to Noah and his three sons, to Abraham, Isaac and Jacob, to Moses and the children of Israel in Egypt. This same Yahweh also appeared to the judges, like Gideon, to Samuel, David, to Solomon and to Isaiah, Jeremiah, Ezekiel, to Daniel and many other prophets whose writings and experiences are found in the Old Testament. The Hindu scholar Rambachan, quoted by Morphew, claimed: "When students can affirm that God does reach out to people through other religions, their understanding of the spiritual connections among religious people take shape. At the same time, they begin to develop a new curiosity about Christianity."[36]

If this be true that in various different religions, its devotees have revelations from God, and religions like Zoroastrianism, Buddhism, Hinduism, Jainism, Taoism, Confucianism, Judaism and other religions that might be mentioned, which have such completely different views on major religious issues, must it not follow that God is a God of confusion in giving revelations that contradict each other? The truth of the matter is, that in both the Old and New Testaments only one plan of salvation is depicted and that those that differ are false. The Apostle Paul wrote to the congregations of Galatia, who were being invaded by the Judaizers, Christian Jews who taught that in addition to believing in Christ, it was mandatory to observe circumcision as well as keeping the requirements of the ceremonial law: "But though I myself or an angel from heaven were to preach to you any Gospel other than that which I did preach to you, let him be accursed (Galatians 1:8-9)." Paul called the Judaizer's teaching "another Gospel" and not the true Gospel.

Religious Views Not To Be Forced on People

While we are not physically to persuade people holding different religions than Christianity by force to become Christians, and while in a democracy all religious have the right to propagate their religious teachings, it nevertheless does not follow that Christians must show sympathy for Judaism, Mohammedanism, Buddhism, Taoism, Hinduism, Confucianism and the religious cults and concede that their religious concepts are just as good as the divine instructions found in the Word of God. All false religions are departures from God's Word and in no way to be regarded as containing true revelations from the Triune God. Jesus clearly indicated that He did not come to bring peace but the sword (Matthew 10:34).

Should Lutherans Be Sympathetic
Toward Non-Christian Faiths

Liberal Lutherans who advocate sympathy toward non-Christian religions and help the promotion of paganism, and claim that belief in the atonement of Christ is not necessary and reject the idea that Christ is not the only way to heaven, cannot be labelled Christians or Lutherans. No intelligent person can read the works of Martin Luther and assert to be a follower of his, who advocates and promotes religious positions, which are contrary to the clear teachings of the Bible relative to the plan of salvation.

How Important Is Worldwide Religious Harmony

According to Morphew to criticize and attack non-Christian religions is wrong, because it does not promote worldwide religious harmony but instead fosters hatred.[37] If the Christian faith, which true Lutheranism promotes, were only one of a number of human philosophical systems, then such a position might be correct. However, it is the claim of both Old and New Testament writers that they were setting forth divine revelations, which if men rejected them they would be punished. Morphew's position is that of theological liberals who in the 1930 objected to the sending of missionaries to heathen lands. Christ gave the command before His ascension that His followers were to make disciples of all nations (Matthew 28:20).

The Gulf Between Christianity and
Other Non-Christian Faiths

There are tremendous differences between Christianity and Judaism, between Christianity and Buddhism, between Christianity and Hinduism, between Christianity and Confucianism, between Christianity and Taoism, between Christianity and Zoroastrianism, between Christianity and all modern cults, such as Jehovah Witnesses, Mormonism, Christian Science, New Thought and a host of other religious associations that characterize the American and world scene. Over against Christianity they differ about their concept of God, for they deny the Trinity. The Non-Christian religions have different teachings about the place of

God in the universe, the purpose for man's existence, the nature of sin, the manner of getting right with God and what ultimately will be man's final destiny. Max Mueller, professor of Sanskrit and Comparative Philology at Oxford and also editor of *The Sacred Books of The East*,[38] once made this assertion about the difference between Christianity and all other religions:

"I have found the one keynote, the one diapason, so to speak, of all the so-called sacred books whether it be the Veda of the Brahmins, the Puranas of Siva and Vishnu, the Koran of the Mohammedans, the Zend- Avesta of the Parsees, the Tripitika of the Buddhists the one refrain through all—salvation by works. They all say that salvation must be bought with a price and that the sole price, the sole purchase money must be our works and deservings. Our holy bible, our sacred book of the East, is from the beginning to end a protest against this doctrine."[39]

Max Mueller further continued to point out the great fundamental difference between Christianity and the East's sacred books by writing:

Good works are, indeed enjoined upon us in that sacred Book of the East, but they are only the outcome of a grateful heart—they are only a thank offering, the fruits of our faith. They are never a ransom money for the true disciple of Christ. Let us not shut our eyes to what is excellent and true and of good report in these sacred books, but let us teach Hindus, Buddhists, Mohammedans, that there is only one sacred book of the East that can be their mainstay in that awful hour when they pass all alone into the unseen world. It is the sacred Book which contains that faithful saying, worthy to be received of all men, women and children, and not merely of us Christians—that Christ Jesus came into the world to save sinners.[40]

Luther Rejected the Idea that
There were Many Roads to Heaven.

Morphew and those in Lutheranism who teach that Christ is not the only way to heaven will be hard pressed to find such a soul-destroying position in Luther as reflected in his voluminous writings. Luther spoke with great clarity in 1530 in connection with comments on Psalm 118:23, where he stated that the center and cornerstone of Scripture is Christ.[41] The belief in the atoning work of Christ and justification by faith as the method by which lost and condemned sinners are declared righteous is the heart of Lutheranism.[42] Lutherans who deny those teachings are pseudo-Lutherans and not Lutherans at all. Luther and Lutheran beliefs about Christ were masterfully stated in the Reformer's explanation of the Second Article of the Apostles' Creed.[43]

The Lutheran Confessions and the Centrality of Christ

The Lutheran Confessions contain many assertions about Christ as the only way to heaven. Thus in Article XX of the *Augsburg Confession* it is stated:

"We begin by teaching that our works cannot reconcile us with God or obtain grace for us, for this happens only through faith that is, when we believe that our sins are forgiven for Christ's sake, who alone is the mediator who reconciles us to the Father. Whoever imagines that he can accomplish this by works or that he can merit grace, despises Christ and seeks his own way to God, contrary to the Gospel."

Repudiation of the Lutheran Reformation
October 31, 1990 will mark another day when Lutherans will recall the events that began with the nailing of the ninety-five theses to the church at Wittenberg. Between 1518 and 1546 great religious changes would be effected in Europe. Lutheranism would eventually separate itself from the Roman Catholic Church which on December 10, 1520 declared Luther a heretic. Luther in his writings clearly showed the unscriptural character of the church in which he had grown up. His writings as well as the Lutheran Confessions clearly distinguished between the teachings of Rome, Geneva and the promoters of enthusiasm. If the Lutheran Confessions were concerned about the doctrinal differences found in Christendom, they had no doubt about the false teachings of Judaism and Mohammedanism. Yet today, liberal Lutherans not only have made concessions to Romanism, Calvinism, Armenianism, and the charismatics but even have given religious legitimacy to pagan faiths.

The Rejection of the "Solas" of the Lutheran Reformation
The distinctive teachings of the Lutheran Reformation which clearly differentiate the Lutheran Church from the Roman Catholic Church are the "four solas," usually given as "Scripture alone," "Christ alone," "alone by God's grace," by "faith alone." These doctrinal positions. Biblically founded are being jettisoned by modern pseudo-Lutherans. Scripture alone, not tradition or church councils, or the consensus of the Fathers, or the Vulgate text, or decisions by the Pope determine what followers of Christ are to believe. Human reason and erroneous philosophical systems also do not serve as sources for establishing doctrines and ethical rules." When other sacred scriptures are used to establish and promote religious teachings, then the sola Scripture principle is violated.

Solus Christus, Christ alone, is the Savior and Redeemer of the world. When Judaism rejects Christ as God and Lord it thereby places itself in the category of false religions.[46] Mohammedanism, which only recognizes Jesus as a man and prophet beneath Mohammad in rank and denies his virgin birth and resurrection places itself in the class of those religions denying that Christ died for the sins of the world.[47] Hinduism[48] and Buddhism,[49] Zoroastrianism[50] and Confucianism[51] all know nothing of the saving work of Christ. Denying the deity of Christ places all religions in the group of religions that reject the Trinity, around which the entire work of the true God revolves.

Salvation is only due to the grace of God (Ephesians 2:6). Man by his own efforts can do nothing toward his salvation. When human beings believe that by their human efforts they can please God, they are deluding themselves.

The method by which sinners are justified is by faith, which the Holy Spirit creates in a repentant sinner's heart to bring about faith in the objective death of Christ who thereby paid for the world's sins (John 1:22,4). Justification by faith, which is totally due to the grace of God, is not found in any other religions, is a truth which has been abandoned by modern liberal Lutheranism. Basic to sound Biblical teaching is the belief that God's Word alone establishes what men are to believe and how they are to live God-pleasing lives. When the clear assertions of the Old and New Testaments are questioned, rejected, modified or changed, as is done by the use of the historical-critical method, then the foundations of true religion are undermined, emasculated and destroyed.[52] This is especially true when it is taught that Christ is not the only Savior for mankind. Thus the solus Christus principle of Holy Writ has been jettisoned. If Christ is not necessary for salvation, then the idea is fostered that men can save themselves, and as a result they practice autosoterism or contend that man can cooperate in saving themselves. Thus the sola gratia principle of Biblical Christianity and of Lutheranism goes down the drain. Sola fide is the only method by which man is brought by the Holy Spirit to accept Christ as personal Savior. In place of sola fide sinners are taught that by their will power and strength they can come to God by their good works. All four solas of the Reformation have been surrendered. While they are Lutherans who claim to be Lutheran in name, in reality, they have apostatized from the Christian faith.

Present Status of World Lutheranism

The developments of Lutheranism in the second half of the twentieth century are reminiscent of Lutheran conditions after the Age of Orthodoxy, followed in turn by Pietism.[53] The latter prepared the way for the Age of Rationalism when Lutheranism lost its true character. Although the nineteenth century witnesses a revival of Lutheran confessionalism, the rationalism of the eighteenth century was perpetuated in the higher critical movement,[54] which saw the rejection of the four solas or orthodox Lutheranism but spawned not only a negative form of literary criticism, but eventuated in form criticism, content criticism, redaction criticism, structuralism, and tradition criticism.[55] The use of all these types of criticism resulted in the emasculation of the content of Holy Scripture as had not been the case for nearly a thousand years of church history.[56]

The Need to Read the Great Classics of Lutheranism

What liberal Lutherans need to do is to read and study the writings of Gerhard and Chemnitz.[57] *The Conservative Reformation and Its Theology* by Charles Poterfield Krauth would greatly aid getting a correct understanding of Biblical and Lutheran Theology.[58] A good description of the nature and character of the Lutheran faith can be found in Sasse's *Here We Stand*[59] or Sasse's *This Is My Body*, a Scriptural discussion of the Lords Supper.[60] A Scriptural critique of current theological trends can be found in Sendstad's *The Word That Can Never Die.*[61] The great central doctrine of Christianity is powerfully presented by Ed Preus, *The Justi-*

fication of the Sinner before God.[62] Heinrich Schmidt, *Doctrinal Theology of the Evangelical Lutheran Church* shows how the Lutheran Church for four hundred years has taught its doctrine based on Scripture and cites many Lutheran theologians who supported the theology of the Lutheran Confessions.[63] No person can meet the demands of 2 Timothy 2:15, "to handle the Word of God correctly" who does not properly distinguish between Law and Gospel. There is no more competent work that deals with the proper distinctions between Law and Gospel than the classics of C.F.W. Walther.[64] Pieper's *Christian Dogmatics*, 3 volumes,[65] and Adolf Hoeneckes, *Dogmatik*, 4 volumes can show any person desiring to know what God's Word teaches on the whole gamut of Christian theology.[66] Robert Preus, *The Inspiration of Scripture* will show on the basis of 17th century Lutheran theologians what is truly involved in the doctrine of *The inspiration of Scripture.*[67]

Herman Otten has written an excellent book in which he has set forth the great gulf between Biblical theology and modernism as it pertains to all important doctrines and ethical issues, which have implications for churches now and especially what would be their implications for eternity.[68]

The prayer of true Lutherans is: "Gottes Wort and Luther Lehr vergeht nun and nimmer mehr," and **Verbum dei manet in aeternum,**

Footnotes

1. Clark Morphew, "Worldwide religious harmony hampered by the one way dogma," *The News Sentinel*, Saturday, September 1, 1990, F.F 6.
2. **Ibid.**, p. F6.
3. **Ibid.**
4. Bernard W. Ramm, *Protestant Biblical Interpretation* (Revised Edition: Grand Rapids: Baker Book House, 1970), pp. 63-69.
5. Morphew, **op. cit.**, p. F6, column 1.
6. **Ibid.**, p. F6, column 1.
7. **Ibid.**, p. F6, column 1.
8. Ros E. Price, "Idolatry," *Wycliffe Bible Encyclopedia* (Chicago: Moody Press, 1975), 1, pp. 827-828.
9. Nathan J. Stone, *Names of God* (Chicago Moody Press, 1944), 159 pages Herbert F. Stevenson, *Titles of the Triune God. Studies in Self-Revelation* (Westwood, N.J.; Fleming H. Revell Company, 1956), pp. 13-100.
10. F.F. Bruce, "Names of God," J.D. Douglas et. al. *New Bible Dictionary* (Wheaton, IL: Tyndale House Publishers, 1982), p. 430 a.
11. Yahweh as creator, cf. Genesis 1:1-2:3; 2:4-26; Exodus 20:11; 1 Samuel 2:8; Nehemiah 9:6. For a listing of major creation passages cf. Raymond F. Surburg ch. 2 in Paul Zimmerman, Darwin, *Evolution and Creation*: (St. Louis: Concordia Publishing House, 1959), p. 39.
12. Cf. the listing of God's attributes in the Old Testament in A. L. Graebner's *Doctrinal Theology* (St. Louis: Concordia Publishing House, 19010), pp. 21-41.
13. Cf. footnote 8.
14. Isaiah 41:7; 41:29; 42:17; 43:13; 44:8; 44:9; 45:18; 45:19; 45:21; 46:2.
15. Isaiah 52:13; 53:5-6; 53:10; 53:11.

16. Cf. The Epistle to the Hebrews for the fulfillment of Jeremiah's prediction: 8:8-12; 10:16-17.
17. In Matthew's Gospel the whole series of introductory formulas "This happened that it might be fulfilled which was spoken by the prophet: 1:22; 2:15; 2:23; 4:14; 3:17; 12:17; 13:35; 21:4; 26:56; 27:35.
18. *Translation in The New King James Version New Testament* (New York: Thomas Nelson Publishers, 1979), 1032.
19. Helen Barrett Montgomery, *The New Testament in Modern Speech* (Philadelphia: Judson Press, 1924), p. 240.
20. **Ibid.**, p. 249.
21. Mark 14:53-60; 14:65.
22. Mark 15:2-3.
23. Adam Fahling, *The Life of Christ* (St. Louis: Concordia Publishing House, 1936), p. 663.
24. Cf. Walter Kueneth, *The Theology of the Resurrection* (St. Louis; Concordia Publishing House, 1965), pp. 32ff., 31ff., 86 ff., 199ff.
25. *The Acts of the Apostles*, chapter 4:1-4, 4:21.
26. **Ibid.**, chapter 2:41.
27. **Ibid.**, chapter 6:7.
28. **Ibid.**, chapter 3:1-2; 9:31.
29. **Ibid.**, chapter 9:23-29; 13:5; 13:15; 14:1; 17:1; 13:4.
30. **Ibid.**, chapter 9:1; 9:22; 13:1-11; 14:5; 16:19-20; 17:4-7.
31. Cf. Graham Scroggie, *Know Your Bible*, volume II. Analytical New Testament (London: Pickering and Inglis, no date), pp. 230-281.
32. Everrett F. Harrison, *Introduction to the New Testament* (Grand Rapids: Eerdmans Publishing company, 1964) p. 346.
33. *The New King James Version*, **op. cit.**, p. 1179.
34. *The Holy Bible, The New Berkeley Version in Modern English* (Grand Rapids: Zondervan Publishing House, 1969), p. 763.
35. Francis Pieper, *Christian Dogmatics* (St. Louis: Concordia Publishing House 1950), i, pp 19-21.
36. Morphew, **op. cit.**, p. F 6 column 3.
37. **Ibid.**, F6, column 3.
38. Max Mueller, *The Sacred Books of the East* (New York: Charles S. Scribner's Sons, 1395), 12 volumes.
39. As cited by Pieper, *Christian Dogmatics*, **op. cit.**, 1 , pp. 15-16. (Ed. for further information on this statement see p. 2523 of the *Christian News Encyclopedia*. It was probably made by Professor M. Monior Williams).
40. **Ibid.**
41. Ewald Plass, *Luther Speaks* (St. Louis: Concordia Publishing House, 1959), II, p. 353.
42. Tappert, *The Book of Concord* (Philadelphia: Fortress Press, 1959). p. 345.
43. **Ibid.**, p. 345.
44. Tappert, **op. cit.**, p. 42.
45. Raymond F. Surburg, "The Significance of Lutheran Hermeneutics for Protestant Reformation," *Concordia Theological Monthly*, 24:241-261, 1953.
46. Paul E. Kretzmann, *The God of the Bible and Other Gods* (St. Louis: Concordia Publishing House, 1943), p. 175.

47. J. Eider, *Biblical Approach to the Muslim* (Houston: International Headquarters, 13530, no date), pp. 71-79.

48. "Hinduism," Fuerbringer, Engelder and P.E. Kretzmann, *The Concordia Cyclopedia* (St. Louis: Concordia Publishing House, 1927), pp 320-329.

49. Kretzmann **op. cit.**, pp. 62-31.

50. John A. Hardon, *Religions of the World* (Garden City, N.Y.; Doubleday and Company, 1963). 1, 204-219.

51. **Ibid.** 156-192; Kretzmann, **op. cit.**, pp. 34-110.

52. Raymond F. Surburg. "The Historical Method in Biblical Interpretation." *Concordia Theological Monthly*, 22:31-104, February, 1952; Fred Kramer, "The Introduction of the Historical-critical Method and Its Relationship to Lutheran Hermeneutics" (St. Louis; Concordia Publishing House, 1966), in *Aspects of Biblical Hermeneutics*, pp. 43-77.

53. "Lutheran Theology After 1530," Erwin Lueker, Editor, *The Lutheran Cyclopedia* (St. Louis, Concordia Publishing House, 1975), pp. 506-506.

54. **Ibid.**, p. 506.

55. Cf. the bibliography dealing with the different types of criticism in Raymond F. Surburg, "The Principles of Interpretation" (Fort Wayne; Concordia Seminary Press, 1979), pp. 563-573.

56. Johann Gerhard, *Loci Theologi*.

57. Martin Chemnitz, *Loci Theologi*. Translated J.A.O. Preus (St. Louis; Concordia Publishing House, 1939). 2 volumes; Examination of the Council of Trent, Part I. Fred Kramer, St. Louis; Concordia Publishing House, 1971. The Lord's Supper Translated by J.A.O. Preus, (St. Louis; Concordia Publishing House, 1979).

58. C.P. Krauth, *The Conservative Reformation and Its Theology* (Minneapolis; Augsburg Publishing House, 1963). Reprint of 1871 Edition.

59. Herman Sasse, *Here We Stand* (New York; HARPER and Brothers Publishers, 1933.

60. Herman Sasse, *This Is My Body* (Minneapolis; Augsburg Publishing House, 1959).

61. Olav Valen Sendstad, *The Word That Can Never Die* (St. Louis; Concordia Publishing House, 1949.

62. Dr. Ed. Preuss, *The Sanctification of the Sinner Before God*. Translated by Julius A. Friedrich (Distributed by A.P. Deli, *Lutheran Theological Seminary*, Thiensville, Wis. 1934).

63. Heinrich Schmid, *Doctrinal Theology of the Lutheran Church* (Minneapolis; Augsburg Publishing House, 1961). Reprint of 1375 Edition.

64. C.F.W. Walther, *The Proper Distinction between Law and Gospel*. Reproduced by W. H. Dau from 1987 Edition (St. Louis; Concordia Publishing House, 1929.

65. Francis Pieper, *Christian Dogmatics* (St. Louis; Concordia Publishing House, 1950-1953).

66. A. Hoenecke, Dogmatik (Milwaukee; Northwestern Publishing House, 1917), 4 volumes.

67. Robert Preus, *The Inspiration of Scripture - A Study of the Theology of the Seventeenth Century Lutheran Dogmaticians* (Mankato Minnesota; Lutheran Synod Book Store, 1953).

68. Herman J. Otten, *Baal or God* (New Haven, Missouri; Leader Publishing Co., 1965).

Questions

1. Who was Clark Morphew? ____
2. Morphew maintains that Christianity should not make ____ claims.
3. Liberalism rejects the Bible's claim to be ____.
4. Morphew does not seem to grasp that ____.
5. Conservatives are castigated for not getting along with ____.
6. St. Olaf College was once ____.
7. The Old Testament forbids ____.
8. What phrase appears over 2,000 times in the Old Testament? ____
9. Yahweh means ____.
10. What led to the destruction of both kingdoms? ____
11. Many passages of the Old Testament predicted ____.
12. Without Jesus Christ there is no ____.
13. The old Judaism grew into a type of religion eventually found in ____.
14. The great truth about Jesus was that He is ____.
15. Paul called the Judaizer's teaching ____.
16. Christ gave the command before His ascension that His followers were to ____.
17. Liberal Lutherans have made concessions to ____.
18. ____ know nothing of the saving work of Christ.
19. The rationalism of the eighteenth century was perpetuated in the ____.
20. Surburg recommends the reading and study of ____.

What Are Benefits of LCUSA Membership "Ask About the Old Ways"

Christian News, June 29, 1991

"The LORD says this: Stand at the crossroads and look, ask about the ancient ways: Where is the way that leads to good things? Live in it and find rest for your souls." Jeremiah 6:16 (Beck, An American Translation).

This passage is part of an early sermon preached by the prophet Jeremiah to the people of Jerusalem and Judah in the early part of Josiah's region. Josiah was the last good king of Judah who attempted to bring about a religious reform in a kingdom that had been guilty of serious apostasy from its God, Jehovah. In 626 B.C., during the 13th year of Josiah's reign, Jeremiah received his call from Jehovah. In 621 B.C. the book of the Law was found in the Temple in Jerusalem, a discovery which caused Josiah to be alarmed when he read the book's contents and compared its teachings and demands with the religious practices and beliefs current in Judah. The prophetess Huldah played a part in this attempted reformation. Most likely Jeremiah also supported it, although it did not take him too long to realize that the reformation really only touched the surface. In his sermon in chapters 2 and 3 he accused the southern nation of serious backsliding. In the sermon in chapters 5 and 6 Jeremiah depicted the great danger in which the Judeans found themselves. The prophet's appeal was to them to give up their sinful ways and to return to the practice of the religion that had once obtained among them.

Jeremiah was greatly alarmed at the future prospects of his compatriots, who faced the destruction of the Temple, the city of Jerusalem, and either death or captivity. Why did Jeremiah consider the situation so grave? The reason the prophet of Anathoth gave was that the Judeans had completely forgotten the covenant and its stipulations that they had agreed to when God chose them as his special people. At Mount Sinai, Israel had entered into a marriage relationship with its God, the Israelites had agreed that God was their husband and they were his wife. This involved the fact that they would only recognize Jehovah (or Yahweh) as their God and would avoid recognizing or worshipping the gods of their heathen neighbors. Moses, the mediator of the Sinaitic covenant, gave them regulations, directives and laws designed to fence Israel off from its idolatrous neighbors of the Ancient Near East. In Exodus 19:5-6 the LORD outlined Israel's mission in the Near Eastern World on behalf of Jehovah.

However, after its entrance into Canaan, in the days of the Judges, between 1375-1075 B.C., many apostasies occurred and thus Israel time and time again broke the marriage covenant by going "a whoring after other gods." The very dangers against which Moses in his farewell address had warned the descendants of Abraham, they did not avoid and did exactly what the LORD told them not to do. Instead the Canaanite fertility cult with its immoral practices was embraced. Between 1375 till 626 B.C. the history of Jacob's descendants was a history of many failings

128

away from Jehovah who had delivered them from the Egyptian house of bondage. By the time of Jeremiah there had been so any defections and the denunciations of the prophets of the eight pre-Christian century (Amos, Hosea, Isaiah, Micah) had fallen on deaf ears, the Northern Kingdom had gone into captivity because of its sins and ceased to be a nation, so that in the latter years of the seventh century the situation in Judah was extremely critical from Jehovah's perspective. According to the thinking of the Lord the Judean situation had to be seriously dealt with. With the preaching of Jeremiah and Ezekiel Judah was being given one last chance. Either repent, or be punished! It was either back to "the ancient ways," or forward to death, doom and destruction!

Analogy with LCMS History

The Lutheran Church-Missouri Synod (LCMS) was founded 134 years ago in Chicago (1847). The LCMS has grown from twelve congregations to an international church numbering over 6,000 congregations, a synod which according to the 1981 Annual has over two million baptized members. Members, past and present, have witnessed during the thirteen decades of its existence the appearance of a number of different philosophies and psychologies of religion. Its professors, theological leaders, pastors, teachers and laity have evaluated them, rejected them and defended the great principles of Lutheranism: **Solus Christus, Sola Scriptura, Sola Fide, Sola Gratia**. From the very inception of its history, the LCMS has aimed at the ideal of strict adherence to the Scriptures and the Lutheran Confessions. However, since 1947 (the centennial year of LCMS existence) a change has occurred in that certain individuals become enamored of the ecumenical movement and its theology, with the result that between 1957-1974 a serious attack was made upon the theological heritage of the LCMS by men who studied at secular universities and heterodox seminaries. These individuals determined to change the direction of the LCMS, an attempt that was paralleled in the American Lutheran Church by a group who called themselves the "young Turks" (cf. *Dialog*). The last twenty-three years have been characterized by tension in fighting, theological warfare and finally in the withdrawal of 267 congregations, totaling over 113,000 members and the formation of a new Lutheran organization, called The Association of Evangelical Lutheran Churches (AELC). Since the Milwaukee convention of 1971 there have taken place a number of crucial conventions, such as the New Orleans (1973) and the Anaheim (1975), where the challenge to the reorientation of the LCMS was met head on and the attempt to take over the Synod failed.

Although there are many who did not leave the Synod and join the AELC, there are still remaining many within the Synod who sympathize, support and abet the theological views and church practices of those who left the LCMS and who now do everything in their power to criticize the doctrinal stance and the church practice of the Synod; their support of the LCMS's program is at best lukewarm, if not downright hostile.

In view of recent historical developments the word of Jeremiah to his

129

fellow religionists is also appropriate for the delegates and those exercising influence at the July 3-9 convention in St. Louis: "Stand at the cross roads and look. Ask about the ancient ways: Where is the way that leads to good things? Live in it and find rest for your souls."

At Mt. Sinai Jehovah had made a covenant with Abraham's descendants whom he had brought out of the Egyptian house of bondage. Jehovah expected Israel to abide by the stipulations of the Sinaitic covenant, of which Moses was the mediator. Time after time in his various sermons Jeremiah refers to the fact that Israel had broken this covenant and violated its stipulations.

The Congregation of Synod Made A Covenant with Each Other

All congregations, pastors, teachers who are members of the LCMS have entered into a covenant with each other when of their own free-will, they signed the constitution and its by-laws. Honesty and integrity require all signees of this constitution to abide by its spirit and requirements. Deliberately to violate its purposes and the rules for governing the Synod is unethical!

What are the major objectives of the LCMS? They are set forth in the constitution as follows: 1. The conservation and promotion of the true faith (Ephes. 4:3-4; I Cor. 1:10), and 2. A united defense against schism and sectarianism (Rom. 16:17). An analysis of the actions and activities of many of the LCMS during the last three decades will reveal that they did not attempt to conserve the true faith as understood by the Synod for over a hundred years nor did they promote it. The doctrinal position of the LCMS has been set forth in a number of doctrinal statements both before 1959 (the San Francisco Convention) and since 1959. Since the St. Paul Convention (1956) doctrinal tension has been mounting, promoted especially by those committed to bringing the LCMS into the mainstream of ecumenical Protestantism. A comparison of what was done by certain synodical officials, professors, teachers and lay people with the synodical position shows that they set about not only *to* undermine the LCMS doctrinal stance, but to impose upon the congregations and members of the Synod teachings which disagreed with those of the Scriptures and the Lutheran Confessions. The doctrinal position of the LCMS was set forth in 1947, the centennial year of the Synod's existence, in the volumes of *The Abiding Word.* By departing in a number of important ways from the hermeneutics as well as of the understanding of Biblical doctrine and church practice, there resulted a different understanding of the true nature of the Bible (now considered errant), a different comprehension of certain basic doctrines and a diametrically opposed view about with whom fellowship was possible. The result was that the innovators violated the Synodical constitution and its by-laws.

Conditions For Membership

A return to keeping the covenant agreement made with others in the LCMS, who take the words of the constitution and its by-laws seriously and follow them, would require:

1) Living up to the conditions for membership required by any person having subscribed to the Synodical constitution and its by-laws. If this were really done by all, then the harmony which for many years characterized the LCMS would be restored.

Now what are the conditions that in the last three decades have been violated by certain members and congregations? Here are some of the most important ones: "Renunciation of unionism and syncretism of every description." In the last two decades the religious press of the United States has reported numerous instances when members of the LCMS's clergy have joined in worship services and religious programs with members of other church bodies, who when evaluated by the theological teachings of the Lutheran Confessions, do not teach correctly the doctrine of the sacraments, the person and work of Christ, the nature of the Bible, the doctrine of creation, the doctrine of the church and ministry, the way of salvation, the work of the Holy Spirit and the Second Coming of Christ. The Lutheran Confessions are misinterpreted and made to teach just the opposite of what they were intended to teach when first written.

There are those today in the LCMS (as well as those in The Lutheran Church in America and in The American Lutheran Church) who have forgotten what the Reformation was all about. They ignore all confessional statements which have accurately described the differences between Rome and Wittenberg, between the Church of the *Augsburg Confession* and the theology of the Roman Church with its nearly two thousand years of theological developments. In Rome, doctrine is being further revealed, as may be seen relative to the doctrines dealing with Mary (Mariology). In Rome the revelation of God is not yet final. This means that either Lutherans do not really understand the theology of Rome or they do not really know or believe Lutheran doctrine.

Justification by infused grace as taught by Rome is not justification by faith apart from works. Justification and sanctification are mixed in Rome; in Lutheranism justification precedes sanctification. Further, twentieth-century Rome has embraced and condoned the use of the historical-critical method which makes it a bedfellow with theological liberals. ALL members of the LCMS need to return to "the old ways" relative to their attitude toward Rome.

Our Lutheran forefathers also held that there were significant differences between Lutheranism and the theological teachings held by the Reformed and Arminian Churches and also between Lutheran doctrine and that of the Enthusiasts. Recognition of and fellowshipping with conservative people from the Calvinistic and Arminian camps means that those in the LCMS who are doing it, are not living up to the historic Lutheran attitude toward those who have different ideas about Baptism, the Lord's Supper, the nature of the church the Second Coming of Christ, the nature of the Bible. Again: faithfulness to the Synodical covenant requires avoiding those whose doctrines which are not considered to be in line with Holy Writ. This, of course does not mean, that other Christians are not members of the Una Sancta or belong to the fellowship of communion of saints of the Apostle's Creed.

2) To return to the old ways and living up to the synodical compact would further mean not only abiding by the teachings of the Lutheran Confessions, but would also require employing the system of interpretation of hermeneutics employed by Luther, Melanchthon, Gerhard, Chemnitz and many Lutheran divines and past outstanding exegetes. This would mean employing the historical-grammatical method and avoiding the historical-critical method. For the last 13 decades of Synodical history the historical-grammatical method was the system that controlled the preaching, teaching and exposition of the Bible in Lutheranism, not only in the LCMS but in all Lutheran Churches before a new spirit invaded these churches not too many years ago.

Liberal Protestantism abandoned the historical-grammatical method in favor of the historical-critical, which is a methodology composed of a number of types of criticism which the last two hundred years have spawned. They are: a liberal type of literary criticism, a later-developed form criticism, followed by redaction criticism, tradition criticism, contents criticism, and more recently a still more radical type known as structural criticism. The latter is critical of all those types of criticism the past developed. This historical-critical method has undermined the Bible's reliability, led to all manner of theological aberrations and introduced uncertainty into Christian doctrine. The result has been that the Church has been presented with a changing Christ for a changing world. That which is true today, is not true tomorrow! The new hermeneutic has created tensions in Lutheranism and has fomented divisions that have bedeviled the history of the LCMS for the last thirty years. Thus we find that many miracles of the Bible are rejected or reinterpreted, the person and work of Christ undermined, theistic evolution supported, new anti-Scriptural views about sex condoned, abortion, divorce, and homosexuality considered not wrong; in fact, even a friendly attitude has at times has been manifested over against anti Trinitarian cults.

If delegates and congregations were to go back to the "old ways," they would recognize that between the official position of the LCMS and the official stance of The American Lutheran Church (TALC) on a number of important issues there now exists a great difference and that since Denver (1969) a gulf has developed on proper Scriptural interpretation, the doctrine of office of the ministry (Woman's ordination), the proper use of sex , and religious unionism.

Benefits of Membership in LCUSA?

Relative to The Lutheran Council in the USA (LCUSA), delegates and congregations might seriously ask themselves what have been the benefits of membership to LCUSA, when three of the four major constituent bodies are denominations that employ the historical-critical method and that are committed to church union apart from doctrinal unity. Just what of significance has emerged from the so-called theological studies that have been produced by the Division of Theological Studies? In a number of instances documents have been sent forth that were not in agreement with the historic position of the LCMS. Could not the monies expended

132

to support LCUSA be employed more wisely and beneficially?

3) For congregations and delegates to return to the "old ways" would also mean exclusive use of doctrinally pure agendas, hymnbooks, and catechisms in church and school. Sound educational materials that are faithful to the teachings of the Lutheran Confessions and to the Bible should be the concern of all members and congregations of the Synod. When writers of educational materials are influenced by philosophies of education and psychologies of education that are not Scripturally- sound and also at the same time use the historical-critical method in interpreting the Bible, the results, as the past has shown, are not conclusive to doctrinally-sound and faith building books and helps.

4) A return to the "old ways" by all congregations of Synod would mean living up to the objectives of the Synod, as stated in its constitution, namely to be served by pastors trained in seminaries that are orthodox. Since 1974 this has been challenged. Christ Seminary in Exile, supported by AELC and congregations and people within the LCMS, has graduated pastors who reject the historical position of the LCMS and yet wish to serve within that church body with whom they are not in theological sympathy. Men trained in the historical-critical method and who favor gross unionism should serve in churches outside of the Synod. Akin to this matter is permitting congregations and pastors to hold dual membership in the AELC and in the LCMS simultaneously.

A return to adhering to the objectives of the constitution and its by-laws, really agreeing with the historic LCMS's position, would rectify a situation that has become intolerable in that it has produced a church that does not wholeheartedly live up to the Lord's will, a church that does not give a clear sound.

Questions
1. What was found in the Temple of Jerusalem in 621 B.C. ____?
2. When was the Lutheran Church-Missouri Synod founded ____?
3. The great principles of Lutheranism are ____.
4. What happened in the LCMS between 1957-1974? ____.
5. After 267 congregations withdrew from the LCMS many ____.
6. It is unethical for an LCMS congregation to ____.
7. What was set forth in *The Abiding Word*? ____?
8. Justification by infused grace as taught by Rome is not ____.
9. Rome has embraced the ____ method.
10. True Lutherans employ the ____ method and avoid the ____.
11. What introduced uncertainty into Christian doctrine? ____
12. A return to the "old ways" by all congregations of the LCMS would mean ____.

Whatever Happened to
"The Festival of the Reformation?"

Christian News, October 18, 1993

This year true Lutherans will celebrate the 476th anniversary of the nailing of the 95 theses to the church door of Wittenberg, which turned out to be the beginning of what church historians have called The Protestant Reformation, but by Roman Catholic pundits The Protestant Revolt.

The Lutheran Church is unique among the churches of the world in appointing a festival of the Reformation. This festival which a number of church agendas in the past regarded of major rank, may be traced back to the annual commemoration in domestic circles of the translation of the Bible into the German language, or to the annual Thanksgiving service commemorating the introduction of the Reformation in specific districts which Bugenhagen appointed in several of the Church Orders (Brunswick 1528, Hamburg, 1529, Luebeck, 1531). Similar services of thanksgiving were instituted by Elector Joachim, 1563 in the Pomeranian Church Order, 1568. In some places in Germany services were held on the eve of Luther's birthday (November 10) or on the anniversary of Luther's death, February 18, 1546. In Wuerttenberg and Baden the festival was observed on the Sunday following June 25, the date of the delivery of the *Augsburg Confession*, June 25, 1530.

The Thirty Years War obliterated these observances, but in 1667 Elector George II reestablished the festival in that he designated October 31 as the day for its observance. The 31st of October, or the Sunday either preceding or following became general practice in Germany and in other Lutheran lands.

When Lutherans celebrate the Festival of the Reformation they are doing what the author of the Letter of Hebrews encouraged his readers to do, namely, "Remember your leaders, the men who spoke the message of God to you; consider the issue of their lives, and imitate their faith." (Heb. 13:9)

In recent years the 31st of October was not called "The Festival of the Reformation," but simply "day of the Reformation." Formerly *The Lutheran Hymnal* produced and authorized by the Synods comprising The Evangelical Lutheran Synodical Conference of North America spoke of "The Festival of the Reformation," as did also *The Common Service Book* of the former Lutheran Church in America. *The German Hymnal* used by congregations of The Lutheran Church-Missouri Synod listed October 31 as "das Fest der Reformation."

By contrast the new hymnal of The Evangelical Lutheran Church in America (ELCA) and *Lutheran Worship*, the hymnal prepared by The Commission on Worship of The Lutheran Church-Missouri Synod, 1982, speaks on page 115, of "Reformation Day" (Ed. The LCMS's *Lutheran Service Book*, published in 2006, speaks of "Reformation Day," p. xi).

Now it must be conceded that both recent Lutheran hymnals do list

Reformation Day, October 31, as an event to be remembered. But there is a difference between "festival" and "day." The word "festival" suggests a special happy, a joyous celebration. Webster defines "festival" as: "A day of feasting or celebrating." The word day, of which each year has normally 365, and 366 in a leap year, does not necessarily suggest the reason for celebration and therefore is a bland word by comparison. In the past, especially in better than the last half century, Lutherans had cause for rejoicing when they thought and remembered the great historical events which occurred between 1517 and 1546 when God's servant Martin Luther was used by God to restore to the Christianity of Europe the great saving truths of the Bible. One might say there was effected the restoration of apostolic Christianity.

The Protestant Reformation was a doctrinal revolution, one which was greatly needed. Christ and His salvation had been obscured to a point that the true way of salvation had been lost. The essence of Luther's theology has been summarized in four slogans: 1. Sola scriptura (Scripture alone, 2. Sola gratis (by grace alone), 3. Sola fide (by faith alone), and 4. Solus Christus (Christ alone). Here the world has the heart of the plan of salvation.

Luther restored the Scriptures as the sole authority in ethics. For the first five hundred years the Bible was the sole authority in the entire Christian Church. As the Church developed from a simple type or church polity to a complicated hierarchical system with its pomp and glory, changes relative to the question of authority were added. A vain leadership took over in the Church. Traditions which did not have their source in God's Word came to in some instances to replace the Biblical teachings.

In addition to the Bible, the Roman Church also added the consensus of the Church Fathers, the decisions of church councils. The faulty Vulgate in key passages (Genesis 3:15) and the encyclicals of the Papacy became determinative. The Teaching Magisterium of the Church claimed to have the guidance of the Holy Spirit, thus allowing for the setting forth of new teachings. This represents quite an extension of the source of divine revelation and source of authority. These pluses to the Holy Scripture as further sources for Christian doctrine and ethics soon caused darkness and trouble.

Church history has shown how one new teaching after the other was made binding on the consciences of the people who were members of the Roman Catholic Church. In 590 Pope Gregory developed the doctrine of purgatory. In A.D. 800 Radbertus formulated the doctrine of transubstantiation, bread and wine were said to be changed into the body and blood of Christ by the action of the priest as he consecrated the elements in the Eucharist. In A.D. 993 the worship of saints began; in A.D. 1070 the decree forbidding priests to marry was promulgated. In A.D. 1170 the cup was taken away from the laity, and yet since Vatican II we see a restoration of the cup by a church which claims to be under the guidance of the Holy Spirit reversing itself. The Vatican Council of 1870 declared the infallibility of the Pope when speaking **ex cathedra**. In 1854 the immaculate conception of Mary was promulgated by Pius IX. A hundred years later the assumption of Mary by Pope Pius XII in 1950 became official church doctrine.

Some of these new doctrines were promulgated after Luther's time, but it was Luther who declared that only the Word of God (sola scriptura) could establish doctrines and ethical precepts. Luther, as far as the Old Testament was concerned, went back to the Hebrew canon and not to the Alexandrian which also included ten of the fourteen Apocryphal books. The Bible forbids adding or subtracting from what God has revealed. The Scriptures alone are allowed for the establishment of doctrines and directions for ethical living.

Lutherans have reason to celebrate because of Luther's finding again the Biblical doctrine of sola gratis (only grace), that human beings are saved only by the grace of God. As St. Paul clearly taught: "By grace are ye saved through faith; and that not of yourselves: it is the gift of God Ephesians" 2:8-9.

The Roman Catholic doctrine of sacramental grace, namely that the sacraments infuse God's grace, and then with their help human beings can earn or merit their salvation, is not the Biblical doctrine of being saved alone by God's grace. God's grace is totally effective, and by faith men and women, children and infants are totally justified in God's sight. Connected with sola gratia is also associated sola fide (by faith alone). Again God's inspired apostle Paul wrote: "Therefore, we conclude that a man is justified by faith apart from works" (Romans 3:24).

This faith is created by the Holy Spirit in a person so that faith is the hand that grasps God's forgiveness. By faith in Christ's atoning work on Calvary's cross man is declared righteous instantaneously. In Luther's day justification and sanctification were mixed, but the Wittenberg Reformer showed that the life of sanctification only begins when the sinner has been declared righteous.

Lutherans have reason to celebrate because of the solus Christus principle, namely that only Christ and no other person can effect a person's salvation. Christ as He is described in the Gospels, the Book of Acts, in the Pauline and General Epistles and in the Apocalypse has solely brought about our salvation; the saints and Mary cannot contribute one iota to mankind's salvation. Luther's theology is very different in its essentials from the religious views taught in the fifteenth and sixteenth centuries, as found the decisions of the Council of Trent (1545-1563), and later in decisions of Vatican I (1870) and Vatican II (1962-1965).

Many Lutherans and Protestants do not see any reason to celebrate and consequently do not speak of October 31st as a day to celebrate, but if they observe the 31st, it's just a day. Since a number of Lutheran denominations have joined together and also become members of The National Council of Churches and the World Council of Churches, they no longer appreciate Luther's stance on avoiding such as cause division contrary to the doctrine of the Scripture (Rom. 16:17). They cannot at all appreciate Luther's objections to fellowship with the Reformed. The Roman Catholics or the Enthusiasts, all of which has happened and still is occurring on the part of Lutherans. Today very often Reformation Day is employed to advocate and support the very things Luther wrote and acted against. Today Reformation Day is being used to promote ecumenism.

The truth is Lutherans have much to celebrate even though the Reformation occurred 476 years ago. Here are jewels we have received as a result of the Lutheran Reformation:

1. The Open Bible.
2. The general priesthood of all believers.
3. The certainty of salvation.
4. The evangelical parsonage.
5. The correct understanding of the sacraments.
6. The right of private judgment.
7. The separation of church and state.
8. General education for all people.

May it always remain true: Gottes Wort und Luther's Lehr Vergehet nun and nimmer mehr.

(God's Word und Luther's doctrine may (they) now and never depart.)

Questions

1. Martin Luther was born in the year ____ and died in the year ____.
2. Why did the writer of Hebrew say about remembering your leaders? ____
3. What is the difference between "day" and "festival?" ____
4. The Protestant Reformation was a ____ revolution.
5. For the first five hundred years the ____ was the sole authority of the entire Christian Church.
6. What took over the Church? ____
7. When was the doctrine of purgatory developed? ____
8. When was the decree forbidding priests to marry developed? ____
9. The Vatican Council of 1870 declared ____.
10. When was the immaculate conception of Mary promulgated? ____
11. Lutherans have reason to celebrate because ____.
12. Faith is the hand that ____.
13. Who alone can effect a person's salvation? ____
14. Today Reformation Day is employed to advocate and support ____.

The Papacy

Dear Pastor Otten:
You may possibly want to publish this in *Christian News*. In an attempt to counteract all the propaganda and Scriptural misrepresentation that the public media are given about the doctrine of the papacy and the claim of the Roman Catholic Church to be apostolic in origin.

Fraternally,
Raymond Surburg

The Infallibility of the Pope

The 125th Anniversary of Vatican I and Its Promulgation of the Dogma of Papal Infallibility and The Reaction of Non-Catholics

Christian News, December 4, 1995

The nineteenth century's only Roman Catholic council was held during 1869 and 1870. It began on December 8, 1869. This was the first council since the conclusion of the Council of Trent which concluded rather abruptly in 1563.[1] Since the Tridentine Council Rome has taught the headship of the Pope of Rome. The gain the Pope made relative to his headship of the Church was finalized at Vatican I when the Roman Pontiff was declared to be Christ's representative on earth and that when His Holiness spoke **ex cathedra** on matters of dogma and morals, this was as definitive as if Christ Himself had recorded in the New Testament. The magisterium, through whom the Holy Spirit supposedly spoke, affirmed the primacy and infallibility of the Pope.[2]

When Pope Pius IX issued the call for an ecumenical council, this was the first in slightly three hundred years. It shows how powerful the Pope had become since the Tridentine Council when the Council of Trent was adjourned.[3] It was the largest gap between councils since the churchly gathering at Nicea, not called by the Pope, but by the emperor Constantine.[4] Pope Pius IX invited not only all of the Roman bishops, abbots, having episcopal jurisdiction, but also the Greek Orthodox bishops and Protestant bishops and leaders.[5] Latourette, the Protestant church historian, wrote about this papal invitation: "It was made clear that the Orthodox and Protestant participants that if they accepted that, by that act they would be acknowledging the supremacy of the Pope."[6] Obviously none of those non-Catholics came. In contrast to previous councils, no secular princes were asked, partly because they had broken their concordat with Rome.

The big issue of Vatican I was the promulgation of the infallibility of the Papacy.[7] Other matters also were on the agenda. It ended hastily as

138

had the Tridentine in 1563. To appreciate the events that led up to the infallibility dogma, pronounced on July 18, 1870, it is necessary to follow the developments in Central Europe in the nineteenth century. In 1854 Pius IX had declared the Immaculate Conception of Mary[8] and Pius asserted that all Christians must accept and believe this man-made doctrine. This dogma was binding on all believers and rejection of it subjected the denier to anathema: To further the veneration of the Virgin Mary it was hoped that the council would declare her assumption, just like present day Roman Catholics are looking for the promulgation of Mary as Mediatrix of mankind. The promulgation of the assumption of Mary was only secured by papal decree, by Pope Pius XII on November 30, 1950.[9]

Who Has the Authority to Establish New Dogmas?
About the time of Vatican I there was no unanimity as to who had the power to declare new doctrines. According to Roman Catholic doctrine, all doctrines that have been and may in the future be set forth are found seminally in Holy Writ, which included the Apocrypha. Politically the Pope was viewed as a temporal prince. Across Europe there was great suspicion that the concern for papal supremacy and infallibility marked a reassertion of the old claims of the dominion of the church over the state.[10] Culturally it was the period when Romanticism was in the ascendant and anti-intellectualism had an opportune time for a firmly traditional council. Theologically, Pius IX believed it was time for a decisive step forward (although the minority regarded it as a step backward).[11]

There developed within Roman Catholicism two parties: the Gallican and the Ultramontane. The Gallican position held that only the body of bishops and no particular bishop, not even the Pope of Rome, could make infallible judgments on matters of doctrine. With this stance stood French, Austrian, and German episcopates. Gallicanism began with J. B. Bossuet (1627-1704) end continued with conciliar theologians D'Ailly and Gerson, who at the Council of Constance promoted the supreme authority of a general council.[12] Gallicanism rejected the temporal claims of the Pope. The conciliarists believed the Pope was not subject to a general council.

The Ultramontanists took the opposite stance, and this position was advocated and supported by the Italians. Its classical exponent was Bellarmine in the nineteenth century W. C. Ward, editor of **The Dublin Revue and Veuillot, Editor of L'Universe.** Vatican I saw the defeat of Gallicanism and the establishment of the complete authority of the Pope over the church of Rome.[13]

Factors Contributing to the Advancement of Papal Supremacy
At the beginning of the nineteenth century the Roman Catholic Church was torn by opposition and distracted in its views. The Jesuit order, the backbone of the Papacy, had been abolished. In France, the French Revolution enemies had confiscated much church property. Monasteries were abolished, the priests despised and persecuted; church

services were frequently disturbed and Pope Pius XI was left to die in prison in 1799.[14]

This situation was to change considerably by the end of the nineteenth century. Asserted a Lutheran church historian: "At the beginning of the twentieth century the Roman Church had been restored to a strength and splendor such as it had not enjoyed in the Middle Ages."[15]

The New Awakening of Roman Catholic Prestige, 1830-1830

Pope Pius VII (1800-1823) pursued a policy of restoring the prestige of the Roman Catholic Church by reestablishing the Jesuit order in 1815.[16] He selected a capable secretary of state, Consalvus, who was a jurist. In 1816 Pius condemned Bible societies and Protestant Bible translations. Napoleon Bonaparte realizing the value of the French Church made a Concordat and in 1802 the French emperor formulated a new church constitution, known as the **Organic Articles**. These two documents made the Roman Catholic Church the religion of the French people. The bishops of France were supported by the State. These two documents constituted church law in France till 1905.[17]

The State of the Roman Catholic Church in Germany

However, by contrast, in Germany the Roman Catholic Church lost strength and prestige when all church property was given to the secular states.

Furthermore, the Roman Church lost three million members as well as the basis of its political power. In 1806 the Holy Roman Empire ceased to exist; after over a thousand years it came to an end.

A New Era for the Papacy

With the fall of Napoleon in 1814, a new era began with the Pope again at liberty to select his own policy for the Congress of Vienna (1814-1815) restored the States to the Church. Calsaveri by clever diplomacy acquired a new status for the Roman Church in many European countries. Many countries wished to restore peace and order, looked upon the Roman Pontiff as the traditional bead of Christendom.

In its restoration of power in the world it was aided by Romanticism and Ultramontanism.[18] The former represented a new emphasis on the emotions and advocated a return to the simpler life of earlier days. The new appreciation of ancient and medieval things was emphasized and the spirit of the French revolutionists was abandoned. The Roman Church with its seventeen centuries of history appealed to many supporting the Romantic movement. As a result of the Oxford Movement in England a number of Episcopalians embraced Rome, headed by John Henry Newman (1801-1890), who brought with him into the Church of Rome one hundred and fifty clergymen from the Church of England.[19]

Piux IX and the Promotion of Vatican Council One

Theologically Pius IX believed in 1869 that the scene was right for a decisive step forward by the promotion of the Gallican Stance on the supremacy and primacy of the Pope. In the opinion of Pius IX and his followers the time had come to put the cap-stone on the edifice of papal absolutism. The latter had been built up over hundreds of years by the use of the forged Pseudo-Isodorean Decretals and the claims of such powerful Popes as Gregory VII, Innocent III and Boniface VIII.

Liberalism and Ultramontism in Conflict With Each Other

Liberalism in the nineteenth century might be described as a reappearance of Rationalism. Its principles emphasized freedom of the press, freedom of conscience, freedom of organization and strict separation of church and state. Several Ultramontanists, including Lamennis, Lacordance (1861) and Montlenbar (d. 1870) believed that these ideas could be used to promote papal supremacy.[70] Could papal supremacy and infallibility be harmonized with religious tolerance, political freedom and modern science? Gregory XVI (1831-1846) in his papal bull of 1832, the **Mirari** condemned liberal views[20] and thus a conflict arose between Liberalism and Ultramontism. Ultramontism strongly advanced the cause of the Papacy. Historic events in England, Ireland, Germany, Austria and France enabled the Pope to control the Roman Catholic Church in all lands.

Pope Pius IX (1846-1878) won a number of outstanding victories. He proclaimed as binding teaching the dogma of the Immaculate Conception of Mary, who was preserved from the taint of original sin.[21] Henceforth, every good Catholic was to believe in the Virgin Mary as mediatrix and intercessor with God. This was clearly asserted in the encyclical of Pope Pius IX, in the **Lux Veritatis**, issued on Christmas Day, 1831.

In 1864 Pius IX issued his "**Syllabus of Errors**." This encyclical refuted eighty serious errors, including freedom of conscience, freedom of the press, Protestantism, Bible societies, civil marriage, free scientific investigation, separation of church and state, non-sectarian schools and religious toleration.[22] The **Syllabus of Errors** closed by condemning the idea that the Roman Pontiff had to adjust his views to progress, to liberalism and civilization as lately introduced.[23]

The crowning achievement of Pius IX came when in 1870, when the Vatican Council declared magisterially that when the Pope spoke **ex cathedra** on church doctrine and on morals this was binding on all Christians.[24] Thus Vatican I is noted specifically for its promotion of the inerrancy and infallibility of the Papacy, which changed the course of Roman Church forever. Vatican I approved a "dogmatic constitution of the Catholic faith." And this was proclaimed by the Pope as immutable truth.[25]

Facts About the Vatican Council

Vatican Council I was opened on December 8, 1869 among great splendor in Rome with 700 present.[26] Only the Roman Catholic Church could put on such a resplendent scene as those witnessed who participated. Over a thousand clerics had the right of attendance, the 276 Italian bishops outnumbered the 265 from the rest of Europe. One hundred and ninety-five diocesan bishops were particularly dependent on the Pope; in fact one-fourth were housed by the Pope himself.[27] Many of the bishops were theologically inferior and were thus open for pressure from the majority party. In the Pope's document it was claimed that Protestantism, rationalism, and nationalism were a danger to the true church, and it defined the true relationship of reason to faith. At no time were more than 800 present at any one session.[28]

The Formal Proclamation of the Infallibility of the Papacy

There was a great struggle relative to declaring Papal infallibility. Opponents were the great historian Hefle, two Austrian cardinals, Dupanloup of France, Moriarity of Ireland and many others.[29] From outside the council they were supported by J. H. Newman and Doellinger. On July 13, 1870, 471 voted non-placet, 62 agreed in principle but not in detail, while 76 abstained.[30] On July 13, 1870, the constitution **Pastor Aeternus** was passed by 533 placets to two non-placets.[30] Many left Rome so that they would not have to vote. If over 1,000 bishops could have been present, constituting the magisterium of the Roman Church, then a little better than 505 voted on this grave doctrinal matter. The two non-placets later agreed with the majority. The great theologian Doellinger was excommunicated because he refused to accept the dogma of the Papal Infallibility. A split occurred in the Roman Church and there came into existence The Old Catholic Church, which rejected the Primacy of Peter and the Pontiffs Infallibility.

Pius IX wrote the first constitution on the Church of Christ in **Pastor Aeternus**, with the approval of the council.[31] This document affirmed "that the primacy of the Church of God was immediately and directly promised and given to Blessed Peter, the Apostle of Christ. The successors of Peter are the Bishops of the Holy See of Rome. These Bishops therefore by the institution of Christ Himself obtain the primacy of Peter over the whole church," and the document says that it at all times has been necessary that every Church-that is to say the faithful throughout the world should agree with the Roman Church. The **Pastor Aeternus** went on to declare that to "the jurisdiction of the Roman Pope... all of whatever right and dignity, both individually and collectively, are bound 'to submit, not only in matters which belong to faith and morals but also those pertaining to the discipline and government of the Church throughout the world.'"[32] The **Pastor Aeternus** also asserted that no appeal could be taken from the Roman Pontiffs decisions to an ecumenical council, thus asserting the superiority of the Pope over the latter. The Pope was emphatically pronounced to office, not merely of inspection and direction but also had the supreme power of jurisdiction over the Universal Church.[33]

Council Splits the Roman Church
Formation of Old Catholic Church[34]

Old Catholic Church which in 1957 was estimated as having 350,000 members, was the direct result of the Vatican I's decision to promulgate the Doctrine of Papal Infallibility. Old Catholic Church is a movement in German-speaking Europe, especially in Bavaria, which broke away from the Roman Church because of the views set forth in *Pastor Aeternus*. This off-branch was to be found after 1879 in Germany, Switzerland and Austria and in other countries of the world.

Luther, Calvin and the Protestants rejected Papal infallibility already in the sixteenth century. The Church of the Augsburg Confession went so far as declaring the Papacy as the Great Antichrist, "The Man of Sin," spoken of by St. Paul in II Thessalonians 2:3-12.[35]

The Hierarchy the Source of Doctrines

It is evident from the proceeding of the Vatican Council that the real source of doctrine is the Church, that is, the hierarchy and not The Bible. As the official interpreter of the Bible and Tradition the Roman Church decides what the Romanist must believe. But the Protestant asks: "How can fallible men and an erring Church determine and fix doctrine?" Rome answers: "The church is infallible when it teaches." But the believers ask: "Where in the Bible is such a claim substantiated?"[36]

Besides Tradition, sources for doctrine are numerous, and they are: the decisions of church councils, especially the decrees of the Council of Trent (1545-1563), those of Vatican I (1869-1870) and Vatican II (1964-1965), the Roman Catechism, the official liturgical publications, Papal Bulls and Encyclicals and canon law. The New Roman Catholic Catechism of 1994 has over 800 page of materials. Much in these sources either contradicts Biblical teachings or creates new doctrines and practices not found in Holy Writ.[37]

While Roman Catholicism uses the Bible (including the Apocrypha), its doctrinal system contains so many views contradictory of God's Word, so that mankind finds it difficult to be saved, especially when justification by faith is anathemized and a Christology is advanced which robs Christ of the glory and honor which is His Tradition, only given the Roman Church, and not accessible to mankind, contradicts clearly revealed doctrines and moral practices of Holy Writ.

Here is a listing of false teachings promoted under the aegis and with the Roman Pontiffs agreement during the last 1400 years: Institution of purgatory (593), the claim that the Roman Pontiff is over kings and becomes an earthly ruler (754), the insistence of the celibacy of the priesthood (1075), the selling of Masses for money (1100), the use of the inquisition, to hunt out heretics (1184), the sale of indulgences (1190), the doctrine of transubstantiation (1215), the adoration of the host of the Eucharist (1226), the Bible placed on the list of Forbidden Books by the Council of Toledo (1229), the Papal Bull **Unam Sanctam**, denying the laity the cup (1415), the placing of Tradition as of equal authority with the Bible, the condemnation of justification by faith at the Council of Trent, the invention of scapulars (1600), the Immaculate Conception of Mary (1854), the separation of church and state condemned (1864), Papal infallibility declared (1870), the decree invalidating mixed marriages not performed by a priest, the Assumption of Mary (1950).[38]

Christ the Sole Authority in the Church

Paul in Ephesians 1:22f; Col. 1:18; Matt. 28:20; I Tim. 6:3f, 1 Peter 4:11 all testify that Christ alone is the head of the Church. Peter admonished: "If any man speak let him speak as the oracles of God." The Christians, the royal priesthood, I Peter 2:9, are not subject to any human authority in spiritual matters, Matt. 23:7f., Luke 22:25f.; I Cor. 3:21f.; I Cor. 7:23: "You are bought with a price; be ye not the servants of men." 2 Cor. 1:24; 8:8; I Peter 5:3: "Neither as being lords over God's heritage." The Christian people governs itself, Acts 6:5. "The saying pleased the entire multitude," 15,22f, 21:22; Peter cited the agreement of all the prophets. This truly is the authority of the Church. The author in *Popular Symbolics* wrote: "The Roman Catholic polity, subjecting the Christians to the government and rule of the hierarchy, exercises the supreme (only) authority, making laws and decisions binding upon the Church, abrogates the sole authority of Christ and despoils the Christians of their priestly and royal estate."[39] While Jesus used Peter mightily in organizing the Church in Judea, Samaria, Caesarea and in Asia Minor, there is no indication that Peter was placed over other Apostles or that he was instructed to appoint a successor and that procedure was to remain till the Second Coming of Christ. There are no **ex cathedra** decisions made by Peter. In fact, it cannot be proved that Peter was in Rome from 49-68. The story of Peter's successorship is a myth.

As to Papal Infallibility, the Word of God teaches that there is but one who is infallible, Ex. 3:14; Matt. 24:35; Rom. 3:4; James 1:17 and that the apostles, inspired, are the infallible teachers of the Church at all times, John 17:20; Eph. 2:20, and that any departure from their teachings constitutes error, Gal. 1:8f. History shows that the papacy is guilty a hundredfold of such departure. The Smalcald Articles P. II, IV, if 9f says: "The Church can never be better governed and preserved than if we all live under one head, Christ, and all the bishops, equal in office... be diligently joined in unity of doctrine, . . . This teaching shows forcefully that the Pope is the very Antichrist, 2 Thess. 2:4."[40]

(Ed. The speech which Bishop Josef Strossmayer delivered at the Vatican Council in 1871 opposing papal infallibility is in the *Christian News Encyclopedia*, pp. 1433, 1434. It was published in the LCMS's *Lehre und Wehre* in February 1889, *CNE*, p. 2995).

Footnotes

1. J. Derek Holmes and Bernard W. Bickers, *A Short History of the Catholic Church* (New York: Paulist Press 1984), p. 169.
2. Richard P. McBrien. *Catholicism* (New York and San Francisco: Harper & Row, 1981), p. 1259.
3. Holmes and Bickers, **op. cit.**, p. 169.
4. **Ibid.**, p. 169; Philip Schaaf, *The Creeds of Christendom With a History and Critical Notes* (New York: Harper & Brothers, Publishers 1877) I, p. 136.
5. Holms and Bickers. **op. cit.**, p. 243.
6. Kenneth Scott Latourette, *A History of Christianity* (New York: Harper & Brothers, 1953), p. 1094.

144

7. **Ibid.**, p. 1094.

8. *Catechism of the Catholic Church* (Rome: Urbi Editrice Vaticana, 1994), pp.

9. **Ibid.**, pp. 966, 974.

10. Lars P. Qualben, *A History of the Christian Church* (New York: Thomas Nelson and Sons. 1910). pp. 377-378.

11. J. W. Charley, "'Papacy." in S.B. Ferguson and D. Wright, *New Dictionary of Theology* (Downers Grove: InterVarsity Press, 1988), p. 490a.

12. A. Mickey, "Gallicanism," Walter A. Elwell, Editor, *Evangelical Dictionary of Theology* (Grand Rapids: Baker Book House, 1984), p. 438.

13. R.D. Linder, "Ultramontism," **Ibid.**, p. 1121.

14. Nelson, **op. cit.**, pp. 376-377.

15. **Ibid.**, p. 377.

16. Nelson, p. 377; P, Koehler, *Lehrbuch der Kirchengescichte* (Milwaukee Northwestern Publishing House, 1917), p. 605.

17. Holmes and Bickers, **op. cit.**, pp. 220-221.

18. **Ibid.**, pp. 218-219.

19. I. S. Renie, "Newman, John Henry," *Evangelical Dictionary of Theology*, **op. cit.**, p. 67.

20. Lindner, "Ultramontism," **op. cit.**, p. 1121.

21. Ludwig Ott, *Fundamentals of Catholic Dogma*, Edited in English by James Canon Bastible (St. Louis: Herder Book Company, 1957), pp. 199-202.

22. McBrien, **op. cit.**, pp. 11,642.

23. **Ibid.**, pp. 642-643.

24. Ott. Fundamentals of Catholic Dogma, **op. cit.**, p. 286.

25. Karl Heussi, *Kompendium der Kirchengeschichte, Elfte Auflage*, (Tuebingen: Verlagvon J.C.B. Mohr [Paul Siebeck]. 1957), pp. 454-455.

26. Schaff. **op. cit.**, I, p. 138.

27. Bickers and Holmes, p. 243.

28. Schoff, **op. cit.**, p. 141. *A Short History of the Catholic Church* by J. Derek Holmes and B.W. Bickers, **op. cit.**, p. 243.

29. Frederick A. Norwood, *The Development of Modern Christianity* (New York and Nashville: Abingdon Press, 1956), p. 153.

30. Holmes and Bickers, **op. cit.**, p. 243.

31. Latourette, **op. cit.**, 1095.

32. **Ibid.**, p. 1094, Schaff, **op. cit.**, I, pp. 147ff.

33. Latourette, **op. cit.**, p. 1094.

34. G. S. M. Walker. "Old Catholics," E. F. Harrison. G.W. Bromiley and C.F. Henry, Baker's Dictionary of Theology (Grand Rapids: Baker Book House, 1960), p. 386a; Norwood, **op. cit.**, p. 153.

35. A Brief Statement of the Doctrinal Position of the Ev. Lutheran Synod, of Missouri, Ohio and Other States (CPH, 1932 paragraph 43).

36. F. E. Mayer, *American Churches, Beliefs and Practices* (St. Louis: CPH, 1946).

37. **Ibid.**, p. 12.

38. Based on Theodore Hoyer, *Why I Am Not a Roman Catholic* (St Louis: CPH, 1953), 10 pp.: *The Split Between Roman Catholicism and Christ* (New York: The Lutheran Press, no date), pp. 1-2.

39. Th. Engelder, W. Arndt, Th. Graebner and F. E. Mayer, *Popular Symbolics* (St. Louis: CPH, 1934), p. 115.

145

40. The Smalcald Articles in Theodore G. Tappert's, *The Book of Concord* (Philadelphia: Fortress Press, 1959), pp. 298-301. Paragraph dealing with Antichrist.

Questions

1. The nineteenth century's only Roman Catholic Council was held in ____.
2. What does Rome teach about the infallibility of the Pope? ____
3. In 1854 Pope Pius declared ____.
4. The Assumption of Mary was secured by papal decree in ____.
5. The two parties which developed within Rome were ____.
6. When did the Holy Roman empire cease to exist? ____
7. As a result of the Oxford Movement a number of Episcopalians joined ____, headed by ____.
8. Ultramontism advanced the cause of ____.
9. What did the "Syllabus of Errors" refute? ____
10. How many were present at Vatican I? ____
11. The Old Catholic Church rejected ____.
12. The Church of the Augsburg Confession declared the Papacy the ____.
13. The *New Catholic Catechism of 1994* contradicts ____.
14. Rome anathematizes ____.
15. What are some of the false teachings of Roman Catholicism? ____
16. The Bible teaches that ____ alone is infallible.
17. The Pope is the very ____ of 2 Thess. 2:4.

Observations on Martin Luther's
Prefaces to the Books of the New Testament
(In Commemoration of the
479th Anniversary of the Lutheran Reformation)

Christian News, **October 28, 1996**

Luther was a voluminous writer. Some of his writings were most important for his age as well as subsequent times. His prefaces to the books of the Old and New Testaments have always interested Luther devotees. Inasmuch as the New Testament contained the ultimate revelation of the grace of God in Christ Jesus, Luther translated the New Testament first before embarking on rendering the Hebrew and Aramaic Old Testament into German. Plass claimed that before translating the New Testament on the Wartburg where Luther had been spirited, that he had before him a German translation of 1475 and the Latin Vulgate and especially the original Greek New Testament, issued by Erasmus in 1516.[1] Because of his thorough knowledge of the Vulgate as a result of 20 years of studying it, Luther translated the New Testament from the Greek into German in about three months. From mid-December 1521 to about mid-March Luther performed this outstanding feat. Dr. Reu, a Luther specialist, asserted: "It still remains an achievement that Luther could not have accomplished this without the special assistance of the Holy Spirit."[2]

On September 21, 1522, the first printed edition of the *German New Testament* was off the press and it is generally known as the "Septembertestament."[3] Luther's name was not printed on the title page, nor was the date of publication indicated. The title page did inform that the place of publication was Waitemburg.[4] Luther received no compensation for his great literary effort. The title page had a woodcut with the inscription "Das Neue Testament Deutsch." *The Septembertestament* of 1522 was a book of 222 leaves, in folio size, with 45-46 lines to a page. The numbering of leaves begins with the text of Matthew's Gospel and reaches the end of Acts. The first part was introduced with Luther's preface to the whole New Testament and with the instruction in which are the finest books of the New Testament."[5]

The Content of the New Testament Prefaces
A five and one-half page of observations introduces the various New Testament prefaces. In this study the writer is using the translation of Charles M. Jacobs, found in volume 6 of The Holman Casele Edition of *The Works of Martin Luther*, and the New Testament prefaces are found on pages 439-489, plus footnotes, ending with page 491.[6] In some cases there has been given the preface found in the 1545 Edition, as is done relative to First Corinthians, the preface to the Epistles of Saint James and Saint Jude, Preface to the Revelation of Saint John[7]. All others are from the 1522 New Testament. In the case of the Apocalypse both the 1522 and the 1545 editions are reproduced.

Martin Reu considered the general preface of the entire New Testament so significant that he reproduced the entire introductory preface for the entire New Testament in his book *Luther's German Bible, A Historical Presentation With a Collection of Sources*.[8] It begins with a notable preface, which stresses with great emphasis the fact that though the New Testament contains laws and precepts for the true guidance of life and direction for good works that are wellpleasing to God, nevertheless, we are not to expect or seek in it a new law book, but a Gospel, a good tidings of salvation wrought by Christ and appropriated by faith alone. Of his theological stance Reu observed: "So at the very beginning there is a declaration of the fundamental view of Scripture, which, in contrast to the medieval view of the Bible, had gradually been given Luther."[9] The emphasis of this fundamental idea is so valuable and so characteristic of the new view of Scripture that we must give the most important passages at this point. Thus Luther began his New Testament's general preface like this: "It would be known, in the first place, that the idea must be given up that there are four gospels and only four Evangelists. The division of the New Testament book into legal, historical, prophetic and wisdom books, is also to be rejected entirely. Some make this division, thinking that by it they are somehow comparing the New with the Old Testament. On the contrary, it is to be held firmly that."[10]

Modern Biblical scholarship has always distinguished between the four gospels, for Matthew, Mark, Luke and John were written by different people, of whom two were apostles and could report what Jesus had said and done from personal experience, while two were dependent on other people's information and even on written sources (as Luke). Though this is true, the Biblical reader could speak about there being just one Gospel, because the Holy Spirit caused Matthew, Mark, Luke and John to pen their record of the words and deeds of Jesus, the Christ. The New Testament is characterized by different literary genre, ultimately there was one Word of God running through the length and breadth of the New Testament.[12]

The prefaces of the New Testament books are significant for the light they shed on Luther's hermeneutics.[13] As early as 1513 Luther asserted that Holy Writ was the inspired Word and the only final authority in religion. The Reformer adopted the principle that only the original languages, the Hebrew and Aramaic of the Old Testament and the Greek of the New Testament were the reliable sources for the Establishment of Christian doctrine and Christian ethics and not the Vulgate, translated by Jerome and periodically corrected after the fifth century. The Old Testament was utilized to illustrate and supplement the New Testament. Luther rejected the manifold sense of Holy Writ. He combined into one the literal sense the anagogic and prophetic. This was supported by the conviction that most of the Psalms were literal in their meaning and referred to Christ, Who was yet to come. Beginning in 1517 in his *Seven Penitential Psalms*, he no longer used the manifold four senses of Scripture.[14] As a result of his new principles of interpretation he was led to distinguish between Law and Gospel and recognized in Christ crucified as the unity of all Scripture.[15] For Luther it became very important to distinguish between Law and Gospel. These are principles with which Roman Catholicism does not agree, as well as modern liberal Protestant theology.

In the 1522 opening of the general preface to the New Testament Luther announced his fundamental view of the Bible. Thus he wrote: "It would be right and proper that this book should appear without preface and without any other name than that of its authors, and only its own name and its own language. But many wild interpretations and prefaces have driven the thought of Christians to a point where no one any longer knows what is Gospel or Law, Old Testament or New. Necessity demands, therefore, that it should have an announcement, or preface, by which simple man can be brought back from old notions to the right road, and taught what he is to expect in this book, so that he may not seek laws and commandments where he ought to be seeking the Gospel and God's promises."[16]

What Is the Gospel?

The German Reformer defined the Gospel this way: "The New Testament is a book in which are written the Gospel and the promises of God, together with those who do not believe them, for the Gospel is a Greek word and means in Greek, a good message, good tidings, a good report, which one tells with rejoicing. So when David overcame the great Goliath, there came among the Jewish people the good report and encouraging news that their terrible enemy had been smitten and they had been rescued and given joy and peace, and they sang and danced and were glad for it."[17]

In describing the Gospel or Good News, Luther continued to declare: "So the Gospel, too, sounded forth into all the world by the apostles, telling of some true David who strove with sin, death and the devil, and overcame them, and thereby rescued all those captive in sin, afflicted with death, and overpowered by the devil. He made them righteous, gave them life, and saved them, so that they were given peace and brought back to God. For this they sing and thank and praise God, and are glad forever, if only they believe and are steadfast in faith."[18]

Old Testament Proclaims the Gospel

The word "testament" is Luther's translation for the Greek diatheke, often rendered as "covenant." A "testament" is a word which describes what a dying man bequeaths to his heirs. So Christ before His death bequeathed the Gospel, to be preached in all the world. By this command Jesus gave to the whole world, those that believe the possession, everything that He had that is, His life, in which he swallowed up death; His righteousness, by which he blotted out sin; His salvation, with which He overcame everlasting damnation; A poor man, dead in sin and tied for hell, can hear nothing more comforting than this precious and tender message about Christ, and from the bottom of his heart, he must laugh and be glad over it, if he believes it is true.

This Gospel, so prominent in the New Testament, was also promised

149

in the Old Testament. This Gospel, the testament of the prophets, was foretold in the Old Covenant Bible, for Paul told the Roman congregation: "I am separated to preach the Gospel of Christ, which he promised before through His prophets in the Holy Scripture, concerning His Son, who was born of the seed of David etc..."

Luther thereupon refers to the first Messianic prophecy in Genesis 3:15 where God promised Eve: "I will put enmity between thee and the woman, and between thy seed and her seed; he shall tread on thy head and thou shall tread on the head and thou shall sting his heel." Christ is the seed of the woman who would tread on the devil's head, i.e., sin, death, hell and all his power for without Christ, the Seed of Eve, no man can escape sin, death or hell. The Reformer cites a number of Old Testament passages in the Old Testament that speak about Christ. In Genesis 22, God promised Abraham: "Through thy seed shall all the nations of the earth be blessed," (22:10) and Luther uses Galatians 3:16 to prove that God was not supporting the idea that the Jews would be a blessing to the world, but that all nations would be justified by faith in Jesus Christ. He cited John 11:26 for the necessity of believing in the atoning death of Christ: "He that believeth in me shall never die" (John 11:26). Luther believed that God made a promise to David in II Samuel, when He said: "I will raise up thy seed after thee, who shall build a house to my name, and I will establish the throne of his kingdom forever." "That is the kingdom of Christ, of which the Gospel speaks, an everlasting kingdom, kingdom of life, salvation, and righteousness, and all those who believe shall enter into it from out of the prison of sin and death."[20]

The Reformer also expressed the opinion that many prophets have spoken about the promises of the Gospel, as Micah does in chapter 5:2 or as He does in Hosea 13, "I will redeem them from hell and rescue them from death; death, I will be a poison to thee; hell, I will be to thee a pestilence."[21]

According to the Wittenberg Reformer, the Gospel is nothing but the preaching about Christ the Son of God and of David, who by his death and resurrection has overcome all of mankind's sins as well as eternal death and hell, for those who believe in Christ. The Gospel can appear in short sentences or in extended lengthy messages.[22]

It is important that Christ be not depicted as a Second Moses, or make the Gospel a set of rules and regulations, as had been done before and during Luther's time. The Gospel does not make demands of people but tells them what God has done for their salvation. In the Bible, both Old and New Testaments, the Gospel is not a book of law, but really preaches the benefits of Christ freely bestowed on those who believe that Christ paid the punishment for mankind's sins. Good works are to be done by the justified sinners to prove that, true and genuine faith exists. Averred the Reformer: "To know His works and the things that happened to Him, is not yet knowledge of the Gospel, for if you know only these things you do not yet know that he has overcome sin, death and the devil." Seeing what Christ has done for him will prompt the Christian to follow Christ's example.[23]

Luther's Opinion Relative to the
Best Books of the New Testament

The Wittenberg University professor held the following as the best New Testament books: John's Gospel, St. Paul's Epistles, especially Romans, and St. Peter's First Epistle; they, opined Luther, were the true kernel and marrow of all books. He recommended that these books should be read first and most and by daily reading, make them as familiar as his daily bread. In these books many works and miracles of Christ are described and in them the reader will see how in a masterly fashion faith in Christ overcomes sin, death, and hell, and gives life, righteousness, and salvation. There is found the real nature of the Gospel.[24]

If Luther had a choice between the works or preaching of Christ he would rather choose His preaching, for Christ's works did not help him. For this reason Luther favored John's Gospel because it has many words uttered by the Lord. So also the Epistles of Paul and St. Peter far surpass the other three Gospels — Matthew, Mark and Luke. In brief, St. John's Gospel and his First Epistle, St. Paul's Epistles, especially Romans, Galatians and Ephesians, and St. Peter.[25] The First Epistle shows you about Christ all that the reader needed to know about the inheriting of eternal life. In this respect James's Epistle is a "strawy epistle," because it says little about Christ.

General Observations About Luther's
Prefaces of the Books of the New Testament

After the Reformer's views about the New Testament and its doctrines, he then has prefaces for twenty-three of the books of the New Testament. The last four books of the New Testament canon were not accepted as apostolic and therefore, not authoritative relative to Christian doctrines. These were Hebrews, James, Jude and the Book of Revelation or the Apocalypse. The books for which Luther composed prefaces were: Acts, the thirteen Epistles of St. Paul, with Romans receiving 15 and a half pages in the Jacob's translation. 1 and 2 Thessalonians, Galatians, Ephesians, Philippians, Colossians, 1 and 2 Corinthians, 1 and 2 Timothy, Titus, Philemon, 1 and 2 Peter, Saint James and Jude, and the Revelation of John. Most of the prefaces were found in the *Septembertestament*; in the case of 2 Corinthians and Revelation, the 1945 version was also utilized by Jacobs in his translation. Most of the prefaces are brief and succinct. In addition to the hermeneutical principles previously given, there should be added that justification by faith was utilized to determine the value of a New Testament writing and the fact that Old Testament predicted facts and events that are fulfilled in the New Testament. Luther found parallels to the same teachings and happenings in both the Old and New Testaments.

Most of the Pauline prefaces are brief, some being a half page or at best three-quarters of a printed page. Romans is by far the longest covering fifteen and a half pages. The Revelation of St. John, not accepted as canonical by Luther, receives eight pages, more than any other New Testament Epistle, except Romans.

151

Most of the prefaces contain a brief summary of an Epistle's contents, considering the importance of Galatians and Ephesians they do not appear to be given space that he gave to some uncanonical New Testament writings. From the Reformers prefaces it would be difficult to ascertain why and when these Biblical books were penned. It would be difficult to construct a life of Paul from the Epistles. It was Luther's conviction that Hebrews, James, Jude and Revelation were not inspired by the Holy Spirit. There is evidence that Luther would not have agreed with many modern New Testament scholars who have questioned the authorship of Ephesians, the Pastoral Epistles and other isagogical theories commonly found in books of introduction written by modern liberal scholarship.[26] A criterion for the Reformer was: How much Christological teaching is found in a book of the New Testament. Of non-canoncial Hebrews he asserted: "My opinion is that it is an epistle of many pieces put together, and it does not deal with any one subject in an orderly way."[27]

Although Luther did not accept Hebrews as canonical, he nevertheless said: "It was a fine epistle. It discusses Christ's priesthood masterfully and thoroughly, out of the Scriptures and interprets the Old Testament finely and richly."[28] Again further Luther asserted: "Therefore it should not be hindered, even though wood, straw, or hay be mixed with them (I Cor. 3:12), but except that is fine with all honor; though to be sure we cannot put it on the same level with apostolic epistles."[29]

Luther on the Canonicity of James

The Wittenberg professor claimed that the ancients rejected the apostolic character of James, and be opined: "I praise it and hold it a good book because it sets up no doctrine of men and lays great stress upon God's law. But to state my opinion about it though without injury to anyone, I consider that it is not the writing of an apostle."[30]

Luther on the Canonicity of Jude

The Reformer noted a similarity between Jude and 2 Peter. He asserted that the ancient Fathers threw out this Epistle from the main body of Scripture. "Therefore remarked Luther, it is an epistle that need not be counted among the chief writings which are to lay the foundation of the faith."[31]

The Book of Acts, the Bridge Between the Gospels and the Remainder of the New Testament

The Preface to the Book of Acts appeared in the 1534 edition of the New Testament. Unlike many modern scholars Luther believed in the Lucan authorship of Acts, being the continuation of volume I of Luke's two volume opus. Luther accepted Luke's statement that both the Gospel and Acts were written for the Gentile Theophilus. In Acts, Luke traced the history of Christ's kingdom from the Ascension in A.D. 30 till Paul's first Roman imprisonment in the imperial Roman city. The Acts preface Luther began this way: "This book should be read and regarded not as though Dr. Luke had written of the personal words and lives of the apostles for an example of good works and good lives only."[32] The Reformer tells sixteenth century followers that by this book, St. Luke teaches the whole Church, to the end of the world, the true chief point of Christian doctrine, namely that we must all be justified only through faith in Jesus Christ, without any addition of law or help from good works.[33]

The main purpose of Acts was to stress so mightily that Gentiles and Jews are justified through the Gospel only and not through the law. By means of doctrine about faith and the example of faith all men are saved in the same manner. This Peter confesses in Acts 10:28; 15:9. God gave the Holy Spirit through the Gospel to Jews and Gentiles. In Luther's opinion the Book of Acts is a commentary on the Epistles of St. Paul. The events and works in Acts show that not the law, not works, justify men, but only faith in Christ *Sola fides justificat*, "faith alone justifies."[34] All the examples and instances of the doctrine of justification by faith contained in the Book of Acts are certain and comforting testimonies. Luther cited the cases of Paul of Tarsus, the conversion of Sergius Paulus on Cyprus, the actions of the first council of Jerusalem as illustrations of justification by faith.[35]

The Preface to the Congregation in Rome

Here is Luther's evaluation of the Roman Epistle: "This Epistle is really the chief part of the New Testament and the very purest Gospel and is worthy not only that every Christian should occupy himself with it every day, as the daily bread of the Soul."[36] To adequately understand the 16 chapters of Romans the Reformer contended that the reader must have a knowledge of its language and comprehend what St. Paul means by the usage of words, like law, sin, grace, faith, righteousness, flesh, spirit etc.; otherwise no reading of the law has an advantage. Luther devoted a number of pages to the explanation of Paul's use of the concepts of law, righteousness, faith and good works, flesh and spirit. Asserted the Wittenberg Reformer: "Without such an understanding of these words, you will never understand this letter of Paul, or any other book of Holy Scripture."[37]

Paul's preface to the Church at Rome is the longest of the canonical books prefaces, occupying 15 printed pages in Jacob's translation. Luther correctly recognized the fact that the first eleven chapters treat a whole series of fundamental doctrines, and chapters 12-16 Paul is mainly concerned with Christian conduct according to God's Word. In his concluding paragraph he summarizes the main observations and deductions that he had made on the various chapters and concluded: "Therefore it appears that Paul wanted to comprise briefly in this one epistle the whole Christian and evangelical doctrine and to prepare an introduction to the entire Old Testament; for without doubt, be who has this well in his heart has the light and power of the Old Testament with him. Therefore let every Christian exercise himself in it habitually and continually. To this may God give His grace. Amen."[38]

In his summarization and exposition of The Roman's Epistle Luther uses passages both from the Old and New Testaments. Luther follows the hermeneutical principle that Scripture interprets Scripture. He also uses the principle that the same Christian doctrines are found in numerous books and therefore the Bible contains parallel passages dealing with the same subject matter. Melanchthon's *Loci Communes* of 1555 may have been inspired by Luther's remarks.[39] Hayes in the introduction to Paul's Preface to St. Paul's Epistle to the Romans described Luther as an "ocean minded man."[40] "The waves of influence set in motion by Divine Providence through him keep touching all shores where men who desire to know the things of God, to have right relations with God, or even to share actively in the thought and life of modern times."[41] Paul is the greatest interpreter of Christ, while Luther, by work and voice and pen, is the greatest interpreter of both.[42]

The founder of Methodism by his own words was given assurance of salvation by Luther's *Preface to The Epistle of Romans*. Wesley in his journal wrote that on May 24, 1738, he unwillingly went to a Moravian Society in Aldersgate Street and there this is what happened: "About quarter to nine, while he was describing the change which God works in the heart through faith in Christ, I felt my heart strangely warmed. I felt I did trust in Christ, Christ alone, for salvation; and assurance was given me that He had taken away my sins, even mine and saved me from the law of sin and death."[43]

Preface to the Book of Revelation

Next to Romans, Luther's preface to Revelation is the longest of all New Testament prefaces, even though Luther regarded the present last book of the New Testament as not canonical. Scholars have two different prefaces for Revelation, the shorter one of 1522 and the much longer one of 1545, in which the Reformer endeavors to outline chapter by chapter the difficult teaching of the Apocalypse. In the 1522 Luther said that he would not bind a person to his opinion or judgment: "I say what I feel I miss more than one thing in this book, and this makes me hold it to be neither apostolic nor prophetic."[44] He averred that he took the same stance on the Fourth Book of Esdras and cannot see how the Holy Ghost produced it. The Reformer cited many Church Fathers who felt as he did, even though St. Jerome praised it highly. After twentythree years by 1545 he did not change his mind about the canonicity of Revelation. He claimed that many different scholars of the past did not accept Revelation as canonical[45] and cited Eusebius' *Ecclesiastical History*, Book III,25 which this fourth-century historian did not include the Apocalypse as a part of the New Testament canon.[46]

In the 1545 preface Luther gave a short disquisition on Biblical prophecy.[47] The Wittenberg Reformer distinguished three kinds of prophecy. One kind involved was the interpretation of the writings of the prophets. Another kind of prophecy foretells happening and events to come which are not contained in Scripture. This latter kind of prophecy Luther claimed was threefold in its manifestation: It expresses its predictions in words, without symbols. Thus Moses, David and many prophets announce the future coming of Christ. The apostles predicted the coming of Antichrist, and did this with symbols, but accompanied them with an interpretation of words. Thus Joseph and Daniel interpret dreams in express words. The third kind of prophecy does not use words or interpretations as does the Book of Revelation.

In his attempt to interpret the Book of Revelation Luther used one of the four different approaches exegetes have employed in explaining the Apocalypse,[48] which are: 1. The praeterist, which regards the greater part of the prophecies fulfilled in the first century; 2. The Futuristic, according to which the greater part is unfulfilled and deals with events to yet be fulfilled; 3. The Idealistic which believes the Book is the historic unfolding of great principles in conflict through all ages; and 4. The Church History approach, which holds that major historical happenings will occur between the first and the later centuries. Luther adopted the Church history approach.[49] Since Luther's death his church history approach has affected subsequent Lutheran exegesis of Revelation as may be seen from reading C.M. Zorn's *Offenbarung St. Johannes*,[50] Louis Harms, *Die Offenbarung St. Johannes*[51] or Louis Fuerbringer, *Einleitung in das Neue Testament*.[52]

In relegating four books to the end of the New Testament and not numbering them, thus declaring his doubts about their canonicity, Luther was following the classification of Origen who used **homologoumen** (universally recognized) and antilegoumen a (not universally recognized), although Luther recognized as canonical 2 and 3 John, which Origen did not. Eusebius expressed doubts about Hebrews; relative to Revelation Eusebius was following the Syrian canon with only 22 books.

During the Middle Ages there was no doubt about the divinity of the 27 books now in our printed Bibles, also in the edition of the Greek New Testament. In cleansing the Old Testament canon he removed the books of the Apocrypha. Luther revived the Oriegenic distinction between **homologoumena** and anti-legomena. Martin Chemnitz and M. Flacius followed the Reformer in this matter. However, later dogmaticians allowed these distinctions recede into the background. Instead of using the term anti-legomena they employed the term deutero. Rationalists employ the word canon in the sense of list. Lutherans in America have followed Luther and held that the distinction between **homologoumena** and **antilegomena** must not be suppressed. The author of the article on "the canon" warned that caution must be exercised not to exaggerate this distinction.

Piersch in **Deutsche Bible**, 2 of the Weimar Edition listed 95 separate editions of the New Testament appearing between 1522-1546, and ten editions of the complete Bible. Reu asserted: "If we may again reckon 3,000 copies for each edition, we have a total of no less than 315,000 copies printed during these years. That is something unique in the earlier history of printing. In comparison the figures we believe correct for the medieval Bibles seem quite small. Even in the number of copies of the New Testament circulated among the people of the Reformation commenced a new era."[53]

Through Luther's **Septembertestament** of 1522 and the complete

Bible of 1534 and their introductory prefaces, a new era began for Christianity and they were a great instrument for the dissemination of the true Gospel of Our Lord Jesus Christ.

Footnotes

1. Ewald Plass, *This Is Luther* (St. Louis: Concordia Publishing House, 1948), p. 351.
2. Martin Reu, *Luther the Scripture* (Columbus, Ohio: Wartburg Press, 1944), p. 158.
3. Roland Bainton, *Here I Stand* (Nashville: Abington Press, 1960), p. 327.
4. E.G. Schweibert, *Luther and His Times* (St. Louis: Concordia Publishing House, 1950), for the title page fo the Septembertestametn, p. 530.
5. Martin Reu, *Luther's German Bible* (Columbus: The Lutheran Book of Concern, 1934), p. 162.
6. *Prefaces to the Books of the New Testament*, Translated by Charles M. Jacobs, in *The Works of Martin Luther* (Philadelphia: A. J. Holman Company and The Castle Press), pp. 439-491.
7. **Ibid.** pp. 462-465 (I Cor.); S. James and Jude, pp. 477-479; Revelation, 479-491.
8. Reu, Luther's *German Bible*, **op. cit.**, 166-169.
9. **Ibid.** p. 167.
10. Prefaces in Holman-Castle, **op. cit.**, VI, p. 439.
11. W. Graham Scroggie, *A Guide to the Gospels* (London: Pickering & Inglis, 1948), pp. 127-163.
12. Luther's Prefaces, Holman-Castle, **op. cit.**, p. 444, footnote 3.
13. Cf. Raymond F. Surburg, "The Significance of Luther's Hermeneutics for the Protestant Reformation," *Concordia Theological Monthly*, 24:241-261, April, 1953.
14. Reu, Luther's *German Bible*, **op. cit.**, p. 130; cf. esp. pp. 124-133.
15. **Ibid.** p. 133.
16. Holman-Castle, *Luther's Works*, VI, 439.
17. Reu, Luther's *German Bible*, **op. cit.**, p. 167.
18. Holman-Castle, *Luther's Works*, VI, 440.
19. **Ibid.** p. 440.
20. **Ibid.** p. 441.
21. **Ibid.** p. 441.
22. **Ibid.** p. 441.
23. **Ibid.** p. 443.
24. **Ibid.** p. 494.
25. **Ibid.** p. 443.
26. Paul Feine, Johannes Behm, Revised by Werner Georg Kuemmel, *Introduction to the New Testament* (Nashville: Abingdon Press, 1965), p. 265 for Ephesians: pp. 256-272 for the Pastoral Epistles; Norman Perrin, *The New Testament. An Introduction* (New York: Harcourt Brace Jovanovich, 1974), pp. 129-133; 264-267.
27. Holman-Castle, *Luther's Works*, VI, p. 477.
28. **Ibid.** p. 477.
29. **Ibid.**, p. 477 .
30. **Ibid.** p. 477...C78.
31. **Ibid.** p. 478.
32. **Ibid.** p. 445.
33. **Ibid.** p. 446.
34. **Ibid.** p. 446.

35. **Ibid.** p. 446.

36. **Ibid.** p. 447.

37. **Ibid.** p. 453.

38. **Ibid.** p. 462.

39. Clyde L. Manschreck, *Melanchthon on Christian Doctrine: Loci Commumes, 1555* (New York: Oxford University Press, 1965), pp. xii. ff.

40. Dr. Martin Luther, *Preface to St. Paul's Epistle to the Romans*, translated by Rev. Charles E. Hay (Philadelphia: United Lutheran Publication House, 1903), Forward, p. iii.

41. Hay, **op. cit.**, p. iii.

42. **Ibid.** p. iii.

43. As cited by Hay, **op. cit.**, pp. iii-iv.

44. Holman-Castle, *Luther's Works*, **op. cit.**, VI, 488 (The 1522 preface).

45. **Ibid.** p. 480 (The 1545 preface).

46. **Ibid.** p. 481. For Greek text cf. Kirsopp Lake, *Eusebius. The Ecclesiastical History* (London: William Heinemann, 1926), p. 257. One of the volumes in the Loeb Classical Library.

47. Holman-Castle, *Luther's Works*, VI, pp. 479-480.

48. W. Graham Scroggies, *Know Your Bible: Vol. II: The New Testament* (London: Pickering & Inglis, No. date), pp. 367-368.

49. *Luther's Works*, in Holman-Castle, pp. 479-488; Louis Harms, *Die Offenbarung St. Johannes* (Hanover: Druck und Verlag der Missionshandlung, 1918), p. 171.

50. C. M. Zorn, *Offenbarung St. Johannes* (Zwickau. S.) Verlag von Johannermann, 1910.

51. Louis Fuerbringer, *Eileitung in das Neue Testament* (St. Louis: Concordia Publishing House, 1927), p. 109.

52. "Canon," in Erwin Luecker, *The Lutheran Cyclopedia* (St. Louis: Concordia Publishing House, 1975), p. 132.

53. **Ibid.** p. 133.

Questions

1. Luther was a ____ writer.
2. Luther translated the New Testament from the Greek in about ____.
3. Did Luther receive any compensation for his translation? ____
4. Contrary to modern scholarship the Biblical reader could speak of only ____ Gospel?
5. There was just one ____ running through the New Testament.
6. Luther maintains that most of Psalms referred to ____.
7. For Luther it is most important to distinguish between ____.
8. What is the Gospel? ____
9. A "testament" describes ____.
10. Luther uses Galatians 3:16 to prove that ____.
11. It is important that Christ not be depicted as ____.
12. According to Luther, the best New Testament books were ____.
13. James is a "strawy epistle" because it says little about ____.
14. Did Luther accept Revelation as canonical? ____
15. Did Luther along with many modern New Testament scholars question the authorship of Ephesians and the Pastoral Epistles? ____

16. What did Luther believe about James? ____
17. The main purpose of Acts was to ____.
18. According to Luther, the Book of Romans is ____.
19. Luther follows the hermeneutical principle that Scripture ____.
20. What approach did Luther use to interpret the Book of Revelation? ____

21. Should the distinction between homologoumena and antilegomena be suppressed? ____

Where Am I Going? (1546-1996)

The Four Hundred and Fiftieth Anniversary of Luther's Death

Christian News, January 20, 1997

Luther was born on November 10, 1483 in Eisleben and died on February 18, 1546 in the same city at the age of 62 years and a little over three months beyond his last birthday. He thus lived not too long a life by modern twentieth-century statistics for the longevity of men.

On February 18 at one o'clock Luther awoke and was in great pain. He wrung his hands and said: "O my God, how I agonize, dear Jonas. I think I will die in Eisleben where I was born and baptized." Then great beads of sweat rolled down his forehead. Suddenly he opened his eyes and prayed: "Lord Jesus Christ, accept my soul, O heavenly Father, though I must leave this body and be torn from life, yet I know for since I shall abide eternally with Thee, no one can take me out of Thy hands." Then Luther's strength left him. Dr. Jonas and minister Coelius asked him: "Reverend Father, do you remain fixed in the faith in Christ and the doctrine you have preached?" "Yes," he replied.[1] Then the angel of death entered the room and the soul of Martin Luther goes to his eternal rest. In describing Luther's death, Plass wrote: "The fire leaves these leonine eyes, the lips stiffen into silence, the cheeks grow white, but friends comment with baited, awesome breath on the look of serenity that settles on the face of the dead one. Some say he died of a stroke; others speak of certain complications of the lungs. Still others say: 'God took him. **They are right**.'"[2]

Luther on Issues Dealing With Death and the Hereafter

Ewald Plass in his three volume work. *What Luther Says*,[3] in volume one, has devoted pages 363-386 to the subject of death, the universality of death, the reason for death, the significance of death for believers and unbelievers, erroneous views about death, the necessity of preparation for the Grim Reaper, how to get to heaven, how to avoid hell, the existence of the intermediate state, and the non-existence of purgatory. Plass has listed the views of Luther on the topics of eschatology just enumerated. Numbers (called **Item**s in this essay) 1065-1141: Luther's beliefs on one aspect of eschatology are important, as to how Christians can successfully and joyfully leave this "vale of tears."[4]

On this 450th landmark event of Luther's life, namely his death, it certainly is appropriate to present his views dealing with one of life's most important questions. "Whither am I going?"

Death Is Not Natural

Death was not originally intended for human beings, but is the penalty for sin.[5] On October 20,1532 Luther stated that death is not natural, as for example, as the sun rises or a pig or dog grows and dies. But Scripture teaches that our death does not come in a natural way, but is the fruit of and punishment for sin of our father Adam. In fact, man's death is in a class by itself, it does not come by chance. Death is the reward of inherited and actual sins.[6]

Wrong Ideas About the Cause of Death
Between 1532 to April 1533 Luther delivered 17 sermons on I Corinthians 15, published by G. Roers. It was the contention of the Reformer that many theologians of his day rationalized about death, that the latter is a sort of haven in which people are shut up and are safe from the labors and calamities to which life is common.[7] Those who hold this opinion are blind to the teaching on the real cause of death.[8]

Pagan Views on Death
Luther warned that death cannot be laughed off.[9] The Epicureanism, which had as one of its maxims: "Eat, drink and be merry, for tomorrow we die," is held by many. No, everywhere the human race sees death, so observed Luther in a sermon on Luke 7:11-17, "the miracle of the raising of the young man of Nain." This was a sermon used a number of times by Luther in the course of his teaching and preaching ministry. One fact is certain in life, all human beings must die.[10]

The Need for Preparation for Death
Throughout his life a Christian should prepare for his last hour.[11] Do not wait till a person is on his death bed. It would be unwise for a person to lead a fast life and indulge in all manner of excesses and then expect that suddenly on his death-bed this will be reversed. This is the way the Reformer envisioned the life of a Christian: A Christian is a person who through faith begins to pass out of life into heaven as soon as he is baptized. For him Christ is already the Way, the Truth and the Life and does not cease to be these things till the last hour. Indeed, a Christian always proceeds this way, led by the truth, to the goal of eternal life.

Death Can Come in Different Ways
One day in September 1532 Luther stated that death, the Grim Reaper, can come by many different avenues.[12] It can affect practically any member of the human body. A mortal sickness may affect most members of the human body. In view of this, it is important that a Christian be vigilant because the Devil has sworn to kill us. But he will not effect anything on the pious.

People's Failure to Prepare for Death
In a sermon on Luke 7:11-16 the Reformer remarked that people witness different people being carried to the grave, yet they make no preparation to meet death.[13]

Luther's life was constantly in danger since 1521 when he defied the Pope and emperor and was placed under the ban of the empire, which meant that any person was considered doing a good deed who killed Luther. That meant that the last 25 years he had to be careful in Germany where he traveled, lest he be caught and killed. Melanchthon reported that Luther said: "I am ready to die when and where God calls me and I shall then and there die as the enemy of all enemies of my Lord Jesus Christ."[14]

The Real Cause for Death

All human beings know that they must die. The wise among the heathen complained about this but did not know the cause.[15] The majority of people think that death happens by chance, just as animals are born, grow up and eventually die. However, on the basis of Genesis chapters 2-3 Luther pointed out that death came from an occurrence in Paradise or Eden, from the bite of the forbidden fruit, that is from our first Parents, who disobeyed God. Before the Fall there was no death in the world (cf. Romans 5:12).

Luther's Use of I Corinthians 15

Luther preached a number of sermons on I Corinthians 15:1-57, the great resurrection chapter of the New Testament. On April 27,1532 the Reformer made this comment on I Cor. 15:56: "If you ask whence death came and whereby it so easily frightens people, you hear at this place that sin is the killer, nothing else. Sin is nothing less than the spear and cannon balls, yea, the thunder and lightning of death. Sin kills".[16]

The Defense Against Sin

In commenting on Luke 2:29-32, the *Nunc Dimittis* of Simeon, Luther asserted that the Savior gives a defense against sin. Simeon confessed: "Mine eyes have seen Thy salvation. Now I depart in peace."[17]

Spiritual Agony Is the Real Death

To feel death means to experience the terrors of death; the latter is not merely the separation of body and soul. Christ has removed the fear of death and so death becomes a sleep.[18] He who believes in Christ shall not die or see death (John 11:26).[19]

Human beings fear death because they are afraid of meeting God, for if they loved God, they would not fear to meet their Maker. However, I John 4:18 teaches: "Perfect love casteth out fear." It is God who must perform the miracle of taking away the fear of death.[19a]

Death Rampant In Magdeburg, 1538

In 1538 many individuals were dying in Magdeburg as the result of an epidemic.[19] On November 28, 1538 Luther wrote Nicolas Amsdorf. Relative to this situation, Plass wrote: "Honest realist that he is, the Reformer is so far from denying or minimizing death that he frankly concedes that even the best Christians, who see sin in all its depths and damnableness must struggle with it."[20]

Saints Fear Death

The fear of death is natural, for death is a penalty; therefore it is something sad.[21] "The reason Christians are afraid, is because of the wrath of God. While unbelievers live and die in security, being of the conviction that death ends all, and thus there is nothing to fear. The Roman orator and man of letters, Cicero expressed it like this: "After death we shall be as nothing at all, or shall be altogether blessed."[22]

The Necessity of Preparing for Death

The Bible clearly indicates the necessity of preparation for death. The non-Christian relies upon his life and deeds, but these are no support for death and the judgment which occurs at death.[23] By contrast, the Wittenberg Reformer consoled himself with the fact of his baptism, also that he has received forgiveness through absolution and the forgiveness bestowed in the Lord's Supper and that he commended his soul to Christ, His Savior. The Christian is prepared for death because he is in Christ.[24]

In 1524 Luther wrote the hymn: "In the midst of Earthly Life," which is hymn 590 in *The Lutheran Hymnal* of 1942 and in Kirchengesangbuch Life of the Lutheran Church-Missouri Synod it is hymn 418.[25]

God the Determiner of Life's Length

"My times are in thy hand (Psalm 31:15)," is a verse which should be a comfort to Christians showing that it is not a tyrant but God who has determined individual's life span. Because of this truth, Christians do not greatly worry about death, but do like children, whenever it pleases the Lord to call his own to Himself.[26]

The Christian and Sudden Death

Luther preached many sermons on Luke 7:11-16, the miracle of the raising of the young man of Nain. In one of these sermons he declared that believers should not be alarmed if and when death strikes a Christian unannounced. [27]

The Great Difference Between the Death of the Believer and That of the Unbeliever

The following verse expresses the unbeliever's view of death:

I live, how long I do not know
Must die, but know not when I go;
Pass on, but know not where it will be
My cheerfulness surprises me.[28]

The Christian knows where he is going. As a Christian, Baptism, Absolution and the Sacrament of the Lord's Supper have been given him; for with Christ he has everything.[29] In 1542 Luther spoke of the lot of unbelievers in a collection of funeral hymns. Without faith the unbeliever has no hope and is downtrodden.

After death the non-Christians must expect eternal death and the wrath of God in hell. By contrast the believer, who has been redeemed

162

by the precious blood of Christ, can by faith despise death. The coffin can be considered to be nothing but a soft bed of ease and rest. Death is merely a sleep (John 11:11; Matt. 9:28).[30]

Luther's Consolation Book of 1520
Luther addressed a consoling booklet to sick Frederick the Wise, in which the latter was assured that although it seemed as if the righteous die, they are really at peace. Death is the beginning of real life. It is as Jesus promised: "If a man keep My saying, he shall never see death."

In his exposition of John 14:20, written in 1537, the Reformer assured Christians that because Christ and the Father are one, and therefore those who are with Christ by their faith can overcome death, as it is assured by Christ.[31]

The Christian Looking Forward to his Death
In a sermon on Luke 7:11-16 Luther tells what thoughts a Christian must have (1) I must die but after death I am eternally saved; (2) No matter where and how I die God has determined my death. This same confidence rests upon Christ, the Savior, who has paid for my sins and reconciled me to God.[32]

Crossing Over From Life to the Other Side
In an explanation of John 14:6 (1531) Luther compared the crossing of the Red Sea by the children of Israel and the Christians passing over to heaven and eternity.[33] Nothing could Israel do to pass through the waters of the Red Sea. God performed a miracle. So nothing that a believer can do will enable him to reach the promised land of heaven. Only faith in Christ will be enabled to pass over into heaven.[34]

Man Is Not Saved By His Own Suffering
The agony of the act of dying, the reformer claimed, cannot atone for past sins or wash away wrong doings of a lifetime. This erroneous idea was common in Luther's day.[35] In 1519 Luther preached a sermon on preparing for death and advised a person not to think of only of past sins but on his death bed to think of the death of Christ and what it has achieved for Christians. In death one should die like St. Stephen who prayed: "Into Thy hands I commend my spirit (Acts 7:58)."[36]

In a sermon preached on Luke 2:1-12 (a Christmas sermon), delivered in 1528, Luther advised his hearers to cling to the Word. In death, a Christian must cling to Christ alone and boldly trust the Word of God.[37]

In a comment on Isaiah 38:10 (1532) the Reformer urged that faith must look up to the cross of Christ.[38] The true preparation for death is to exercise faith in Christ. Christ Crucified has overcome and overthrown sin, hell and Satan. Looking at the Cross the dying believer sees death as it is in Christ. Just as in the days of Moses the people bitten by the poisonous snakes were healed by looking at the bronze serpent (Nu. 21:9), so The Christian by looking at Christ will die peacefully (John 3:16).[39]

163

"I Am the Way" (John 14:6) Used by Luther

Texts like John 14:6 gave Luther the opportunity to emphasize the sufficiency of Christ for salvation.[40] The Ten Commandments will not lead to salvation, although they are necessary and keeping them will please God. But keeping the Decalogue is not walking the "Way" as one journeys from death into life, from the temporal and sinful world into the heavenly and spiritual mode of being. Faith says: "I believe in Jesus Christ; I live, I die, I remain in Him alone."[41]

When individuals face their last hour, when all work must cease, Jesus suggested that they pray: "Forgive us our trespasses," and hold to Him Who is the Way, the only Way,[42] a safe bridge to the hereafter. Luther dwelt considerably on John 14:6 and made clear that Christ was a person's sole and only hope for everlasting life.[43]

Luther's Use of the Ascension as Comfort for Death

In 1527 Luther preached on Ephesians 4:8ff on Ascension Day, in which he depicted Christ as the Victor over death.[44] As a result of Christ's entry into heaven, death has become an entrance to eternal life, and add to this the death we suffer is no more real, that is a terrible death, but a picture of death, aye, a sweet slumber.[45] Luther wrote a beautiful hymn, "In Peace and Joy I Now Depart," No. 137 in *The Lutheran Hymnal* of the Synodical Conference of North America.[46]

Luther used Christ's Last Words on the Cross

"Father, into Thy hands I entrust My Spirit" (Luke 23:46). Simeon in Luke 2:41 expressed his willingness to depart. Luther took Simeon's prayer as his own and was prepared, resting on it, to depart this life, confessing that there are many mansions in God's house.[47]

Luther's Look at Burials and the Grave

On December 22, 1532 Luther preached a series of sermons on I Corinthians chapter 15. In connection with verses 36-37 Luther showed his contemporaries how to regard death and the grave.[48]

Like seed thrown into the ground disintegrates and then comes forth as a new life, so the Christian should look upon death and the burial; later the aches and pains that caused the death of the body, will come forth as a glorious body. The shorter the time of the earthly body on earth, the longer will be the joys of eternity. Christians must learn a new language and speech in talking about death and the grave when they die.[49] We are like pure kernels of grain when we die, which will grow as immortal and imperishable. For a Christian dying is like going to sleep.[50]

Luther Favored the Word "Cemetery"

Luther contended that the word "cemetery" was a good name for the place where the remains of Christians are placed.[51] The Church Fathers called churchyards "cemeteries," that is places where Christians slept. "Cemeteries" are called bedrooms and beds. Cemeteries are sleeping places. Those who sleep during the night, awake in the morning.[52] Jesus said of Jairus' daughter; "Give place; for the maid sleepeth" (Mark 5:41).[53]

Resurrection Follows Sleep
In a sermon on Matthew 9:18-26, the incident of Jairus' daughter's resurrection, the Reformer reasoned that we shall not remain sleeping in the grave, but arise from the grave and corruption. Christians shall be made alive and shall meet their Savior Jesus Christ.[54]

The Encouragement of I Corinthians 15
Luther on the basis of I Corinthians 15 believed that while appearances seem to deny the fact of the resurrection, the Christian with the eye of faith says: "O Grave, where is your victory?" Sin has been atoned for and on Judgment Day death will be abolished.[55]

Luther's Advice About Conduct at Funerals
The Reformer in a sermon on Luke 7:11-16 preached on the manner people should conduct themselves at funerals. When a Christian dies, the hour of deliverance for evil has come.[56] Through Christ a Christian shall be saved for eternal life. A Christian can say with St. Paul: "I have a desire to depart and be with Christ (Phil. 1:2-3)."[57] Christian dying is entering Glory. It merely depends upon our Lord God's removing the wall that still separates us from bliss; then everything will be pure heaven and blessedness.[58]

Luther's Use of Romans 6:3-11 Relative to Death's Fear
Faith has brought spiritual and moral resurrection.[59] For a Christian to fear death is foolishness and is due to the sinful flesh and blood which people have, which cannot comprehend that pestilence, death, and the grave are God's laying you gently as a child into a cradle, in which you may sweetly sleep until the Last Day.[60]

Personal Pangs When Taking Leave of Loved Ones
When Luther's daughter Magdalene died at the age of fourteen, her father wrote that the Christian must comfort himself with Rev. 14:13: "Blessed are the dead which die in the Lord."[61]

The Christian Should Welcome Death
A Christian views death differently than an unbeliever does. Christians view death like a journey and a departure from this vale of tears. Each day Christians should ask God for a blessed hour.[62]

Comfort for Frederick the Wise
In 1520 Luther sent his ruler Frederick the Wise a comforting booklet in which the Reformer stated that death ends the worst of Evil Sinning.[63] The other blessing of death is this that it ends not only evils and sufferings of this life but best of all, all the vices and sins to the believing soul, that makes death desirable. This fact the elector was told should also make a Christian kindly disposed to the so-called King of Terrors.

Death Is Not Death But Life

To believe that death brings life is a matter of faith.[64] It is only the eyes of faith which can take such a stand. These were thoughts that Luther expressed in an exposition on the sacrifice of Isaac, recorded by Moses in Genesis 22:11. To take such a position requires a high order of faith.[65]

Death Is the Death of Death

In the *Tessaradecas Consolatoria* (fourteen points of consolation) Luther bids the ailing Elector to remember that for the Christian dying means entering into afterlasting life.[66] Death is its own undoing. Through death sin is destroyed by its own fruit and thus illustrates Ovid's *Necis artificem arte perire sua* (by his own art the artist perishes).[67]

The Paradoxical Ways of God

In a sermonic exposition of Genesis 32:24-28 Luther showed that Jacob became Israel only after the Angel of the Lord made the patriarch as undone.[68] So God acts with regard to us, when He wants to put reason to shame, by saving us from death. He leads us into it. God puts reason to shame—to give room for faith.[69]

Old Testament Saints Believed in an Afterlife

Luther believed that the patriarchs believed in an afterlife, on the basis of the expression in Genesis 35:29 and 49:20 that patriarchs Isaac, Jacob and Abraham "were gathered unto their fathers."[70] Luther contended it was certainly true of Abraham.

What After Death?

Concerning a life beyond the grave Luther relied on Christ's assertion: "He that believeth in Me, though he were dead, yet shall he live (John 11:25)." Or the Pauline assurance: "Whether we live or die, we are the Lord's" (Romans 14:5).[71] There will be no days or years in the intermediate state.[72]

Life in the Intermediate State

Luther believed that "being in the Lord" the believer between burial and the resurrection existed, but the Scriptures do not inform the readers what exactly is involved. Thus he reasoned in an explanation on Ecclesiastes 9:10.[73]

Much About the Hereafter Is a Mystery

Although Bible readers know there is an intermediate existence of believers, the Word of God has not told us facts we would like to know. What kind of life does the soul live? Was it a kind of life of rest? On this subject, Plass claimed, the Reformer arrived at paradoxical views.[74]

Luther and Purgatory

Luther contended that the Bible did not mention purgatory. He claimed it was rather a fabrication of the devil, that papists may have found economic values in advocating purgatory.[75] The Reformer's greatest objection was that the implication of the theology of the existence of purgatory was what made the redemption of Christ insufficient.[76]

Footnotes

1. E. G. Schwiebert, *Luther and His Times* (St. Louis: Concordia Publishing House, 1954), p. 750.
2. Ewald M. Plass, *This Is Luther* (St. Louis: Concordia Publishing House, 1948), p. 382.
3. Ewald M. Plass, *What Luther Says, An Anthology.* St. Louis, Concordia Publishing House. 1950, Vol. I *Absolution to Giving*, pp. 1,536, Vol. II *Glory to Prayer*, pp. 537-1101, Vol. III *Prayers to Zeal*, Index, pp. 1103-1167.
4. **Ibid.**, Vol. I, pp. 363-386.
5. **Item** 1065, p. 363, SL8, 1157.
6. D. Martin Luther, *Kritische Ausgabe* (Weimar, 1883-) hereafter referred to as W W 36, 557; and also *D. Martin Luthers Saemtliche Schriften*, 23 volumes in 25, ed. Johann G. Walch, modern German (St. Louis: 1880-1910, hereafter referred to as SL).
7. **Item** 1067, p. 363.
8. W 40, III, 513f-SL 5, 751f.
9. **Item** 1068, p. 364.
10. **Item** 1069; W 22, 289-SL 11, 1671.
11. **Item** 1072; W45, 506f.-SL 8, 317f.
12. **Item** 1073, p. 365; D. *Martin Luther's Werke. Tischreden* (Weimar, 1912-1921). W-T2. No, 2669b.
13. **Item** 1074, p. 366; SL 13a, 1333; *D. Martin Luther's Saemmtliche Werke* (Frankfurt and Erlangen, 1826-1857) referred to as the Erlangen Edition, hereafter referred to as E.
14. **Item** 1075, p. 366; Found in Koestlin-Kaweraum Martin Luther, II, p. 388.
15. **Item** 1076, p. 366; W 22, 284 SL 11, 1664f.
16. **Item** 1077, W. 36, 689-SL 8, 1267.
17. **Item** 1078, p. 3666. W. 52, 156f-SL 13a, 224f.
18. **Item** 1078, p. 366; W. 43, 218-SL 1, 1512. **Item** 1070; W. 43, 218-SL 1, 512.
19. **Item** 1079, W. 43, 218-SL1, 1512.
19a. **Item** 1080; W. 45, 158.
20. Plass, *What Luther Says*, I, p. 367b.
21. **Item** 1082; W. 111, No. 408.
22. **Item** 1084, p. 368; W-T3, N. 3140a-SL22, 1310, No. 22.
23. **Item** 1086; W. 22, 307f, SL 12, 906f.
24. W. 22, 307f; SL 12, 906f.
25. Plass, *What Luther Says*, i, p. 369.
26. **Item** 1088, p. 369b.
27. **Item** 1089, p. 370 E. 3,552f-SL 13a, 1338f.
28. **Item** 1090, 1091.
29. W 45, 500-SL 8, 309f.
30. **Item** 1092; W. 35, 478-SL 19, 1424f.
31. Plass, *What Luther Says*, I, p. 371b, W 6, 118-SL 10,1862f

32. **Item**, 1095; E3, 554f-SL 13a, 1340.
33. **Item** 1096
34. E. 35f-SL 13a, 1340.
35. **Item** 1098; W. 17, II, 175-SL 11,528.
36. **Item** 1100; W-T No. 117.
37. **Item** 1101, p. 374.
38. **Item** 1103; SL 6, 462.
39. W 25, 243-SL 6,462.
40. **Item** 1104, p. 375.
41. W 45, 506-SL 8, 317.
42. **Item** 1105; W 493-SL 8.
43. W 45, 498f-SL 8, 307.
44. **Item** 1107, W 23, 714-SL 5 1363f.
45. **Item** 1107, W 23,714-SL 5, 1363f.
46. The hymn is given in its entirety in Plass, *What Luther Says*, 1, pp. 376b-377a.
47. **Item** 1109. W-T 4, No. 4833.
48. W. 36, 641f-SL 8, 1228f.
49. **Item** 1110.
50. W. 36641f.-SL 8, 1228f.
51. **Item** 1112.
52. **Item** 1112: W. 46, 470.
53. **Item** 1113.
54. **Item** 1114.
55. **Item** 1115; W. 12, 685f-SL 8, 1264.
56. **Item** 1116; E. 543f-SL 13a, 1329f.
57. **Item** 1117.
58. **Item** 1118; W. 52, 505-13a, 926.
59. **Item** 1119, page 381.
60. W. 22, 1-1f-SL 12,769.
61. Plass, *What Luther Says*, I, p, 382, footnote 17; W-BR, 10,169-21b, 2797f.
62. **Item** 1121, page 383; W. 48, 63f-SL 9, 1783f.
63. **Item** 1123, page 383; SL 10,1880.
64. **Item** 1125, page 383.
65. W. 43, 218f-SL 1, 1514.
66. **Item** 1126, page 383.
67. **Item** 1126, page 383.
68. **Item** 1128, p. 384; W. 6,124-SL 10, 1883f.
69. W. 24, 574-SL 3, 511.
70. Plass, *What Luther Says*, I, p. 384.
71. **Item** 1129, W-T 5, No, 5534.
72. **Item** 1137, p. 387.
73. **Item** 1129, W. 20,162-SL 5, 1539.
74. **Item** 1132; W. 43, 360-SL 1, 1759.
75. **Item** 1138, p. 387; W. 44, 812-SL 2, 2071.
76. **Item** 1141; W-T-3, No. 3695.

Questions

1. Luther was born on ____ and died ____.
2. Did Luther die in the faith he preached? ____
3. What fact is certain in life? ____
4. Before the Fall there was no ___ in the world.
5. He who believes in Christ shall not ____.
6. The fear of death is ____.
7. The Christian is prepared for death because ____.
8. Without faith the unbeliever has no ____.
9. According to Luther, the coffin can be considered ____.
10. On his deathbed a Christian should think of ____.
11. For the Christian dying is like ____.
12. Cemeteries are ____.
13. A Christian views death like a ____.
14. Purgatory is a fabrication of the ___.

The Jewels of the Reformation Remembering the 480th Anniversary of the Reformation

Christian News, November 3, 1997

In the liturgical calendar used in Lutheran churches, October 31 is a red-letter day. It was on October 31 that Doctor Martin Luther, professor of theology at the University of Wittenberg, nailed ninety-five theses or propositions for debate on the front door of the church at Wittenberg. This event is usually regarded as the beginning of the Protestant Reformation, termed by Rome as The Protestant Revolt. From October 31, 1517, until February 18, 1546, Luther was the leader of a religious movement, which eventuated in the coming into existence of The Evangelical Lutheran Church.

In 1997, it will be that 480 years have elapsed since Luther's posting of his 95 theses. Lutheranism in this period has undergone many defections from as well as defenses of the theology of Martin Luther. There have been periods when the true Biblical theology was perverted and buried under such movement as pietism, Kantian rationalism, negative Biblical higher criticism and the Erlangen theology. Over against these departures from Luther's Biblical views there have been individuals who returned back to Luther and promoted the central doctrines of Lutheranism. When one compared the early years of the twentieth century with the closing years of the same century, the observant and astute student of Lutheranism will note how in the latter part of the twentieth century Lutheranism in America and in the world has departed from the theology of Lutheranism as set forth in the various symbols found in *The Book of Concord*.

One of the saddest developments in recent years has been the fact that the largest Lutheran Church in the United States has declared altar and pulpit fellowship with various Reformed or Calvinistic Churches and soon also with The Episcopalian Church of the United States. The Evangelical Lutheran Church in the United States (ELCA), with a membership of over 5,000,000, has rejected the historic Lutheran position with its opposition to the symbolical interpretation of the sacraments of baptism and the Lord's Supper, and recognized the spiritual presence but not real presence of Christ in the Lord's Supper. Religious unionism, an anathema to Luther, is now practiced even with one denomination which is not Trinitarian. Lutheran theologians of ELCA have attacked every basic Biblical doctrine set forth in the Lutheran Confessions. Positions fought for by Luther and held for centuries have been jettisoned and used human philosophy, caving in to the Zeitgeist and replaced the clear teachings of Holy Writ with human philosophy and feelings. Sad to say some Lutherans are members of the Jesus Seminar which is rewriting the New Testament and repudiating the teachings of God's word. There are Lutherans who wrongfully believe that the Roman Catholic Church has the correct understanding of the Pauline doctrine of justification by faith.

There are those in Lutheranism who would unite with Rome and even recognize the Roman Pontiff as Christ's successor on earth.

The author of Hebrews in 13:6-9 called upon his readers: "Remember your former leaders that brought you the Word of God, imitate their faith." While the writer of Hebrews did not have Luther in mind, but those people who brought the Gospel of Jesus Christ as well as Christ's teachings as given through His apostles, yet it is appropriate to apply this admonition and encouragement to Luther and the other reformers, because it was through them that the understanding of the true Word of God was restored and Jesus was given the primacy and importance Christ demands of those who would be true members of His kingdom. In view of religious conditions, on this the 480th anniversary of the beginning of the Protestant Reformation, the writer calls upon all Lutherans:

Remember Your Former Leaders—Luther and His Associates Who Restored The True Biblical Doctrine

It is important that twentieth century Lutherans see what had happened to the Church founded and redeemed by Christ. Prior to His ascension into heaven Jesus gave His disciples the great commission: "Go and make disciples of all nations, baptizing them in the name of the Father, the Son and the Holy Ghost, teaching them to observe all things whatsoever I have commanded you" (Matthew 28:18-20).

Before His death, Jesus promised His disciples the Holy Spirit who would guide them into all truth and bring to their remembrance what Jesus had told them. The Lord also called Paul of Tarsus to bring the Gospel to the Gentiles and caused him to write thirteen letters by the Holy Spirit. Matthew, John, Paul, Peter, James and Jude all were apostles who wrote twenty-three New Testament writings. Mark was a friend of Peter, Luke of St. Paul. Matthew and John together with Mark and Luke authored the four gospels, our major source for the life, ministry, and teachings of Jesus of Nazareth. The New Testament also recognized the Scriptures of the Old Testament as Word of God and the thirty-nine books of Old Testament (24 in Hebrew) together with the twenty-seven books of New Testament constitutes the source for Biblical and Christian theology. From the Bible its readers should learn that the work of salvation was the work of the Triune God and after conversion and justification how Christ's followers were to live as children of the heavenly Father.

Already in the apostolic or New Testament period theological aberrations and errors manifested themselves. Legalistic Judaism, gnosticism affected a number of churches. In the course of time Christian theology began to depart from the doctrines and ethical teachings of the New Testament.

In the second and third centuries the church saw the development of the episcopacy, according to which one clergyman, called a bishop, assumed jurisdiction over a number of congregations in a geographical region. By the fourth century the Bishop of Rome and the Bishop of Constantinople had become supreme. A rivalry developed between the

171

head of the Western Latin Church and the Eastern Orthodox Church.

The Bishop of Rome, later called Pope, claimed that he was Christ's representative on earth and that all peoples, kingdoms and kings were subject to him. His interpretations of Scripture had to be accepted. New doctrines promulgated **ex cathedra** were binding on the consciences of Christian people. In the course of the centuries, prior to the Reformation, the decisions of church councils, the consensus of the Church Fathers on certain teachings, the oral tradition (as known by the Pope) were added to the Bible, and also included were 14 apocryphal books. As a result of these additional sources for Biblical teachings and theology, many Biblical teachings were reinterpreted and others not found in Holy Writ were added supposedly by the Holy Spirit to the sources for the doctrines people needed to know and live by. By adding these additional sources, this addition of a "plus" authority soon caused darkness and trouble. For the first five hundred years the Bible was the sole authority of the entire Christian Church. As the church developed from a simple type of church polity to a complicated hierarchical system, pomp, glory, and vain leadership entered her history. Traditions which did not have their source in the Word of God but which were man-made by church assemblies were added and given the same authority as the Bible.

Here are some instances of man-made doctrine. In A.D. 590 Pope Gregory developed the doctrine of purgatory. In A.D. 800 Radburtus formulated the miracle theory of trans-substantiation, that the priest changed the bread into the body of Jesus and the wine into the blood of Jesus. In 835 indulgences were introduced. In A.D. 983 and worship of saints began, while in 1070 came the decrees for celibacy, good works and priestly forgiveness. In 1170 the cup was withheld from the laity, even though the Lord said: "Take drink you all of it." A Pope felt he had the right and the power to decree that only priests have the right to partake of the wine. Not only did the Middle Ages see the transubstantiation theory from being introduced, it also led to the celebration of the Mass, in which the priest claims to crucify Christ anew. In Roman Catholic Churches there are repeated sacrifices of Christ in an unbloody manner, sacrificed for the living and the dead. But that constitutes a blasphemy on the death of Christ which was all sufficient. The author of Hebrew assured Christians: "For Christ once suffered for sins, the Just for the unjust that He might bring us to God." This teaching that numerous times Christ is being sacrificed in an unbloody mass, is anti-Biblical.

One of the great problems for the true Church of Christ was the claim that the Bishop of Rome was Peter's successor as Christ's representative on earth. The claim of the Pope's headship of the Church was based upon the statement of Christ to Peter: "Thou art Peter (Petros) and upon this rock (petra) I will build my church and the fortresses of hell will not prevail against it." If the Bible reader reads this Matthean passage and especially the context in which it occurs, it will be found that Christ was asking His disciples as to the views people at that time held concerning Him. After a number of disciples responded and related to Christ the opinions prevalent among the people, Peter responded with his great confession: "Thou art Christ, the Son of the Living God." It was upon this confession (petra), and not on the person of Peter that the Christ was to build His Church. It is as St. Paul told the Corinthians: "Other foundation can no man lay than that which is laid, which is Jesus Christ" (I Cor. 3:11). Paul, in his Church Epistle, assured the Ephesians: "Ye are no more strangers and foreigners, but fellow citizens with the saints and of the household of God; and are built upon the foundation of the Apostles and Prophets, Jesus Christ Himself being the chief Cornerstone." Paul notes specifically upon the foundation of the Apostles, of whom Peter was just one (Eph. 2:19-20). There is no statement that Peter as the head of the Church was to appoint a successor, who in turn would appoint a successor and that this be done unto the end of the age. The Bible forbids adding or subtracting from what God has revealed in Holy Writ. The Scriptures alone and nothing but the Scriptures are allowed to establish doctrines and give directions for Christian living.

Luther as Professor of Holy Writ

On October 18-19, 1512, Luther was awarded the degree of Doctor of Holy Scripture. Between 1512 and 1518 Luther lectured on Genesis, Psalms, Romans, Galatians and Hebrews. During this period Dr. Schwiebert claimed that Luther evolved from a scholastic theologian to a Biblical humanist. The same Valparaiso scholar contends that that was in 1514 when Luther discovered the principle of justification by faith in his study of Psalm 71. Although at that time he did not completely understand all the implications of his discovery, he did realize that he had found the gate to heaven. As Luther's new theology began to develop, he began to win over the whole faculty of the University of Wittenberg and by 1517 Luther was becoming a scholar who based his whole theology of religious beliefs solely on Holy Scripture.

Gradually in his dialogue with the Roman church-authorities of his day, Luther became convinced that only one reliable authority for a Christian was to be found in the Bible, minus the Apocrypha, never recognized by the Old Testament Church as part of the Old Testament canon. On April 18, 1521, at his final hearing at Worms, Luther asserted that unless he was shown from Holy Scripture that his writings contained errors, he would not recant or withdraw them as containing errors and heresies. Before 1521 Luther had published 88 writings and in the 25 years beyond the Diet of Worms he published 332 more, he never changed his position that Holy Scripture and only Holy Scripture determined doctrines and also directive for Christian living. At Worms Luther stated:

"Unless I am overcome by testimonies of Scripture or by evident reason, for I believe that neither Pope nor Councils alone because it is an established fact that they have erred a number of times, and have contradicted one another— I am overcome by the Scriptures which I have cited, and my conscience is caught in the worship of God. Recant I cannot and will do nothing because it is uncertain and insincere to act contrary to your conscience."

173

When Luther took this step of claiming that he would not be moved from his stance, unless the Word of God taught and supported it, Luther was advocating what has come to be known as the SOLA SCRIPTURA principle. This new insight constitutes one of the most precious jewels the Protestant Reformation has given its followers and future generations.

All other important doctrines and ethical directives are based upon Holy Scriptures. "If you abide in my Word, then you are my disciples," averred Jesus. The Lutheran Confessions establish doctrine only by the Scriptures of the Old Testament and the Apostolic New Testament. Luther's Scripture—alone position was radical one and singularly separates Rome from historic confessional Lutheranism.

While Rome accepts an enlarged version of Holy Writ (by including the Apocrypha as a part of the Old Testament canon) it has a second major source for the establishment of theological teachings. It is called TRADITION. The latter is derived from the consensus of the Church Fathers on a given teaching, supported by mistranslations of the Vulgate, the Apocrypha, the arguments established by scholastic philosophy and the decisions of Church Councils. With the addition of these many new sources, any person acquainted with the complexities of Roman Theology can realize why there are great differences between Rome and Wittenberg. With the Reformed tradition, which uses reason to create and promote teachings on the work of the Holy Spirit, the symbolic or figurative use of the sacraments of baptism and the Lord's Supper. Wittenberg also differed with Geneva as to what the Word of God really taught.

By insisting that the twenty-four books of the Hebrew Old Testament (which equals the thirty-nine of Protestant Bibles) and the twenty-seven books of the New Testament were the only source for doctrinal teachings and ethical instructions for the conduct of a God-pleasing life, a large number of teachings and dogmas Luther was taught as a child, as a monk and as a priest are automatically eliminated. Especially as professor of Holy Writ Luther realized that many theological positions and practices of the Roman Church had to he abandoned because they were not found in the Word of God or commanded in the latter.

In Luther's writings there are 1,221 references to the Scriptures. They are placed where Luther makes pronouncements about the Old Testament and the New Testament. In their entirety they form an inexhaustive reader on Luther's attitude toward the Bible. Every one of these breathes a profound reverence for the Scriptures as a whole but to every doctrine and even to minute details of Scriptural teaching, Luther argued that a person must come to a halt where God's Word stops. Said Luther: "The rest we must simply leave aside; such things cannot be ventured into without danger." Again the Reformer asserted: "Whoever takes away the Word and does not accept it as spoken by God takes away everything."

When Luther stressed the meaning of a text, he meant that the text must be understood in its plain sense, literal and grammatical. When Emser, Luther's opponent, argued for the "Scriptural" meaning, Luther responded: "The Holy Spirit is the simplest writer and speaker in heaven and upon earth. Accordingly, His words cannot have but one simple meaning which we call the written or literal meaning. The literal meaning must be abandoned only when Scripture itself compels it."

It was the Scripturalness of Luther's teaching that won him so many followers. It gripped men's hearts and won for him his earliest coworkers. Luther's slogan became. Nothing but Scripture (Nihil nisi Scriptura) Nothing beyond Scripture (Quod non biblicum, non est theologicum). That which is not Biblical, is not theological. For Luther the entire testimony of the Old and New Testaments was CHRIST. Luther was convinced that it was God's will that people should know God's Son as their personal Savior. Accordingly, Luther argues that all the Bible must be used in favor of Christ and not against him. If the Bible was not related to him, it was not Scriptural. One of the blessings of Luther's reformatory efforts was to place Christ in the center of Christian theology. Roman Catholics and liberal Protestants (including Lutherans) no longer believe that Christ is the only way to heaven. Rejecting Christ as the world's only Savior, as is now permitted by Rome and liberal Protestants and Lutherans, is a serious departure from the faith once delivered to the saints.

For Luther the entire testimony of the Old and New Testaments was to Christ. The Reformer was convinced that it was God's will that people should know His Son Jesus Christ as their personal Savior. Luther argued that all of the Bible must be used in favor of Christ, not against Him. If it did not relate to Him, it was not Scriptural.

Another reason why Lutherans ought to remember their former spiritual leaders—Luther, Melanchthon and other co-reformers is because Luther especially rediscovered the Biblical answer to the question which the jailor of Philippi asked Paul: "What must I do to be saved?"

During his younger days Luther was greatly concerned about his soul's eternal salvation. The question which haunted Martin Luther was: How could he be accepted by God as a righteous and just person? To find an answer to this crucial question, Luther gave up the study of law and became an Augustinian monk. He tried fasting and performing good works, but they did not assuage his anxiety. It was Staupitz who directed Luther to Christ and His wounds. It took Luther many hours and days to find the true Gospel of salvation. Finally, by God's grace, the Reformer found the true meaning of the righteousness of God revealed in the Gospel. He had been taught that the righteousness of God was an attribute of God who in his essence was righteous and by reason of which God abhorred all unrighteousness.

When Luther discovered that grace was free, that it was grace that motivated the Father to send His Son to die for the sins of the world and that salvation was offered free to all people, then Luther discovered that a man is justified by faith alone, without works.

That salvation was by grace alone is the second jewel that Luther has bestowed on Lutherans and Protestants.

Salvation Is by Grace Alone (Sola Gratia)
Through Paul God had taught: "By grace are you saved and that not

175

of yourselves, it is the gift of God." Man does not need to earn his salvation nor can he. "Behold, the Lamb of God that taketh away the sins of the world." Christ has paid the penalty for the world's sins. Forgiveness is offered unconditionally without any demands whatsoever to be met on man's part. The Word of God states: "If a man be in Christ (that is, accepts Christ), he is a new creation."

Luther had been taught that grace was freely given and was infused into the individual. New powers were thus given the soul and with these added powers the believer could merit, even earn justification with God. This, however, was a life-long process and the individual Roman Catholic could never be certain that by the end of his life he had done enough to completely meet God's demands. But the Bible states that the moment the Holy Spirit caused a person to believe in Christ's atoning work, in that moment the sinner is declared justified. The sinner is given the status of a righteous person, he does not inwardly become or turn into a righteous person. The work of salvation is one hundred percent the work of Christ. Man contributes nothing to his salvation.

Sola gratia, only by the grace of God, God's undeserved mercy promoted God to declare believers sinless and righteous, created by faith in Christ Jesus. As Paul wrote: "Now to one who works, his wages are not reckoned as a gift but as his due. And to one who does not work, but trust him who justifies the ungodly, his faith is reckoned as righteousness."

The fact that Christians do nothing to be God's children is purely due to God's mercy and grace. By emphasizing this important and essential Biblical truth, Luther has presented his followers with another jewel.

Sola Fidei (Big Faith)

How does the sinner receive the forgiveness of sins and become justified or declared righteous?

When Luther proclaimed the truth that man was a lost and condemned creature, is declared righteous and that by faith appropriates God's gracious offer, he was dealing with the very heart of the plan of salvation.

How is a person saved? By God's grace or infused grace plus works? There is a world of difference between the Roman Catholic's concept of justification and justification by faith made possible by God's grace. Only by faith which has as its object the redemptive work of Christ on Calvary is the means for the effectuation of being declared righteous and becoming a member of God's family. The faith that apprehends God's offer of forgiveness is a gift of the Holy Spirit. This gift is offered all repentant sinners who accept Christ as their savior and Redeemer. Faith is the hand by which the Christian accepts God's offer of forgiveness and subsequent justification, which is not a medicinal act by which the sinner is supposed to gradually be purged from sin and reach perfection by making use of infused grace, but is a judicial, forensic act like that of a judge who squashes an indictment against a criminal. Justification by faith is another precious jewel Luther made available to the Lutheran Church.

Solus Christus, the Fourth Sola

The three solas. Scripture alone, by grace alone, by faith alone also undergird a fourth sola, Christ alone. Christ is the heart of Scripture, justification by grace was due to Christ's salvatory efforts for mankind and justification by faith has Christ as its object. Thus Christ alone is the world's savior, redeemer, teacher and guide. Jesus is the name by which we must be saved. "Nor is there salvation in any other, for there is no other name under heaven given among men by which we must be saved."

Jesus is the name that sets the tone for everything a Christian does. "Whatever you do in word or deed, do all in the name of the Lord Jesus, giving thanks to God the Father through Him (Col. 3:17)." The name of Christ is the name at which one day in the future, every knee shall bow. "That at the name of Jesus should bow, of those in heaven, and those on earth, and those under the earth, and that every tongue should confess that Jesus Christ is Lord to the glory of God the Father" (Phil. 2:10-11).

The Priesthood of All Believers

Another jewel Luther gave his followers was the teaching of the Priesthood of All Believers. The Roman Catholics in Luther's day and so even today after 480 years contended that there was a class of intermediaries between God and man, the priesthood. They alone had the God-given right to administer the seven sacraments through which infused grace was transmitted. The Roman Church adopted the Old Testament idea of the priesthood, who were the people appointed by God to offer especially the sacrifices that effected atonement between Yahweh and the Israelites. However, on the first Good Friday, when the veil in the Temple was rent in twain, it meant that from that time the believer would have direct access to God. In the light of Calvary St. Peter could write Christian congregations in Asia Minor: "But you are a chosen race, a royal priesthood, a holy nation, God's own people, that you may declare the wonderful deeds of him who called you out of darkness into his marvelous light" (RSV). With one sweep of the pen, Peter asserted the equality of all Christians before God. You and I, and every other believers can go to God, day or night with our confessions and God will forgive us directly.

Congregational Singing Introduced

Another jewel bestowed by Luther on his followers was the fact that he restored the lost art of congressional singing and the Christian hymn again was given a place in public worship. Philip Schaff, the great historian, wrote: "To Luther belongs the extraordinary merit of having given to the German people in their own tongue the Bible, the Catechism and the hymnbook, so that God might speak directly to them His Word and that they might directly answer him in their songs."

The Council of Constance, the one that had John Huss burnt alive in 1415, had decreed: "If laymen are forbidden to preach and interpret the Scriptures, much more are they forbidden to sing publicly in the churches."

177

Luther is the author of thirty-six hymns, of which "A Mighty Fortress Is Our God" has achieved the greatest fame. This hymn has been translated into more languages with the exception of the Bible and will always remain the classical example of Christian hymnody. Heine called it the "marseillaise of the Reformation." Frederick the Great called it "God's Almighty grenadier march." The magnificent chorale to which the hymn is sung is also Luther's work. Never have words and music been combined to make such a tremendous appeal. Great musical composers have turned to its stirring theme again and again. Mendelsohn has used it in the last movement of his Reformation Symphony; Meyerbeer employed it to good advantage in his masterpiece "Les Hugenots." Wagner used it in his Kaisermarsch, written to celebrate the return of the German troops in 1870.

Luther inspired many other German composers to write hymns and others to supply the new ones with melodies. Hymnody has been a mighty force for spreading the Lutheran faith and also making it firm in the hearts of those following the Lutheran Reformation's theology. Luther's hymnological heritage is one of the jewels of the Reformation.

By following Peter who had a wife and taking seriously the requirements for an episcopos or presbyter, that he should have one wife, Luther established the evangelical parsonage, thus eliminating celibacy as a requirement for the priesthood, and the modern press had made clear how insistence on the celibate life has led to immorality, homosexuality and boy's abuse. By marrying Catherine von Bora he showed how a wife and children made for a healthy situation in the life of a congregation.

The author of Hebrews called upon Christians, "Remember your leaders, those who spoke to you the word of God; consider the outcome of their life, and imitate their faith." On February 17, 1546, Luther became very ill. Luther experienced a number of heart seizures. After his third heart seizure he recited a number of Bible passages and repeatedly commended his soul into the hand of God. Finally, Jonas asked Luther with a penetrating voice: "Reverend Father, are you willing to die in the name of the Christ and the doctrine which you have preached." Luther rallied his whole strength and said: "Yes, so distinctly that the whole group heard it." Then Luther died. Luther should be imitated and not denounced and denigrated!

Questions

1. What event is generally regarded as the beginning of the Reformation? ____

2. In the latter part of the twentieth century Lutheranism departed from ____.

3. What was anathema to Luther? ____
4. Are some Lutherans members of the Jesus Seminar? ____
5. Surburg called upon all Lutherans to ____.
6. The Pope claimed that he was ____.
7. When was the doctrine of purgatory developed? ____
8. When were the decrees of celibacy made? ____

9. Did Christ build his Church on Peter? ____
10. Luther based his whole theology on ____.
11. What is the SOLA SCRIPTURA principle? ____
12. What is Rome's second major source of doctrine? ____
13. In Luther's writings there are ____ references to Scripture?
14. What won Luther many followers? ____
15. Roman Catholics and liberal Protestants including Lutherans no longer believe that ____.
16. The second Jewel that Luther bestowed on Lutherans and Protestants is ____.
17. Faith is the hand by which ____.
18. How is a person saved? ____
19. What is a fourth sola? ____
20. Another jewel Luther gave his followers was ____.
21. Luther restored the lost art of ____.
22. The Council of Constance decreed ____.
23. Luther is the author of ____ hymns.
24. Hymnody has been a mighty force for ____.
25. Luther established the evangelical ____.
26. Celibacy has led to ____.
27. Luther should be ____.

Luther Still Speaks

(Dr. Martin Luther (Born November 10, 1483;
Baptized November 11; Died February 18, 1546;
Glorified February 18, 1546)

Though Dead, He Still Speaks Through His Prefaces of the
German Bible, Through His *German Bible*, Through His Two
Catechisms, Through the Smalcald Articles, Through His
Voluminous Writings 100 Volumes in the Weimar Edition)

Christian News, November 10, 1997

Since the New Testament contained the ultimate revelation of the grace of God in Jesus Christ, Luther translated the New Testament from the Greek before attempting to make the Hebrew-Aramaic Old Testament available to the German people in their native tongue.[1] Luther had as far as can be determined a German translation of 1475 and the Latin Vulgate before him in addition to the New Testament, also the Greek New Testament of Erasmus of 1516.[1a] Because of his thorough knowledge of the Bible in the Vulgate acquired through 20 years of reading and studying, Luther translated into German the entire New Testament on the Wartburg in three months; it occurred between mid-December 1521 to about mid-March 1522. Reu believes: "It still remains an achievement that Luther could not have accomplished it apart from the special assistance of the Holy Spirit."[2]

On September 21, 1522, the first printing of the German New Testament was off the press and is generally known as the "September Testament." Luther's name was not printed on the title page, nor is the date of the publication given. The place of publication is given as Wittenberg. Luther received no pay for his literary effort. The title page has a woodcut with the inscription "Das Neue Testament Deutch." It was a book of 222 leaves in folio size, with 45-46 lines to a page. The numbering of the leaves begins with the text of Matthew's Gospel and reaches the end of Acts.[3] The first part is introduced with Luther's preface to the whole New Testament, his instruction; "which is the finest and best known New Testament books." This preface stresses with great emphasis the fact that though the New Testament contains laws and precepts for the true guidance of life and directions for good works that are well-pleasing to God, nevertheless we are not to expect or seek in it a new law-book, but a Gospel, a glad tidings of the salvation wrought by Christ and appropriated by faith alone. For most books of the New Testament Luther wrote prefaces, designed to aid the German readers as to what of significance they could find in a Biblical book.

The prefaces to the books of the New and Old Testaments have been printed separately because of their making plain how Luther interpreted and understood the Bible, which he translated between 1521 and 1534.

The Holman Edition of *The Works of Martin Luther,* volume VI, has made available the prefaces of the Old Testament and also of the New Testament. The translations were the accomplishment of Charles M. Jacobs. In Volume VI page 439 till page 489 (plus three pages of footnotes) there is a general introduction to the New Testament.[4] This then is followed by a preface to the Acts of the Apostles, and then by the longest of all prefaces, dealing with Romans (23 pages) and concluded with the Apocalypse. The Book of Revelation has a nine-page preface, even though Luther did not consider it of apostolic origin, but listed it together with James, Jude, and Hebrews as non-canonical.[5]

Most of the other prefaces were written for the 1522 edition, but Acts was composed in 1534; for a number of books he wrote another preface for the 1545 German New Testament as was the case with the Preface to the New Testament, 1 Corinthians, the Epistle of Saint Jude and St. James, and the Revelation of St. John.

New Hermeneutics in Evidence

Luther New Testament prefaces reflect Luther's new understanding of the principles of hermeneutics (interpretation).[6] As early as 1513 he asserted that Scripture was the Word of God and the only final authority in the theology or religion. Luther also adopted the principle that the original languages of the Bible and not the Vulgate were final. It was the Greek of the New Testament that determined what the New Testament taught relative to salvation and the conduct of the Christian life. Against the stance of his time, Luther rejected the fourfold sense of Scripture. The Reformer combined into one the sensus literalis, anagogicus and propheticum.

This was made possible by his conviction that most of the Psalms in their literal meaning referred to Christ, who has yet to come. Luther also insisted that a text has but one meaning and cannot be given a multiple interpretation. Beginning with 1517 in his *Seven Penitential Psalms* he no longer used the fourfold meaning in Scriptural interpretation. Further, Luther learned to distinguish between law and Gospel, and recognized in Christ crucified the unity of Scripture. Justification by faith apart from the deeds of the law was the central doctrines of Holy Writ. The New Testament determines the meaning of the Old Testament especially when the New Testament defines the meaning of Old Testament books and passages. In fact, Luther was responsible for a hermeneutical revolution which enabled Luther to reject many theological teachings of Rome and inaugurate a theology faithful to the teachings of Christ and the Apostles.[7] Today, there are many critical scholars who refuse to accept Luther's hermeneutics.

At the very beginning of his "The Preface to the New Testament" Luther announced his fundamental view of Scripture. Reu claimed that Luther's view of Scripture was so fundamental that he quoted the most important passages. In the 1522 preface Luther wrote: "But many wild interpretations and prefaces have driven the thought of Christians to a point, where no one any longer knows what is Gospel or Law, Old Testament or New. Necessity demands, therefore, that it should have an announcement, or preface, which the simple man can be brought back from the old notions to the right road, and taught what is to be expected in this book, so that he may not seek laws and commandments where he ought to be seeking the Gospel and God's promise."[8]

Not Four Separate Gospels by Just One

Luther averred that the notion that there are four distinct Gospels must be given up. Yet modern Biblical scholarship knows that there are in the New Testament four separate and distinct Gospels, two penned by Apostles Matthew and John and two by non-Apostles Mark and Luke. John Mark had contact with Peter and Doctor Luke with the Apostle St. Paul. The four Gospels were written at different times by Matthew, Mark and Luke before the destruction of Jerusalem in A.D. 70, and John possibly in the early nineties.

How could Luther really say "that the idea that there are not four gospels when in the Greek New Testament they are clearly distinguished?" Luther argued that since the Holy Spirit inspired Matthew, Mark, Luke and John to write their Gospels, and record what is known about the earth life of Jesus of Nazareth, Son of God and son of man, all four Gospels pertain to the One Life of Jesus. It further was the Reformer's conviction that the division into legal, historical, prophetical and wisdom books should be rejected. Scholars have categorized the books for their literary characteristics. No matter to which literary genre a New Testament is assigned, it is the final analysis the inerrant Word of God and not the work of men.

The Meaning of "Gospel"

The New Testament is a book in which are written the Gospel and the promises of God, together with those who do not believe them, for the Gospel is a Greek word, and means good message, good tidings, a good report which one sings and tells with rejoicing. So when David overcame the great Goliath, there came among the Jewish people the good report and encouraging news of their terrible enemy had been smitten and given joy and peace, and they sang and danced and were glad for it.

So the Gospel, too, is a good story and report sounded forth into all the world by the apostles, telling of a true David who strove with sin, death and the devil and overcame them, and thereby rescued all those who were captive in sin, afflicted with death, and overpowered by the devil; He made them righteous, gave them life, and saved them so they were given peace and brought back to God. For this they sing, and thank and praised God, and are glad forever, if only they believe firmly and are steadfast in faith.[9]

Luther asserted that this Christian faith was promised in the Old Testament by the prophets, and that is what Paul asserted in Romans 1: "I am separated to preach the Gospel of Christ, which He promised before through His prophets in the Holy Scriptures concerning His Son, who was born of the seed of David, etc." The Reformer devoted over two pages

182

to the Messianic prophecies of the Old Testament, discussing especially Genesis 3:15; Genesis 22:18, as shown by Galatians 3:16, II Samuel 7:12ff, Micah 5:2 and Hosea xiii:14. As a result of this evidence Luther wrote: "The Gospel, then is nothing but the preaching about Christ, Son of God and of David, true God and man, who by his death and resurrection has overcome all men's sin, and death and hell, for us who believe in Him. The Reformer devoted an entire page describing what the Gospel is, where it is found in the New Testament and what was involved in appropriating Christ's forgiveness. He warns against making Christ a Second Moses and thus nullifying the salvatory work of Christ. Relative to emphasizing Christ's atoning work, Luther listed the following books as creating and fostering the true way of salvation. They were: John's Gospel and St. Paul's Epistles, especially that Romans and St. Peter's first Epistle and these Luther called "the true kernel and marrow of all the books." Because James did not show the plan of salvation and set forth justification by faith the Reformer said James was "an epistle of straw."[10]

Preface to the Acts of the Apostles (1534)

Luke, who wrote Acts, tells his readers why he had written to Theophilus what Jesus had said and done in his first treatise, the Gospel of Luke. In Acts he traces the spread of Christianity from A.D. 30 to A.D. 60, concluding with Paul's imprisonment in Rome. Luther began his preface on The Acts of the Apostles this way: "This book should be read and regarded not as though St. Luke had written of the personal works and lives of the apostles for an example of good works and good lives only; though this is the way it has sometimes been taken." Luther told his 16th century followers that this second volume of Luke should teach the whole church to the end of the world, the true chief point of Christian doctrine, namely, that we must be justified only through faith in Jesus Christ, without any additions of law or help from good works.

The main purpose of Acts was to stress so mightily that Gentiles and Jews are justified through the Gospel and not through the Law.[11] Luke's church history gives examples of the doctrine of justification by faith and so all men are saved in the same manner. Thus Peter testifies in Acts 10:28; 15:9. God gave the Holy Spirit through the Gospel to Jews and Gentiles. Luther asserted that Acts is a commentary on the Epistles of St. Paul. The events and words in Acts show that not law, not works justify human beings, but only faith in Christ Jesus, **Sola fides justificat** (Faith alone justifies). All the examples and instances of justification by faith contained in Acts are sure and comforting. Luther cites Paul of Tarsus, Cornelius, and proconsul Sergius Paulus, the first council in Jerusalem as illustrations of justification by faith.

The Preface to Romans (1522)

Here is Luther's evaluation of Romans: "This Epistle is really the chief part of the New Testament and the very purest Gospel and is worth not only that every Christian should know it word for word, by heart, but occupy himself with it every day, as the daily bread of the Soul."[12]

Adequately to understand the 16 chapters of Romans, Luther contended that the reader must have a knowledge of its language and comprehend what Paul meant by the usage of the words like law, sin, grace, faith, righteousness, flesh and spirit, etc., otherwise no reading of the law has any advantage. Paul spent a number of pages in explaining Paul's use of the law, righteousness, faith and good works, flesh and spirit. "Without such an understanding of the words, you will never understand the letters of Paul, or any other book of Holy Scripture"[13] (p. 453). In the Holman *Works of Luther* the Romans preface occupies pages 447 to 462. In 1903 the United Lutheran Publication House published a translation by the Rev. Charles E. Hay, 29 pages, in pamphlet format.[14] This was selected from all prefaces because it was considered the most theological and representative Pauline Epistle that elucidated the plan of salvation.

Luther begins this preface in this way: "This Epistle is really the chief part of New Testament and the very purest Gospel, and is worthy not only that every Christian should know it word for word, by heart, but occupy himself with it every day, as the daily bread of the soul. It can never be read or pondered too much, and the more it is dealt with the more precious it becomes, and the better it tastes."[15] Any person wishing to ascertain the teachings and theology of Romans should carefully study this Roman's preface. It amounts to a minor commentary of Paul's most theological Epistle.

Luther concluded his Romans preface with these words: "Thus in this Epistle we find most richly the things that a Christian ought to know; namely, what is law, Gospel, sin, punishment, grace, faith, righteousness, Christ, God, good works, love, hope, the cross, and also how we are to conduct ourselves toward everyone, whether righteous or sinner, strong or weak, friend or foe. All this is ably founded on Scriptures and proved by his own example and that of the prophets. Therefore it appears that St. Paul wanted to comprise briefly in this one epistle the whole Christian and evangelical doctrine and repair an introduction to the entire Old Testament; for, without doubt, he who has this epistle well in his heart, has the light and power of the Old Testament with him. Therefore let every Christian exercise himself in it habitually and continually. To this may God give His grace. Amen."[16]

Preface to I Corinthians (1545)

In this preface, Paul calls upon the Corinthians to cease being divided because Christ is mankind's salvation. Luther inveighs against those who were wise in their own conceits, against fanatics, heretics and those in their own conceit cannot live in harmony with other church members. These troublemakers were so "wild and disorderly" that everybody wanted to be master and teach, and make what he pleased of the Gospel, Sacrament and faith. The result was that Christ is our salvation was forgotten, and that Christ is mankind's salvation and redemption. Luther claimed that in his day the same uncertainty and confusion was occasioned by mad saints and wise men who caused disturbances and offences. Thus mad saints used the Gospel in a clever way and sense. They can never know Christ unless they become fools again and humbly permit themselves to be taught by the simple Word of God. Just like the Corinthians needed the correction which God only could furnish, so also Romanists and others in the sixteenth century. Chapters 5 to 16 are briefly summarized, sometimes a line or two is given to a chapter.

Preface to II Corinthians (1522)

Luther claimed that the two Corinthian Epistles contrasted each other. While in the first epistle Paul rebuked and poured sharp wine in their wounds, thereby terrifying the Corinthian congregation, so by contrast he comforts. Paul praises them once again and poured oil into their wounds and showed himself kind to them. The method and procedure of Paul in dealing with the Corinthians should be imitated by pastors and preachers (cf. chapters 1 and 2).

The remainder of the preface, dealing with chapters 3-13 is briefly outlined and significant observations about its teaching are made. Paul had this to say about the Gospel: "It is the highest and most comforting of all works and is for the profit and good of men's conscience."[17] He shows how it is nobler than the office of the law, and how it is persecuted, and yet increases among believers and produces through the Cross a hope of eternal glory.

Preface to St. Paul's Letter to the Galatians (1522)

In the beginning of the Galatian preface Paul describes the historical situation necessitating the writing of the six chapters of Galatians, one of the favorite New Testament books for Luther. In Chapter 1 Paul defends his apostleship. He states that though any apostle, yes even an angel from heaven, preached differently about justification by faith, apart from the Law, all should be rejected. As an apostle by the grace of Christ, Paul of Tarsus warned against false teachers relative to justification in chapters 1 and 2, in which he clearly concluded that every person must be justified by faith without merit, without the Law, but only through Christ. In chapters 3 and 4 Paul defended the doctrine of justification by faith with passages from Holy Writ. In chapters 5 and 6 the Apostles to the Gentiles taught that the works of love must follow faith.

Preface to the Epistle to The Ephesians (1522)

In chapters 1-3 Paul of Tarsus taught what the Gospel is and how God provided for it alone in eternity. For this purpose God sent His Son so that all who believe in the Son of God are saved from the law, sin and death.

In chapter 4 the Apostle sets forth different doctrines and commandments of men, which are to be avoided so as to remain true to Christ alone. In chapters 5 and 6 the Reformer proceeds to teach that Christians are to practice their faith by fighting the Devil, so that the Cross Christians remain steadfast in hope.

Preface of St. Paul's Letter to the Philippians (1522)

The purpose of the Philippian Epistle is to praise the Philippian Church and also contains an exhortation to abide in the true faith and increase in love. Paul, according to Luther, warns against false teachers. Timothy and Epaphroditus are held forth as exemplars. In chapter 2 Paul rejects the faithless and human righteousness of the false prophets and holds himself up as an example to be followed. In chapter 4 the Apostle exhorts the Philippians to conduct themselves peacefully toward all men and he also thanks them for the gift they had sent.

Preface of St. Paul's Epistle to the Colossians (1522)

It was Luther's judgment that as the Epistle to the Galatians resembles and is modeled on the Epistle of Romans, so the Colossian Letter resembles the Ephesian Epistle and comprises it in outline and contents.

Chapters 2 and 4 are briefly summarized. In chapter 2 Paul warns against the doctrines of men who are opposed to the faith and criticized them in a masterly fashion. In chapter 3 the reader is exhorted to be fruitful in the pure faith. In chapter 4 the Apostle commends himself to their prayers, and sends them greetings and gives words of encouragement.

The Preface of St. Paul's Letter to the Thessalonians I (1520)

In chapters 1 and 2 Paul praises the Thessalonian Church of Macedonia that it had received the Gospel from him as God's Word. He praised them for their suffering endured for Christ. Especially does he appreciate the suffering they had endured at the hands of the Jews. In chapter 2 Paul sends Timothy to Thessalonica to find out whether they were remaining faithful to Christ. In chapter 4 the Thessalonians were exhorted to guard themselves against sin. In chapter 5 Paul writes about the Last Day, how it will come suddenly and give suggestions for the government of other people and what attitude they were to show toward the lives and teachings of other people.

The Pastoral Epistles: Preface of St. Paul to I Timothy (1522)

The purpose of I Timothy is "to give a model to all bishops of what they are to teach and how they are to rule the church in every station, so that it may not be necessary for Christians to rule according to their own human opinions."[18] In chapter one bishops are instructed to avoid false teachers and also to resist the false teachers of the law, who in addition to Christ and the Gospel demanded the works of the law for salvation. In the same chapter Paul gives a brief summary, namely the whole Christian doctrine concerning the purpose of the law and the purpose of the Gospel.

In chapter 2 Paul insists that prayer be made for all men, that women are not to preach in church and wear costly adornment and women be obedient to their husbands. In chapter 3, Paul lists the requirements for bishops or priests and their wives. In chapter 4, Paul by inspiration prophesied the coming of false prophets and denounces those who forbid marriage and foods together with them and their doctrines. In chapter 5, Paul describes rules to guide widows and young women. Further he also prescribes how godly and blames worthy bishops or priests are to be held in honor or punished. In chapter 6, Paul exhorts bishops to cleave to the pure Gospel and to avoid unprofitable and curious questions.

Preface to the II Epistle to Timothy (1522)

This was Paul's "swan song," his farewell writing in which he exhorted Timothy to continue preaching the Gospel. This was necessary because in the first Christian century many are falling away and false spirits were springing up all around in the Roman Empire. Because of this bishops must be watchful and preach the word. Luther believed that the situations described in chapter 3 were being fulfilled in the early sixteenth century in the clergy.

Preface of Paul's Letter to Titus (1522)

Luther noted that Titus was a short epistle, but a model of Christian doctrine, containing those beliefs a Christian should know.

Chapter 1 sets forth what kind of a person a bishop should be. It complements the requirements given in I Timothy. In chapter 2 Paul elucidated what kind of men they should be in every station in life and what they should do, namely, the young, women, men, masters and servants. Paul instincts Titus and others to honor worldly rulers and obey them.

Preface to Philemon (1522)

This short epistle of 25 verses shows Christians how to act tenderly in Christian love. St. Paul takes up the case of Onesimus and asks his Colossian master Philemon to forgive Onesimus and recognize him as a brother in Christ. Luther then makes this application: What Christ has done for us with God the Father, that St. Paul does for Onesimus relative to Philemon. For Christ laid aside His rights and overcame His Father with love and humility, so that He had to put away His wrath and His rights and receive us into favor, for Christ's sake, who so earnestly advocates our cause and takes our part so tenderly. For we are all his Onesimi, if we believe.

The Preface to the First Epistle of Saint Peter (1522)

The first Epistle of Peter had a number of objectives according to the Wittenberg professor, namely, to convert Gentiles, to cause the congregations of Asia Minor to remain steadfast in the Christian faith and to endure all manner of suffering and increase in good works. Luther claimed that in chapter 1 Saint Peter makes strong the faith of the readers by the promise and power of the future salvation, which was proclaimed by the Old Testament prophets. Since the Asia Minor Christians have been born anew through the living and eternal Word of God they should lead holy lives.

In chapter 2 St. Peter stresses Christ as the Head and Cornerstone and His followers are encouraged to sacrifice themselves to God through Christ who sacrificed Himself. This is the chapter from which Luther drew his teaching of the general priesthood of all believers. In the second half of the chapter Peter calls upon various classes of society to be obedient to constituted authority. Christ was the example citizens, slaves and women were to imitate.

In chapter three, the Gospel on family relations is discussed. How men and women in the marriage relationship are to respond to each other; Christians, in general are to be humble, be kind to one another, just as Christ was because of mankind's sins.

Chapter four deals with victorious living in the power of Christ. The followers of Christ were to subdue the flesh, with sobriety, watching, temperance and prayer and in their suffering to be comforted with Christ's sufferings. In chapter five Peter admonished bishops and priests to live with humility and care for people, and the leaders of the Church are warned against the Devil who aims to destroy believers.

Preface to the Second Epistle of St. Peter (1522)

Luther believed that the purpose of II Peter was to show that the faith without works is dead. The Reformer believed that Peter was encouraging Christians to test themselves about good works so that they may know that they are in the faith. Then the Reformer held that Peter praises the Gospel and that no doctrines are of private interpretation.

In chapter 2 Peter warns against false teachers, who by their teaching and works deny Christ. These false teachers were motivated by avarice, pride, audacity, fornication and hypocrisy. Luther claimed that Peter foresaw the clergy of his day. In chapter 3 Peter speaks of the glorious hope of the Second Coming. In the future men will deny the inevitability of the **Parousia** (Second Coming) and mock about it.

Luther's Summary of II Peter

"Briefly, chapter I shows what the Church should be like at the time of the pure Gospel; chapter II shows how it was to be in time of the pope and the doctrines of men; Chapter III shows how, afterwards, people will despise the Gospel and all doctrine, and believe nothing, and that is now in full swing, until Christ comes."[19]

Preface to the Three Epistles of Saint John (1522)

The Reformer considered the First Epistle of John a genuine apostolic writing and that it ought to follow immediately upon the Gospel. While in the Johannine Gospel John treats of faith, the First Epistle teaches that faith without works is not genuine faith. Luther believes that John in his five-chapter letter inveighs against the Cerenthians, Gnostics, and also against the Antichrist. Already at John's time the humanity of God's Son was being attacked. In applying this epistle to the sixteenth century Luther asserted: "For although men do not now publicly deny with the lips that Christ is come into the flesh, they do deny it with their hearts, by their doctrine and life."[20] In the Reformer's opinion those who held that they could be saved by their own works actually deny the purpose for Christ's assuming flesh and blood. The truth is that we can only be righteous as a result of His shedding His blood.

John in his First Epistle fights both theological positions, but John takes a middle course by teaching that believers are free from sin through faith and afterward do good works not expecting a reward for them.

Relative to The Second Epistle of John and The Third Epistle Luther claimed they are not epistles of doctrine but give examples of love and faith.

Luther Distinguished Between Canonical and Non-Canonical New Testament Books

Luther followed Eusebius who did not accept all the 27 books of the New Testament as apostolic.

Luther, while listing them at the end of his *German Bible*, did not hold Hebrews, James, Jude, and Revelation as apostolic (Cf. Eusebius Church History, Book III, Ch. 25).[21] The theologians of the Ancient Church distinguished between **Homologoumena** and **Antilegomena.** Theodore Mueller claimed: "Nevertheless, though the canonical character of the Antilegomena was questioned by some, each received sufficient testimony to entitle it a place in the canon, from which all spurious apostolic (pseudepigrapha) were rightly ruled out."[22]

The same St. Louis Seminary scholar wrote: "When the ancient Church differentiated between Homologoumena and Antilegomena, this was purely a historical procedure, involving nothing more than the question whether certain books were written by such and such an apostle of Christ or not."[23] The Lutheran Confessions quote from Hebrews, James, Jude and Revelation as Scriptural and binding proof for doctrines advocated.[24]

Luther's Dubious Canoncial Books The Preface of the Epistle of Saint James and St. Jude, 1545 (1522)

The Reformer claimed that the ancients rejected the book, but he averred: "I praise it and hold it a good book, because it sets up no doctrine of men and lays great stress on God's law."[25] He devoted a page and a half to show why he did not consider it the writing of an apostle. First he was convinced that James contradicted St. Paul on justification by faith, while James, Luther believed, taught salvation by works of the law. Secondly, the Reformer could not find the Passion, Resurrection or the Spirit of Christ in the five chapters of James. Because James's Epistle did not teach Christ it was not apostolic. "What does not teach Christ is not apostolic, even though St. Peter or Paul taught it; gain, what preaches Christ would be apostolic, even though Judas, Annas, Pilate and Herod did it."[26]

Luther believed that on a number of teachings James and Paul and Peter were in conflict. Concluded the Wittenberg Professor: "Therefore, I cannot put him among the chief books, though I would not thereby prevent anyone from putting where he pleases; for there are many good sayings in him."[27]

189

Preface to the Epistle of Jude

This is at the end of his James' preface. Luther was of the opinion that it is an extract from St. Peter's second epistle, so likely are all the words. Luther claimed that Jude writes of the apostles as a disciple coming long after them and cites sayings and events found nowhere else in Scripture. It was for that reason the ancient Fathers did not accept Jude as apostolic. Furthermore, the Apostle Jude did not write in Greek, nor did he do missionary work in Greek-speaking lands, but instead went to Persia. "Therefore, although I praise the book, it is an epistle that need not be counted among the chief books, which are to lay the foundation of faith."[28]

Preface to the Revelation of Saint John (I), 1522

Luther wrote two different prefaces for the Book of Revelation, the first in 1522, and the second in 1545. Luther asserted that other individuals could hold what they wished as to the canonicity of Revelation. He did not believe it was prophetic or apostolic. Because apostles do not deal with visions, but prophecy in clear plain words, the Apostle John could not have written it. The Reformer contended that the Gospel was set forth in clear terms and not in figures and visions. He put the Revelation on the same level as the Fourth Book of Esdra, concerning which two books he cannot understand how the Holy Ghost produced them. The Reformer found it offensive that in chapter 22:18f people are warned not to add or subtract from this book. Luther knew that Jerome praised it highly but did not share the latter's enthusiasm for the Apocalypse. The professor of Wittenberg believed that Christ is not known or taught in it. His reason for not accepting it as the Word of God was that "therefore I stick to the books which gave me Christ, clearly and purely."

Preface to the Revelation of Saint John (II) 1545

This preface is the second longest of all of Luther prefaces, nearly nine pages in the Holman edition (Jacob's translation, pp. 479-488).

In the 1545 preface Luther gives his interpretation of the 22 chapters comprising this last book of the Greek New Testament. Any person reading this short explanation of Revelation will notice that Luther must have changed his mind by 1545 as to the Christian value of this apocalyptical book. He devoted nearly two pages to its value for the Christian Church. Luther claimed one can profit from its teachings and make good use of it.[29]

In the interpretation of Revelation there have at least been four different schools of interpretation:

(1) the Praeterist; (2) the Historic; (3) the Futurist and (4) the Symbolic. The first interprets the vision as having reference to episodes in Jewish and Christian history up to the fall of Rome; the second, that we have here in vision the entire course of all the centuries of the Christian era. This is also called the church history school, an understanding Luther adopted and which thereafter influenced Luther exegetes; the third postpones the significance of the vision of events accompanying the second coming of Christ; the fourth holds that in signs and symbols we

have the never-ending conflict between good and evil.[30]

The 1545 preface is interesting as showing how Luther understood this apocalyptical book and some novel views expressed by Luther.

In the first part of the preface Luther elucidates on his conception of "prophecy." He asserts there are different kinds. One is prophecy that interprets the writings of the prophets. Paul speaks of this kind in I Corinthians XII and XIV, and in other places. This is the most necessary kind and we must have it every day, because it teaches the Word of God, lays the foundation of the Church, and defends the faith; in a word, it rules, preserves, establishes and administers the preaching-office.[31]

Another kind foretells things to come and are not previously recorded in the Scriptures. This it does without employing symbols and figures, in direct words. David, Moses and many of the prophets prophesy of Christ and Christ and the Apostles prophesy of false teachers, the Antichrist, etc. Another kind does it with symbols, placed alongside their interpretations. Joseph and Daniel thus interpret dreams. Yet another kind does it without either words or interpretations, "like the Book of Revelation and like the dreams and symbols that people have from the Holy Spirit." Wrongfully Luther claimed Joel's prophecy cited in Acts 2 is not explained and is not as Luther asserted a concealed and dumb prophecy. Relative to Revelation Luther believed that it is not certain as to how to interpret this book which many have attempted to do.

Since it is the purpose of Revelation to deal with the future of the Church, and especially to set forth the tribulations to come upon the Church, it is best to find in the events of church history the meaning of the Apocalypse.[32]

Luther is on firm exegetical ground as he interprets the first three chapters, which has the seven letters to seven different congregations of Asia Minor. He holds that the angel of the seven churches are bishops or teachers. Chapter 4 and 5 give a picture of the future tribulations and plagues to come upon the whole Church. The vision of the seven seals and the Lamb (ch. 4) and the Lamb opening the book while the angels sing are written for the comfort of Christians who may know that the Church is to abide, in the plagues which are to come.[33]

Beginning with chapter 6 John gives the seven seals (ch. 6-7), the seven trumpets (8-12), seven persons (10-12), the seven bowls (13-16), seven dooms (17-21) and seven new things (ch. 22).[34] The chapters from 6-22 have been interpreted differently by modern commentaries. Luther in these chapters takes the church history approach and finds many characters and events of church history reflected in chapter 6 and following. Individuals mentioned by Luther are: Spiridion (ch. 7), Athanasius (ch. 7), Hillary (ch. 7), the Nicene Council (ch. 7), Tatian (ch. 8), the Enchratites (ch. 8), Marcion (ch. 8), Cataphrygians (ch. 8), Manichaeans, (ch. 8), Montanists (ch. 8), Orgen (ch. 8), Arius (ch. 9), the Saracens, the Antichrist (ch. 14). Luther finds the papacy in chapter 14. In chapters 15 and 16 the Reformer believed the Papacy is depicted as attacking the Gospel, on all sides by means of learned and pious preachers, and the throne of the beast, the pope's power. However, the attacks are dark and wretched and despised. Three frogs emerge from the beast and stir up kings against the Gospel. The three frogs are Faher, Eck and Emser, who croak against the Gospel, but they accomplish nothing. They achieve nothing because of the battle of Armageddon. Chapter 17 speaks of the imperial and papal empire, depicted in a single picture and John shows that they both will be damned and condemned, fulfilling by what Paul stated in II Thessalonians 2:8.[35] Chapter 18 announces the destruction of Rome and chapter 19 announces that the enemies of the Gospel will be defeated as the multitudes in heaven proclaim in song.

In chapter 20 Luther claimed that while this was happening, there comes, in chapter 20, the stirrup cup Gog and Magog, the Turks, the red Jews, whom Satan had bound for a thousand years and, after the thousand years, is loose again, brings up; "but they are to go with him into the lake of fire."[36] The thousand years began when the Revelation was written and at the same time the devil was bound. After the Turks the Last Judgment follows quickly, as Daniel VII:7f. shows.

Chapter 21 gives final comfort. Now the holy city is ready and like a bride is led to the eternal marriage. Now Christ alone is Lord and all the godless are damned and go with the devil into hell."

The preface to Revelation closes with a section treating of the profit of Revelation, covering two pages, (pp. 486-488). Disregarding many of Luther's interpretations, the value of Revelation for the Christian Church is probably the greatest contribution of Luther's Revelation Preface, a book not considered canonical by Luther, the exegete.

Footnotes

1. F. Heinz Bluhm, *Martin Luther. Creative Translator* (St. Louis: Concordia Publishing House, 1965), 236 pp.; Roland Bainton, *Here I Stand. A Life of Martin Luther* (New York and Abingdon; Abingdon Cokesbury Press, 1950), pp. 325-336; M. Reu, *Luther's German Bible* (Columbus: Lutheran Book Concern, 1934), pp. 1-184.

1a. Ewald M. Plass, *This Is Luther* (St. Louis: Concordia Publishing Company, 1948), pp. 330-331.

2. M. Reu, *Luther and the Scriptures*, **op. cit.** p. 158.

3. Plass, **op. cit.** p. 331.

4. Martin Luther, *Prefaces to the New Testament, The Works of Martin Luther* (Philadelphia: A. Holman Company and Castle Press, 1932), pp. 439-444.

5. **Ibid.** pp. 439-489.

6. Uuras Saarnivara, *Hath God Said? Who Is Right, God Or the Liberals?* (Minneapolis: Osterhus Publishing House, No date), chapter IV, pp. 48-57; Eugene Klug, "Hermeneutical Principles in Luther Theology," Faculty Study Paper, held at Concordia Theological Seminary, May 13,1963; Raymond F. Surburg, "Luther's Attitude Toward Scripture and Basic Principles of Interpretation," delivered at the Joint Faculty Meeting With the Council of Presidents, 1963, also found in Surburg's *A Summary of Lutheran Hermeneutical Principles* (Springfield: Concordia Print Shop, 1969).

7. Raymond F. Surburg, "Significance of Luther's Hermeneutics for the Protestant Reformation," *Concordia Theological Monthly*, 24,241-261 (1953).

8. Holman, Vol. VI, p. 439.

9. **Ibid.** p. 441.

10. **Ibid.** p. 444.

11. **Ibid.** p. 445.

12. **Ibid.** p. 447.

13. **Ibid.** p. 453.

14. Charles E. Hay, Preface to *St. Paul's Epistle to the Romans* (Philadelphia: United Lutheran Publication House, 1903), 29 pp.

15. Holman, VI, **op. cit.** p. 447.

16. **Ibid.** p. 462.

17. **Ibid.** p. 465.

18. **Ibid.** p. 470.

19. **Ibid.** p. 475.

20. **Ibid.** p. 476.

21. Kirsopp Lake, Eusebius, *The Ecclesiastical History* (London: William Heinemann; New York: G. Putnam's Sons, 1926), Greek text, pp. 256-258; English translation, pp. 257, 258.

22. J. T. Mueller, *Christian Dogmatics* (St. Louis: Concordia Publishing House, 1955), p. 130.

23. **Ibid.** p. 131.

24. Theodore G. Tappert, *The Book of Concord* (Philadelphia: Fortress Press, 1959), p. 64.

25. Holman, VI, **op. cit.** p. 472.

26. **Ibid.** p. 478.

27. **Ibid.** p. 479.

28. **Ibid.** p. 479.

29. **Ibid.** p. 486.

30. Ludwig Fuerbringer, *Einleitung in das Alte Testament* (St. Louis: Concordia Publishing House, 1927), p. 109. Helen Barrett Montgomery, *New Testament in Modern English* (Philadelphia: Judson Press, 1924), p. 650; George A. Hadjiantoniou, *New Testament Introduction* (Chicago: Moody Press, 1957), pp. 340-341.

31. Holman, VI., **op. cit.** pp. 479-480.

32. **Ibid.** p. 480.

33. **Ibid.** p. 481.

34. Based on chart in Samuel M. Miller, *The Revelation of Jesus Christ* (Minneapolis: Published by the Author, 1926), p. 98.

35. Holman, VI, **op. cit.** p. 485.

36. **Ibid.** p. 485.

37. **Ibid.** p. 486.

Questions

1. Martin Luther was born on _____ and died on _____.
2. How many volumes are there in the Weimar edition of Luther's writings? _____
3. How long did it take Luther to translate the New Testament? _____
4. How much pay did Luther receive for his translation? _____
5. Which books of the Bible did Luther list as non-canonical? _____
6. The only final authority in theology, according to Luther, is _____.
7. What was final for Luther? _____

8. According to Luther, the Psalms in their literal meaning referred to
____.

9. The central doctrines of Holy Writ were ____.
10. There are not four separate Gospels but ____.
11. Luther warns against making Christ a ____.
12. Luther said James was ____.
13. The chief point of the book of Acts is ____.
14. Luther's preface to Romans amounts to ____.
15. What does Paul teach in chapter 2 of I Timothy? ____
16. The theologians of the ancient church distinguished between ____ and
____.

17. The Lutheran Confessions quote from ____.

Luther and the Vulgate Biblical Version

Christian News, February 23, 1998

Luther has been accused of the great sin of having abandoned the Word of God, even changing it on occasion, because he forsook the employment of the Vulgate, which had been the Bible of Western Christianity for over a thousand years. Two followers of Rev. Gordon Winrod, living in Cassville, Missouri, in an attack on this writer's article: "Luther Still Speaks," (*Christian News*, November 11,1997) wrote: "We are told that Luther had a thorough knowledge of the Bible in the Vulgate acquired through 20 years of studying, yet he adopted the principle that the original languages of the Bible and not the Vulgate were final, inexplicably overlooking the fact that Hebrew and Greek manuscripts available to him, were older and more reliable than anything available to him, and that the Vulgate had stood as the true Bible for over a thousand years."[1] Winrod in Letter #300, asserted: "Luther's crowning crime, securely sealing forever his eternal damnation, was what he did to God's Word. Therein is the proof more than any other thing, that he was against Jesus. His German 'Bible' is the evidence that he was against Jesus. He hated the name of Jesus. His *German Bible* is the evidence against him."[2]

Where in Luther's writings is there any statement that Luther hated Jesus?[3] Since Luther used the Massoretic text which Jerome also employed and also utilized Erasmus' edition of the Greek New Testament, based in 1517 on the best manuscripts Erasmus had available, the Wittenberg Reformer used as basis the best possible sources from which to make his German translation. At Worms, Luther in 1521, when called upon to renounce the errors in his writings, replied that unless he were shown from reason and from the Holy Scripture the errors of his theology, he was appealing to the Vulgate, on the basis of which he had come to realize the unchristian character of much Roman Catholic theology.[4] The Bible which he referred to in his "Here I Stand" reply was the Vulgate. Thus it is shown that Luther had a high respect for the Latin Vulgate.

The History of the Vulgate Textual criticism has given considerable material for the establishment of the original beginnings of the Vulgate. The Clementine Vulgate, the standard edition now used by Roman Catholics, is for the Old Testament based on the Massoretic text, but the New Testament is partly based on the Old Latin, a translation, prior to the coming into existence of the Vulgate, thus the Vulgate is a primary translation for the Old Testament, but for the New Testament employed as its basis the Old Latin, and even though corrections were made by Jerome of the New Testament, it is a secondary rendering while Luther's German translation was made directly from the Hebrew and Greek and therefore is superior to the Vulgate, in that it is completely based on the original Biblical languages.

Greek was not only the language of culture but the normal language for intercourse in the Roman Empire, in which Christ and the Apostles lived.[5] All 27 books of the New Testament were composed in Greek and addressed to people living in Palestine, Asia Minor, Greece, Dalmatia, Italy, Gaul and Spain. Thus Bruce wrote: "For the first two centuries the need for having a Latin version of the Bible does not seem to have been felt in Rome or Italy."[6] In Constantinople, in the Eastern Churches, Greek was the language employed by the Church and its Bible for the Old Testament was the Greek Septuagint, while Greek was also the language in which God's Word in the New Testament was recorded. In Syria and Mesopotamia, where Syriac was spoken by Christians, one finds that the Jacobites and Nestorians translated the Bible into Syriac.[7] In Egypt the Bible was rendered into the various Coptic dialects, where Bohairic, Sahidic, Fayumic and other dialects were spoken and church services were held in them.

Across the Mediterranean, however, lay the Roman province of Africa, covering the territory now occupied by Tunisia, Algeria, and Morocco. This area, prior to the Islamic conquest of the seventh century, contained some of the most flourishing churches in the Roman Empire. North Africa became famous for its Church Fathers, such as Tertullian, Cyprian and the greatest of the North African theologians Augustine, who died 430, when the Vandals were about to plunder North Africa, followed by the seventh-century Islamic Conquest.

The success of the Vandals and Mohammedans may be attributed to the absence of a Bible in the vernacular Berber tongues, because in places where there were Bible translations, such as in Egypt, which had various Coptic versions and Syria and Mesopotamia, where there were Syriac versions, the Muslim Conquest did not succeed in obliterating Christianity.[8]

In North Africa, Latin and not Greek was the leading official language of administration, and the language of the upper strata of society. In Carthage, originally destroyed by the Romans in 164 B.C., and rebounded a hundred years later, Latin was employed. When the Gospel of Jesus spread to North Africa, a version of the Bible in Latin was necessary.[9]

Early Pre-Vulgate Latin Versions

Unger claimed: "Whether this consists of one verse or more than one is definitely not known, for extent manuscripts differ to such an extent as to raise the question whether or not or that they had their origin in a single source."[10] The Old Testament was put into Latin around A.D. 150. This version was made from the Greek Septuagint and slavishly follows it, even to the reproduction of evident blunders. The Apocrypha were added unrevised to Jerome's Vulgate and are thus preserved. Tertullian (d. 230), Cyprian (d. 258), and Augustine (d. 430) quoted from the Old Latin in their writings."[11]

Augustine speaks of an "Italian version" which may indicate another old translation prior to Jerome's Vulgate. Some scholars consider this reference as an allusion to the Vulgate New Testament, which had been published for about ten years when he wrote it. The Jesuit scholar

McKenzie asserted about the Old Latin as follows: "No great merit can be attributed to the Old Latin. It was made from the LXX and the translators had little Latin and less Greek. It was slavishly literal and often unintelligible. The translators were not educated men and produced without intending it one of the greatest monuments of vulgar unlettered Latin of the period. The uncritical and careless multiplication of copies soon produced a state corruption which demanded attention."[12]

The state of affairs forced Pope Damascus to invite Jerome to correct this confusing situation relative to the Old Latin Version.

St. Jerome as Translator of the Vulgate

In the New Testament Jerome simply amended the Old Latin text from the original Greek, confining his revision only as he himself asserts in the Preface to the Gospels, which seems to change the meaning. As far as the Old Testament was concerned, Jerome made two revisions of the Psalter (the Psalms). The first of these revisions he made in 385, before he left Rome and it was a cursory revision of the Old Latin according to the Septuagint, and **Psalterium Romanum** (the Roman Psalter). The second Psalter revision was made after 385, revised according to Origen's Hexaplaric text and was called **Psalterium Gallicanum**, because it came into common use in Gaul. Other Old Testament books were revised according to the Greek Septuagint.[13]

Jerome's Use of the Hebrew for the Old Testament Vulgate

The last phase of Jerome's Bible translation activity began at A.D. 390. Before leaving Palestine he began translating the Old Testament in Hebrew. Jerome's study of Hebrew began in Antioch prior to 379. He endeavored to perfect his knowledge of Hebrew with a view of rendering the entire Old Testament (minus the Apocrypha) into the Hebrew and Aramaic. He settled at Bethlehem, in Palestine, and secured the help of Jewish rabbis and his study showed him how unsatisfactory were the Septuagint Old Testament texts as well as the Old Latin.[14] It was with a renewed sense of importance that he undertook to translate the Hebrew books as well as the Aramaic portions found in Ezra and Daniel, Jerome's Preface, called Prologus Galeatus, shows how Jerome felt about his translating activity in Bethlehem.

Jerome began with Samuel and Kings in 390. By 393 had also completed Job, the Prophetical books, and Psalms. From 393-396 he finished Ezra, Nehemiah and Chronicles. In 398 he rendered into Latin Proverbs, Ecclesiastes and Canticles. In 405 he completed the Pentateuch, Joshua, Judges, Ruth and Esther. Upon request of his friends he hastily translated Judith and Tobit, together with the rest of Esther. Because the Apocryphal Books were not in the Hebrew Old Testament, he did not wish to undertake translating them into Latin, and give the impression that they were canonical."[15]

The Composite Character of Jerome's Vulgate

Jerome's Vulgate was a composite work. It comprised a translation of

197

the 24 Books of the Hebrew canon, except Psalms. Secondly, it contained the Psalms in Old Latin, revised with the help of Origen's Heaplaric text of the Septuagint. Jerome's Hebrew Psalter never became popular because the churches preferred the Roman Psalter, a slight revision of the Septuagint. Thirdly, the Gospels consisting of the Old Latin text revised with the aid of the original Greek. Fourthly, the rest of the New Testament, 23 books were only superficially revised. The Apocrypha were added but Jerome did not considered them canonical and therefore, not authoritatives.[16]

The Initial Reception of the Vulgate in Fifth Century

Clergy and laity who had become use to the Old Latin Version severely criticized Jerome's new translation, especially the rendering of the Gospels, although hostility was not so vehement against the rest of the New Testament. However, when Jerome's translation of the Old Testament appeared, there broke out a storm of protest because there were differences between his renderings and those of the Old Latin. Jerome defended his translation over against the Old Latin.[17] In 420 died, greatly disillusioned by the reception the major project of his life had received in the churches. For four centuries Jerome's Vulgate struggled with the Old Latin for the adherence and recognition of the church people. It was only in the eighth century that Jerome's Vulgate was finally recognized as the Bible of Western Christianity.[18]

The Corruption of the Vulgate

During the long course of its usage, the text of the Vulgate became corrupt and subjected to revisions a number of times. McKenzie has this to say about the transmission of the Vulgate: "The problems of the Vulgate can be said only to have begun with its production. It was multiplied by careless copying, and the recensions of Cassiodorus (570), Alcuin (800), Theodulf (821), Lanfranc (1089), and Stephen Harding (+1134), failed to establish a reliable text" (p. 917).[19] When Paris became an important theological center, there was established a text, known as the Paris text, which came into general use and was the text which was used in the printing of the Gutenberg Bible at Mainz, 1450-1452.[20] It was frequently reprinted in subsequent editions of which there were 100 before 1500. Two Roman Catholic scholars became dissatisfied with the text at their times, and these were Sanctes Pagnini and Cajetan who undertook to make new Latin versions in the early sixteenth century, at Luther's time. The Paris text was made from current unrevised manuscripts of the time and contained many errors.[21] In 1546 the Council of Trent declared the Vulgate to be the definitive text when matters of doctrine and ethics were to be decided.[22] A decree of The Tridentine Council called for a revision which was not accomplished until Pope Sixtus produced what is known as the Sixtine Edition. This was shortly recalled and was replaced in 1592 by the Clementine Vulgate, differing in some 3,000 instances from the Sixtine. The Clementine has become the standard edition in use in Roman Catholicism for four hundred years. The Rheim-Douay English

Roman Catholic Bible of Great Britain (1585-1610) was an English translation of the Vulgate[23] and was designed to oppose the many English Bible translations between 1525-1610. In the sixteenth century a number of new Latin translations appeared, done by such men as Pagninus, Sebastian Muenster, Castalio, Erasmus and Beza.

Since 1907, the Roman Catholic Church began work on a critical edition of the Latin text at the instigation of Pope Pius X. Today this work is carried on by the Benedictine monastery of St. Jerome. The Clarendon Press has begun to publish the Vulgate New Testament, initiated by John Wordworth and Dean J. White. Bruce claims that "much more information is available nowadays on the original text of Jerome's translation, and thus information is used to good purposes" in the new critical editions of the Benedictines and of the British scholars.

In 1948 the Hierarchy of England and Wales and the Hierarchy of Scotland authorized the publication of Bishop Knox's translation of the Vulgate in the Light of the Hebrew and Greek Originals,[24] thus showing that the original Biblical languages found is the Old Testament (Hebrew and Aramaic) and the Greek New Testament were important. Since the issuing by Pope Pius XII of his encyclical Divino Afflante Spirituto to go to the original sources, two major English Bible translations, namely The Jerusalem Bible[25] and The New American Bible[26] have translated the Old Testament and the New Testament from the original languages and therefore would reject Winrod's contention that only the Vulgate constitutes the real Word of God.

Footnotes

1. Mr. and Mrs. Robert Krause in a letter, titled; "Agree With Winrod, Luther Hated Jews," *Christian News*, January 12, 1998, p. 15, columns 3 and 4.
2. Gordon Winrod, "Luther Was Forerunner of Ant-Christ - Hated Jesus." "Loved the Jews," reproduced in the *Christian News Encyclopedia*, V, p. 3976.
3. As rebuttal of Winrod's false assertion, cf. Ewald Plass, *What Luther Says*, (St. Louis: Concordia Publishing House, 1959), I, pp. 145-206, on "Christ."
4. E. G. Schwiebert, *Luther and His Times* (St. Louis: Concordia Publishing House, 1950), pp. 504-505.
5. Benjamin Kedar, "The Latin Translations," in Marin Jan Mulder, *Mikra. Text, Translation Reading and Interpretation of the Hebrew Bible in Ancient Judaism and Early Christianity* (Philadelphia: Fortress Press, Aasen/Maastrich: Van Gorcum, 1988), p. 299.
6. "The Latin Bible," in F.F. Bruce, *The Book and the Parchments* (Old Tappan: New Jersey, Fleming H. Reveall Company, 1962), p. 202.
7. H. Wheeler Robinson, *The Bible in Its Ancient and English Versions* (Oxford: At the Claredon Press, 1940), p. 83.
8. Bruce, **op. cit.,** p. 202.
9. "Vulgate," John McKenzie, *Dictionary of the Bible* (Milwaukee: Bruce Publishing Company, 1965, p. 936 b.
10. Merrill F. Unger, *Introductory Guide to the Old Testament* (Grand Rapids: Zondervan Publishing House, 1953).
11. Bruce, **op. cit.,** p. 203, p. 169.

12. McKenzie, **op. cit.,** p. 917.
13. "Vulgate," in Hartmann, *Encyclopedia Dictionary of the Bible* (New York: McGraw-Hill, 1963), p. 2555.
14. Bruce, **op. cit.,** pp. 204-205.
15. Unger, **op. cit.,** p. 172.
16. McKenzie, **op. cit.,** p. 917.
17. Bruce, **op. cit.,** p. 206; Robinson, **op. cit.,** p. 115.
18. Bruce, **op. cit.,** p. 206.
19. McKenzie, **op. cit.,** p. 917.
20. **Ibid.,** p. 918.
21. **Ibid.**
22. Philip Schaff, *The Creeds of Christendom* (New York: Harper and Brothers, 1889), II, p. 241.
23. Dr. Challoner and Dr. H. H. Cans, *The New Testament of Our Lord and Savior Jesus Christ*, translated from the Vulgate (New York: The C. Wilderman Company, 1905).
24. Published by Sheed & Ward, Inc., New York, 1956) under the title *The Holy Bible*.
25. *The Jerusalem Bible* (New York, Garden City: Doubleday & Company, 1966), edited by Alexander Jones.
26. The Saint Joseph Edition of *The New American Bible* (New York Catholic Book Publishing Company, 1970). This translation sponsored by the Bishop Committee of the Confraternity of Christian Doctrine of the U.S.

Questions

1. According to Rev. Gordon Winrod, what was Luther's crowning crime? ____
2. Luther used the ____ text.
3. Did Luther have a high respect for the Vulgate? ____
4. Luther's German translation was taken directly from ____.
5. All 27 books of the New Testament were composed in ____.
6. North Africa became famous for such Church Fathers as ____.
7. The success of the Vandals and Mohammadans may be attributed to ____.
8. The Old Testament was put into Latin in ____.
9. Jerome settled in ____ for his translating work.
10. The Apocryphal books are not in ____.
11. When was Jerome's Vulgate recognized as the Bible of Western Christianity? ____
12. What did the Council of Trent declare about the Vulgate? ____

Psalm 46 and Its Significance for the Lutheran Reformation

Christian News, October 26, 1998

Among the 150 poems comprising the Psalter, there are a number of Psalms which have become especially famous. The most famous is Psalm 23, "The Shepherd Psalm." Psalm 2 sets forth two different lifestyles, and may be said to capitalize the theology of the Psalter. Psalm 119, the longest chapter in the Bible, in 176 verses, in a kaleidoscopic way depicts the uniqueness and wonders of God's Torah or Word of God. New Testament writers frequently quote verses from many different Psalms and many of these enunciate the deity of Jesus and likewise portray Christ as the promised Messiah of the Old Testament.[1] Various Psalms authors have comforted Jews and Christians since their publication. A number of Psalms were paraphrased and used in Lutheran worship services.[2]

Martin Luther has paraphrased a number of Psalms and had them used in the singing during worship services.[3]

For the Festival of the Reformation it has been customary to use "A Mighty Fortress Is Our God," and it generally agreed that this famous chorale is a paraphrase of Psalm 46.

Old Testament scholarship believes that Psalm 46 was born out of an event which was active in the minds of those for whom it was composed. Psalm 46 and the following two poems were hymns of triumph, written on the occasion of a great deliverance. Stewart Perowne claimed: "I am inclined to think they celebrate the same event, the sudden and miraculous destruction of Sennacherib under the walls of Jerusalem. That proud king swept the land."[4] City after city in Judah had fallen to the Assyrian king. Only the capital Jerusalem held out. Like a swollen river he had overflowed all the land's channels, and had even caused the waters to its neck. At this crisis, deliverance had come for Yahweh, the Lord of Hosts, was in the midst of Jerusalem. God sent His mighty angel, who in one night killed 185,000 of the Assyrians and completely thwarted the plans of Sennacherib. Such deliverance filled the children of Israel with great joy and was reminiscent of the days of Moses and David, when Yahweh had done great things for His people. Dr. Marion McHull gave the following analysis of Psalm 46, claiming it was one of the most popular of the Psalms[5]:

Verse 1-3 Amidst the most terrifying convulsions of nature, over against which man is helpless, he has no fear, because he has God as a place to go for protection, and in tight places God rushed out to meet him vehemently.

Verses 4-7 A river, the overflow of which makes glad the city of God. God is in the midst of that city. Therefore, it is a city of safety.

Verses 8-9 Come and see his works.

Verses 10-11 Let's go. Let God be exalted.[6]

Time of Origin of "A Mighty Fortress, The Battle Hymn of the Reformation"

Polack claims that the weight of evidence points to the year 1529 as the date of the hymn's origin. The occasion for the composing of "A Mighty Fortress Is Our God" was the convening of the Diet of Spires, which met on April 20, 1529, when the German princes made a formal protest against the revocation of their liberties and thus were given the name of Protestants.

Laukmann in Koch wrote: "Luther with this hymn entered a protest before all German people against any endeavor to obstruct the Gospel."[7]

"A Mighty Fortress Is Our God" has been called "The Battle Hymn of the Reformation" or "the Marseilles of Protestantism." Luther's hymn appeared in Klug's Gesangbuch, Wittenberg, 1529, titled *Der Psalm Deus noster refugium et virtus*, and in *The Lutheran Hymnal* is more than a paraphrase; actually, it is a new composition on the text composed by the Sons of Korah. The tune for this hymn is called "Ein feste Burg," and was Luther's own composition. It appeared in King's *Geistlich Lieder*, Wittenberg, 1529, and also in *Kirchengesaenge*, Nuremberg, 1531.[8]

"Ein feste Burg ist unser Gott" is used in world Lutheranism, found on the continents of North America, Central America and South America, Europe, Asia, Africa and Australia and certain islands of the seas and oceans. No hymn has been translated into so many different languages as this hymn of Luther. "A Mighty Fortress" exists in over 80 different translations. Many great writers have attempted to put Luther's German hymn into English. Thomas Carlyle made a translation beginning with the words "A safe stronghold our God is still." Eraser's magazine, 1831, was the first publication to make available Carlyle's rendering of "ein feste Burg."[9] Another outstanding rendering into English was by F. H. Hedge, beginning: "A mighty fortress is our God, a bulwark," which was included in *Gems in German Verse*, 1852. The translation found in *The Lutheran Hymnal* and in *Lutheran Worship* is a composite translation. This is the translation which is widely used throughout Lutheranism. Averred Polack: "Its value lies chiefly in its reproduction of the sturdy soundness of Luther's Original."[10]

Since October 31, 1517, Luther was constantly in great difficulties. On June 15, 1520, the famous Bull *Exsurge Domine* was drafted and gave Luther sixty days to recant; the Bull went into effect on January 3, 1521. This was followed by Luther publicly burning Rome's Canon Law and the Bull. Many of Europe's outstanding universities declared Luther guilty of many heresies. At the Diet of Worms, because Luther refused to recant what he had written, he was placed under the ban of the empire, which meant that any person killing Luther was performing a meritorious deed.

With the Universities against his theology, the Pope sentencing him to hell, if he did not repent, and the mighty Holy Roman Empire against him, it did not take too much imagination to see how the Wittenberg Reformer could have despaired. At such a time, it is reported that Luther said to Melanchthon: "Come, Philip, let us sing the 46th Psalm," and the two friends lustily would sing:

"Ein feste Burg ist unser Gott."[11] From singing it they would receive courage and continue the battle against the powers that were opposed to Luther and the true Gospel, which was being proclaimed by his followers.

Dr. Benson made this assertion about this hymn: "Such a hymn, with such a tune, spreads quickly, as may well be believed, quickly, as if angels had been the carriers. But they were men that spread Luther's hymn of faith and courage from heart to heart and from lip to lip." Joseph Hunecker, a musical critic, declared: "This hymn thunders at the very gate of heaven in its magnificent affirmation of belief."[12]

Great men of history have rendered great tributes to Martin Luther's mighty chorale, which has also been called "The Marseilles of the Protestantism." Frederick the Great named "A Mighty Fortress Is Our God" "God's Almighty Grenadier March." A very apt description of the power and uniqueness was expressed by the English man of letters, Carlyle, who said as follows: "There is something in it like an Alpine avalanche or the first murmur of earthquake, in the very vastness of which dissonance at higher unity is revealed... It is evident that to this man all Popes, cardinals, emperors, devils, all hosts and nations, were but weak, weak as the forest with all its strong trees might be to the smallest spark of electric fire."[13]

The hymnological authority, Dr. Polack made this assertion about "A Mighty Fortress Is Our God": "The good this hymn has done, the faith it inspired, the hearts it has comforted, the influence it has exerted cannot be measured and will first be revealed to us in eternity, where the saints of God will praise their Lord and Redeemer for many blessings, not the least will be the privilege of having known and sung this hymn."[14]

Charles Haddon Spurgeon summarized this psalm as follows: "Happen what may the Lord's people are happy and secure; this is the doctrine of this psalm, and it might help our memories, be called 'The Song of Holy Confidence' were it not that from the great Reformer's love this soul-stirring hymn it will be best remembered as Luther's Psalm."[15] Martin Luther said: "We sing this Psalm to the praise of God against all fanatical spirits against the gates of hell, against implacable hatred of the devil, and against all the assaults of the world, the flesh and sin."[16]

The following translation reflects the vigor of Luther's version:

A sure stronghold our God is He
A timely shield and weapon;
Our help He'll be, and set us free
From every ill can happen.
And were the world with devils filled.
All eager to devour us.
Our souls to fear shall little yield.
They cannot overpower us.[17]

Footnotes

1. Cf. Paul's *Epistle to the Romans*, W. Graham Scroggie, *Know Your Bible, Vol. II Analytical New Testament* (London: Pickering and Inglis, No Date), p. 171; Cf. also Hebrews, Scroggie, **op. cit.,** p. 265.
2. Scroggie, **op. cit.,** pp. 285-286.
3. Cf. hymns in *The Lutheran Hymnal* on Psalms 12, 67, 128, 130.
4. J. Stewart Perowne, *The Book of Psalms* (Grand Rapids: Zondervan Publishing Company, 1976. Third printing, 1996), I, p. 379.
5. Marion McHull, *Two Thousand Hours in the Psalms* (Chicago: John A. Dicksen Publishing Company, 1934), p. 167.
6. **Ibid.,** p. 166.
7. W. G. Polack, *Handbook to the Lutheran Hymnal* (St. Louis: Concordia Publishing House, 1982), p. 192.
8. **Ibid.,** p. 193.
9. **Ibid.,** p. 193.
10. **Ibid.,** p. 193.
11. **Ibid.,** p. 193; D. A. Fuller, *Psalms - Charles Haddon Spurgeon* (Grand Rapids: Kregel Publications, 1965), p. 218.
12. As cited by Polack, **op. cit.,** p. 193.
13. **Ibid.,** p. 193.
14. **Ibid.,** p. 194.
15. Fuller, **op. cit.,** p. 218.
16. As quoted by Fuller, **op. cit.,** p. 218.
17. As given by S. W. Christophers in *Hymn Writers and Their Hymns*, as cited by Fuller, **op. cit.,** p. 218.

Questions

1. "A Mighty Fortress Is Our God" is a paraphrase of ____.
2. Psalm 46 may have referred to ____.
3. In one night the angel of the Lord killed ____.
4. When were the German Princes called Protestants? ____
5. Which hymn has been translated into the most language? ____
6. Martin Luther's mighty chorale has also been called ____.

Messianic Prophecy

Messianic Prophecy

December 17, 1986

Relative to our discussion of Messianic Prophecy, I published two articles in the *Springfielder*. "Messianic Prophecy and Messeniasm" vol. 37 No. 1 June, 1973. pp. 17-34 and "The Interpretation of Isaiah 7:14" *The Springfielder* vol. 38 No. 2, Sept 1974. pp. 110-118.

You might find them useful to reprint in connection with the debate with St. Louis Exegetical Department. If you do not have them I would be glad to send them to you.

Surburg

Messianic Prophecy and Messianism
(Reprinted from Vol. XXXVII, No. 1, June 1973 *The Springfielder*)

THE TERM "MESSIANIC PROPHECY" is being avoided by most recent Bible dictionaries and articles dealing with the subject of the Messiah in the Old Testament and the term "Messianism" is being substituted.[1] The Old Testament term "Messiah" is the simple reproduction of the Hebrew original *Mashiach,* which means "anointed." The Septuagint and the Greek New Testament both translate the Hebrew *Mashiach* by the term *Christos,* with the same meaning. In the English translations of the Old Testament *Mashiach* is usually rendered by the word "anointed." The English word Messiah is found only twice in the King James Version (Dan. 9:25, 26); "Messias," the Greek form, also appears twice (John 1:41; 4:25). In the Old Testament the reader will find "the anointed of the Lord" (Lamen. 4:20), "His anointed," (Ps. 2:2), "Mine anointed" (1 Sam. 2:35), "the Lord's anointed" (1 and 2 Sam.). These might have been translated as "the Messiah of the Lord," "His Messiah," "the Lord's Messiah." Our New Testament employs *Christos,* rather than the term "anointed." In Old Testament times the term "anointed" was applied to prophets, priests and kings. Even non-Hebrews were so designated because God had chosen them for a particular task, such as Cyrus (Is. 45:1). The high priest of Israel (Lev. 4:3,5,16), the messianic Prince (Daniel 9:25), and the patriarchs (Ps. 105:15) were also called "the anointed."

G. T. Manley claims that "the Messianic hope, which is born very early in the story of the human race, is represented throughout the whole Old Testament as something which had its source in God. The hope is given to man. Hence the messianic references of the Old Testament Scriptures present a very wide field of divine redeeming activity."[2] Messianism as a rule portrays the Messianic idea as a development of the people which has its beginning no earlier than the time of David, and not as a part of God's redemptive activity for man.

The New Testament describes the origin of the coming of the Messiah as something that was foreordained in eternity, long before the universe and the earth were created. The death of Jesus, through whose shed blood men are cleansed, according to Peter "was destined before the foundation of the world but was made manifest at the end of times for your sake" (1 Peter 1:19,20). The fall of man was foreseen by the Triune God and when Eve and Adam fell, God in His mercy announced to our first parents that a person would come from Eve's offspring who would crush the Tempter's head.

Roman Catholic and Protestant writers (representing many different denominations and churches) have written books in the past dealing with Messianic prophecy and all begin their presentations with Genesis 3:15, known as "the First Gospel."[3] The prediction that someday a man from the seed of Eve would bruise and crush the head of the Serpent (used by the Devil) becomes more explicit as the centuries march on. Abraham was told that through his seed (Hebrew, "zerah") the nations of the earth would be blessed. According to the interpretation of Paul in Galatians 3:16 the word "seed" does not refer to many but to one, "and to your offspring," which is Christ. In Genesis 49 Jacob predicted "that out of Judah would come a ruler, unto whom the gathering of the people would be" (v. 10). Balaam, a contemporary of Moses, in his fourth oracle announced the coming of a king, who would be victorious over his enemies (Num. 24:18 ff.). In Deuteronomy 18:15 Moses predicted the coming of a greater prophet than he was, to whom the people would listen. In I Samuel 2:10 Hannah spoke about the Lord's *Mashiach,* the Anointed, at a time when the kingship of David was still decades away. At the end of the Song of Hannah, she exclaimed: "Yahweh will judge the ends of the earth; and exalt the power of his anointed." In 2 Samuel 7:12-17 Yahweh gave David a remarkable prophecy about the future of the latter's dynasty, predicting the coming of David's greater Son, the Messiah (Passages from the Davidic covenant are cited by various New Testament writers as having had Christ in mind).

The writings of Isaiah, Jeremiah, Ezekiel, Daniel, Hosea, Micah, Haggai, Zechariah, Malachi and a number of Psalms were all recognized as containing Messianic prophecies. The stay of Jonah in the great fish's stomach was a type of Christ's burial and resurrection.

Luther in his writings believed that Christ was found in the Old Testament beginning with Genesis 3:15 and ending with prophecies in Malachi 1, 3 and 4. It was the conviction of the authors of the *Formula of Concord* that Law and Gospel were teachings that went back to the garden of Eden. Thus in Article V of the *Formula of Concord* it is written:

> Since the beginning of the world these two proclamations have continually been set forth side by side in the church of God with the proper distinction. The descendants of the holy patriarchs, like the patriarchs constantly reminded themselves not only how man in the beginning was created righteous and holy by God and through deceit of the serpent transgressed God's laws, became a sinner, corrupted himself and all his descendants, and plunged them into death and eternal damnation, but also revived their courage and comforted themselves, with the proclamation of the woman's seed, who would bruise the serpent's head; likewise, of the seed of Abraham, by whom all nations should be blessed; likewise, of David's son, who should restore the kingdom of Israel to be a light to the nations, 'who was wounded for our transgressions and bruised for our iniquities and with his stripes we are healed.'[4]

In this passage the confessors refer to Gen. 3:15; 22:18; 28:14; Ps. 110:1; Is. 40:10; 49:6 and Is. 53:5 and interpret them as Messianic.

I.
THE DECLINE OF MESSIANIC PROPHECY
IN THE TWENTIETH CENTURY

Today an inadequate idea of the scope and emphasis of the Messianic message of the Old Testament is generally prevalent. Predictions about the person, work and kingdom of God's Messiah are of necessity prophetic in character. Since in the estimation of some, prophecy is restricted to the sixteen canonical books of the Major and Minor Prophets, all predictive statements about the coming of the Messiah are limited to these books, thus eliminating many important prophecies in the earlier historical books of the Old Testament. Others suppose that Messianic prophecy is merely a matter of sporadic and emotional utterance, without any intimate relation to the comprehensive literature and vital thought of Israel.

Already in 1926 Professor Edward Mack wrote about the dearth of literature in the twentieth century concerning Messianic prophecy:

> In recent years the conflict of opinion over the literary and historical problems of the Old Testament has diverted attention from the real content of this most important record of ancient religion. Compared with the mass of this controversial and merely propaedeutic literature, the amount of material available for study from modern writers is meager. The inquiring reader finds few text-books covering the field, and in his quest must glean here and there from introduction and interpretative works. Strangely enough, modern Old Testament theologies contain scant purely Messianic discussion.[5]

Wilbur M. Smith, in his introduction to Aaron Kligerman's *Messianic Prophecy in the Old Testament* stated:

> During the nineteenth century, the Christian Church was blessed with a number of great works on the Messianic prophecies of the Old Testament, by such scholars as Delitzsch, Hengstenberg, Kurtz, and Riehm, in Germany; and R. Payne Smith, David Baron, Edersheim, and Saphir, in England, the last three of which were Christian Jews. In the twentieth century, however, at least until the last few years, the literature on Messianic prophecy, outside strictly academic circles, has been very thinephemeral contributions which were but inadequate, disconnected collections of extracts from the writers of the preceding century, with expository comments of no particular importance.[6]

One of the sad developments of twentieth century critical biblical scholarship has been the surrender of the idea that in the Old Testament God the Holy Spirit made the fact of the necessity of Christ as Redeemer known to the saints of the old dispensation. Dr. Charles Augustus Briggs, who was involved in a heresy trial in the Presbyterian Church and forced to resign because of promoting higher criticism, wrote a book on Messianic Prophecy. In the beginning of this volume he stated:

> Messianic Prophecy is the most important of all themes, for it is the ideal of redemption given by the Creator to our race at the beginning of its history, and it ever abides as the goal of humanity until the Divine plan has been accomplished.[7]

Modern Protestant scholarship which followed the leading of Dr. Briggs in the adoption of a critical approach of the Scriptures has now reached a point where Old Testament scholars deny that there are any clear predictions of Messianic prophecy in the Old Testament Scriptures. The Old Testament teachings about the Messiah are not presented as a matter of revelation but as a result of insights Jewish writers had throughout the preChristian centuries which led especially to beliefs about a personal Messiah in the two centuries before the birth of Christ. The brief article by the former Professor Edwin Lewis of Drew Theological Seminary in *Harper's Bible Dictionary* treating of the Messiah portrays this view. Genesis 12:3 which states that in Abraham's seed all the nations of the world should be blessed, interpreted by Paul as a prediction of the fact that through Christ men would be justified by faith and thus incorporated into the body of Christ (Galatians 3:8), is understood merely as setting forth an expectancy of the coming of the Kingdom of God. Thus Professor Lewis described the beginning and development of what is commonly known as "Messianism":

The Old Testament is the story of the growth of this expectancy, and of changes in the way it was understood. One form limited the promise to the physical line of Abraham: 'the chosen people' were 'the sons of Abraham.' With the emergence of Saul as the first Hebrew king, the national and political conception was quickened (I Sam. 8:1-12:55). The brilliance of the reign of David, Saul's successor, and his own personal character, set the pattern of Messianic thought for later centuries (II Sam. 7:1-29). The conviction grew that the Kingdom of God, in which the Abrahamic covenant would be consummated, would be a kingdom like that of David, and its ruler would be 'a son of David,' a king like David, only greater (Is. 9:2-7; Jer. 23:5-8; Ezek. 34:20-31; cf. Ps. 89:3, 19-37, 132:1-18).[8]

After the destruction of the northern kingdom in 722 B.C. the southern kingdom of Judah was left alone to carry on the Davidic tradition and hope. The thought grew that if the Abrahamic promise was to be realized, some person would need to deliver God's people from their enemies. So Lewis states great importance was attached to the word "save" in the Old Testament, especially as used in the Psalms (28:9; 69:35; 72:13f; 106:47), and in Isaiah (25:9; 33:22; 35:4; 37:20; 63:1-5; cf. Jer. 42:11). The Israelites looked for a deliverer from their "enemies, threatening worldly powers. Sometimes God is represented as effecting this deliverance; sometimes it will be God's anointed, a veritable Messiah" (Ps. 72).[9]

According to Lewis with the prophets there grew up the idea that God is not merely the God of Israel but of all peoples. Jahweh's concern was for all people. After the destruction of Jerusalem in 587 B.C. and the virtual destruction of the Jewish state, the idea arose, sponsored already by Jeremiah, that the Abrahamic hope would be fulfilled in a religious community and not in a political organization. God was going to establish a brotherhood in which the "new covenant" would be written on the hearts of every man (Jer. 31:31-34). This idea was further fostered by the Exile in Babylonia under priestly influence. During the exilic period two Messianic concepts developed side by side. One looked for a restoration of the Israelite nation, which found its chief mark in the observance of the "Holiness Code" (Lev. 17-28), a product allegedly of the Exile. In this conception there was practically no place for a personal Messiah; the closest approach to the idea of a Messiah was the "prince" in Ezek. (44:3; 45:7; 46:2-18; 48:21f). Ezra and Nehemiah tried to promote the thought of a Messianic ritualistic people of God, who adhered and were loyal to the "Law."[10]

According to Lewis during the Exile a more spiritual concept was also fostered; a number of the psalms emphasize the necessity of spiritual deliverance. The prophet known by critics as the Second Isaiah gave his fellow religionists glowing descriptions of a return from captivity but also wrote four famous servant passages (42:1-4; 49:1-6; 50:4-9; 52:13-53:12). In these "the Servant" is described as a sufferer. Modern critical scholarship does not identify the Suffering Servant with Jesus Christ, but with a "purified Israel" or with the idea of "a remnant of Israel." This Israel will be a community not after the flesh but after the spirit, and would extend the benefits of the true Israel to all mankind through his own (the servant) sacrificial and self-forgetting love (53:10-12).[11]

The priestly and particularistic conception prevailed following the era of Ezra-Nehemiah. Yet there were some who held to the spiritual conception. In the Deutero-Zechariah (chs. 9-14) there is a marked emphasis on a national restoration, with "Jerusalem conceived as the center of the world." Zech. 9:9 states that "thy king cometh unto thee" but in the text verse the reader is told that He will create universal peace and "that his dominion shall be from sea to sea." In the second century B.C. (190 B.C.) Daniel teaches that one called "a Son of Man" will be granted "an everlasting kingdom," one embracing "all peoples and languages" (7:13,14).[12]

In the apocalyptic literature of the two preChristian centuries the Messiah is often associated with "the Day of the Lord." Sometimes the apocalyptic writers depict the Messiah as leading the armies of heaven; other times he is portrayed as Judge; and still other writers depict the Messiah as the ruler of a kingdom that follows resurrection and judgment. In the apocalyptical writings the Messiah is always depicted, so Lewis contends, as the instrument of God for the deliverance of His people. It is God who provides the Deliverer, the Messiah, who achieves deliverance. New Testament critical scholars claim that such ideas were current in the first century A.D. The Zealots were convinced that the Messiah would be a political deliverer who would achieve national deliverance by force. The Pharisees, on the other hand, held that the Messiah would appear in God's appointed time and would be a "Son of David," one who would fulfill the Law, which they revered. The Apocalyptic form of the Messianic hope was very prevalent and according to Lewis "strongly influenced early Christianity."[13]

Lewis stated about Jesus' belief of being the Messiah that the Nazarene appropriated this concept to Himself, although Jesus did not know in what sense He was the Messiah. His Messiahship was revealed to Him at the Baptism. In the subsequent Temptation in the wilderness He wrestled with this matter as to what constituted His Messiahship.[14]

Professor Otto A. Piper of Princeton Theological Seminary in an article dealing with the developments in the field of Biblical scholarship in the twentieth century made the following assertion:

> In the field of exegesis the critical method has led to one-sided interest in textual, philological, and historical problems. Exposition has confined itself primarily to the Prophets and Psalms; in the works of Duhm, Steuernagel, G. A. Smith, Eissfeldt, Hans Schmidt and Hoelscher the prophets have been considered as the representatives of a superior morality, while the element of messianic prediction has been, as a rule, disregarded. The traditional view was upheld by Keil, Delitzsch, and Riehm, and has been revived by Hebert, T. H. Robinson

and W. Fischer.[15]

According to Professor Dentan of Yale Divinity School the concept of the Messiah was derived ultimately from ancient Near Eastern ideas of kingship, which, he claims, were more or less naturalized in Israel during the Davidic dynasty. "To the world of the ancient Near East, the king was a divine or semi-divine figure from whom radiated powers which made for prosperity in peace and victory in war. Since these grandiose ideas of kingship were constantly being disappointed by the actual kings of David's line, it was only natural that they should be transferred to an ideal king of the future and by the time the monarchy came to an end in 586 B.C. this figure had probably already become a fixed feature of Hebrew eschatological expectation."[16]

Thus according to Dentan, when it was no longer feasible for the Jews in the exilic and postexilic periods to dream of political action, they compensated for their disappointment by centering their hope completely on the idea that God would intervene in the affairs of men and set up His eternal rule. It was ideas like these which set the background for a tremendous growth of Messianic hopes, which took place just before the beginning of the Christian era.[17] *The Oxford Dictionary of the Christian Church* in its article on the "Messiah" knows of no Messianic hope prior to the Davidic days. It was especially in the later monarchy when the political fortunes of Judaism were on the wane, that prophets like Isaiah and Jeremiah bolstered the faith of their coreligionists by depicting for them the coming of a future king of the house of David who would be glorious, wise and who would provide security for his people.[18]

E. F. Scott, a liberal New Testament scholar, stated in his book, *The Kingdom and the Messiah* that it always had been an article of Christian belief that the Old Testament Scriptures were inspired throughout by the hope of the Messiah. This belief, which he claims grew naturally out of the apologetics of the early Christian Church passed over into the ordinary theology of the Church.[19] "The testimony of Jesus is the spirit of prophecy." Scott and many Old and New Testament critical scholars claim that while Christ is the fulfillment of the religion of Israel and although the student can trace an unconscious anticipation in its earlier history, this larger witness which the Old Testament bears to Jesus Christ must not be confused with a specific hope in a Messiah. Thus he wrote: "When we examine the Old Testament according to strict historical methods, we are compelled to assign an altogether secondary place to the Messianic idea. It originated with the prophets, but only assumed its characteristic form in later Judaism." His position was stated by him one page later in the words:

When we thus exclude from Messianic prophecy all that is fanciful and extraneous, we find that it recedes within narrow limits. So far from constituting the chief theme of Scripture, it holds a subordinate and almost incidental place. The dominant conception of the Old Testament writers is that of the kingdom which is to be established in the latter days. In their thought of this kingdom they were influenced by the existing historical conditions; and associated the restored Israel with the house of David.[20]

According to Dr. Scott the Book of Psalms was the great repository of Messianic texts, a position that was countenanced by current Jewish theology. When Jesus used psalm passages to support his Messiahship he was simply falling back upon "the scribal interpretation." The interpretation which found the Messiah foretold in various psalms like the 2, 16, 22, 45, 72, 110 was erroneous because it amounted to eisegesis, when a later theory was read into them, giving them a meaning that formed no part of the original intention of the author.

Critical scholarship has propounded still other divergent views about the source of the Messianic hope in Israel. According to the school of Wellhausen (P. Volz, K. Marti, W. Nowack, A. von Gall) Israelite Messianism is a postexilic phenomenon, which was influenced by teachings found in the Persian religion.[21] In Zoroastrianism there is the doctrine of world renewal, the hope of a redeemer who would achieve salvation for the people by the purification of the world, the annihilation of evil, and the resurrection of the dead. This hope of a Savior arose in the postexilic period of Judaism. Sigmund Mowinckel conceives of the Messiah as an eschatological figure, which according to this Scandinavian scholar was unrelated to the hope that men in Israel associated with the kingship. Mowinckel proposed that the Messianic hope developed only after the fall of the Davidic dynasty in 587 B.C.

By contrast two outstanding form-critical scholars, H. Gunkel and H. Gressmann, believe that Israelite Messianism is older than the time of Amos (ca. 750 B.C.). Like Mowinckel they also endeavored to find the source for the Messianic concept outside of Israel. They found it in Urzeit, the ancient Oriental myths about a primeval king, whose return was expected at the time of the end of the world. They asserted that "Endzeit ist Urzeit." The texts given in *Ancient Near Eastern Texts* (pp. 441-452) do not give evidence that the Mesopotamians were expecting an eschatological Savior, as alleged by Gunkel and Gressmann. The texts in ANET are not predictions or prophecies about a future prince who will bring salvation, but to give the evaluation of J. T. Nelis are "either predictions of the successes of the reigning prince, or warnings addressed to him, or good wishes expressed in prophetic style, to a new king that he may be victorious over his enemies and may further the peace and welfare of his people, expressions, therefore, of the hope that conditions will be better under the new king than they were under the other, or, on the other hand, these texts are mere *vaticinia post eventum,* pseudo-predictions of events which have already taken place and thus likewise concerned with historical kings."[22]

Another school of thought looks for the root of Messianism in ancient Oriental ideology of the king. G. Widengren, I. Engnell, A. R. Johnson, and others regard the king as the son or incarnation of a god, or even identified him with a god, and each year in the ritual the king's son was subjected to a rite of humiliation and suffering, which was supposed to be a dramatic representation of the conflict between deity and the forces of chaos and signified the renewal of the vital energy of the universe. The idea of divine sonship is said to have been adopted by Israel writers in their concept o.f the Royal Psalms (Ps. 2:7; 10:3) also by Isaiah in his description of the king's son in 9:5: "Unto us a son is given and the government shall be upon his shoulder: and he shall be called Wonderful, Counsellor, the mighty God, the everlasting Father, the Prince of peace." The humiliation of the king is supposed to have been taken over by the Ebed Yahweh Oracles in Isaiah, while the idea of the king as an actualization of the primeval king, which is identified with the *Urmensch,* was revived in Israel in the figure of the Son of Man (so Bentzen). Some scholars have questioned the correctness of Widengren's portrayal of the king ideology. That in Israel the belief in the recurring periodic renewal of the energies of the earth was held is pure speculation, there is no evidence whatever for this assumption.

E. Sellin, followed by W. Eichrodt, W. Caspari, L. Blecker and L. Durr, begins Israel's Messianic hopes with the Mt. Sinai revelation. This group believes that when Yahweh made a covenant with His people, the Hebrews, He thereby gave assurance that in the future He would intervene time and again in the fortunes of His people. Since Yahweh was indivisible in His nature, He would accomplish this intervention through a great personage, called the Messiah. In the image of this Messiah this group of German scholars saw a projection of the concept of the *Urmensch* into the eschatological future, traces of which are according to Sellin, found in such passages as Dan. 7:13f.; Job 15:7; Is. 9:5; Micah 5:1; Num. 24:17.[23]

In the centuries before the birth of Christ there is evident in the pseudepigrapha the belief in the coming of the Messiah. The Qumran writings clearly indicate the belief in the coming of a Messiah; some interpreters of the Qumranic literature believe that two different Messiahs were expected by the Qumranite sect, a kingly one, and a priestly one.[24] From the Gospels it becomes very apparent that the Jews were looking forward to the Messiah. From Matthew 2:6 it is clear that the scribes consulted by Herod believed that Bethlehem was to be the Messiah's birthplace as foretold by Micah 5:2. John the Baptist was no doubt referring to the Messiah when the former announced to the Pharisees and Sadducees: "I baptize you with water for repentance, but he who is coming after me is mightier than I, whose sandals I am not worthy to carry, he will baptize you with the Holy Spirit and with fire." The angel Gabriel told Mary about the Holy One to be conceived in her womb: "He will be great, and will be called the Son of the Most High; and the Lord God will give to him the throne of his father David, and he will reign over the house of David forever and of his kingdom there shall be no end." Here the archangel Gabriel is referring to the promise given to David in the Davidic covenant, 2 Samuel 7:12-17.

Zacharias in the Benedictus asserted that "the Lord God of Israel has raised up a horn of salvation in the house of his servant David as he spoke by the mouth of his holy prophets from of old, that we should be saved from our enemies . . . to perform the mercy promised to our fathers and to remember his holy oath which he swore to our father Abraham"

(Luke 1:69-73). Here Zacharias is referring to Genesis 12:3: "In thy seed shall all the nations of the earth be blessed," and not as the RSV and other modern translations have it: "In thy seed shall all the nations bless themselves." In Luke 3:15 the reader is apprised of the fact that some people believed that John the Baptist was the Messiah. When Andrew found his brother Peter he said to him "We have found the Messiah" (which means Christ). Philip finds Nathaniel and says to him: "We have found him of whom Moses in the law and also the prophets wrote, Jesus of Nazareth, the son of Joseph." In John 4 the Samaritan woman is reported as saying: "I know that the Messiah is coming (he who is called the Christ), when he comes he will show us all things." The Samaritans it should be remembered only accepted the Torah of Moses as their Scriptures, and yet on the basis of the Pentateuch these people found the Messiah foretold. After having accepted the Messiah, the Samaritan woman returned to her village and said to the people: "Come see a man who told me all that I ever did. Can this be the Christ?" (4:29)

II.
THE NEW TESTAMENT VIEW OF MESSIANIC PROPHECY

The conviction held by the Early Christian Church, the Medieval Church, the Church of the Reformation and post-Reformation periods that numerous prophecies in the Old Testament Scriptures regarding the birth, coming, nature, ministry of Jesus of Nazareth were based upon the clear light thrown upon ancient prophecies by the New Testament. It will be instructive to examine the attitude of the preachers and writers of the New Testament toward the Messianic passages in the New Testament. Thus Professor Mack contended about this interpretative procedure: "The Christian student with his confidence in the authority and accuracy of the New Testament, has the right to begin his argument with it; and more than this, it is his bounden duty to do so."[25] The New Testament provides a good guide for a study of Old Testament prophecy for the following reasons: 1. The New Testament writings come out of an epoch that was close to O. T. days, by men, all of whom with the possible exception of Luke were Jews. As members of the Jewish faith they should have possessed a good knowledge of its traditions and an understanding of the hopes and aspirations of their nation. 2. Like a telescope, the New Testament brings the promises of the Old Testament closer to us, it makes their outline clear and real. 3. The New Testament claims to be the true interpretation of the Old Testament. When the Samaritan woman shifted the topic of conversation about the nature of Old Testament hope to the subject of the Messiah, Jesus said to her: "I that speak to thee am He." When John the Baptist asked whether Jesus was the promised Messiah of the Old Testament, Jesus sent back the answer: "I am He who is fulfilling the Messianic promises of Isaiah" (Matt. 11). Paul, in describing the problem of the Jew in his day, claimed that in Jesus "the veil is done away" (II Cor. 3).

Christ and His apostles had a great reverence and respect for the Old Testament Scriptures. To them the twenty-four books of the Hebrew Old

Testament canon were "The Scriptures."

1. The Method of John the Apostle

In Revelation 19:10 we read: "the witness of Jesus is the spirit of prophecy." The witness to Jesus by angels, apostles, and martyrs found in Revelation is the same witness as the witness of prophecy. In comment on this verse Dr. Lenski wrote: "Some restrict this ('The prophecy') to the prophecy contained in these visions of Revelation, but the substance is that of all Scriptures."[25]

2. The Method of Philip the Evangelist

No passage of the New Testament is more helpful in showing us how New Testament Christians interpreted the Old Testament than the episode involving Philip, who was sent by the Holy Spirit to convert the Prime Minister of Candace, Queen of Abyssinia. He had attended one of the great festivals of Judaism in Jerusalem. The festival visitor had procured a copy of the Prophets, which he was reading on his way home to Africa. Philip the Evangelist, led by the Spirit of God, came near to Gaza, as he was reading the 53rd chapter of Isaiah. When Philip had joined him and heard him reading the Isaian passage, asked the African Prime Minister if he understood what he read? They then read the chapter together; coming to verses 7 and 8, Philip was asked: "Of whom speaketh the prophet this?" These were the verses of the Great Servant passage that spoke of the atoning death of Jesus Christ. Luke reports Philip's answer as follows: "Starting from this very passage, he told him the Good News about Jesus" (v. 35). If this was not truly speaking of the suffering, death, resurrection of God's Messiah, then Philip was guilty of reading a meaning into the chapter it was not intended to have.

3. The Method of Paul

Paul had a great influence on the New Testament Scriptures. Fifteen out of twenty-seven writings shows his influence. This includes the two books by his friend and companion, Luke the physician. Paul made liberal use of the Old Testament. His epistles are saturated with the Old Testament, with its doctrines, its ideals, and its phrases. As one Old Testament scholar has written: "His letters might be called interpretations of the Old Testament in terms of Jesus Christ, even though he wrote chiefly to Gentiles." Frequently Paul appealed to Messianic prophecies in order to present Christ as the Savior of mankind. He believed in the inspiration of the entire Old Testament. "For all Scripture is inspired by God and is useful for teaching the truth, rebuking error, correcting faults, and giving instruction for right living, so that the man who serves God may be fully qualified and equipped to do every kind of good work" *(Good News for Modern Man)*. In describing the religious training Timothy had received from Lois and Eunice, Paul wrote to Timothy: "For you know who your teachers were, and you know that ever since you were a child you have known the Holy Scriptures, which are able to give you the wisdom that leads to salvation through faith in Christ Jesus." These words clearly enunciate the truth that the Old Testament Scriptures enabled the reader to come to faith in Christ Jesus. If there are no direct predictions about the Messiah, how could the Old Testament Scriptures then lead to salvation in Christ Jesus?

In many places Paul, who claimed to be an inspired apostle of Jesus Christ, appealed to its prophecies as fulfilled in Jesus Christ. Only a few of the many passages will be cited here to support the Christological hermeneutics of the Old Testament by Paul. In Acts 13:13-41 Luke has given an epitome of a Pauline sermon at Antioch in Pisidia. To the people in the Pisidian synagogue, Paul said: "We declare unto you good tidings, how that the promise which was made unto the fathers, God hath fulfilled the same unto us their children, in that he hath raised up Jesus again, as it also is written in the second psalm." In this sermon Paul quoted both from the Second and Sixteenth Psalms and interpreted them as containing prophecies about Christ. Yet today modern scholarship will not recognize Paul's interpretations.

Toward the end of his Caesarean captivity, Paul appeared before Festus and King Agrippa. The latter had been raised as a Jew and was trained in the Scriptures. Since Agrippa was considered learned in the Law, Paul could appeal on common ground. And these are the remarkable words of Paul: "Having therefore obtained help of God, I continue unto this day, witnessing both to small and great, and saying none other things than those which the prophets and Moses did say should come : that Christ should suffer, and that He should be the first that should rise from the dead, and should show light unto the people, and to the Gentiles" (Acts 26:22-23).

Another good illustration of Paul's interpretative methodology of finding Christ foretold in the Old Testament Scriptures, occurred when he came to Thessalonica on his second missionary journey. In that city, in the synagogue, Paul preached. "And Paul, as his custom was, went in unto them, and three sabbath days reasoned with them out of the scriptures, opening and alleging that Christ must needs have suffered, and risen again from the dead, and that (said he) this Jesus, whom I preached unto you, is Christ" (Acts 17:2-3).

Paul began his great letter to the Romans in this way: "From Paul, a servant of Christ Jesus, and an apostle chosen and called by God to preach his Good News. The Good News was promised long ago by God through his prophets, and written in the Holy Scriptures. It is about his Son, our Lord Jesus Christ: as to his humanity, he was born a descendant of David; as to his divine holiness, he was shown with great power to be the Son of God, by being raised from the dead," (vv. 1-4). These words clearly testify to Paul's belief that Christ's divinity and humanity were foretold in the Holy Scriptures (The Old Testament). The plan of salvation as set forth in the euangellion was foreknown because it had been revealed to the writers of the Old Testament books.

In the last chapter of Acts Paul is portrayed as being in Rome, where the Jews were allowed to visit Paul. One day a confrontation took place between Paul and a large number of Jews. Luke reports: "From morning till night he explained (to them) and gave them his message about the kingdom of God. He tried to convince them about Jesus by quoting from the Law of Moses and the writings of the prophets" (v. 23).

In setting forth the essentials of the Gospel that Paul had proclaimed to the Corinthians, he asserted in chapter 15 of his first letter: "I passed on to you what I received, which is of the greatest importance: that Christ died for our sins, as is written in the Scriptures; and that he was buried and raised to life on the third day, as is written in the Scriptures." (vv. 3-4)

4. The Method of Peter

In the early chapters of Acts, Luke has provided us with samples of the preaching of Peter, primus among the apostles. Peter's sermon at Pentecost, the first Gospel sermon, was based entirely on prophecies of the Old Testament: first, the outpouring of the Spirit, as foretold by Joel; then the resurrection of Christ, from the sixteenth Psalm; and finally His exaltation to power at the right hand of God, as prophesied by David in Psalm 110.

In the second sermon of Peter, Acts 3, the apostle made his appeal in a similar way, calling upon his hearers to accept Jesus as the promised Christ of the Old Testament: "Those things which God before had showed by the mouth of all his prophets, that the Christ should suffer, He hath so fulfilled." (v. 18) When Peter and John were brought before the Sanhedrin for healing the lame man, Peter full of the Holy Spirit, said to the leaders and elders: "Then you should all know, that all the people of Israel should know, that this man stands here before you completely well by the power of the name of Jesus Christ of Nazareth-whom you crucified and God raised from death. Jesus is the one of whom the scripture says, 'The stone that you builders despised, turned out to be the most important stone.' Salvation is to be found through him alone for there is no one else in all the world whose name God has given to men, by whom we can be saved." (Acts 4:10-12)

When Peter and John returned from their examination before the Jewish leaders, the group of believers prayed in unison: "Master and Creator of heaven and earth, and sea, and all that is in them. By the means of the Holy Spirit you spoke through our ancestor David, your servant, when he said:

'Why were the Gentiles furious,
'Why did the peoples plot in vain?
The kings of the earth prepared themselves,
Against the Lord and his Messiah'" (Acts 3:24-26).

In his Pentecost sermon to the Gentiles in the house of the centurion Cornelius, Peter said: "And he commanded us to preach the Gospel to the people, and to testify that he is the one whom God has appointed Judge of the living and the dead. All the prophets spoke about him, saying that everyone who believes in him will have his sins forgiven through the power of his name" (Acts 10:42-43). In his first letter to the congregations of Asia Minor in writing about the wonderful salvation which had been made available to the believers through the death and resurrection of Jesus Christ, Peter states: "It was about this salvation that the prophets made careful search and investigation; they were the ones who prophesied the blessings that God would give you. They tried to find out when the time would be and how it would come; for the Spirit of Christ in them pointed to this time in predicting the sufferings that Christ would have to endure, and the glory that should follow. God revealed to these prophets that their work was not for their own benefit, but for yours, as they spoke about the truths, which you have now heard. The messengers of the Good News, who spoke by the power of the Holy Spirit sent from heaven, told you these truths," (ch. 1:10-12).

5. The Appeal of Christ to Prophecy

The foregoing array of New Testament passages by various New Testament individuals should have been impressive to support the contention that the coming of the *Mashiah,* the Christos, was foretold by God centuries before God's Anointed One's appearance. There is still a more impressive type of evidence, and that is the use of prophecy by Christ Himself. "The use of prophecy by Christ Himself is the most remarkable part of the New Testament claim to be the fulfillment of the Old. Christ was continually quoting Old Testament promises as fulfilled in Himself."[25b]

To the leaders of the Jewish people Jesus said one day in controversy with them: "You study the Scriptures because you think that in them you will find eternal life. And they themselves speak about me" (John 5:39). How could Jesus make such a statement if his hearers did not believe that the Old Testament Scriptures contained specific statements about the Messiah? And Jesus claimed to fulfill the prophecies about the coming of the Messiah.

When Jesus visited Nazareth after his baptism, he attended the synagogue as was his custom. He read to them from the scroll of the prophets; he read the passage from the beginning of Isaiah 61. After reading the lesson from the Haphtorah, with the eyes of the multitudes fixed on him, he spoke these momentous words: "This day is the Scripture fulfilled in your ears." His hearers understood full well what Jesus was claiming by this statement, namely, that He was the *Mashiach,* the Anointed One, the Servant of the Lord, who was the most imposing figure of the Old Testament prophecy.

Again when John the Baptist was in prison toward the end of his life, he sent two disciples to Jesus with the question: "Art thou He that should come, or must we wait for another?" The answer of Jesus was to quote words that spoke of the Christ in chapters 35 and 61 of Isaiah.

Especially important are the words of Jesus, as reported by Luke in chapter 24 of his Gospel, where on Easter afternoon Jesus opened the eyes of Cleophas and his friend to see the Lord but also gave them proof of His Messiahship from the Old Testament when he said:

"O foolish ones, and slow of heart to believe all that the prophets have spoken; ought not the Messiah to have suffered these things, and to enter into His glory? And beginning with Moses, and all the prophets, he interpreted unto them in all the Scriptures, *the things concerning Himself*' (v. 26). Later that evening, coming to the Eleven in Jerusalem, He reminded them how often He had showed in the Old Testament the very things which had happened to Him: "These are the words which I spoke unto you while I was yet with you, that all things must be fulfilled, which were written in the law of Moses, and in the Prophets and in the Psalms concerning Me. Then He opened their understanding, that they might understand the Scriptures" (Luke 24:44).

III.
MESSIANIC PROPHECY IN LUTHERANISM
IN THE TWENTIETH CENTURY

In 1935 The Parish and Church School Board of The Lutheran Church in America published *The Old Testament-A Study,* by Professor Herbert C. Alleman. In discussing the Old Testament, Alleman quoted Kirkpatrick to the effect: "Prophecy was no premature unrolling of the future .... But from first to last it pointed forward to a great divine purpose slowly being evolved in the course of the ages, to 'some far off divine event,' towards which the history of Israel and the history of the world were moving."[26] He claims that no reader can come to the Old Testament without feeling that the history is not complete. In the course of time the Hebrews came to believe in a personal Messiah. It was only through a personal Messiah that God's reign on earth could be realized. "As a child he was to be the gift of God 'Immanuel-God With Us' (Is. 7:14); of the house of David (Is. 11:1); one upon whom would rest the Spirit of Jehovah (Is. 11:2-5); a prince out of Bethlehem (Mi. 5:2); one to whom the nations would come to learn righteousness."[27] Alleman seems to begin his discussion of the Messiah with the passages in Isaiah but says not one word about any promises prior to the eighth century B.C. He claims that the classic words of Isaiah have become the description of the mission of Jesus. Nowhere does he, however, state that the Old Testament writers foretold the Messianic days by direct prophecies.

In 1948 *Old Testament Commentary* Professor Alleman and Professor T. W. Kretzschmann wrote the article on "The Messiah in the Old Testament Scriptures."[28] This is much more complete and satisfactory than the brief discussion in the book for Sunday School and Bible Class teachers. Regarding Gen. 3:15, the protevangelium, these two scholars wrote: "The word Messiah does not occur here, but the idea is clearly implied. This verse has been known in Christian theology as the *protevangel,* or the first announcement of the Gospel of redemption. Protestant theology generally has taken the passage as a promise to mankind of victory over Satan in the headship of Jesus. The older theology may have erred in the particularism of its conception of prophecy, but it did not err in the general conception of victory over sin which is here announced. The New Testament writers took the verse as an adumbration victory (cf. Rom. 16:20; Heb. 2:14; I John 3:8). The theme of our Bible is salvation, and it is one of the high touches of its art that theme should be announced in the story of our first catastrophe."[29]

These same professors close their article on the Messiah by showing from John 5:45-46; Luke 24:27; Luke 24:44 that Jesus claimed that many prophecies of the three major divisions of the Old Testament Scriptures were fulfilled in His life, especially His death and resurrection. Despite the clear assertions of Jesus Christ, Alleman and Kretzschmann state: "It is not to be understood that the Old Testament forecasts of God's purpose of salvation were always literal predictions." We agree with these two scholars that "Jesus Christ is the key to the Old Testament. It is by His testimony that we know that He is the Messiah."[30]

Whether this is still the position of Old Testament scholars at LCA seminaries is questionable. In 1937, Augsburg Publishing House published a volume by Byron C. Nelson entitled, *On the Way to Emmaus,* in which Nelson sets forth the divine-human Christ as revealed in the prophecies of the Old Testament.[31] The former position of this large Lutheran body, now a part of TALC, may also be seen in R. A. Ofstedal's *God's Plan in Prophecy.*[32] It would seem that literature appearing between 1960 and 1970 by members of TALC shows a shift toward rejecting direct Messianic prophecy in the Old Testament. One of the most startling statements read by the essayist is that of Professor Quanbeck, who in an essay read at a Lutheran professors' conference in 1962 asserted:

The primary manifestation of the Word of God is Jesus Christ but the Word comes to man also in the Scriptures and in the Church's proclamation. To see Christ as the content of God's address is to find the perspective for interpreting the entire Bible. This perspective is not to be arbitrarily imposed upon in a capricious application of allegorical methods. It is rather the recognition that the Old Testament, for example, contains a number of theologies, but that from these theologies our Lord selects one and gives it his sanction. It is entirely possible to derive from the Old Testament a theology of achievement which understands religion as character development. It is also possible to insist that the Servant passages of Isaiah refer to the nation and not to an individual. But Jesus interprets the Old Testament as a message of God's gift of life and the Servant songs as finding their fulfillment in his own person and career. Nothing in the Old Testament itself compels a scholar to come to Christological interpretation of these passages, as the flourishing of Jewish Biblical interpretation today shows. He who accepts Jesus as Messiah, however, accedes to the tremendous claims that Jesus made for himself, and these involve a comprehensive interpretation of the Old Testament.[33]

If all these assertions are permissable from the standpoint of Lutheran confessional theology, what happens to Christ's own declaration: "I am the way, the truth, and the life, no man cometh unto the father but by me." Why did Jesus denounce the leadership of the Jewish people in the great woe Chapter, Matthew 23? Was Peter mistaken when before the Jewish leaders he claimed: "Neither is there salvation in any other or any other name given under heaven among men by which we can be saved?" (Acts 4:12) Surely, Peter was not presenting the Jewish leaders with a group of options.

In 1969 Augsburg Publishing House made available in an English translation Claus Westermann's *Das Alte Testament und Jesus Christus.*[34] In the opening chapter of this small booklet Westermann totally rejects the methodology of Luther, the Lutheran Confessions and of many older Lutheran exegetes. Finding in isolated texts such as Genesis 3:15, Isaiah 7:14, predictions of the Virgin Birth and birth of the Messiah is wrong, for to quote Westermann "such interpretation based on comparison of isolated texts brings a strong factor of unreliability into the attempt to determine the Old Testament's relation to the message about Christ." On page 34 of the English translation Westermann states that during the history of Christianity the messianic prophecies have come to be considered by far the most specific and least ambiguous promises of Christ. However, asserts the German scholar, "when one examines the texts of these promises line for line, this is certainly not the case, for the divine activity mediated by this Savior-King was not deliverance, but blessings."[35]

He claims that the servant of God passages are much closer to Jesus of Nazareth than are the messianic prophecies.

In his essay, "Prophecy and Fulfillment," Rudolf Bultmann discusses the manner in which the New Testament writers understood the Old Testament. Thus he wrote:

> The primitive community lived in the conviction that the prophecies of the Old Testament had been fulfilled in its time, that is, the appearance of Jesus Christ, in his death and Resurrection, and in the same way in its own existence and destinies; or, insofar as the fulfillment still remains outstanding, that they will shortly be fulfilled in the *parousia* of Christ.[36]

"According to the conception which prevails in the New Testament and in the tradition of the church, prophecy is understood to be the forecasting of a future happening, and fulfillment is the occurrence of what has been forecast. And if prophecy is authorized by God, it is to a certain extent a promise of God's, which finds its fulfillment in what happened later."[36a]

Bultmann claims that two truths are self-evident from the New Testament 1) that the future of which the Old Testament speaks in its prophecies of the *eschaton* is the Messianic age, which has been fulfilled in the Christian community; 2) The Old Testament does not contain prophecy in those passages that are prophecies in the common sense but the Old Testament is a book of prophecy as a whole, for as St. Paul says: "For whatever was written in former times was written for our instruction" (Rom. 15:40).

Bultmann then proceeds to show that the New Testament writers were guilty of faulty hermeneutics and comes to the conclusion that the arguments of the New Testament writers are erroneous when they found happenings in Jesus' life foretold in the Old Testament Scriptures. Bultmann, a nominal Lutheran, has therefore given us another example of the rejection of the belief of the Messiah in the Old Testament. However, in the final analysis it therefore comes down to this: does a Christian theologian accept the interpretations of God's Word or does he place human wisdom and human knowledge over that of God?

A Lutheran, Mowinckel, belonging to the Uppsala School of Sweden, has written a book that dealt with Messianic prophecy and that since

1958 has become available under the title, *He that Cometh.*[37] In many respects this is a very scholarly book. However, it is a good example of what is meant by the advocacy of Messianism. According to Mowinckel the Christian Church, following the lead of the New Testament, has wrongly interpreted many Old Testament passages as treating of the Messiah and the Messianic kingdom. The use of the historical-critical method makes impossible interpreting Genesis 3:15; 12:3; 49:10 and many other passages as predictive of the Messiah.[38] For S. Mowinckel the Messiah was a purely eschatological figure, quite unconnected with the hopes which were cherished about the historical kings of Judah and he was of the opinion that the true Messiah received its genuine form only after the fall of the Davidic dynasty.

The Lutheran Claus Westermann, a German Old Testament scholar, does not follow the traditional Lutheran position on Messianic prophecy. In his *Handbook of the Old Testament* he has just five references to the Messiah and proceeds in two of them to reject the Messianic interpretation.[39] All Psalms, identified as Messianic by the New Testament, are said not originally to have permitted that interpretation, but was later read into the Royal Psalms.

Nov. 27, 1972

Footnotes

1. John I. McKenzie, *Dictionary of the Bible* (Milwaukee: Bruce Publishing Company, 1965), pp. 568-572; Louis F. Hartman, *Encyclopedic Dictionary of the Bible* (New York, Toronto and London: McGraw-Hill Book Company, 1963) pp. 1511-1525; George Arthur Buttrick, *The Interpreter's Dictionary of the Bible* (New York and Nashville: Abingdon Press, 1962), K-Q, pp. 360-365.
2. G. T. Manley, *The New Bible Handbook* (Chicago and Toronto: The Inter-Varsity Christian Fellowship, 1949), p. 265.
3. Franz Delitzsch, *Messianic Prophecies in Historical Succession* (New York: Charles Scribner's Sons, 1891); E. W. Hengstenberg, *The Christology of the Old Testament* (Grand Rapids: Kregel Publications, 1956, 4 volumes); L. Fuerbringer, *Exegesis of Messianic Prophecies* (St. Louis: Concordia Mimeo Company, no date); Max Reich, *The Messianic Hope of Israel* (Chicago: Moody Press, 1945); Georg Stoeckardt, *Adventspredigten, Auslegungen der fornehmsten Weissagungen des Alten Testaments* (St. Louis: Concordia Publishing House, 1887); Edward Mack, *The Christ of the Old Testament* (Richmond: Presbyterian Committee of Publication, 1926); Aaron Kligerman, *Messianic Prophecy in the Old Testament* (Grand Rapids: Zondervan Publishing House, 1957); George Spitz, *Messianic Prophecy* (Cleveland : Central Publishing House, 1923); Paul Heinisch-William G. Heidt, *Christ in Prophecy* (Collegeville, Minn.: The Liturgical Press, 1956); Ronald Knox, *Waiting for Christ* (New York: Sheed and Ward, 1960); Norman Geisler, *Christ: the Theme of the Bible* (Chicago: Moody Press, 1968), pp. 1-68.
4. Theodore G. Tappert, *The Book of Concord* (Philadelphia: Muhlenberg Press, 1959), p. 562.
5. Edward Mack, *The Christ of the Old Testament* (Richmond, Va.: Presbyterian Committee of Publication, 1926), p. 9.
6. Aaron Judah Kligerman, *Messianic Prophecy in the Old Testament* (Grand Rapids, Michigan, 1957), Introduction.
7. Charles Augustus Briggs, *Messianic Prophecy* (New York: Charles Scribner's Sons, 1891), p. vii.
8. Madeleine S. Miller and J. Lane Miller, *Harper's Bible Dictionary* (New York:

Harper & Brothers, Publishers, 1952), p. 440.

9. **Ibid.**
10. **Ibid.**
11. **Ibid.**
12. **Ibid.**
13. **Ibid.**, p.441.
14. **Ibid.**
15. O. A. Piper, "The Bible," *Colliers Encyclopedia,* 3:300.
16. Robert C. Dentan, "Bible-Religion and Theology (7)," *Encyclopedia Americana,* 3:646.
17. **Ibid.**
18. "Messiah," *Oxford Dictionary of the Christian Church* (New York: Oxford University Press, 1957), p. 890b.
19. E. F. Scott, *The Kingdom of God and the Messiah* (Edinburgh: T. & T. Clark, 1911), p. 29.
20. **Ibid.**, p. 34.
21. J. T. Nelis, "Messianism," Hartmann, *Encyclopedic Dictionary of the Bible, **op. cit.**,* p. 1512.
22. **Ibid.**
23. **Ibid.**, p. 1513.
24. Charles F. Pfeiffer, *The Dead Sea Scrolls* (Revised and Enlarged Edition; Grand Rapids: Baker Book House, 1962), p. 53.
25. Edward Mack, *The Christ of the Old Testament* (Richmond: Presbyterian Committee on Publication, 1926), p. 18.
25a. R. C. H. Lenski, *The Interpretation of St. John's Revelation* (Minneapolis: Augsburg Publishing House, 1943), p. 546.
25b. Mack, **op. cit.**, p. 28.
26. Herbert C. Alleman, *The Old Testament - A Study* (Philadelphia: The United Lutheran Publication House, 1935), p. 201.
27. **Ibid.**, 201.
28. Herbert C. Alleman and Elmer E. Flack, *The Old Testament Commentary* (Philadelphia: The Muhlenberg Press, 1948), pp. 65-74.
29. **Ibid.**, p. 65.
30. **Ibid.**, p. 74.
31. Byron C. Nelson, *On the Way to Emmaus* (Minneapolis: Augsburg Publishing House, 1937), 81 pages.
32. R. A. Ofstedal, *Ten Studies in God's Plan of Prophecy* (Minneapolis: Augsburg Publishing House, 1942). 115 pages.
33. Warren A. Quanbeck, "The Bible," *Theology in the Life of the Church* (Philadelphia: Fortress Press, 1963), p. 34.
34. Claus Westermann, *The Old Testament and Jesus Christ.* Translated by Omar Kaste (Minneapolis: Augsburg Publishing House, 1970).
35. **Ibid.**
36. Rudolf Bultmann, "Prophecy and Fulfillment," *Essays on Old Testament Hermeneutics,* edited by Claus Westermann (Richmond: John Knox Press, 1963), p. 50.
36a. **Ibid.**
37. Sigmund Mowinckel, *He That Cometh.* Translated by G. W. Anderson (New York and Nashville: Abingdon Press, 1958). 528 pages.
38. **Ibid.**, pp. 10-20.
39. Claus Westermann, *Handbook to the Old Testament.* Translated and edited by Robert H. Boyd (Minneapolis: Augsburg Publishing Company, 1967).pp. 203, 224.

Questions

1. The term ____ is being substituted for messianic prophecy.
2. The New Testament describes the origin of the Messiah as something

that ____.

3. Genesis 3:15 is known as the ____.
4. According to Paul in Galatians 3:16 the term "seed" refers to ____.
5. In Deuteronomy 18:15 Moses predicted the ____.
6. What did Yahweh give David in 2 Samuel 7:12-17? ____
7. The stay of Jonah in a great fish was a type of ____.
8. According to the authors of the *Book of Concord* the Law and Gospel were teachings that went back to ____.
9. What has declined in the twentieth-century about prophecy? ____
10. Modern critical scholarship identified the Suffering Servant with ____.
11. The Zealots are convinced that the Messiah would be ____.
12. In Zoroastorianism there is the doctrine of ____.
13. How does the RSV translate Genesis 12:3? ____
14. Christ and his apostles had a great reverence and respect for ____.
15. What did Philip tell the Prime Minister of Candace about Isaiah 53? ____
16. Paul made liberal use of ____.
17. The plan of salvation had been revealed to ____.
18. What did Peter say in his Pentecost sermon to the Gentiles? ____
19. Jesus claimed to fulfill the prophecies about ____.
20. What is now questionable about the prophecies ____.
21. Claus Westermann totally rejects ____.
22. According to Mowinckel, the Christian Church has wrongly interpreted ____.

The Interpretation of Isaiah 7:14

(Reprinted from *The Springfielder,*

Vol. XXXVIII, No. 2, September 1974)

THE NEW ENGLISH BIBLE of 1970 has translated Isaiah 7:14 as follows: "Therefore the Lord himself shall give you a sign; a young woman is with child, and will bear a son, and will call him Immanuel."[1] *The Revised Standard Version* of 1952 and 1959 rendered this passage similarly: "Therefore the Lord himself will give you a sign. Behold, a young woman shall conceive and bear a son, and shall call his name Immanuel."[2] *The American Translation,* produced by the Divinity School of the University of Chicago, translated Is. 7:14: "Therefore the Lord himself will give you a sign; behold! A young woman is with child, and is about to bear a son; and she will call him 'God with us.'"[3] The translation sponsored by The Jewish Publication Society of America has a similar rendering: "Therefore the Lord Himself shall give you a sign: behold, the young woman shall conceive, and bear a son, and shall call his name Immanuel."[4] The Moffatt translation interpreted the Hebrew as follows: "There is a young woman with child, who shall bear a son and call his name 'Immanuel' (God is with us)."[5]

Generally it may be stated that critical scholars, rejecting the idea of predictive prophecy, embracing a wrong concept of Messianic prophecy and refusing to accept the New Testament's interpretations of Old Testament prophecies, adopt the "young woman" interpretation for the Hebrew word *almah.*

Almah in the Ancient Version

How did the ancient versions understand Isaiah 7:14? The Septuagint translated: "Dia touto dosei Kyrios autos humin semeion. Idou *he parthenos* (a virgin) en gastri lepsetai, kai texetai huion, kai kaleseis to onoma autou Emmanuel."[6] The Syriac Peshitta (according to the translation of George Lamsa) rendered Is. 7:14: "Therefore the Lord himself shall give you a sign; Behold, a virgin shall conceive and bear a son, and shall call his name Immanuel."[7] The Latin Vulgate translation of St. Jerome has: "Propter hoc dabit Dominus ipse vobis signum: ecce virgo concipiet, et pariet filium, et vocabitur nomen ejus Emmanuel."[8] The Latin *virgo* means "virgin." Throughout the Middle Ages and the time of the Reformation this was the meaning given to the Hebrew *almah,* namely, that the word meant "virgin," a member of the female sex of marriageable age who never had sexual intercourse with a man.

Martin Luther rendered Is. 7:14 as follows: "Damm so wird euch der Herr selbst ein Zeichen geben: Siebe, eine Jungfrau ist schwanger, und wird einen Sohn gebaren, den wird sie heissen Immanuel."[10] In German the term "Jungfrau" is used of a woman who has remained unmarried. The King James Version was following the Septuagint understanding of almah when it rendered the latter as "virgin." The British Revised Version of 1885 has the same translation as the Authorized Version. All

Roman Catholic translations have either rendered almah as "virgin" or "maiden." *The Oxford Historical Dictionary* gives the meaning of "maiden" as "virgin."[11] The Rheims-Douay translated Is. 7:14: "Therefore the Lord himself shall give you a sign, Behold a virgin shall conceive and bear a son: and his name shall be called Immanuel." *The Jerusalem Bible* of 1966 has: "The Lord himself therefore, will give you a sign, it is this: the maiden is with child and will soon give birth to a son whom she will call Immanuel."[13] The Knox Version rendered: "Sign you ask none, but sign the Lord will give you. Maid shall be with child, and shall bear a son, that shall be called Immanuel."[14] The Confraternity Version of 1970 does likewise.[15]

The 1959 and 1969 versions of the Berkely Bible translated Is. 7:14 as follows: "Therefore the Lord Himself will give you a sign: Behold, the virgin shall conceive and shall bear a son and shall call His name Immanuel."[16] Young in his *Commentary on Isaiah* translated the Hebrew: "Behold the Lord Himself will give you a sign: A virgin is with child and she will call his name Immanuel."[17] Dr. Leupold likewise in his recent commentary rendered *almah* as "virgin."[18]

Those translations in modern times that render *almah* as "young woman" are simply following the rendering of Aquila, Theodotion and Symmachus who substituted *neanis,* "young woman" for virgin in their new translations or revision of the Hebrew O.T. into Greek, designed to replace the traditional Septuagint translation, because first and second centuries Christians were using Old Testament Messianic prophecies according to the LXX and claiming that they (including Is. 7:14) were fulfilled in Jesus of Nazareth.

The Historical Background for Almah Passage

The name Immanuel appears for the first time in Isaiah Chapter 7:14-17. The allied armies of Israel and Syria held Jerusalem in the iron grip of a siege, which had brought the city to the verge of despair. Already the allies had decided upon a foreigner, who should be seated on the throne of David, when the city would fall, one called "the son of Tabeel," (Is. 7:6). King Ahaz and his staff had gathered, it seems, to consider some last expedient for deliverance, when the prophet Isaiah appeared among them. His message from the Lord was that Ahaz might dismiss his fears, for the two kings must soon abandon the siege, and that their own destruction was hurrying on. Seeing unbelief in the faces of his hearers, Isaiah offered a sign from the Lord, any sign that they might ask from heaven above to hell below. Ahaz, who was hostile to Isaiah's religion and to his policy for (Judah), rejected the prophet's gracious offer with scorn. Isaiah knew that Ahaz, refusing to trust Jehovah, had put his faith in Assyria, and bought its intervention with a ruinous tribute. Possibly Ahaz had tidings, or at least some hope, that just then the Assyrian was invading the land of Syria. So in hypocrisy or scorn he answered the prophet: "I will not ask, neither will I tempt Jehovah." Then, the prophet, turning upon the apostate king, said: "Therefore the Lord Himself will give you a sign (whether you ask for it or not)."

This is the historical setting of the appearance in revelation for the first time of the Immanuel sign. The foremost element in the interpretation of Is. 7:14ff, must be that it is not a sign of blessing to Ahaz, the apostate, but of judgment or deprivation.[19] The emphasis of the sign is not upon the birth of Immanuel, but upon the time condition; before the child can come to years of moral discretion and accountability, — twelve years with the Jews-Israel and Syria will be conquered and in captivity. After that, instead of deliverance through Immanuel, Ahaz and wicked Judah will be judged and punished: "Jehovah will bring upon thee, and upon thy people" days darker than those through which they were then passing.

Ahaz had refused to ask for a miraculous sign. In announcing judgment on the immediate house of David, Jehovah at the same time proclaimed a miraculous happening, the birth of His Son by a virgin. The prophet sees in a vision *the* virgin pregnant and about to bear a son, whom she will call *Immanuel.*

Professor Gehman and those who follow his viewpoint claim that to take Is. 7:14 as a prediction would fail to do justice to the historical situation, that the prophet's words to Ahaz had to have relevance for the immediate situation in which they were uttered. Those who accept Matthew's statement that the conception of Christ by the Virgin Mary was in fulfillment of what Isaiah had predicted are accused by Gehman of being guilty of subjective exegesis.[20]

To find a prophecy of the Virgin Birth of Christ in Is. 7:14 is not fanciful exegesis. The salvation set forth by Christ and the Apostles was the theme of Old Testament prophecy. In writing to the congregations of Asia Minor, Peter said:

"This salvation was the theme which the prophets pondered and explored, those who prophesied about the grace of God awaiting you. They tried to find out what was the time, and what were the circumstances, to which the spirit of Christ in them pointed, foretelling the sufferings in store for Christ and the splendours to follow; and it was disclosed to them that the matter they treated of was not for their time but for yours. And now it has been openly announced to you through preachers who brought you the Gospel in the power of the Holy Spirit sent from heaven. These are things that angels long to see" (I Peter 1:10-12, NEB).[21]

The same apostle, speaking before the Jewish council, claimed that the Old Testament prophets had foretold the suffering and glorification of the Messiah, identified with Christ by Peter. "And so said all the prophets, from Samuel onwards; with one voice they all predicted the present time."

Professor Gehman has stated in his article on "Immanuel" in the *New Westminister Dictionary of the Bible* that "the prophet spoke in a historical situation, and that Isaiah would not have been understood by his contemporaries if in some mysterious manner he had referred to an event that was to take place 700 years in the future."[22] There are many more statements in the prophetic literature that contain assertions about the

227

future which were not always understood by those to whom they were addressed. That is no adequate criterion for rejecting the clear interpretation of Matthew that Isaiah had definitely foretold the unique manner of Christ's conception on the grounds that the immediate hearers needed to understand the words. Ahaz had been guilty of unbelief; his condition would make him obtuse to many statements the prophet might utter. Isaiah's prediction was understood no doubt by many future Israelites as a new prophecy.

Any correct interpretation of Isaiah 7:14 must take three points into consideration: (1) The birth must be a sign. (2) The mother of the child is one who is both unmarried and a good woman. (3) The very presence of the Child brings God to his people. "Immanuel" is a title which according to both Luther and Calvin can only be applied to one who is both God and man in one person. For these reasons the prophecy can only be found fulfilled in that Person who meets all the conditions set forth in Isaiah 7:14.

Wrong Interpretation of Isaiah 7:14

The so-called "young woman" of Is. 7:14 is said to have been one of the women of Ahaz' harem or the mother of Hezekiah, but if we accept II Kings 16:2; 18:2 as historical statements, immediately a difficulty arises in making the year c. 734 the year of Hezekiah's birth, who by that time was a number of years old.

Another faulty interpretation is the identification of Almah with the wife of Isaiah, for she already was the mother of Shaer-Yashub, and in Is. 8:3 she is called a prophetess. This view according to Gehman must be rejected.[23]

Some scholars believe that Isaiah pointed to some pregnant woman, who stood nearby, but surely that would have been an indelicate act and rules out *almah* being a virgin.

Others claim that the young woman was some undefined person, and that her personality was unimportant. Immanuel, was simply the symbol of a new age that would dawn for Judah. However, in 8:18 Immanuel is addressed as a real person and in 8:10 there is a play on his name.

Still others have proposed the idea that *almah* represents the house of David, that the term is a personification of the descendants of David's line. In the prophetic literature Israel is sometimes represented as a virgin (bethulah) in Amos 5:2; Jer. 18:18; 31:4,21. This view it is felt by Gehman would at least connect the prophecy with a local and historical situation.

Some have also advanced the theory that Isaiah was simply announcing that within nine months a woman was going to have a child and that she would call her baby Immanuel as an act of faith that God would save his people from the Assyrians.

The exegetical interpretations just cited all reject Matthew's clear assertion that it had been Isaiah's intention to announce the Virgin Birth. There is an interpretation, accepted by a number of expositors, which endeavors to do justice to both the historical situation and the fulfillment as given in Matthew 1. These expositors believe that Isaiah announced the birth of a child by a young woman who would be a sign that within a very short time the threat of Israel and Syria would come to naught and that God would deliver His people from their enemies, and that this woman was a type of the Virgin Mary.

The Use of Almah in the Hebrew Old Testament

The word *almah* occurs six times in the Old Testament. We pass by those references of the form in the plural *alamoth* as a part of certain psalm titles. Scholars do not know exactly what the meaning is of this title. In Gen. 24:43, in reference to Rebekkah, the word *almah* is used and it becomes clear in that chapter that it is synonymous with *bethulah*. The same is true of Ex. 2:8, in the case of Miriam, Moses' young sister, where Miriam is designated an *almah*. The same is true of Psalm 68:25, obviously a reference to women of honorable repute at the sanctuary. In the Song of Solomon, in 1:5 *almah* certainly does not imply a woman of questionable reputation, inasmuch as she is described as a woman to be desired. The same can also be said about the use of the term *almah* in 6:8, where the word is employed to such as stand over against both queens and concubines. Thus virginity is implied. Dr. Von Rohr Sauer in an article in the *Concordia Theological Monthly,* August, 1953, page 558 asserted the following about the use and meaning of *almah* in Isaiah 7:14: (1) *Almah* is never used of a girl before she attains to puberty, as the etymology of the word shows. (2) *Almah* is never used of a girl after she has become a married woman, as the usage in the Old Testament shows. (3) This means that a girl is called an *almah* only during a very restricted period of her life, namely, from the point of her becoming mature to the point of her becoming married. (4) It is proposed that this is precisely the period in which the Hebrew girl normally possessed the characteristics of maidenhood. (5) It is further proposed that the word "maid" or "maiden" is an accurate translation of the word *almah,* which implies virginity without stressing it, as *bethulah* does. (6) It is finally proposed that this translation is supported by the probability that the sign in Is. 7:14 is a miraculous sign.

A Ugaritic Text and Almah

An interesting text has come from the Rash Shamra or Ugaritic literature, where the goddess Nikkal is described as "A virgin will give birth . . . a damsel will bear a son."[24] In this passage *bethulah* and *glmt* (= Hebrew almah) are used synonymously. These two designations are used of the goddess Nikkal before her marriage to a god took place. It is of little importance that the child is to be born after the marriage; what is significant is the fact that before her wedding Nikkal is characterized by two words *btlt* and *glmt*. These two Ugaritic words are practically synonymous. At least, there was no hesitation in applying this word *btlt;* in the Ugaritic texts it is the standing designation for the virgin Anat. *Glmt* is never used in Rash Shamra of a married woman, and hence it was well adopted to serve as a parallel expression to *btlt*. The new evidence from

Rash Shamra in no wise supports the contention that *almah* may be used of a married woman. It was the conclusion of the late Robert Dick Wison of Princeton Seminary that in extra-Biblical Semitic literature *almah* never meant a young married woman.[25]

Almah the Proper Noun for Designation of Virginity

Dr. Edward Young claims that of all the Hebrew words that Isaiah could use to describe the virgin birth, *almah* was actually the only suitable word.[26] Thus there were available the following words: *yaldah, naharah, bethulah, ishshah, kalah* and *almah. Yaldah* was used of a young child and thus would not be appropriate to describe a woman that had the capability of bearing a child. In Joel 4:3 the word is employed of one who is a mere child.

The word *naharah* is the ordinary word for "girl." Its usage is broad and therefore would not have been suitable in this Immanuel prophecy. *Naharah* may refer to both married and unmarried women. It may be used of a concubine as well as of an evil woman. Thus it was unsuitable for predicting a virgin birth.

Then there is the word *bethulah* which those contend should have been employed if Isaiah wanted to announce a virgin birth. In the Rash Shamra texts as has been shown the word without exception refers to an unmarried woman. This however, is not the case in Biblical Hebrew. Dr. Young has examined the usage of the word in O.T. Hebrew and claims that:

> A close examination of the Biblical data reveals the fact that in Old Testament times there were two classes of women who might bear the designation *bethulah.* One of these was the young girl who may have been of marriageable age, but who was technically a virgin in that she had not known a man. The other was the *bethulah meorasah* or betrothed virgin. This distinction is made clear in a passage such as Deuteronomy 22.[27]

A study of Deuteronomy 22 indicates that it is a chapter designed to preserve the sanctity of the married estate. The various laws set forth in chapter 22 leave the reader with the distinction of a *bethulah* not engaged to a man and a *bethulah meorasah,* "a betrothed virgin," who is also defined as the "wife" of the man to whom she is betrothed. In Hosea 4:13,14 the word *kalah,* "bride" refers to a woman already married. On the other hand, Isaiah 49:18 refers most likely to a woman who is a betrothed virgin before the actual ceremony has been performed. On the strength of such writers as Epstein, Neufeld and Mace who have written on ancient Hebrew marriage customs, Young claims that "it is difficult to discern precisely what constituted the change from the status of 'betrothed virgin' to that of a married wife."[28]

Joel 1:8 complicates the matter further, where we read: "Lament like a virgin, girded with sackcloth over the husband of her youth." On the basis of this passage it would be proper to speak of a *bethulah behulah.* Such an inference is warranted in view of the fact that the virgin in Deut. 22:24 is called a wife (ishshah). The language employed in these two passages would seem to imply that whatever the difference was between the state of betrothal and the actual marriage state was merely of a formal nature. That there does not appear to have been a great difference between a "betrothed virgin" and a married woman is also shown by the severe penalty the law imposed upon unfaithfulness by a betrothed virgin. According to the Mosaic Law she was not merely guilty of fornication but guilty of adultery.

When the Old Testament speaks of a true virgin, it adds the qualifying phrase "who had not known a man." In Judges 21:12 this phrase is used to indicate that the girls (nahrah) were truly virgins and not betrothed. Otherwise this language would be unnecessary if the word *bethulah* without exception meant "virgin." Rebekkah is described as a *bethulah,* as a woman whom no man had known (Gen. 24:16). This qualifying phrase "neither had any man known her" would seem to indicate that Rebekkah was not a betrothed virgin. This phrase removes any doubt about her virginity which is not implied by the mere use of the word *bethulah.*

In view of the uncertainty connected with *bethulah* it becomes clear why Isaiah employs *almah,* which implies an unmarried woman of marriageable age, who has never had sexual relations. Probably the best translation for *almah* is the English "damsel" or "maiden." While Scott,[29] Leslie'[30] and others claim that *almah* designates a married woman, one wishes that they would furnish philological evidence for this assertion. The O.T. philological evidence does not support this rendering.[31]

In discussing the meaning of Isaiah 7:14 it should also be remembered that the name *Immanuel* occurs three times in chapters 7-11, and for this reason this section of Isaiah has been called the "Immanuel book." The second Immanuel passage we have in chapter 9:1-9. In this passage the prophet announces that Immanuel's ministry will be in Galilee. Matthew states that this prophecy was fulfilled in the preaching in Galilee, during the first year of His public ministry.

Isaiah ascribes to Immanuel the following titles: "Wonderful Counsellor, Mighty God, Everlasting Father, Prince of Peace. Of the increase of his government and of peace there shall be no end, upon the throne of David, and upon his kingdom, to establish it, and to uphold it with justice and with righteousness from henceforth even forever." The titles given here surely could not be assigned to any human king. Nor would the nature of Immanuel's reign be possible for any human Israelite king.

In this passage there are also the distinctive features of the Davidic covenant; he shall sit on David's throne, his kingdom is everlasting; and he is God's son, as Jehovah had promised.

In Isaiah 11:1-9, the third Immanuel passage, new features appear in Isaiah's picture of the Messiah. He is to be the house of Jesse; the Spirit is poured out upon him abundantly; righteousness and justice are the foundations and strength of his reign; and peace will fill the earth.

In chapters 7, 8, and 10 the prophet has predicted the desolation of Judah which the Assyrian will effect. Before the mighty Assyrian, the houses of Israel and Judah have fallen as trees of the forest before the axes of the woodmen. Only the bare stumps remain to accentuate the desolation. Then begins the message of hope in the eleventh chapter; one of these stumps has life in it, and will put forth again, for there shall come forth a shoot from the stump of Jesse.

This coming King "shall not judge after the sight of his eyes, neither decide after the hearing of his ears." Righteousness is declared to be the strength of his reign by the figure of girded loins or waist.

Finally, his reign of righteousness will heal the wounds of the world and establish everlasting peace.

Footnotes

1. *The New English Bible with Apocrypha* (New York: The Oxford University Press, Cambridge University Press, 1970), p. 817.
2. *The Holy Bible Containing the Old and New Testaments. Revised Standard Version* (New York: Thomas Nelson & Sons, 1952), p. 534.
3. *The Bible, An American Translation* (Chicago: The University of Chicago Press, 1931), p. 1145.
4. *The Holy Scriptures According to the Massoretic Text - A New Translation* (Philadelphia: The Jewish Publication Society of America, 1917), p. 487.
5. James Moffatt, *A New Translation Containing the Old and New Testaments* (New York and London: Harper & Brothers, 19 35), p. 755.
6. Alfred Rahlfs, *Septuaginta, Libri poetici et propheticie* (Stuttgart: Privilegierte Wurttenbergische Bibelanstalt, 1950), II, p. 575.
7. *The Holy Bible from Ancient Near Eastern Manuscripts. Containing the Old and New Testaments. Translated from the Peshitta, The Authorized Bible of the Church of the East* (Philadelphia: A. J. Holman Company, 1957), p. 705.
8. *Biblia Sacra. Juxta Vulgatam Clementinam* (Roma, Tournai, Paris: Typis Societatis S. Joannis Evang., Desclee et Socii, 1956), p. 8 56.
9. *Die Bibel oder die ganze Heilige Schrift des Alten und Neuen Testaments,* 501 Auflage (Halle a.d.s.: Druck und Verlag der V. Cansteinisch en Bible Anstalt, 1922), p. 675.
10. *The Holy Bible Containing the Old and New Testaments, Translated Out of the Original Tongues* (Oxford: At the University Press, 1892), p. 508.
11. *The Oxford Historical Dictionary* (Oxford: At the University Press, 1933), XII, pp. 230-231.
12. *The American Catholic Edition. The Holy Bible* (New York: Benzinger Brothers Inc., 1958), p. 709..This version contains the Rheims-Douay translation of Isaiah.
13. *The Jerusalem Bible* (New York: Doubleday & Company, Inc., 1966), pp. 1153-1154.
14. Knox. *The Holy Bible. A Translation from the Latin Vulgate in the Light of Hebrew and Greek Originals* (New York: Sheed & Ward, Inc., 1956), p. 634.
15. *The New American Bible.* Sponsored by the Bishops Committee of the Confraternity of Christian Doctrine (New York and Cleveland: The World Publishing Company, 1970), p. 621.
16. *Holy Bible. The New Berkeley Version in Modern English.* Gerrit Verkuyl, Editor-in-Chief (Grand Rapids: Zondervan Publishing Company, 1969), p. 691.
17. Edward J. Young. *The Book of Isaiah* (Grand Rapids: Wm. B. Eerdmans Publishing Company, 1969), I, p. 278.
18. H. C. Leupold, *Exposition of Isaiah,* Volume I, chapters 1-39 (Grand Rapids: Baker Book House, 1968), p. 153.
19. G. Stöckhardt, *Der Prophet Iesaja. Die ersten swölf Capitel* (St. Louis: Concordia Publishing House, 1909), p. 85.
20. Henry Snyder Gehman, *The New Westminster Dictionary of the Bible* (Philadelphia: Westminster Press, 1970), p. 419.
21. *The New English Bible. New Testament* (New York: Oxford University Press, Cambridge University Press, 1961), pp. 396-397.

22. Snyder, **op. cit.**, p. 4 19.
23. **Ibid.**, p. 419.
24. Cyrus H. Gordon, *Ugaritic Literature* (Roma: Pontificium Institutum Biblicum, 1941), pp. 63-64.
25. Robert Dick Wilson, "The Meaning of Almah (A.V. "Virgin) in Isaiah VII. 14," *The Princeton Theological Review,* 24: 308-316, April, 1926.
26. Edward J. Young, *Studies in Isaiah* (Grand Rapids: Wm. B. Eerdmans Publishing Company, 1954), pp. 178-185.
27. **Ibid.**, p. 179.
28. **Ibid.**, p. 179-180.
29. R. B. Y. Scott, "The Book of Isaiah," *The Interpreter's Bible.* George Arthur Buttrick, editor (New York and Nashville: Abingdon Press, 1956), v, p. 219.
30. Elmer A. Leslie, *Isaiah. Chronologically Arranged, Translated and Interpreted* (New York and Nashville: Abingdon Press, 1963), p. 49.
31. Modern Hebrew dictionaries simplify reflects what is considered the scholarly interpretation of *almah* in the standard commentaries. cf. Ludwig Koehler and Walter Baumgartner, *Lexicon in Veteris Testamenti Libras* (Leiden: E. J. Brill, 1958), p. 709. Where almah is said to be a marriageable girl or young woman (until the birth of her first child). No passage cited demonstrates the latter part of the definition; William L. Holladay, editor, *A Concise Hebrew and Aramaic Lexicon of the Old Testament* (Grand Rapids: Wm. B. Eerdmans Publishing Company, 1971), p. 274.

Questions

1. The New English Bible, the Revised Standard Bible, The American Translation of the Chicago Divinity School, the translation sponsored by the Jewish Publication Society of America and the Moffat translation translated **almah** in Isaiah 7:14 with ____.
2. Luther translated **almah** in Isaiah 7:14 with ____ which means ____.
3. The name Immanuel appears for the first time in ____.
4. Immanuel is a title which can only be applied to ____.
5. What did Von Rohr Sauer say about Isaiah 7:14 in the August 1953 *Concordia Theological Monthly?* ____
6. Robert Dick Wilson concluded ____.
7. Edward Young wrote that the Hebrew word **almah** Isaiah used was the ____ suitable word.

Additions to the 1974 Article, 'The Interpretation of Isaiah 7:14'

Christian News, January 5, 1987

Recently the editor of *Christian News* asked the undersigned whether he regarded Isaiah 7:14 as a rectilinear Messianic prophecy. In response he stated that his views about the rectilinear nature of Isaiah 7:14 were the same as those expressed in his article that appeared in *The Spring-fielder*, Volume xxxviii, 1974, No. 2, pp. 110-118, entitled "The Interpretation of Isaiah 7:14."

Relative to this article, written twelve years ago, the author of that journal article would like to make certain clarifications, give explanations about certain statements, and also add some other thoughts pertaining to the subject of rectilinear or direct versus the typological interpretation of Isaiah 7:14.

The Historical Background of the *Almah* prophecy relative to "the historical background for the *Almah* passage," the writer would like to call attention to the fact that the LORD sent two different messages, at two different limes, to Ahaz through His prophet Isaiah. The first message was sent at the beginning of Syro-Ephraimitic War. Thus the opening verses of chapter 7 read according the Beck translation: "During the time when Ahaz son of Jotham, son of Uzziah, was king of Judah, Rezin, King of Aram, and Pekah, the son of Remaliah, King of Israel went to Jerusalem to fight against it, but they couldn't keep it up. When the dynasty of David was told 'The Arameans are camping in Ephraim,' the hearts of the king and his people shook like the trees in the forest in the wind" (7:1-3). Rezin and Pekah wanted to force Judah into a military alliance against the Assyrians ruled by Tiglath-pileser III who had designs of expansion which included the small countries of Canaan (II Kings 15:37; 16:5). While Ahaz and his son Shear-jashub were examining the water supply for Jerusalem in anticipation of an attack on Jerusalem, Isaiah appeared "at the end of the canal from the upper pool, on the road to the Laundryman's Field" (Beck translation). Through his prophet Isaiah, the LORD called upon Ahaz to place his entire trust in him, because within a relatively few years, the two kings from the north would cease to be a threat to anyone. It appears that Ahaz had made up his mind to appeal to the Assyrians for help against his two northern opponents.

In Isaiah 7:10-14 there is a record of the second meeting of the prophet with Ahaz and also the special offer by the LORD to give Ahaz evidence that He could help Ahaz against his enemies as well as showing him that he needed not to appeal to the Assyrians for help. But here the question arises: What were the specific circumstances when these words were uttered? How much time elapsed between Isaiah's first and second messages to Ahaz? Some believe that the second message followed soon after the first; others hold that it was uttered some time later. Rezin and Pekah did attack Jerusalem and Judah as is apparent from II Chronicles 28. It is possible that 7:10-14 may have been spoken during the beginning of the siege of Jerusalem.

Regardless of what view a person takes, as to when the word were spoken, God did offer to give Ahaz evidence by the performance of some remarkable sign, which would demonstrate the LORD'S power and ability to keep His promise to Ahaz. Ahaz had already made up his mind to appeal for help from the Assyrians and so hypocritically rejected the LORD'S offer. Then the LORD responded: "Listen now house of David", he said, "Is it too little for you to weary men that you must also weary my God?" Then came the famous prediction of the virgin conception and birth. Beck translates 7:14 as follows: "Therefore the Lord Himself will give you a sign: Look the virgin will conceive and have a Son and His name will be Immanuel (God is with us)."

Arguments of the Opponents of the Direct Prophecy View

Rationalists who do not believe in the supernatural or the miraculous, claim that Isaiah 7:14 refers to a young woman of the eighth century B.C. who either was pregnant when the words were uttered or would become pregnant and for some unknown reason would call her son Immanuel. The proponents of the "double prophecy" view hold that Isaiah 7:14 is, first of all, a prophecy of a coming birth of a child by a woman, who is a contemporary of the prophet Isaiah. Then there was a later fulfillment, which occurred when Mary became pregnant without the benefit of a man. One might therefore speak of a primary and a secondary fulfillment of the prophecy of Isaiah 7:14.

The proponents of the primary view argue that Isaiah 7:14 must meet a need of the time of the Syro-Ephraimitic War. The prophet must give Ahaz a message that would have significance for the situation in which Judah and Jerusalem found themselves. A prophecy about an event that would transpire some seven hundred years later would be meaningless. In answer to that objection the response has been made that the prophecy did have meaning for the eighth century and all the centuries unto the prophecy's true fulfillment, the Virginal Conception and the Virgin Birth of Christ. Isaiah has greatly added to the store of Messianic prophecies which God gave between Genesis 3:15 and the prophecies about Christ in Luke chapter 1. The believers Judah had received from the Lord through Moses, Hannah, David, Hosea, Amos and Micah prophecies about that Person, called "the Seed of the Woman" who would crush Satan. Just like Micah foretold the city where Christ was to be born, so here in Isaiah 7:14 the true Israelites learn the significant fact about the unique way God's Messiah would enter human existence. Thus Isaiah 7:14 was relevant to the true believers in Judah and Jerusalem who were looking for the coming of the promised Messiah.

Problems for the Typological Interpreters of Isaiah 7:14

If the virgin spoken of in Isaiah 7:14 is a type of Mary as the typological advocates have claimed, it would appear that the point of comparison between the type (the prophecy) and its anti-type (the fulfillment) breaks down on how the virgin in Isaiah 7:14 became pregnant. The virgin must have had sexual relations with some man and the child, to be called Immanuel thus had a father and mother. However, in Matthew 1:18-25 and also in Luke 1:32-35, Mary is depicted as becoming pregnant without having sexual intercourse with Joseph. Thus the virgin of Isaiah 7:14 is not a real type of Mary.

Others claim that the important fact of Isaiah 7 is to be found in the name which the *almah* of 7:14 gave her child, namely, Immanuel. Somehow this woman of which Isaiah spoke would come to the conviction that in a time of crisis God was with his people and King Ahaz. But the New Testament identifies this name with Mary's virgin-born son who is further said to be Jesus, "for He shall save His people from their sins" (Matthew 1:21).

The word "Immanuel" occurs altogether three times in Isaiah, chapters 7-8. There are two passages in chapter 8 which identify Immanuel with God. The name Immanuel used for Christ sets forth the unique teaching that in one person Christ united two natures: the divine and the human. This has been called "the theanthropic union," and Isaiah 7:14's Immanuel cannot be identified with any person except Christ, who was not only a man, but God who assumed man's human nature. There are two occurrences in chapter 8 that identify this Immanuel of 7:14 with God Himself. In the first part of chapter 8 there is found a prophecy by Isaiah to Ahaz that the Assyrians whom he trusted and for whose help he had appealed, would be the foes to overwhelm Judah and Jerusalem. The prophecy ends like this: "It will flow into Judah flooding it as it passes on till it reaches up to the neck. When he spreads his wings, he will fill the breath of your land, O Immanuel." (Beck translation). The land of Canaan the territory of Judah and Jerusalem only belonged to God, to Immanuel, the creator of heaven and earth (Cf. John 1:1-3). The land did not belong to the child supposedly born to this anonymous woman.

Inserted between this prophecy of destruction and 8:13-22 is a short oracle of hope spoken for the true believers which says the following: "Be provoked , people and confused. Listen, all you distant countries, listen and be confused. Make your plans and it will come to nothing, make your statement and it will not come true, for God-is-with-Us." (in Hebrew, Himmanuel [with us-God]). So there Immanuel is clearly used of God.

The Results of the Syro-Ephraimitic War

In II Chronicles 28 the writer of the two books of Chronicles has recorded information relative to Ahaz not found in II Kings or Isaiah. Thus in II Chronicles 28 it appears that there is a record of the successful attack by the Kings Rezin and Pekah. The result was a disastrous defeat for Ahaz, with the result that one hundred and twenty thousand men were killed and two hundred thousand people taken captive (28:3-8). In view of this catastrophe how could a woman name her child "God-is-with-us?" It would have been more appropriate to Call the child "God-is-against-us."

A number of commentators have labelled chapter 7-12 "the Immanuel Book," and there are three major Messianic passages in it: chapter 7:14;

9:56, and 11:1-16. In 9:5-6 we have "The Wonder Child with the Remarkable Names" thus a prophecy of the birth of the Messiah, also telling of the nature of His Kingship, and in 11:1-16, a description of the King's Gifts and Abilities and the Spiritual Nature of Messiah's Kingdom. All three Messianic prophecies are rectilinear and not typical.

The Use of the Greek Verb "Pleroo"
and Direct Prophetic Fulfillment
The Evangelists and especially Matthew employ the word "pleroo" in the sense of "fulfilled." New Testament lexicographers list a number of different uses in various contexts for the verb "pleroo." Arndt-Gingrich, Abbott-Smith and others list the meaning of "fulfill by deed, prophecy as one use of pleroo." Thus the formula, "this happened that it might be fulfilled" refers to a prophecy that was made in Old Testament times and fulfilled in connection with Christ. The following passages are cited by Arndt-Gingrich with this sense: Matthew 1:22 (refers to Is. 7:14), 2:15; 2:17,23; 4:14; 8:17; 12:17; 13:35; 21:4; 26:54,56; 27:9; in Mark the following passages: 14:49; 15:28; In Luke: 1:20; 4:21; 21:22; 24:44; in John: 12:38; 13:18; 15:25; 17:12; 19:24,36; Acts 1:16. In reading these verses the readers does not get the impression that the Old Testament passages first have a different primary meaning and then assumed a secondary fulfillment in the New Testament. When Old Testament Messianic prophecies are interpreted as doubly fulfilled this is not done on the evidence of the New Testament, but on considerations relative to the Old Testament text, based on hermeneutical presuppositions which either question the canonical unity of the Bible or of the refusal not to allow the New Testament to be determinative for the in interpretation of Old Testament passages cited in the New Testament.

Hindson's Study of Isaiah 7:14
In 1978 there appeared a study of Isaiah 7:14, *Isaiah's Immanuel, A Sign of His Times or the Sign of the Ages?* This was published by the Presbyterian and Reformed Publishing Co., Philipsburg, New Jersey. The book has on a hundred pages and is an expansion of Hindson's Master's thesis and studies made since reception of that degree. He has a listing of many books, monographs and studies of the Isaiah 7:14 passage. It is a very thorough study. His conclusion was that Isaiah 7:14 is a direct, rectilinear prophecy.

Raymond F. Surburg

The New Hermeneutic Versus the Old Hermeneutics in New Testament Interpretation

(Reprinted from the *Springfielder*,

Vol. XXXVIII, No. 1, June 1974)

The New Hermeneutic Is a Development in continental theology after World War II. It has developed from the hermeneutics of Rudolf Bultmann.[1] In order to understand the new hermeneutic it is necessary to look at the thought of Bultmann. In the 1920's Bultmann joined Barth in protesting against the old liberalism. When Barth published his famous *Römerbrief* (1919) Bultmann welcomed it as a breakthrough in Biblical interpretation. However, the friendship with Barth did not last too long because Barth did not employ the historical critical method even though he was not in principle opposed to its use. Bultmann had been thoroughly indoctrinated in critical methodology and his entire scholarly endeavor was shaped by its use. Bultmann took the position that nothing which contradicts science can be accepted even though clearly taught in the Bible. Bultmann's hermeneutics was thoroughly opposed to any form of supernaturalism, which in essence means cutting out the very heart of that which is distinctive about Biblical teaching, whether found in the Old or the New Testaments.[2] Any doctrine which goes against reason must therefore be rejected. Obviously miracles cannot be taken seriously. Doctrines like the incarnation, resurrection, ascension and a visible return of Christ are out of the question for any person who desires to be intellectually respectable. This rules out the concepts of prophecy and eschatology.

Over against the Old Testament Bultmann took a very negative attitude.[3] Christians may entirely ignore the Old Testament or if they believe it should be used, then its value would be as law to show need for the Gospel. The Old Testament is a totally human document, at best preparing the way for Christianity. For Bultmann there is no such concept and reality as holy history or theology of history, only events of salvation. Since Bultmann espoused existentialism early in his life, even before coming into contact with the existentialist philosopher Heidegger, he rejects all precritical notions according to which man casts his religious experiences into the form of an external, worldly, historical event.[4] For the Marburg professor this is a myth and the interpreter must get rid of the form that the myth has assumed and yet retain the religious intention of the myth.[5] In this respect, Bultmann differs from the old liberalism of Harnack, one of Bultmann's teachers. With Kierkegaard Bultmann held that the inner side of religious experience was existential in character; thus here also he departs from the earlier twentieth-century theological liberalism.[6] The myth must be peeled off in order to find the existential meaning within it.

Dr. Ramm claims that Bultmann's "existentialism in turn leads him to the notion that the Word of God must be address which summons a man to decision either for or against the address. Hence the message of the New Testament as address is kerygma. This in turn must lead to powerful kerygmatic preaching from the sacred text."[7] Bultmann's theological system is a synthesis of these different strands and enabled him to win away from Barth the theological leadership of European scholarship as found in Germany and Switzerland.[8]

The new hermeneutic has utilized all of Bultmann's contributions. The proponents of the new hermeneutic are convinced that Bultmann's hermeneutic constitutes a new breakthrough in relationship to the old hermeneutics, to which there can be no return.[9] However, the new hermeneuticians believe that Bultmann did not realize all the implications that must follow if his positions are valid. Ernst Fuchs, Gerhard Ebeling and Gadamer are all convinced that the new hermeneutic is the answer to correct Biblical interpretation. Philosophically and theologically the new hermeneutic is more comprehensive than anything so far advocated. The older Biblical and sacred hermeneutics was too narrow in its understanding of the issues of the interpreting of a Biblical text.[10] Earlier already, it is claimed, Schleiermacher and Dilthey had suggested that interpretation was far more comprehensive than traditionally conceived and practiced. Historical-philosophical interpretation was inadequate according to this new school of interpretation. Wilhelm Dilthey, greatly influenced by Hegel, claimed that the stream of history had to be experienced in one's self before *Verstehen* or comprehension could occur.[11] *Erldarung* was placed in opposition to mere *Verstehen.* It was the philosopher Heidegger who is supposed to have grasped this more comprehensive function of hermeneutics.

The new hermeneutic follows Heidegger in its claim that language itself is interpretation.[12] Fuchs, Ebeling and their followers also claim that language is existential in character. When an individual speaks he is said to be interpreting, thus the language act is hermeneutical. It is at this juncture where the problem arises for many students of the new hermeneutic for they note that here a radical shift occurs. Hermeneutics is no longer fundamentally the setting forth of principles by which the text of Scriptures is understood, but a profound investigation of the hermeneutical function of speech. In some instances the older hermeneutics is employed but there is much more involved in the interpretation of ancient Biblical texts.

The new hermeneuticians wish to eliminate the older psychologism and historicism that has characterized the older theological liberalism that has been found wanting by Bultmann and the post-Bultmannians.[13] According to psychologism the text and events are interpreted in psychological terms; historicism on the other hand was guilty of explaining everything in terms of the law of causality. Both approaches were considered deficient because of the relativistic stance from which they spoke. By understanding the word ontologically the new hermeneutic believes it has avoided this dilemma.

The big problem in trying to understand the new hermeneutic is the manner in which its proponents use the vocable "word." It is difficult to grasp the various nuances of this word. Sometimes "word" seems to mean existential truth which reveals itself in speech. At other times it means speaking itself; yet at other times it refers to the existential truth contained in the text. Sometimes "word" is said to be the Word of God that breaks forth from a sermon. Some of the advocates of the new hermeneutic seem to imitate the procedure of the logical positivists who classify sentences into different categories. In reading the literature one notes that some sentences are *programmatic,* that is, they endeavor to state the structure of hermeneutics and understanding as such. Still other sentences are existential because they do not merely attempt to impart information but their purpose is to involve the reader in participation and profound communication. Still other sentences are *factual* or *scientific,* their purpose is to inform, whether it be on a popular level or a more theoretical (e.g., light is composed of rapidly moving photons). Other sentences are formal and only set forth relationships as in logic, mathematics, or grammar.

It is within this context of "word" that the new hermeneutic delineates its existential understanding of the Word of God. For Ebeling and Fuchs, the word of God is more a movement than an idea. Within the text of Scripture God communicates existentially; the Word of God must be dug out of the text by exposition and exegesis of the text. The Word of God is received by the listener as such when he makes a decision and accepts it by faith. In describing the new hermeneutic Ramm wrote: "Existential considerations permeate each step of the procedure. For this reason the new hermeneutic is very critical of the so-called neutral, objective, scientific approach to exegesis as represented by Oscar Cullmann. No such exegesis is possible. The expositor must come to the text with existential understanding of religious matters (Vorverständnis), but he may not come with a prejudice (Vorurteil) as to what the text must say (as allegorical exegesis)."[14]

The new hermeneutic, following Bultmann, claims that faith cannot elaborate its content. Bultmann and the post-Bultmannians teach that the New Testament authors had true faith and that they are only witnesses to the Christ event. According to the new hermeneutic the New Testament writers were not exempt from error; in reporting the Christ event they introduced materials that cannot be accepted today. Bultmann insisted that the New Testament writings needed to be demythologized, that myth vitiated the reports of the information regarding the life of Christ. The foreign materials (foreign to the existential communication of the Word of God in the texts) must be criticized as to the contents (known as Sachkritik, content criticism), which is a characteristic of the new hermeneutic.

In this respect Barth is much better than Bultmann and his followers. While Barth does not hold to the old Protestant doctrine of inspiration as held by Calvin, Luther and other reformers,[15] he does believe the content of the text. Barth, for example, believes in the existence of angels,[16] while for the Bultmannians this simply cannot be accepted in a scientific age. Since people do not rise from the dead once they have become deceased, Bultmann rejected the statement that Christ rose from the dead. Such a belief the modern interpreter may reject because it is contrary to the scientific understanding of the way nature functions. Content criticism became an essential element in the demythologization program of Bultmann as outlined in his famous essay of 1941. The content criticism of the new hermeneutic goes even beyond that of Bultmann's demythologization and is applied to the entire New Testament.

Bultmann had made much of the proclamation of the kerygma in preaching. The new hermeneuticians extend the kerygmatic proclamation of the New Testament to Christian preaching. According to this new school of interpretation the preacher must pose certain questions to the text, questions that man's existentialistic situation prescribe. The text in turn must ask questions of the interpreter. There must be an existential encounter with the text. Christian preaching, however, must also be relevant for not only the text but also the historical and cultural situation of the hearers determines the kerygmatic proclamation of the sermon. For the new hermeneuticians the essence of kerygmatic preaching is announcing God's love and forgiveness in Christ, and calls upon the hearer to decision of faith.

The new hermeneutic is not limited to theology but claims also the areas of philosophy and other branches of human knowledge. Ebeling, Fuchs, Gadamer, Funk claim that the new hermeneutic should also be the foundation for the reconstruction of philosophy, for a new program in epistemology. The liberal arts need also to be built upon the new foundation furnished by this new system of interpretation. The new hermeneutic in theology does not merely mean some additional insight regarding the science of hermeneutics; it is completely revolutionary to the extent that its proponents claim it actually is a new theology.[17]

Evaluation of The New Hermeneutic

What shall we say of this new hermeneutic? A very important question in theology is the significant question: What is the source of theology? What is the source for religious authority? There is no more important question! We have grown accustomed to answering that Scripture alone is the source and norm of all doctrine. We believe that the Bible is God's Word. On the pages of the Old and New Testaments God has seen fit to reveal to us what He would have us believe concerning Himself, concerning His nature, concerning His acts, concerning His plan of salvation. Being God's infallible Word the Bible is the source of Christian doctrine, the only source and norm. We call this the *Sola Scriptura* principle, a very important issue in the Reformation, in the confessional writings that followed, and in the writings of the seventeenth-century dogmaticians.[18] And very closely related with this *Sola Scriptura* principle is its corollary; namely, since there is no higher authority than God's Word itself, and since there is no additional revelation to which we may appeal, the basic hermeneutical principal must be "let Scripture interpret Scripture," *scriptura scripturam interpretatur.*[19]

However, it is just at this point that the new hermeneutic moves away from the traditional position and goes in a completely different direction. It calls the traditional view which we have outlined as the static concept as opposed to the dynamic. In fact, Ernst Fuchs, Ott and others have gone so far as to label the traditional view "a manifestation of unfaith." If this objection were motivated from the concern that doctrine sometimes has been simply taught for doctrine's sake; if this criticism would be prompted because often doctrine has been intellectualized and not related to life, then we would be in hearty agreement with the criticism of the old theology as being static!

But a reading of the literature advocating the new hermeneutic will show that Ebeling, Fuchs, Gadamer, Robinson and others are not merely interested in making the applications in sermons more life related, but they are saying that the Gospel message itself needs reformulating.[20] All those teachings of the Gospel message that modern man finds difficult to accept are to be trimmed away. It is actually a different Gospel that Ebeling, Fuchs, Ott, Bultmann, Robinson are proclaiming, in which all such external forms as faith in a preexistent Jesus, the Virgin Birth, a physical resurrection of Jesus, a vicarious atonement, a second coming of Christ in the clouds must be removed. [21] Even a hasty perusal of the new hermeneuticians will make it clear that it is this type of Gospel that men like Bultmann, Ebeling and Fuchs are convinced should be offered to our generation, a Gospel that will not require them to accept the so-called mythological form of the New Testament message but only its basic contents, a Gospel which will not require modern man to sacrifice his thinking!

Bultmann has written:

Let us think simply of the newspapers. Have you ever read anywhere in them that political or social or economic events are performed by supernatural powers such as God, angels or demons? Such events are always ascribed to natural powers, or to good or bad will on the part of man, or to human wisdom or stupidity . . . therefore modern man acknowledges as reality only such phenomena or events as are comprehensible within the framework of the rational order of the universe. He does not acknowledge miracles because they do not fit into this lawful order. When a strange or miraculous accident occurs, he does not rest until he has found a rational cause.[22]

Bultmann's conclusion, followed by all the new hermeneuticians, is to scrap the supernatural because modern man cannot accept it.

This means that for Bultmann, Ebeling, Fuchs, Robinson, and others the source of religious authority is Scripture and modern culture. According to these men the New Testament exegete or preacher is to begin with the New Testament kerygma, i.e. the faith of the early church, but then this faith must be shaped so that it becomes acceptable to modern culture and philosophy. When this new formulation and message are proclaimed and men respond to it, then it is "language event" (so Ebeling); according to Fuchs it is "word event." They both agree on this, that when this reformulation is made and men respond, then the message is Word of God;

this is what for Fuchs and Ebeling represents a dynamic word versus a static word.

For any Bible-believing Christian who follows the literal interpretation, this is quite different from the historic Protestant principle that Scripture is the only source and norm of Christian doctrine. It surely is not in harmony with the stance of Luther and the Lutheran Confessions. Many scholars, therefore, both in Europe and in America find the new hermeneutic objectionable on the ground that it changes the saving Gospel of Jesus Christ. In 1952 at the assembly of the United Lutheran Church of Germany (the confessional grouping of Lutheran provincial churches) a pastoral letter condemned the theology of demythologizing as "false doctrine."[23] This confessional stand by the bishops was then followed by an officially sponsored volume in which a number of theologians explained their views in greater detail. In response Bultmann and his German followers retorted by claiming that the Lutheran bishops had betrayed the Reformation and attempted to show that Luther was on their side.

No one will accuse the American theologian Nels Ferre as being a conservative theologian. In his book, *Searchlights on Contemporary Theology,* the Vanderbilt University theologian wrote:

All attempts to claim that Bultmann has done away merely with an outworn cosmology, leaving the ontology of the Gospel undisturbed is stuff and nonsense.[24]

Bultmann is not merely "bringing Christianity up-to-date by differentiating between outworn and indestructible events of the Christian faith. He is the pioneer of the most radical retranslation and transcalculation of faith itself into existential categories."[25]

S. H. Ogden, who appears to be sympathetic to some extent with the new hermeneutic, is ready to admit that the new hermeneutic is a revival of liberalism. He writes:

We have aligned ourselves with that 'liberal' tradition in Protestant Christianity that counts among the great names in its history those of Schleiermacher, Ritschl, Hermann, Harnack, and Troeltsch and many more recently Schweitzer and the early Barth and, in part at least, Bultmann.[26]

Walter Marshall Horton, in his recent publication *Twentieth Century Christianity* classified Bultmann and his disciples as Post-Barthian Liberals. It is quite evident that the new hermeneuticians have retained a residue of the Liberalism of the 19th century.[27] Both liberals and conservatives are in agreement that the new hermeneutic is neo-Liberal.

In other respects the new hermeneutic is also deficient and in error when evaluated in the light of the interpretative principles used in the Lutheran Confessions. Thus in its restriction of its understanding of the supernatural it destroys prophecy and with that any real significance of the Old Testament for the Christian Church, and thus is a return to the position of Marcion in the 2nd century. By its emphasis upon existentialism, most of the traditional dogmatic teachings are eliminated. By its interpretation that faith is purely a relationship between persons and need not have a doctrinal content, the whole foundation for Christian doctrine has been undermined.

Dr. K. Runia of Australia, in an essay delivered at the Annual Public Lecture of the Tyndale Fellowship of Australia, gave the following evaluation of Bultmann and the new hermeneutic:

> In denying all this (the doctrine of the atonement) the new school of demythologizing performs one great destructive reduction of the Gospel. Not only are all aspects that are not susceptible of existential interpretation eliminated from the Bible, but those that are open to such an interpretation are reinterpreted in such a way and to such an extent that the real Gospel completely vanishes into the midst of essential self-analysis. David Cairns has put it very pointedly in these words: "The actual result is to bring before modern man a Gospel without the Gospels, so that not without justification we may quote Mary Magdalene and say: 'They have taken away my Lord, and I know not where they have laid him.'"[28]

The only teachings of the Apostles' Creed that have remained intact, according to Bultmann, are the assertions that he suffered, was crucified, died and was buried. The Virgin Birth, the conception caused by the Holy Spirit, Christ's resurrection, ascension and visible return are all denied.

The Relationship of the New Hermeneutic to the Old Testament

While Bultmann and his followers primarily operated with the Books of the New Testament and developed an approach that has revolutionized the understanding of the New Testament writings, yet it should be acknowledged that in some respects Bultmann was indebted to critical Old Testament scholars for some of the basic hermeneutical approaches he used.

The rejection of the supernatural was not first promoted by Bultmann and his devotees, but dated back to the days of the Enlightenment, when the uniqueness of the Old Testament was questioned and much of its historical data was reinterpreted as myth and saga. In some respects the anti-supernaturalism of Bultmann was already adopted by the negative literary critics of the eighteenth and nineteenth centuries. Old Testament criticism rejected the idea that the coming of the Messiah was foretold in many passages of the Old Testament, a stance the New Testament writers aver time and time again. This was also the position of Christ, who claimed that in His ministry He was fulfilling direct Messianic predictions about His person and work. Bultmann is simply following critical Old Testament scholars when he denies the existence of Messianic prophecy in the Old Testament. In fact, like critical Old Testament savants, Bultmann rejects prophecy per se, because that would be contrary to what we know about the ability of men to anticipate and know the future and against the idea of a closed universe.

It was Hermann Gunkel, a German Old Testament scholar, who developed the hermeneutical approach known as form criticism (German: Formengeschichte). As early as 1901 Gunkel had set forth his ideas on

Form Criticism in the introduction to his commentary on Genesis. The ideas explicated in this commentary denied to Genesis any historical and factual value, but argued that in the Genesis volume there were different kinds of sagas employed. The Sitz-im-Leben for the different types of literature had to be determined and then the interpreter had to try to understand how the smaller units of literary types had been embodied into cycles of tradition. Gunkel operated with myth, saga, legends. The character of the Pentateuch, Joshua, Judges and I Samuel was changed by Gunkel's new hermeneutic. Books like Jonah, Esther and Daniel were relegated to the non-historical category by virtue of the fact that all three were said to represent a special type of literary genre, which forbade them, as was once the case, from being understood as recording true historical happenings.

In both Old and New Testament interpretation today the new hermeneutic is being employed. The result has been that there is being fostered in theological seminaries and school of religions an understanding of the Bible that has little resemblance to that once held by the various communions of Protestantism, by Roman Catholicism, and by Lutheranism as reflected in its confessional writings in *The Book of Concord* of 1580.

Footnotes

1. Alan Richardson, *Religion in Contemporary Debate* (Philadelphia: Westminster Press, 1966), pp. 90-91.
2. Carl Braaten, *New Directions in Theology Today.* Vol. II. *History and Hermeneutics* (Philadelphia: The Westminster Press, 1966).
3. Rudolf Bultmann, "The Significance of the Old Testament for the Christian Faith," in *The Old Testament and Christian Faith,* edited by Bernard W. Anderson (New York: Harper & Row, Publishers, 1963), pp. 8-35.
4. Cf. Raymond F. Surburg, "Rudolf Bultmann and the Old Testament: His Approach and Interpretation," *The Springfielder,* 30:3-26, Winter, 1967.
5. **Ibid.,** p. 14.
6. Herman Ridderbos, *Bultmann.* Translated by David H. Freeman (Grand Rapids, Baker Book House, 1960), p. 9.
7. Bernhard Ramm, "The New Hermeneutics," in Ramm and Others, *Hermeneutics* (Grand Rapids: Baker Book House, 1971), p. 132.
8. **Ibid.,** p. 133.
9. **Ibid.**
10. Martin Scharlemann, "Hermeneutic(s)," *Concordia Theological Monthly,* 39:614, October, 1968.
11. "Wilhelm Dilthey," in *An Encyclopedia of Religion,* edited by Vergilius Ferm (New York: Philosophical Library, 1945), p. 228.
12. Richardson, **op. cit.,** pp. 81-88.
13. Ramm, **op. cit.,** p. 135.
14. **Ibid.,** p. 136.
15. Cf. Karl Barth, *The Word of God and the Word of Man* (New York: Harper & Brothers, 1957).
16. Karl Barth, *Church Dogmatics,* III, 3, p. 369ff.
17. This will become apparent from reading the volume of Robert Funk, *Language, Hermeneutic, and the Word of God. The Problem of Language in The New Testament and Contemporary Theology* (New York : Harper & Row, Publishers, 1966), 305 pp.

18. W. H. T. Dau, "The Heritage of Lutheranism," in *What Are Lutherans Thinking,* edited by E. C. Fendt (Columbus: The Wartburg Press, 1947), pp. 14-15.
19. W. Arndt, "Hermeneutics," *Concordia Cyclopedia,* edited by Erwin L. Lueker (St. Louis: Concordia Publishing House, 1954), p. 463.
20. Cf. the following books dealing with the new hermeneutic: Gerhard Ebeling, "Hermeneutik," *Religion in Geschichte und Gegenwart* (third edition), III, 242-262.
———. *The Nature of Faith.* Philadelphia: Fortress Press, 1961.
———.*The Word and Faith.* Philadelphia: Fortress Press, 1963.
Ernst Fuchs, *Hermeneutik.* Second edition. Bad Constatt: R. Muelerschen, 1958.
James H. Robinson, and John B. Cobb, *The New Hermeneutic. New Frontiers in Theology.* Vol. II. New York : Harper & Row, 1964.
21. Cf. the essays by Elwein, Kinder, and Künneth which have been published in *Kerygma and History,* edited by Carl E. Braaten and Roy A. Harrisville (New York: Abingdon Press, 1962.)
22. Rudolf Bultmann, *Jesus Christ and Mythology* (New York: Charles Scribner's Sons, 1958), pp. 37-38.
23. Ernst Kinder, *Ein Wort Lutherischer Theologie zur Entmythologisierung,* (Minchen, 1952).
24. Nels Frederick Ferre, *Searchlights on Contemporary Theology* (New York: Harper & Row, 1961), p. 109.
25. **Ibid.**
26. S. H. Ogden, *Existence and Faith, Shorter Writings of Rudolf Bultmann.* Selected; translated and introduced by Shubert M. Ogden (New York: Meridian Books, 1960), cf. Introduction.
27. Cf. Howard W. Tepker, *The New Hermeneutic* (Springfield, Illinois: Concordia Seminary Print Shop, 1966), pp. 6-13.
28. K. Runia, "Dangerous Trends in Modern Theological Thought," *Concordia Theological Monthly*, 25:337-338, June, 1964.

Questions

1. The New Hermeneutic developed from ____.
2. Bultmann's Hermeneutic was opposed to any form of ____.
3. What was out of the question for Bultmann? ____
4. Bultmann insisted that the New Testament writings needed to be ____.
5. ____ is the sole source of Christian doctrine.
6. Let Scripture interpret ____.
7. Ebeling, Fuchs, Ott, Bultmann are proclaiming ____.
8. What did Hermann Gunkel develop? ____
9. What is being fostered in theological seminaries and schools of religion today about the Bible? ____

The Hebrew Passsover:
Its Origin, Biblical History and Typological and Christological Fulfillment
(A Study for Holy Week and Easter)
Christian News, March 17, 1986

Sacred festivals or feasts held an important place in Jewish religion.[1] They were the religious services which were accompanied by joy and gladness. In Leviticus 23 they are fully described and they were called "holy convocations." The following were the major. Old Testament festivals: 1. The Feast of the Weekly Sabbath; 2. The Passover or Feast of Unleavened Bread; 3. The Feast of Pentecost; 4. The Feast of Trumpets; or New Moon; 5. The Feast of the Day of the Atonement; 6. The Feast of Tabernacles or Booths, or Ingathering.[2] These were all preexilic and were instituted by Yahweh or Yehovah Himself. In addition, in postexilic times two other festivals were instituted and observed by the Jews: 7. The Feast of Purim and 8. The Feast of Lights, or Hanukkah.[3]

1. The Feast of Passover

The Passover was the first festival instituted by Yahweh or Jehovah. It was probably the most important of all Jewish festivals. God Himself instituted the Passover at the time the children of Israel were about to leave Egypt after a 430-year stay in Egypt. The festival was originally ordained by Yahweh to be observed yearly so that the Israelites would remember the night when God spared all the firstborn of Israel, while the firstborn of Egyptian cattle and people were being killed by the angel of death (Exodus 12:1-30; 43-49).

Critical Old Testament scholarship has endeavored to portray Moses as adopting an earlier pagan practice in devising the passover for his people.[4] Thus Stewart wrote: "Moses quite possibly adopted more ancient ceremonials. Unleavened bread being an agricultural festival, Passover a nomadic and pastoral...Passover may have had its original links with circumcision, demonism, fertility cult or the first born oblation."[5] However, the Bible described this festival as being instituted by God and not by Moses who consequently did not borrow it from any pagan sources.

2. The Origin of the Passover in Egypt

In the Pentateuch it is chapter 12 of Exodus which describes the historical account of the Passover institution and celebration. The Hebrew name was **pesach**, coming from the verb meaning "to pass over." Scholars have attempted to explain the origin of the verb as having been borrowed from different languages. Thus G.E. Mendenhall related it to the Akkadian **pashhu**, which is found in Amarna letter 74:37 to describe the peace and security resulting from the formation of a covenant.[6] B. Couroyer suggested that **pesach** is a translation of two Egyptian words **p'** and **sach** "to blow," "the striking," in reference to Yahweh's striking the land in the tenth plague. This French savant holds that the Egyptian

247

expression has been placed side by side with a Hebrew root comprised of the same consonants, "pasah," meaning "to skip" or "leap over," as in I Kings 18:26 (KJV "Leaped"). So by its connection with the sparing of the Israelites first-born **pesach** came to have the sense of Yahweh's merciful by passing of the houses where the blood was applied.[7]

The Passover was instituted in the month of Abib, later called Nisan, the month of the ripening of ears and the first month of the Jewish Year (Ex. 12:2; Deut. 16:1; Lev. 23:5; Num. 9:1-5; 28:16). Passover was also known as the Feast of Unleavend Bread, thus actually forming a double festival. It was observed on the 14th day of Nisan (our April) and it recalled the Lord's deliverance of the Jews from Egypt. At the same time, the observance also commemorated the establishment of Israel as a nation. The Feast of Unleavened Bread began the day after the Passover and lasted seven days (Lev. 25:5-19). The Passover-Unleavened Bread feast was one of three at which all males were commanded to attend, providing the men were physically fit to travel. In addition those in attendance had to be ceremonially clean (Ex. 23:50; Deut. 16:16); the other two festivals requiring attendance were the Feast of Weeks or Pentecost and the Feast of Tabernacles. These three were known as the "feasts of pilgrimage."

In the observance of the first Passover, on the 14th of Nisan the head of the family set apart a lamb without blemish. On the evening of the 14th the lamb was slain and some of its blood was sprinkled on the doorposts and lintel of the house in which they ate the Passover as a seal against the coming judgment upon Egypt. Then the lamb was roasted and eaten with unleavened bread and bitter herbs. The lamb had to be consumed entirely by a family, and if the latter was too small, the smaller family was to get together with another who would share the Passover lamb. Any portion left was to be burned the next morning. Members who ate the Passover lamb were to eat the meal in haste. They were to be ready so that when the command to leave was given, they could leave at once. Those were the instructions relative to the celebration of the first Passover celebrated in Egypt.

3. Later Observances of Passover

After the establishment of the priesthood by Jehovah and the building of the tabernacle, the celebration of the Passover differed from the first Egyptian one.[8] Some differences were the following: (a) the Passover lamb was to be slain at the Sanctuary, rather than at home (Deut. 16:5-6); (b) the blood was sprinkled upon the altar rather than on the doorposts; (c) In addition to the family sacrifice for its Passover meal there were public and national sacrifices offered each of the seven days of the Feast of Unleavened Bread (Num. 28:16-24); (d) the meaning of the Passover was recited at the feast each year (Ex. 12:24-27); (e) the singing of the Hallel (Psalms 113-118) during the meal was instituted at a later time. Those who were unable to keep the first Passover because of uncleanness or because they were away, were to observe the Passover on the 14th of Nisan of the second month (Num. 9:9-12).

4. Offerings to be Presented at Passover Feast

Those appearing at the Passover celebration were not supposed to appear empty handed, but were required to bring offering as the Lord had prospered them (Ex. 23:14-17; Deut. 16:16-17). To eat unleavened bread after midday of the 14th of Nisan was unlawful. All labor, with however, a few exceptions permitted, was prohibited. Josephus, *The Jewish Wars*, Vi. 9.3 claimed that each lamb was to serve ten to twenty persons. The following was the procedure observed at the celebration of the Passover: No un-ceremonially unclean man or woman was allowed to participate. After an appropriate blessing the first cup was served, followed by the eating of bitter herbs. Then came a second cup of wine, at which time, in compliance with Exodus 12:26, the son asked the father the meaning and significance of the Passover Feast. Then an account of the Egyptian bondage and deliverance was recited in reply to the boy's question. This was followed by the first portion of the Hallel (Psalms 113-114) being sung and the Pascal Lamb was eaten, followed by a third and fourth cup of wine. Then the rest of the Hallel was sung (Psalms 115-118).

The Feast of Unleavened Bread which followed the Passover also remembered the Exodus from Egypt. Yahweh instituted this to remind his people that they had been afflicted in Egypt during their 430-year stay in the land of the pharaohs. The time period would be circa 1876-1446 B.C. The Hebrews were not to forget the haste with which they had left Egypt as they ate the "bread of affliction" (Deut. 16:3). The first and last day of the Feast of Unleavened Bread were Sabbaths on which no work was to be done. The beginning of the grain harvest occurred during Passover time. On the second day of Unleavend Bread (the 16th of Nisan) a sheaf of the first fruits was presented as a wave offering (Lev. 23:9-11) In the course of time, it became customary to call it "the omer ceremony," suggested by the Hebrew word for sheaf, namely, "omer."[9]

5. The Second Mosaic Celebration of the Passover Feast

According to Numbers 9:5 the LORD (Yahweh) spoke to Moses in the wilderness of Sinai, in the first month of the second year, after they had come out of Egypt, saying: "Let the children of Israel keep the Passover." This was done at the command of Yahweh, recorded by Moses as follows: "And they kept the Passover on the fourteenth day of the first month at twilight, in the Wilderness of Sinai, according to all that the LORD commanded Moses, so the children of Israel did (Numbers 9:4)." At that times some came who had touched a dead body and then were un-ceremonially unclean and wanted to know if they were excluded from the Passover celebration. They were told that they would be allowed to observe it on the fourteenth day of the second month. It was a serious matter not to observe the Passover. The LORD'S warning to Israel was: "But the man who is clean and is not on a journey, and ceases to keep the Passover, that same person shall be shut off from his people, because he did not bring the offering of the Lord at its appointed time; that man shall bear his sin."

6. The Passover Celebration in Joshua's Time

Yahweh had promised the land of Canaan to Abram, a prophecy which was only fulfilled some six hundred years later. The LORD gave Canaan to Abraham, Isaac and Jacob as a possession. Remaining in Canaan permanently, however, was conditioned on Israel's faithfulness to the covenant.[10] In His farewell address to the Israelites, God through Moses also announced that the Children of Israel were guilty of forsaking their God, they would be taken captive and no longer be entitled to the land of Canaan.

After thirty-eight years of needless wandering, the new Hebrew generation who had not participated in the great revolt against Yahweh, as described in Numbers 13 and 14, Joshua crossed the Jordan and began the conquest of Palestine. After the new generation entered the Promised Land, the first thing which had to be done, was to circumcise the men who had grown up in the wilderness and had not been circumcised on the eight day, as Yahweh had originally instructed Abraham to do. As a result of sins in the wilderness, Israel was marking time until the death of those who lacked faith to enter Canaan had occurred. God had promised to bring a new generation, born in the wilderness, into fellowship with Him and had not been given the rite of circumcision, the sign of God's covenant with his people, until the unbelieving generation had died out.

With a new generation of Israelites ready to do Yahweh's will the rite of circumcision became meaningful again and was performed there in Canaan and those receiving it, were assured that they were God's people. While in Egypt God had set apart His people for Himself; in the wilderness the same people separated themselves from Yahweh. Canaan was to mark a new start for Joshua and the people he was instructed to lead in the complete conquest of Canaan. The name where this mass circumcising of the men who had crossed the Jordan was at **Gibeath-ha-'araloth**, meaning "Hill of Foreskins." With this religious act, God said the new generation, as recorded by Joshua: "This day I have rolled away the reproach of Egypt from you (5:9)." The Israelites were now in covenant relationship with Him. Now that the nation was right with God and obedient to His command, the Passover was again observed on the fourteenth of Nisan. During the wilderness wanderings, especially after the great rebellion at Kadesh Barnea, the Passover had not been celebrated. Out of fellowship with God neither circumcision nor Passover had any meaning. Thus in Joshua's day in Canaan, Israel, conscious of Yahweh's presence, had made a new beginning.

7. The Passover Celebration in Hezekiah's Time

The next Passover celebration mentioned in the Old Testament occurred in the eighth century B.C. in the days of King Hezekiah of the Southern Kingdom.[11] Hezekiah was the son of Ahaz, one of the most wicked and notorious of all kings of the Davidic Kingdom. During the reign of Ahaz the Yahweh religion probably reached its lowest ebb. Ahaz introduced Assyrian religion and vile pagan practices. God punished Ahaz by causing the Northern Kingdom and the Kingdom of Syria to invade Judah and Jerusalem. According to II Chronicles 28 the forces of Ahaz' two northern neighbors caused the death of 120,000 men and 200,000 captives being apostate.[12] Strangely, his son Hezekiah rejected his father's religion and the practices associated with it, and embarked upon a religious reform and undertook measures to remove the idolatry introduced by Ahaz. II Chronicles gives an account of what measures Hezekiah took to bring his nation back into fellowship with God. Thus the author of Chronicles reports: "And Hezekiah sent to all Israel and Judah, and also wrote letters to Ephraim and Manasseh, that they should come to the house of the LORD at Jerusalem, to keep the Passover to the LORD God of Israel. For the king and his leaders had agreed to keep the Passover in the second month" (II Chron. 30:1-2). When the decision was made to keep the Passover Feast, it was found that there was not sufficient number of priests who were sanctified and thus were qualified to function in the temple in Jerusalem. The king and the congregation then sent invitations throughout the Northern Kingdom, inviting even the scoffers to join their brethren in Jerusalem to participate in one of the greatest Passover celebrations taking place in centuries. Hezekiah associated the deportations to Assyria with the sins of the Northern Kingdom for departing from Yahweh. Hezekiah made an appeal to those in Israel to return to the God of Abraham. The manner in which the appeal to those who had forsaken the LORD was touching. The appeal to repentance and a return to Yahweh was followed by the destruction of the pagan altars erected by King Ahaz. Those "who prepared their hearts," although unable to observe all the ceremonial rules, were permitted to partake of the Passover (31:18,19). The feast which normally held for seven days was extended for another week, for so great was the joy in its celebration (31:23-27). There had been nothing like it since the days of Solomon.

After the celebration of the Passover, the multitudes in their enthusiasms sallied forth and broke down the idolatrous images not only in Judah and Benjamin, but also in Ephraim and Manasseh, in the Northern Kingdom (II Chron. 31:1). Then King Hezekiah had the temple services conducted by priests and Levites according to the model left by David. When the king appealed for contributions for the services of the temple the people responded so generously that priests and Levites had more than enough. For the surplus gifts social storehouses had to be erected. For the wives and families of the Levites generous provisions were made available (31:11-16). Hezekiah was sincere and did that which was good and right before the LORD (31:20-21). In his religious reformation Hezekiah had the help of two eighth-century prophets, namely, Isaiah (cf. 10:5-39) and Micah (cf. Micah 6:1-7:30).

8. The Passover or King Josiah

After Hezekiah, unfortunately there came his son Manesseh who reverted to his grandfather's footsteps.[13] He even outdid Ahaz. In fact, Manasseh surpassed all his predecessors in wicked idolatry by rearing pagan altars even in God's house (II Chron. 33:5,7) and worshipping the stars

(v. 3, cf. II Kings 21:11-16). Because of his wickedness God caused the Assyrian king, Esarhaddon to carry Manasseh captive to Babylon. While in captivity the Chronicler tells his readers that Manasseh repented. The LORD caused Esarhaddon to release Manasseh from his captivity and restored him to his throne in Jerusalem. As a repentant sinner Manasseh now endeavored to serve the LORD and eradicate the paganism which he had introduced, but the damage had been done and the evil could not be removed (Cf. 2 Kings 23:26; 24:3-4). Amon, Manasseh's son, did evil and did not repent. After a short reign of two years he was murdered (vv. 21-24).

Josiah (640/639-609 B.C.) succeeded his wicked father and turned out to be the last good king in the history of the Southern or Davidic Kingdom.[14] The Biblical text refers to him as "the good king Josiah." When he was sixteen years old, he attacked idolatry of every kind (2 Chron. 34:1-4) He destroyed the rites of Moloch, shut the home of the sodomites, and killed the pagan priests upon their own altars he burned their bones (II Kings 23:16,20). Both the writer of Kings and the writer of Chronicles devote considerable space to the activity of Josiah against all forms of idolatry and pagan abominations.

When Josiah was twenty-six years old, in the eighteenth year of his reign, Josiah had the temple cleansed and in connection with its cleansing the book of the Law was found. The year was 621 B.C. As the king heard its contents, he was shocked to see how far the Hebrews had strayed from the will of God as expressed in the Mosaic teachings. Huldah, the prophetess, announced that unless the people repented that all the curses Moses had announced which were to come upon the people, if they forsook Yahweh for other gods, would be fulfilled. Josiah sponsored a public reading of the book of the Law and caused the people to see how grievously they had erred and the people were prevailed upon to renew the covenant between themselves and Yahweh (2 Kings 23:4-20).

An important part of Josiah's reformation was the observance of the Passover, which had been neglected. The author of Chronicles informs us that the celebration in the days of Josiah exceeded that celebration which had been held under the direction of Hezekiah. At the Josianic celebration the Feast was observed according to the laws laid down by David (Cf. 1 Chron. 35:2-19). The ark, which had been removed, was restored to its place. Priests and people had been duly sanctified, and all were in their appointed places (2 Chron. 35:11-17). About a half million people participated in this Passover sponsored by Josiah.[15]

9. The Passover of Ezekiel (45:21-24)

The second last reference to the Passover in the Old Testament is the one found in Ezekiel 45:1-24. The fact that the prophet Ezekiel, an exilic prophet, active from 592-571 B.C., refers in his future vision of the New Testament Church to a Passover, shows that Ezekiel and the people whom he served, were interested in the Passover while they were in the Babylonian Captivity. Chapters 40-48 constitute the last vision granted to Ezekiel.[16] Critical scholars believe that Ezekiel was submitting a blueprint for the Jewish people upon its return to its homeland. The distribution of the land among the 12 tribes was never realized as outlined by Ezekiel. The plans for the building and construction of the temple as described by Ezekiel were never carried out. At best, the vision remained visionary and unfulfilled.

On the other hand the dispensationalists believe that there will be a restoration of the physical Israel to Palestine in the Kingdom dispensation, when the descriptions and directives of these nine chapters will be fulfilled and thus carried out as literally stated. A temple will be built according to the specifications outlined in chapters 40-43.[17] There will also be a priesthood. Sacrifices will be offered. The Old Testament festivals, such as the New Moons, the Sabbaths, and all other appointed seasons of the house of the Lord will be observed. There are three points of interest concerning the Ezekelian Passover, and they are the fuller participation of the secular leader, the fact of the sin offering and the complete change over from a family celebration to a public ceremony. The victims specified include bullocks, rams and kids. The prescriptions about the Passover in Deuteronomy are considerably extended.

In Ezra 6:19ff. the last Old Testament celebration of the Passover is mentioned. Nathan Isaac believes that in postexilic times (537-400 B.C.) the Passover was probably observed more meticulously than ever before. Through the activity of the prophets Haggai and Zechariah the returned exiles were galvanized to complete the rebuilding of the temple during the reign of Darius II (521-485 B.C.).

Since the author of Hebrew teaches that by one sacrifice Christ has forever sanctified those who are sanctified, and that the whole ceremonial law and the Jewish festivals were preparatory for the coming and work of Christ, and since Christ on Good Friday exclaimed: "It is finished," and since the passover lamb has a type of Christ as St. Paul says, "Christ our passover lamb has been sacrificed," the vision of Ezekiel will need to be given a nonliteral interpretation which agrees with the theology of the New Testament, where only two, and not three distinct comings of Christ are outlined (i.e. in Bethlehem and for the last judgment).

10. The Celebration or the Passover in Ezra's Time

Ezra, the scribe, gives a report of a Passover celebration in chapter 6:19-22. This Passover was observed in 515 B.C. and it was conducted according to the instructions given in the days of Moses. It was observed on the 14th day of Nisan, in the first month of the year. The Levites and priests were ritually clean. Ezra reports: "And they slaughtered the Passover for all descendants of the captivity, for their brethren and priests, and for themselves. They observed also the Feast of Unleavened Bread for seven days with joy, for the LORD made them joyful" (Ezra 6:22).

An interesting document has been found at Elephantine in Egypt, dated 419 B.C., and is known as the Passover Papyrus and ostraca,[19] in which the community of Judea was asked for instruction about the celebration of the Passover and the Feast of Unleavened Bread by Jews in

Egypt. That the Jews considered the Passover important during the Second Temple days (515 B.C. and onward) may be seen by reading the Talmud, where an entire tractate is dedicated to this subject, and is called **Pesachim**, on which there is a **gemarah** in both the Palestinian and Babylonian Talmuds. In characterizing these, Nathan Isaacs wrote: "These are devoted to the sacrificial side and to the minutiae of searching out and destroying leaven, what constitutes leaven, and similar questions, instructions which the children of Israel sought 30 days before the Passover."[19] The historian Josephus frequently speaks of the Passover in his writings. The following are some of these allusions in Josephus's works: *The Jewish Antiquities II*, xiv, 6; III, X, 5; IX, ii, 1; XVII, ix, 3; *The Jewish Wars II*, i, 3; V, iii, 1; VI, ix, 3. Josephus also related that great multitudes attended the Passover at Jerusalem. He estimated that in the days Cestius that at least 256,000 lambs were slaughtered.

11. Jesus and the Passover in New Testament Times

According to the New Testament all Israelites were expected to be present in Jerusalem to celebrate the three great festivals of Judaism, namely, the Passover and Feast of Unleavened Bread, the Feast of Weeks or Pentecost and Tabernacles. Even Jews of the Dispersion (Diaspora) would be in attendance. Josephus claimed that at Passover time the population would grow to about three million, a figure scholars considered greatly exaggerated and Jeremias has placed the figure at about 180,000.[20]

A. Jesus and Attendance at the Age of 12

Jesus faithfully attended the major festivals of the Old Testament. Luke states that Jesus went with his parents to Jerusalem when he was twelve years old to celebrate the Passover Festival. On the occasion of this Jerusalem visit Luke reports that Jesus engaged in conversation and dialogue with the learned doctors of the law in the Temple. The Jewish scholars asked Jesus questions and He in turn asked them questions. This is where Jesus parents found Him after they returned looking for Him when he was not found travelling back home with the Nazareth contingent. Luke reports that "all who heard Him were astonished at His understanding and answers." (Luke 2:41). When His mother Mary rebuked Him for not being with the others as they were heading back to Nazareth, Jesus replied: "Why is it that you sought me? Did you not know that I must be about my father's business?"

B. The Four Passovers of the Fourth Gospel

From John's Gospel it becomes evident that Jesus during his earthly ministry attended at least three different Passovers.[21] Then in John 2:13, after the performance of His first miracle at Cana, Jesus went down to Capernaum. Jesus, His mother and His brothers did not remain there very long. Then Jesus proceeded to Jerusalem at the time of Passover. Arriving in the temple, He found those who sold oxen and doves, and also the money-changers, and He made a whip of cords, and drove them out of the temple, together with the sheep and oxen and overturned the tables of the money-changers. To those who sold doves, Jesus said: "Do not make my Father's house, a house of merchandise."

This was the first cleansing of the temple, not to be confused or identified with a later cleansing, which occurred shortly before Christ's suffering and death.[22] The first cleansing took place at the beginning of the Early Judean Ministry, A.D. 27. The Passover of A.D. 27 witnessed Christ preaching and teaching. At this time Jesus performed miracles (called by John as "signs") and resulted in many believing oil His name (John 2:33).

C. The Possible Feast or John 5:1

John 5:1 states: "After this there was a feast of the Jews, and Jesus went up to Jerusalem." Which this feast was cannot definitely be determined. Nearly all Jewish festivals have been suggested by different servants. Fahling asserted about this situation: "But the opinions are chiefly divided between Purim (14th and 15th of Adar, approximately February) and Passover. For the understanding of the passages it matters little which festivals one believes it to have been. In our choice of the Passover in 28 A.D. we are prompted by the Evangelist's evident purpose of supplementing the Synoptic account of the life of Christ. When Jesus departed Galilee as reported in John 4:1-3 we are left with the impression that the forerunner's work was still in progress. We believe that all events of John 4 and 5- the Samaritan ministry, the healing of the ruler's son, and the unnamed Feast are to be inserted before Matt. 4:12, Mark 1:14, and Luke 4:16."[23]

In John 6 in which were recorded the event of the Feeding of the Five Thousand, followed by the walking on the Sea of Galilee and the Capernaum "Life of Bread Sermon" of Christ, we have happenings that took place when the Passover Feast was near, Spring of A.D. 29.

The same Gospel writer also mentions the last Passover that Jesus was to attend before His Passion, which occurred in Spring of A.D. 30. Five times John refers to this feast: (11:55; 21:1; 13:1; 18:28,38; 19:14). In chapter 11:55 John reports that a short time before the Passover, the chief priests and Pharisees met, took counsel how they might kill Jesus (11:47). Many Jews came to Jerusalem to purify themselves so that they might observe the Passover (11:56). John further informs his readers: "Now both the chief priests and the Pharisees had given a command, that if anyone knew where He was, he should report it, that they might seize him" (11:57).

It was six days before the Passover that Jesus came to Bethany where Mary anointed Jesus. Judas complained about the waste involved in Jesus' anointing, in that a pound of very costly oil of spikenard was used, which could have been sold and its proceeds been given to the poor. But Jesus rebuked Judas with the words: "Let her alone, she has kept this for the day of burial. For the poor you have with you always, but Me you do not always have (John 12:8)."

After the Sanhedrin had condemned Jesus to death because of blasphemy, John reports that the Jewish leaders would not enter the Praetorium, "less they should be defiled, but that they might eat the Passover (18:28)."

In connection with the custom which the Romans had that they would release a Jewish prisoner to the Jews at Passover time, when Pilate gave them a choice between Barabbas or Christ, the Jews chose a murderer to be released and demanded that Christ be crucified. The day that Pontius Pilate condemned Jesus to be crucified, was said by John, to be the Preparation Day for the Passover.

D. The Last Passover Christ Celebrated

The first three evangelists give a report of Jesus celebration of His last earthly Passover.[24] Matthew, Mark and Luke give accounts as to the preparation undertaken by Christ for this final Passover. Matthew states in 26:17: "Now the first day of the Feast of Unleavened Bread the disciples came to Jesus saying to Him": "where do you want us to prepare for You to eat the Passover?" Matthew 26:17-19; Mark 14:12-16; Luke 22:7-13 give what Christians know about the preparation for the celebration. Jesus decided to observe the Passover in Jerusalem and asked an unmentioned believer to use a large upper room, who obligingly placed it at the disposal of Jesus. It was on the evening of Thursday, when according to Jewish reckoning, Friday, the fifteenth of Nisan, had begun, that Jesus accompanied by the Twelve, made His way to Jerusalem. After Peter and John had finished the Supper preparations they joined their Lord.

This was the first and last Passover, of which Jesus partook with the full number of the apostolic band. Remarked Fahling: "At the first Passover of His ministry His twelve apostles had not yet been gathered, neither at the second, if, as we assume, the Unnamed Feast was a Passover. And the third Passover Jesus did not attend. At that time after the death of John the Baptist, He was in the utmost parts of Galilee, in the borders of Tyre and Sidon, where of course no sacrifices could be made."[25] Luke is the only Gospel writer who gives an account of what Jesus said before eating the pascal lamb and meal "And he said unto them, with desire have I desired to eat this Passover with you before I suffer." This was to be the first and last Passover that Jesus would eat with the Twelve. One of the disciples would later betray Him and eventually commit suicide. No more festal dinners would Christ enjoy with the Twelve until the perfection of the Kingdom of God would be attained. Jesus's reference to suffering the disciples would not understand. They only had ears for the Kingdom, but not in any suffering by them to establish the Kingdom on earth. As the Host of the day, Jesus opened the feast by filling a goblet of wine, over which customary prayers were spoken and passed it along with the same thought. "Take this and divide among yourselves. For I say unto you, I will not drink of the fruit of the vine until the kingdom of

God shall come."

In the time of Christ the Passover Jamb (usually a year old male sheep) was slaughtered in the temple area. The meal, however, could be eaten in any house within the city. A communal group, like Jesus and His disciples, could keep the Passover together as though they were a family.

From the elements that were left of the Passover meal, unleavened bread and wine. Jesus then proceeded to institute the Lord's Supper or Holy Eucharist.

12. The Typological and Christological Meaning of the Passover

There are passages in the New Testament which set forth the typological and Christological meaning of the Passover Lamb.[26] Which would mean that the Passover Lamb was to be eaten, because in connection of the tenth Plague the blood of a lamb sprinkled on the doorposts of Jewish homes, caused the Angel of Death to bypass those who had carried out Yahweh's command to kill a lamb and smear its blood on the doorposts. Because of the death of an innocent lamb, the life of the Hebrews was spared. It was also God's intention that the Passover lamb should serve as a type of Christ, who as the Lamb of God would take away the sins of the world and who by His substitutionary death paid for the sins of the world. The prophet Isaiah described the suffering Messiah as a lamb that was led to the slaughter. Another New Testament writer spoke of Jesus as "the lamb slain from before the foundation of the world." Utilizing these lamb references Paul could write to the Corinthians: "For indeed our Passover lamb has been sacrificed — Christ Himself (literal translation of the Greek text)." Thus Paul directly declared Christ our Pascal Lamb. Like the Pascal lamb, Jesus was without blemish (Cf. Ex. 12:5 with 1 Peter 1:18-19) not a bone was broken (cf. Ex. 12:46 with John 19:36), His blood was a token before God (Ex. 12:13), and the feast was eaten with unleavened bread (Cf. Ex. 12:18 and I Cor. 5:8).[27]

With the death of Christ upon Calvary's cross, the second aspect of the Jewish Passover was fulfilled and its celebration was no longer necessary. In Colossians 2:16-17 Paul emphasizes the fact of the preparatory nature of the Old Dispensation, the fact that the ceremonial laws no longer were in effect for either Jews or Christians. So the Lord's Supper replaced the Passover celebration, just as circumcision was replaced by baptism.[28]

Up to the Nicene Council in the year A. D. 325, the church observed Easter as the Jewish Passover. Thereafter it took precautions to separate the two, condemning their confusion as Arianism.[29]

Footnotes

1. Gleason Archer, *A Survey or Old Testament Introduction* (Chicago: Moody Press, 1964), p. 230.
2. **Ibid.**, pp. 230-232.
3. "Feast," in Henry Snyder Gehman, *The New Westminster Dictionary of the Bible* (Philadelphia: Westminster Press, 1970), p. 296.
4. Gehman, **op. cit.**, p. 297; Madeleine and J. Lane Miller, *The New Rupert Bible Dic-*

257

tionary (New York: Harper & Row Publishers, 1973), p. 527B.

5. *Encyclopedia Britanica*, Makropedia, Vol. 10, pp. 219ff.

6. *Bulletin of the American Schools of Oriental Research*, No. 133 (1954), 29.

7. B. Couroyer, in Revue Biblique, LXII, (1955), pp. 481-466.

8. Nathan Isaac, "Passover," James Orr, General Editor, *The International Standard Bible Encyclopedia* (Grand Rapids: Wm. B. Eerdmans Company, 1939), IV, p. 2256b.

9. **Ibid.**, p. 2257.

10. A. Cohen, *Joshua and Judges* (London: The Soncino Press, 1950). p. 2A.

11. W. Graham Scroggie, *The Unfolding Drama of Salvation* (London: Pickering & Inglis, 1953), I, p. 349.

12. **Ibid.**, p. 348.

13. R. J. A. Sheriff's "Manasseh," *The Illustrated Bible Dictionary* (InterVarsity Press, Tyndale House, 1980), Part II, pp. 942-944.

14. R. K. Harrison, *A History of Old Testament Times* (Grand Rapids: Zondervan Publishing House, 1957), pp. 183-189.

15. Scroggie, **op. cit.**, pp. 355-356.

16. Cf. Walter H. Roehrs, "Ezekiel," in Carl F. Henry, *The Biblical Expositor* (Philadelphia: A.J. Holman Company, 1960, II, pp. 257-260; (Andrew Blackwood, Grand Rapids, Baker Book House, 1965), pp. 234-235.

17. Merrill F. Unger, Unger's *Commentary on the Old Testament* (Chicago: Moody Press, 1981), II, pp. 1581-1582.

18. Isases, **op. cit.**, p. 2257b.

19. "Passover," in *The New Harper's Bible Dictionary* (New York: Harper & Row, 1973), p. 527b.

20. Joachim Jeremias, *Jerusalem in the Times of Jesus* (Philadelphia: Fortress Press, 1969), p. 83ff.

21. H. Wayne House, *Chronological and Background Charts of the New Testament* (Grand Rapids: Zondervan Publishing House, 1981), p. 107.

22. Cf. Joh Ylvisaker, *The Gospels – Synopsis Harmony* (Minneapolis: Augsburg Publishing House, 1932), pp. 137-141 and 555-557.

23. Adam Fahling, *A Harmony of the Gospels* (Grand Rapids: Zondervan Publishing House, no date), p. 41.

24. Cf. Ylvisaker, **op. cit.,** for a harmonization of events at the Last Supper and its preparation, pp. 633-650.

25. Adam Fahling, *The Life of Christ* (St. Louis: Concordia Publishing House 1936), p. 587.

26. P.E. Kretzmann, *Popular Commentary of the Bible, New Testament* (St. Louis Concordia Publishing House, 1924), II, p. 110.

27. Gehman, *The Westminster Dictionary of the Bible*, **op. cit.**, pp. 705-706.

28. R.A. Stewart, Passover," *The Illustrated Bible Dictionary*, III. 1158c.

29. Nathan Isaacs, "Passover," *International Standard Bible Encyclopedia*, **op. cit.**, IV, p. 2258a.

Books Worth Consulting and Reading

H. Danby, ed. *The Mishnah*, tractate "Pesachim," Oxford: Oxford University Press, 1933, pp. 136-151.

Alfred Edersheim, *The Temple: Its Ministry and Service*. Grand Rapids: Eerdmans, 1950. (reprint), pp.208-24.

J. Jeremias, "Pascha," *Theological Dictionary of the New Testament*. Grand Rapids: Wm. B. Eerdman Publishing Company, V, pp. 896-904.

K. E. Keith, *The Passover in the Time of Christ* (rev.) London: Church Missions to the Jews. 1958.

J. B. Segal, *The Hebrew Passover from the Earliest Times to A.D., 70*. London: Oxford University Press, 1963.

Questions

1. What held a major importance in Jewish religion? ____
2. What was the most important of all Jewish festival? ____
3. This festival was instituted by ____ and not ____.
4. Nisan corresponds to our ____.
5. Remaining in Canaan permanently was conditioned on ____.
6. In the wilderness the people separated themselves from ____.
7. When was the Passover not celebrated? ____
8. When did the Yahweh religion reach its lowest ebb? ____
9. Hezekiah did that which was ____.
10. ____ and ____ helped Hezekiah.
11. Who was the last good king in the history of the Davidic kingdom? ____
12. The dispensationalists believe that there will be a restoration of ____.
13. What are the only two distinct coming of Christ? ____
14. The historian Josephus frequently speaks of ____.
15. The first cleansing of the temple should not be confused with ____.
16. The Passover lamb served as a type of ____.
17. Isaiah described the suffering Messiah as a ____.
18. When did a celebration of the Jewish Passover no longer become necessary? ____
19. What replaced the Passover? ____

The Messianic Prophecies of Zechariah with Special Reference to His Prediction of Holy Week

Christian News, March 21, 1988

The Jews by the time of Christ had adopted for the books of the Old Testament a threefold division: namely, 1) the Law, 2) the Prophets, with Former and Latter prophets, and 3) the writings, which had three subdivisions of poetical books, then scrolls (five books read at various Jewish festivals) and the historical books.[1] The Latter Prophets consisted of: Jeremiah, Isaiah, Ezekiel and the 12 Minor Prophets as one volume. The 12 Minor Prophets covered a period beginning with Joel and Obadiah in the ninth century B.C. and concluding with the period of the post-exilic prophets Haggai, Zechariah and Malachi.[2] Both Hosea and Zechariah have fourteen chapters; these two are the largest in terms of chapters and verses in our English Bible. Both of these prophetic books contain Messianic prophecies. In Hosea they are chiefly found in chapters 1-8; while in Zechariah they are located in both major sections of the book, chapters 1-41 and chapters 9-14.[3] Geisler observed "that Zechariah is filled with Messianic expectation."[4] Moorehead asserted about Messianic prophecies: "Zechariah is remarkable for the fullness with which he treated the subject."[5] Unger was of the opinion that "Zechariah has more to say about Christ than all the other Minor Prophets."[6]

Zechariah, like Ezra and Nehemiah, was aware of the sad fact that the returned exiles were not maintaining the fidelity to God that He demanded. Yes, declension and apostasy were evident among the returnees. Even Ezra and Nehemiah, who were active in Palestine after Zechariah's time, recognized that it was only a remnant which exhibited any genuine faithfulness to the God of Abraham, Isaac and Jacob. In the prophecies of Haggai and Zechariah and Malachi it became evident that "all were not of Israel who were of Israel." It was in only a few of the remnant that these prophets found the true spirit and character of the people of God; and before the voice of prophecy is hushed, Malachi distinguished in the most solemn way the difference between the godly remnant and the mass of the nation, whether people or priests. Accordingly, these prophets, and more especially the last two prophets of the Old Testament, Zechariah and Malachi, turn away from any further hope in the restored captives, and gaze with eager joy and swelling anticipation of the coming Messiah in Whom every promise and prophecy will be made good.[7]

The Divisions of the Book of Zechariah

The fourteen chapters of the book of Zechariah, son of Berechiah, logically fall into two major sections: chapters 1-8 and chapters 9-14. The first section comes from the period of 518-515 B.C., while the second major one deals with the period after 490 B.C. when the Persians invaded Greece between 490-479 B.C.[8] While there are significant differences between the two sections, so that critical scholars have rejected the Zecharian authorship of chapters 9-14,[9] there are enough similarities between chapters 1-8 and 9-14 to warrant maintaining the traditional position that Zechariah was the author of both sections.[10] These have prophecies dealing with the future of the Israelite nation and contain prophecies about the Messiah and the establishment of His spiritual kingdom. The Messianic age, toward which the later books of the Old Testament point, is also found in Zechariah's fourteen chapters.[11] Zechariah surely was one of the prophets whom Peter had in mind when he wrote to the congregations of Asia Minor as follows: "The prophets, who long ago wrote about what God's grace would do for you, made a thorough search to learn all about this salvation. They tried to find out whom and what time the Spirit of Christ in them was pointing out when He exactly predicted the suffering of Christ and the glories that would follow. God told them they were not serving themselves but you in these things."[12] When Jesus told His disciples: "Behold, we go up to Jerusalem and all things prophesied concerning the Son of Man shall be fulfilled," Zechariah was one of these prophets, who at least 480 years before Christ's suffering, crucifixion and death, spoke about the great events of the first Christian century, probably the most important century in world history, especially when a Christian contemplates the eternal results of those historical events.

The Messianic Prophecies of Zechariah

Messianic prophecy was foretold both by symbolical actions (as found in chapters 3 and 6) and by direct prophetic statements as contained in chapters 9-14.[13]

Relative to the interpretation of the contents of the Book of Zechariah we have three major schools of thought. The critical school denies chapters 9-14 to the sixth century prophet and assigns chapters 9-12 and 12-14 to two different authors,[14] and there are no references to the Messiah, to the Christ of the New Testament Scriptures.[15] On the other hand, among those who hold to the unity of the whole book of Zechariah and believe that he, the son of Berechish, is the author and that his book of history and prophecy contains predictions about Christ, there are unfortunately divergent schools of interpretation. Those scholars and individuals who divide Biblical history into seven major dispensations: namely. 1. That of Innocents, 2. Conscience, 3. Human government, 4. Grace, 5. Law, 6. Grace of Church Age, and 7. The Kingdom, contend that many prophecies about Christ in the Old Testament have not yet been fulfilled but will be realized in the Kingdom dispensation.[16] By contrast, the anti-dispensationalist and amillennialist school of interpretation holds that most prophecies have already been fulfilled when Christ came or are being fulfilled in the Messianic Age which will conclude with Christ's final coming to judge the living and the dead.[17]

Freeman's Views on the Messianic Prophecies in Zechariah

Freeman believes that there are at least fourteen different Messianic prophecies in Zechariah. He lists the following as being Messianic: 1.

Christ the Branch (3:8), 2. God's Servant (3:8), 3. the Shepherd (9:6; 11:11); the Smitten Shepherd (13:7), 4. Christ's Entry into Jerusalem (9:9), 5. the betrayal of thirty pieces of silver (11:12-13), 6. the piercing of his hands and his feet (12:10), 7. the return to the Mount of Olives (14:3-8), 8. the Messiah to remove iniquity (Ch. 3), the Messiah to unite the priesthood and the kingship in his own person (10), the Messiah King to be a suffering Servant (Ch. 9,11), the Shepherd to be rejected by Israel (ch. 11), 12. the death of the Shepherd (chs. 12-13), 13. the conversion of Israel (ch. 13), 14. the destruction of Israel's enemies, salvation of Jerusalem and the millennial reign of the Messiah over all the world from Zion (ch. 14).[18]

In this series of fourteen Messianic prophecies a number of them are based on the Scofeldian system of hermeneutics, which claims that the New Testament Church, which Christ founded, was not mentioned in the Old Testament and that Christ originally had come to establish a worldly kingdom in the first century A. D.[19] The rejection of the Jews frustrated this plan of God and of His Son, Jesus Christ. The original plan was then postponed but will be realized in the Kingdom Age, when then the Jews will not reject their King as they did in the days of the Governor Pontius Pilate.[20] Romans 11:26 where Paul speaking of the spiritual Israel stated that all members of the true Israel will be saved. This passage is interpreted as referring to the kingdom age or to the millennium when the physical descendants of Abraham, not Gentiles, will be saved.[21] The second half of Zechariah, chapters 9-14, receives a much different interpretation by the dispensationalists than it does from those who claim the thrust is concerned with the Messianic age.[22]

With the majority of Freeman's fourteen examples of Messianic prophecies, however, amillennialists would agree. Scholars belonging to the Roman Catholic Church, the Eastern Orthodox, various Protestant denominations and Lutherans have held that Zechariah does contain some remarkable prophecies about the Messiah.[23] This can be shown from the inspired writers of the Gospels. The principle, derived from the Bible itself, namely, that Scripture interprets Scripture, shows clearly that in a number of passages in Zechariah, especially in chapters 9-14, there are prophecies about some of the events of the last week of our Lord's life during His states of humiliation.

Christ Found Himself Foretold In the
Old Testament Scriptures

Jesus on Easter Day clearly taught that His suffering and death had been foretold in the Old Testament Scriptures. When Cleophas and his friend complained about the fact that they had placed such great hopes in Jesus of Nazareth and that now all their hopes had been dashed to the ground by Christ's crucifixion and death, Christ then berated them and said: "O foolish men and slow of heart to believe all that the prophets have spoken! Behooved it not the Christ to suffer thus, and then to enter into glory? And beginning with Moses and the Prophets, He interpreted to them all the passages concerning Himself" (Luke 24:25-27).[24] On the same day in the evening Jesus appeared to the disciples, Cleophas, his friend and others who were present. He concludes his conversation with them by declaring: "These are my words which I spoke to you while I was still with you, how all things must be fulfilled which are written in the Law of Moses, and the Prophets and the Psalms concerning me" (Luke 24:44).[25]

The Night Visions of Chapters 1-6 and the Messianic Age

The first six chapters of Zechariah are famous for the experience of Zechariah, when in one night Yahweh granted him eight visions which predicted facts about the future of the returned Israelites in Jerusalem and Palestine but in these visions there were also predictions about the Messiah and the Messianic age. Ludwig Fuerbringer, former President of Concordia Seminary, St. Louis and also an Old Testament professor, in a presentation entitled: "Sacharja, der Prophet der Hoffnung," ("Zechariah, the Prophet of Hope") discussed the eight night visions in an essay presented to The Northern Wisconsin District of the Lutheran Synod of Missouri, Ohio and other states (now known as The Lutheran Church-Missouri Synod) asserted about these visions: "These night visions do not deal with world wars, as many believe, but of God's kingdom and church. World kingdoms are mentioned only in so far as they have meaning for the Church."[26]

The Messianic stream of prophecy takes us back to the Garden of Eden and since throughout the pre-Christian centuries God added from time to time new features to the Messianic picture, some of the titles used in Zechariah Chapters 3 and 6 can be associated and linked with previous Messianic titles in earlier biblical books. Some scholars, however, have found the Messiah referred to both symbolically and directly in chapters 3 and 6 of Zechariah.[27]

The "Branch" in Zechariah 3 and 6

The Messiah was given different titles in the Old Testament prophetic scriptures. One of these is the "Branch." Both Isaiah and Jeremiah ascribed this name to the Messiah.[28] The Hebrew **Tsemach** or synonyms of **Tsemah** are employed by Isaiah in 4:2; 11:1 and by Jeremiah in 23:5 and 33:15 where none other than the Messiah could be meant. In Zechariah 3:1 we read: "And he showed me Joshua the high priest standing before the Lord's Angel, the Satan standing at his right hand to accuse him."[29]

To Joshua the High Priest, the Lord of hosts announced "I will bring forth My Servant, the Branch." The Hebrew **Tzemach** is the same person predicted by Isaiah in 11:1 where the prophet asserted: "A Shoot will come out of the stump of Jesse, and from the roots a Branch will produce fruit and the Lord's Spirit will dwell upon Him, the Spirit of Wisdom and understanding, the Spirit of counsel and might, the Spirit of knowledge and the fear of the Lord,"[30] and also in Jeremiah 23:5-6: "The days will come says the Lord, when I will raise for David a righteous branch, who will rule as king and be wise. He will create fairness and righteousness

263

in the earth. When He comes Judah will be saved and Israel will live safely. This is the name He will be called, "The Lord-our- righteousness."[31] The same name is also used in Jeremiah 33:15-16, except that "the Lord-our righteousness" is said of Jerusalem, i.e. the Christian Church, where the righteousness Of Christ applied to the repentant sinner, is proclaimed.[32]

The Symbolic Messianic Action in Chapters 1-6

There are two symbolic actions in part I, chapters 1-8 where the Messiah is foreshadowed and aspects of His earthly ministry predicted. In the fourth night vision there is described the justification of the High Priest, Joshua. How can a holy and righteous God promise such blessings to a sinful and unworthy nation as Israel? The Lord gives the answer in the fourth night vision. Joshua really represents the people of Israel and the filthy garments he is clothed with are the sins of the people. Satan accuses Joshua before the Lord but God in his mercy removes the sins in one day and clothes Joshua with His righteousness. The Lord then admonished Joshua, as the high priest and representative of the people to walk in His ways, for only then will he have charge of the courts of the Lord and free access to the throne of grace.

Joshua may be said to be a type of Christ.[33] Just as Jesus was later charged with the people's sins, Joshua now stands charged and Satan challenges the right of Joshua to stand before the Lord since he is a sinner. Satan is rebuffed before he can speak a word. "The Lord rebuke thee" are the words the Angel of the Lord, who then commands the filthy garments of Joshua to be removed, signifying that with this act, there is full absolution of all guilt and that Joshua will receive new garments of beauty and grace.

The eighth nocturnal vision reaches a climax in the second half of chapter 6:9-15 where Yahweh requires Zechariah to make a crown of silver and gold offered by the returned exiles and with it to crown the high priest Joshua as king. Thus by means of this striking symbolism the Messianic figure of the BRANCH is shown to combine in one person the offices of Joshua as high priest and Zerubbabel David's descendant, as political leader. The BRANCH (6:8-9) was the name of the coming Messiah of David's family to be called the "Nazarene" (Matthew 2:23).[34]

The Holy Week Prophecies of Zechariah

According to Young, Chapters 9:1-14:21 have as their major theme: The future of world powers and of God's kingdom. Young outlined this second large section of Zechariah as follows:

1. 9:1-10:72 Zion shall be delivered and will triumph over the heathen world. This shall be accomplished by her King Messiah.
2. 11:1-17. The good and faithful Shepherd.
3. 12:1-13:6. A further picture of Israel's future turning unto the Lord.
4. 13:7-14:21. A judgment to purify Israel and the future glory of Jerusalem.[35]

The Prophecy Depicting Christ's
Triumphal Entry into Jerusalem (9:9)

The first prophecy of the second section of Zechariah is found in chapter 9:9: "Be very happy, people of Zion! Shout aloud, people will come to you. He is righteous and victorious, poor, and riding on a donkey, on a young burro, the colt of a donkey."[36]

Mack claimed that this prophecy is the most specific of the Zecharian Messianic prophecies: namely, the one announcing Christ's triumphal entry into Jerusalem on the first day of the Passover week.[37] On that first day of Holy Week Jesus brought about the literal fulfillment of these words of Zechariah by sending His disciples and telling them to bring the colt spoken of by the Second Temple prophet, who uttered his prophetic utterance at least five hundred years before its realization. By this action, Jesus publicly proclaimed Himself as the Messiah and as fulfiller of that Zecharian prophecy. The multitudes and Jesus' disciples understood the significance of that action. Said Mack: "Apart from their goal in Jesus these words have no meaning."[38] Again Mack asserted: "If this is not true, then He was deceived, or a deceiver, and not worthy to be called Lord and Savior. Throughout the last chapters of Zechariah, as through Malachi, runs the phrase "in that day," a characteristic Messianic expression, showing the intensive yearning of that age for the Messiah's coming, the hoping, the waiting spirt with which the books of Old Testament prophecy was closing.[39]

Jesus to be Sold for Thirty Pieces of Silver

In Zechariah 11:12-13 Zechariah predicted: "Then I told Them, 'If you think it right, pay me, but if not, don't. And they weighed out as my pay thirty shekels of silver. 'Give to the potter,' the Lord told me.' A fine price they have set upon me. And I took the 30 shekels of silver and gave them at the Lord's temple to the potter."[40]

Matthew 27:10 cites Zechariah 11:12-13 as fulfilled in the betrayal of Christ by Judas Iscariot for thirty pieces of silver, which were returned by Judas when he realized the enormity of his deed, and the priests used the money to pay for a potter's field. In Matthew 27:6-9 according to Beck's translation: "The high priest took the money. It isn't right to put this into the temple treasury," they said: "It's blood money." So they decided to buy with it the potter's field for the burial of strangers. That's why that field has ever since been called the Field of Blood... Then what the prophet Jeremiah said came true: "I took the thirty shekels of silver, the price of Him, on whom some men of Israel set a price, and I gave them for the potter's field as the Lord directed me."[41]

Who is Right: Jeremiah or Zechariah?

Matthew 27:9-10 and Zechariah 11:13 are said to contradict each other. Surely it is claimed, this is a clear proof that the Bible contains errors and contradictions and therefore it cannot be inerrant as Luther, The Lutheran Confessions, Walther, Pieper and other theologians have taught.[42]

It appears that Matthew ascribed a prophecy which apparently was not uttered by Jeremiah but one recorded by the post-exilic Zechariah and ascribed it to Jeremiah who heads the Latter Prophets. William Arndt in his book, *Does the Bible Contradict Itself?* said that a number of solutions are possible which would remove the charge that Jeremiah and Zechariah contradict each other. In his book he has offered at least two possible solutions. In this apologetical volume, the former St. Louis professor of New Testament Biblical interpretation and Biblical Hermeneutics wrote:

Reading Jeremiah, we find that, while he has not the exact words quoted here, he has words that are somewhat similar, Jer. 32:6-15. It will be noted that he is speaking of the purchase of a field, although he is not alluding to the thirty pieces of silver. The purchase of a field is certainly an important item in the prophecy quoted by St. Matthew. We are justified in saying that a prominent feature of the prophecy as placed before us by St. Matthew is found in Jeremiah. Turning to Zechariah, we find that he does not speak of buying a field, but makes mention of thirty pieces of silver. We see, then, that St. Matthew has drawn together into one two prophecies, the one taken from Jeremiah, the other from Zechariah. We would not find fault with Matthew if he had written: "Then was fulfilled that which was written by Jeremiah and Zechariah," because, inasmuch as buying a field is alluded to in the prophecy quoted, the Book of Jeremiah may justly be said to contain a part of it. But if this must be granted, then we cannot accuse Matthew of contradicting the Old Testament in his statement as to the source of his quotation. No one will take it amiss if a work which has two authors is, in a brief allusion to it, ascribed to merely one of them, especially if this writer happens to be the more prominent of the two.[43]

Thus Arndt pointed out that the well-known Sanday and Headlam's *Commentary on the Epistle of Paul to the Romans* is often referred to as Sanday's *Commentary*. Jeremiah was a far more important and prominent prophet than Zechariah and hence it is not surprising what a prophecy which can be traced back to both of them is called the prophecy of Jeremiah, even though the greater part is taken from Zechariah.[44]

Another reasonable solution to this seeming contradiction between Matthew and Zechariah would be the following: The Jews, in their division of the Old Testament canon into: Law, Prophets and Writings placed Jeremiah at the head of the Latter Prophets whose order was: Jeremiah, Ezekiel, Isaiah and the Twelve Minor Prophets. So a quotation from the Latter prophets of which Zechariah was a part of the Minor Prophets (as one volume) could be quoted as found in the scroll of Jeremiah. Arndt claimed that at the time of the writing of his book that he had in his possession a copy of Luther's *Epistle of Paul to the Galatians* and yet the same book had a number of other Lutheran writings in addition. Both on the inside cover and the title page there was the inspiration: *Luther's Commentary to the Galatians*, although containing more of the Reformer's writings. Hence by analogy, it can be fairly argued that any verses from the

266

prophets might be said to be taken from the Book of Jeremiah.[45]

The Prophecy of Christ's Piercing: Zechariah 12:10

The Gospel of John 19:31-37 reports the death of Jesus, the Messiah, "And then bowing His head, He yielded up His spirit." Jesus died on the day of Preparation for the Passover. The Jews asked Pontius Pilate to take action against the three crucified people, against Jesus and the two malefactors crucified with Him. The Jews did not want their bodies hanging on their respective crosses on a holy day. They requested that their legs be broken and thus hasten death for each of them. Thus John reports: "So the soldiers broke the legs of the first man, and also of the other who had been crucified with Jesus. When however, the soldiers came to Jesus they saw that He was already dead and they refrained from breaking His legs. One of the soldiers then made a thrust at His side with a lance and immediately blood and water flowed out. This statement is the testimony of an eye-witness, and it is true. He knows that he is telling the truth in order that the Scriptures might be fulfilled which declares, 'Not one of the bones shall be broken' (Ex. xii 46) and again another Scriptures says: 'They shall look upon whom they have pierced' (Zech. 12:10)."[46]

In Revelation 1:7 John wrote: "Lo, He is coming in the clouds of heaven, and every eye shall see Him, and so will all who pierced Him, and all the nations of the earth shall gaze who mourn. Even so, Amen." Apart from the New Testament "there is no adequate interpretation of such words as these. Without the New Testament explanation they could never be other than enigmatical."[47]

The Desertion of Christ by His Disciples
In Gethsemane, Zechariah 13:7

The last Messianic prophecy contained in Zechariah is the prediction contained in 13:7: "Smite the shepherd, and the sheep shall be scattered." This prophecy was remembered by Christ in the Garden of Gethsemane and quoted by Him to His disciples, foretelling the events that when the soldiers came to apprehend Christ, all His disciples forsook Him and fled.

Laetsch says of chapter 13:7, that is "a clear prophecy of the offense taken by the disciples when Christ was smitten. So Christ Himself interprets these words (Matt. 26:31; Mark 14:27). They were fulfilled (See Matt. 26:56; Mark 14:50ff.). Yet the Lord would not forsake the sheep. The Lord Himself, acting in and through the person of His 'Fellow' (John 5:19f., 30), will turn His band upon (Gr. N) come to the aid of the little ones (Gr. N.), His despondent, terrified disciples (Luke 24:4f., 11,17Cf., 37; John 20 2, 11ff., 19,6). These weaklings and deserters became the courageous, invincible heralds of the Messiah's kingdom."[48]

Summary of Zechariah's Fore-Glimpses of Christ

His Atoning Death for the Removal of Sin (38-9:13:1). As Builder of the House of God (6:12). His Universal Reign as King and Priest (6:13, 9:10). Triumphal Entry (9:9, quoted in Matthew 21:5, John 12:15). Betrayal for 30 pieces of silver (11:11, quoted in Matthew 27:9,10). His Deity (12:8). His Hands Pierced (12:10; 13:6, quoted in John 19:37). The Smitten Shepherd (13:7, quoted in Matthew 26:31, Matt 14:27).[49]

In view of his predictions about the week when Christ would, suffer, be crucified and die, it is not difficult to see, why Zechariah has been called "The prophet of the Holy Week."

Footnotes

1. Edward J. Young, *An Introduction to the Old Testament* (Grand Rapids: William B. Eerdmans Publishing Company, 1975), p. 30.
2. **Ibid.**
3. Franz Delitzsch, *Messianic Prophecies in Historical Succession*. Translated by Samuel Ives Curtiss (New York: Charles Scribner's Sons, 1891), pp. 130,132.
4. Norman Geisler, *Christ: The Theme of the Bible* (Chicago: Moody Press, 198), p. 100.
5. W. G. Moorehead, *Outline Studies in the Books of the Old Testament* (New York and Chicago: Fleming H. Revell Company, 1894), p. 357.
6. Merrill Unger, Zechariah (Grand Rapids: Zondervan Publishing House, 1963), p. 18.
7. Moorehead, **op. cit.**, p. 351.
8. Gleason Archer, *A Survey of Old Testament Introduction*, (Chicago: Moody Press, 1974), p. 425.
9. Kurt Kuhl, *The Old Testament – Its Origins and Composition* (Richmond: John Knox Press, 1961), p. 224.
10. G.L. Robinson, *The Twelve Minor Prophets* (New York: George H. Doran Company, 1926), p. 155; Archer, **op. cit.**, pp. 425-430.
11. Wilhelm Moeller, *Grundriss fuer Altestamentliche Enileitung* (Berlin: Evangelische Verlagsanstalt, 1958), pp. 257-258.
12. W.F. Beck, *The Holy Bible, An American Translation* (New Haven, MO, Leader Publishing Company, 1976), New Testament, p. 291.
13. P. E. Kretzmann, *Popular Commentary of the Bible, Old Testament* (St. Louis, Concordia Publishing House, 1924), II, p. 708.
14. Walter Harrelson, *Interpreting the Old Testament* (New York: Holt, Rinehart and Winston, 1964), pp. 398-401.
15. Bernard W. Anderson, *Understanding the Old Testament*. Third Edition (Englewood Cliffs: Prentice all, Inc. 1975), p. 482.
16. C. I. Scofield, *The Scofield Reference Bible* (New York: Oxford University Press, 1917), p. 5.
17. F. C. Thompson, *The New Chain Reference Bible*. Third Improved Edition (Indianapolis: B. B. Kirkbride Bible Co, 1934), Cf. Section, New Comprehensive Helps, "Prophecies Concerning Jesus and Their Fulfillment," pp. 246-249.
18. Hobart Freeman, *An Introduction to the Old Testament Prophets* (Chicago: Moody Press, 1968), p. 334.
19. Charles Caldwell Ryrie, *The Basis of the Premillennial Faith* (New York: Loizeaux Brothers, 1953), p. 126.
20. Lewis Sperry Chager, *Systematic Theology* (Dallas: Dallas Theological Seminary, 1948), IV, pp. 265-266.
21. Compare Merrill F. Unger, discussion in chapter 14 of Zechariah in his, *Commentary on the Old Testament* (Chicago: Moody Press, 19810, II, pp. 2050-2062; Cf. also Charles F. Feinberg, God Remembers, A Study of the Book of Zechariah (Wheaton, Illinois: Van Kampen Press, 1950, pp. 248-249.
22. H.C. Leupold, *Exposition of Zechariah* (Columbus: Lutheran Book Concern, 1956), pp. 258-277; Walter R. Roehrs, *Concordia Self-Study Commentary* (St. Louis, Concordia Publishing House, 1973), pp. 656-657.
23. Paul Heinisch, Christ in Prophecy, Translated by Qilliam G. Heidt, Collegeville:

Minnesota: the Liturgical Press, 1956), pp. 167-170; Aaron Judah Kligerman, Messianic Prophecy in the Old Testament (Grand Rapids: Zondervan Publishing House, 1957), pp. 130-135. Josh McDowell, Evidence That Demands A verdict (San Bernadino: Campus Crusade for Christ, 1972), pp. 147-184.

24. Helen Barrett Montgomery, *The New Testament in Modern English* (Philadelphia; Judson Press.

25. **Ibid.**, p. 237.

26. Louis Fuerbringer, "Sacharja, der Prophet der Hoffnung," Synodal-Bericht. Vedrfhandlungen der Evangelischen Synode vonn Missouri, Ohio und Anderen Staaten, Nord Wisconsin Districts, 1918, pp. 35-43, p. 236.

27. L. R. Elliott, "Branch," *Wycliffe Bible Encyclopedia* (Chicago: Moody Press, 1975), I, p. 272.

28. Cf. Horace D. Hummel, *The Word Becoming Flesh* (St. Louis: Concordia Publishing House, 1979), pp. 200, 205,366, 368.

29. Beck, **op. cit.**, Old Testament, p. 1092.

30. **Ibid.**, p. 796.

31. **Ibid.**, p. 901.

32. Kretzmann, *Old Testament Commentary*, **op. cit.**, II, p. 462-463.

33. **Ibid.**, p. 705.

34. Cf. footnote to Matthew 2:23 in Beck, *The Holy Bible, New Testament*, **op. cit.**, p. 3, Which reads: "According to Is. 11:1 the Savior would be a Nezer, a sprout, growing from the roots of the tree of David".

35. Young, **op. cit.**, p. 283.

36. Beck, **op. cit.**, p. 1097 of Old Testament section.

37. Mack, **op. cit.**, p. 127.

38. **Ibid.**, pp. 127-128.

39. **Ibid.**

40. Beck, **op. cit.**, Old Testament, p. 1099.

42. Cf. volume by P. E. Kretzmann, *The Foundations Must Stand* (St. Louis: Concordia Publishing House, 1936), 123 pp.

43. William Arndt, *Does the Bible Contradict Itself?* (St. Louis: Concordia Publishing House, 1926), pp. 51-52.

44. **Ibid.**, p. 52.

46. Translation of Richard Francis Weymouth, *The New Testament in Modern Speech* (Boston: Pilgrim Press, 1943), pp. 264-265.

47. Mack, **op. cit.**, p. 127.

48. Theodore Laetsch, *Bible Commentary, the Minor Prophets* (St. Louis: Concordia Publishing House, 1970), pp. 490-91.

49. Taken from *Halley's Bible Handbook*. New Revised Edition (Grand Rapids: Zondervan Publishing house, 1965), p. 383.

Questions

1. Unger was of the opinion that Zechariah had more to say about ____.
2. The returned exiles were not remaining ____.
3. The anti-dispensationalist and amillennialist school of interpretation holds ____.
4. Joshua may be said to be a type of ____.
5. Jesus was to be sold for ____.
6. Who is right, Jeremiah or Zechariah? ____
7. Zechariah has been called the prophet of the ___.

The Meaning of the Night Visions of Zechariah, the Prophet of Hope, For His Day and for Our Day

Christian News, March 13, 1989

In 539 B.C. Cyrus, king of Persia, conquered Babylon.[1] Moved to Yahweh, the Persian king issued a decree in 536 B.C. (Ezra 1:14), declaring that God's people then in exile in Babylonian should be allowed to return to Jerusalem and rebuild the destroyed house of Yahweh. Nearly 50,000 exiles took advantage of this offer, together with their personal belongings and the temple treasures, they returned to Jerusalem from Babylonia and the other countries where they had previously been settled, to start life a new in the land of their forefathers.[2] They intended to rebuild the temple and the walls of Jerusalem, both destroyed by Nebuchadnezzar in 587 B.C. Among the returnees were Zerubbabel, the grandson of Jehoiachin, and Joshua, descendant of the last chief priest of the temple in Jerusalem. They were to aid Sheshbazzar, Cyrus' representative, in the restoration.

Back from the exile, the people were faced with many problems. By 535 B.C. they had laid the foundations for the temple, but times were hard and the people were poor. The Samaritans wanted to be accepted as Jews and offered to help in the rebuilding. However, when the Samaritans were rejected, and as a result they became bitter and did all they could to hinder the work. As a result of the many difficulties, work was all but abandoned on the temple for almost fourteen years, while the people gave themselves to building their own homes and other selfish pursuits.

After the death of Cyrus the Great in 529 B.C. the latter was succeeded by Cambyses, who ruled till.522 B.C. when a usurper tried to make himself ruler of the Persian Empire.[3] Darius the I records on the Behistun Rock how he defeated Gautama. In 521 B.C. Darius Hystaspis emerged as the new king of the vast Medo-Persian Empire. In Darius' second year Haggai and Zechariah were moved by the Spirit of God to stir the returned Jews from their religious lethargy and galvanize them into action. Haggai in his first message reminded the people that they were not being blessed by Yahweh in their various endeavors because of failure to build God's house. Under divine direction the people began the rebuilding of the temple, an action which roused the suspicions of the officers of the king, so that the matter was taken to Babylon for investigation.

Cyrus' original decree was confirmed and the Persian government gave permission for the temple's rebuilding to go ahead. Haggai challenged the returned exiles from the Lord and between September 1, 520 B.C. till December 25, 520 B.C. four separate messages were given by Haggai particularly to Zerubbabel and Joshua. Three of the four messages were in essence words of encouragement. The people worked for a time but those who had witnessed the first temple became discouraged because the new one was in their sight very inferior (Haggai 2:3) by comparison. But Haggai countered by telling them to take courage for the Lord was with them.

Zechariah, Haggai's contemporary, tells the people that God had not forsaken them. Yahweh was faithful to them and His word. He still had a great purpose for His people, and He will bring that purpose into effect.

While Haggai's work was over in a short time, for his book has but two chapters, Zechariah's contains fourteen chapters and Zechariah goes much further and was used first by Yahweh from 520 to 518 and also possibly at a later time around 490 B.C. to utter prophecies about the future of God's kingdom. Dr. L. Fuerbringer, in an essay delivered at the North Wisconsin District in 1918 said:

He had a special assignment to fulfil in the difficult time which would come more difficult in the future. His assignment was to comfort the people and thus encourage them. He depicts what was still to occur, the future glory of God's people. But in connection with this glory, there would first adhere tribulation. As title for this book, we would place: "Per aspera ad astra;" in German: "On a rough road it goes heavenward," or "Per crucem ad lucem," in German: "Through cross to the crown."

"That is the summary of our book. And while it is so rich in comfort for the people of God, for this reason Luther in his preface called Zechariah one of the most comforting prophets of the Old Testament (XIV, 166)."

Particularly in the second half of the book of Zechariah, in chapters 9-14, the reader, on the strength of the New Testament, will find many Messianic prophecies. Zechariah has been termed the "prophet of Holy Week" because the Gospels cite a number of passages from chapters 9-14 as foretelling the triumphal entry (9:9), the betrayal of Judas for thirty pieces of silver (11:11,12), the desertion of Jesus by His disciples in Gethsemane (13:7), and finally the death of Jesus in chapter 12:10.[5]

The presentation today proposes to treat the eight night visions that Zechariah saw in one night, and see what comfort they had for Zechariah's time as well as for our day. Dr. Fuerbringer cited Dr. Stoeckhardt to the effect that the Scriptures are not monotonous and that especially in the Old Testament the Holy Spirit described New Testament grace in pictures and colors, in order to set forth in the Scriptures the one central truth from all possible angles, namely, that Christ is Son of God and Son of Man, and to sharpen the picture of the great work of redemption, which Christ accomplished.[6] The eight visions granted in one night are closely related to each other. One vision prepares the way for the next, and the following often latching on to the preceding one. These visions deal with the future of Israel and in some instances with the church in the Messianic age.

Three months after Zechariah's initial call to repentance, Yahweh came to the prophet with messages couched in the form of eight visions. The twenty-fourth day of the month Shebat is of significance for on this day five months before the work of the Temple was resumed. This was also two months after Haggai's last message.

Some critical scholars believe that the book of Zechariah originally began with verse 7 because of the biographical information that is repeated, so it is held that the first six verses were added later.[7] Some scholars criticize the phrase "the Word of the Lord," arguing that the following record is not the spoken Word of the Lord to the prophet but only visions, created by the author of chapters 1-8. However, if we accept the book of Zechariah as inspired Scripture, then the first six verses of the chapter are what they claim they are — the Word of God as revealed to Zechariah at the time that verse one says it was.

There are three methods of interpreting the eight nocturnal visions: 1) That which confines their significance to the times of Zechariah; 2) That which spiritualizes very much of the eight visions by application to the church); 3) That which holds that the visions had an application to Israel but makes them refer to events in the future, especially with reference to the Millennium.[8]

Scholars that would interpret all the visions as dealing with the time of Joshua and Zerubbabel and shortly thereafter would be most critical scholars, like Westermann, Gailey, Cornfeld, W. Neil, J. Winton Thomas and many others.[9] As representative of this viewpoint we cite Gailey: "Zechariah may well have been led to use the vision form to present the politically dangerous scheme that appears to be at the heart of his passages. It is not clear today, however, exactly what he sought in the political sphere. He seems to have attempted to establish Zerubbabel as the successor to David in a genuine coronation ceremony in the partially reconstructed Temple."[10]

Some conservative scholars would not limit the revelations contained in the eight nocturnal visions solely to the sixth and fifth centuries B.C.[11] Ellison states that the visions are not solely directed to Zechariah's time or the immediate future, but that a major element for them is timeless (and) stresses major spiritual truths in the light of the prophet's own time.[12]

Leupold stresses the fact that the eight night visions are an orderly sequence of thought and that the following visions point to the fulfillment of previous ones.[13] Leupold, however, does not imply that all parts of the eight visions were necessarily fulfilled within the prophet's lifetime, though he does seem to indicate an orderly sequence of fulfillment which is not all yet to come.[14] Wilhelm Moller finds in most of the eight visions, symbols, types and foreshadowing of the person and work of Christ.[15] Kretzmann spiritualizes and always interprets the visions in relation to the New Testament Church.[16] Relative to the whole book of Zechariah, chapters 1-8, 9-14, Luther wrote: "Here and there throughout his entire prophecy he intersperses quite a lot of material concerning Christ and the apostles and also cites many testimonies from this prophet".[17] Meredith Kline believes that "The central theme of these night visions is the kingdom of God in the midst of the kingdoms of this world. The problem is introduced at that Jerusalem, Old Testament center and symbol of God's kingdom center, bears the scars of defeat and desolation while the nations of the earth are at ease in their indifference to the sovereign claims of the Lord, the God of Israel."[18]

The third group, favoring the millennial times would be Unger, Feinberg, Gaebelein, C. Morgan, Vine, C. Luck and many others.[19]

In the interpretation of the visions of Zechariah it should be borne in mind that although the general teaching of the visions seemed clear, the significance of a number of details is not always clear. This is due, in part, to the fact that the visions, like parables, contain certain features needed to fill out the narrative of presentation, that do not necessarily have interpretative value. Other features are left unexplained.

The question has been raised why God used apocalyptics as a method of salvation. Some critical scholars advance the view that this kind of literary genre was employed to veil the political ambitions of the returned Judeans and this hidden form was used to keep the real intention of the message from the Persian rulers.[20] This is a view we reject. We hold that Yahweh used it to secure the attention of His people and this was the approach he selected. It is one of the diverse manners by which God spake in times past through His prophets.

I.
Introduction to the Nocturnal Visions

The eight night visions are preceded by a call to repentance. "The Lord was angry with your fathers." The evidence of their father's unfaithfulness and God's judgment was about them in the devastation of the land, to which the Jews returned and were now trying to rebuild.

Return to me and I will return to you. Repent-turn around and come back to me and I will bless you. Turn away from your evil way of life and from your wicked deeds.

Listen to my words. Your fathers did not listen, do not be like them! Your fathers, look, where are they? They are gone and missed the opportunity when I called my prophets. Your fathers though they could escape, but My Word set out in pursuit and caught them. They did repent and said that the Lord had told them He would deal with them for their ways and deeds and He did what He said He would do.

Five times in five verses Zechariah repeats that what he is proclaiming is the Lord's Word. This fact emphasizes the seriousness and authority of the message. Some critical scholars, who do not accept the present text of the Old Testament as the Word of God, claim that there is a contradiction between verse 4 and verse 6 of chapter 1. Generally speaking the fathers refused to listen to and repent when the Lord spoke to them through the prophets (v. 4), but as a result of the captivity some did confess and did return. Verse 4 is talking about people before the captivity and verse 6 refers to those who saw their sinful ways and repented after the captivity was indeed a fact and not just a prophecy.

Vision One (1:7-17) The Heavenly Couriers

This vision teaches God's special care for and interest in His people, and affirms explicitly, "my house shall be built" (v. 16). The prophet sees a troop of horsemen, their leader in front, who patrol the earth and report it at rest. It looks as if God is not moved by compassion for His languishing people (v. 12) who are waiting for the great upheaval of the Messianic age (cf. Hag. 2:21,22). The prophet is informed by an interpreting angel that this is not wholly so. God's loving and intense interest ("zeal") is in His chosen people (vv. 14, 16, 17); His displeasure is turned against the arrogant nations who delight in being instruments in Israel's downfall (v. 15). The vision begins like this: "I saw in the night, and behold, a man riding upon a red horse! He was standing among the myrtle trees in the glen; and behind him were red, sorrel, and white horses." Most conservative scholars regard the man of the red horse as Christ.[21] Unger describes him as the pre-incarnate Messiah, the overseer of Israel, and the intercessor for the nation's welfare.[22] According to Leupold, he is the leader of the other messengers, the Angel of the Lord, "the second person of the Trinity appearing in angelic form before the incarnation."[23] Fuerbringer and Laetsch would agree with this identification.[24]

The phrase "Among the myrtle trees" is understood by many commentators as symbolic for the people of Israel. Leupold suggests that the myrtle trees are small and that this portrays Israel's small, insignificant appearance among the other nations.[25]

The Angel of the Lord was in the glen. Both Unger and Leupold conclude that the phrase "in the glen" indicates the low estate of God's people.[26] Leupold limits the significance of the period to the period of restoration,[27] while Unger extends its application on to the second coming of Christ.[28]

The number and color of the horses are interpreted differently by scholars. Ellison concludes that the color merely distinguishes three different groups and has no further meaning,[29] while Gordon suggests that the mention of four colored horses is symbolic of the four quarters of heaven.[30] However, Unger, Leupold and other commentators believe that the colors are of deeper importance. The red signifies bloodshed, war, and judgment. The white is symbolic of glory and victory, while the sorrel is a mixture of both — a mixture of judgment and victory. Leupold also concludes from verse 11 that it was an undetermined number of horses who were involved and not just three or four.

All the earth is reported by the heavenly reconnaissance team as remaining at rest. In this statement there is thus a report of the description of world conditions under the rule of Darius around 520 B.C. Unger claims that this lack of war was disappointing because a great upheavel was to proceed necessarily before Israel's restoration (Hag. 2:6,7).[31] This would explain the cry, "O Lord" ... How long? How long would it take God to fulfill his promises to Israel. The Lord answers with a word of comfort and hope.

In addition to informing Zechariah that the line is stretched out over Jerusalem, and suggesting reconstruction, growth and prosperity, he also announced that the temple will be built.

This vision, coming at a time when Israel was questioning whether her Lord had forsaken her, was to emphasize the fact that he most certainly had not. The angel of the Lord is shown as pleading with Yahweh not to extend further chastisement to his people but to restore them. The prophet is told through the medium of an angel interpreter that Yahweh has nothing but indignation for his enemies and had the determination to do good for his people.

The vision was to bolster up the Israelites by showing them that their time of trial and abuse was coming to an end, that their God has indeed not forsaken them and that his angels were indeed in their company and ready to do battle with their enemies and that they would soon be reinstated in the eyes of others as the Lord's chosen people.

Vision Two (1:18-21) The Four Horns and Four Smiths

The central teaching of this vision is that Israel's foes have finally through war destroyed themselves, and that there is no longer any opposition to the building of God's house.

In the last paragraph of chapter I we have the account of this short vision: "And I lifted my eyes and saw, behold, four horns. And I said to the angel who talked with me; These are the horns that have scattered Judah, Israel, and Jerusalem." Then the Lord showed me four smiths. And I said, What are these coming to do? He answered: "These are the horns which scattered Judah, so that no man raised his head; and these have come to terrify them, to cast down the horns of the nations who lifted up their horns against the land of Judah to scatter it."

It seems that after each vision, the eyes of the prophet were lowered to meditate on what had been shown him. From this the angel aroused him. In Scripture, the horn is a symbol of power and also of pride. There are, however, differences of opinion regarding the details of this vision. Unger claims that "the four horns must then symbolize the four great powers — Babylonia, Medo-Persia, Macedonia, Greece and Rome." In the book of Daniel, horns are pictured as the symbols of world Prowers (Dan. 7:7ff).[32] According to him there are four Gentile world powers that shall rise and fall during "the time of the Gentiles" which began with the captivity of 605 B.C. and will continue to the coming of Christ. Leupold prefers to interpret the four horns as a symbol of worldly power.[33]

If the four horns are to be identified with any nation, one could identify them with the nations who in the past have devastated and destroyed Judah: Egypt, Assyria, Babylon and Persia.

Israel's enemies are going to find their match in the four smiths, craftsmen in iron, whom Yahweh would employ as instruments of divine power for the redemption of God's people. The number four of the smiths may denote the four corners of heaven, suggesting the worldwide character of the forces which oppress Israel, a view common to other prophecies as well (Cf. Dan. 8:8; Hag. 2:6). It was a figurative way of saying that prevailing world-power would be broken and Judah again exalted.

Vision Three (Chapter 2) The Man With the Measuring Line

The purpose of the third vision was to prophetically reassure His people that Yahweh would in due time bring about the rebuilding of

Jerusalem and foster material and spiritual blessings. The vision seems to be a reaffirmation and expansion of the promises in 1:16 and 1:17 of the first vision.

In this vision the prophet sees a man with a measuring line to measure Jerusalem. Fuerbringer concludes that the man is the same one who sits on the red horse in chapter 1, or in other words, Christ.[34]

Lifting up his eyes to the man with the measuring line in his hand, Zechariah said to him: "Where are you going?" The answer given was "To measure Jerusalem, to see what the breadth thereof, and what is the length thereof." While the man is engaged the interpreting angel leaves the prophet in the direction where the measuring was going on, but is met on the way by another angel, most likely sent by the man with the line who gives the order to go and tell the young man from whom he has come that "Jerusalem shall be inhabited as towns without walls for the multitude of men and cattle therein."

The man with the measuring line is the Messiah, Jesus Christ; the symbolism in the act of measuring is the good news that Jerusalem will not only be restored but greatly enlarged. Verse 4 says: "Jerusalem shall be inhabited as town without walls. . ." But more important than outward enlargement is the beautiful promise: "For I, saith the Lord will be unto her a wall of fire round about and will be the glory in the midst of her." It contains the assurance of protection, even though without visible walls, Jerusalem shall be a strong city, because the Lord Himself shall be its defense.

Pusey, Kretzmann, and Laetsch hold the view that the vision does not refer to the earthly Jerusalem.[35] Laetsch writes: "The angel is not here speaking of the earthly Jerusalem." His view is that although the walls of the physical Jerusalem had been destroyed and were later rebuilt by Nehemiah, that the reference here is to the New Testament Church.[36] This shall not need any walls of earthly material, as the Lord is its wall. This church should have a tremendous multitude which no walls could compass. Pusey asserts: "Jerusalem shall be inhabited as towns without walls. Clearly then it is no earthly city; to be inhabited as villages would be weakness, not strength."[37] So rather than describe the earthly city the promise looks to the time of Christ when His church will be enlarged and ever will receive the many souls who worship him. Let everybody hasten to this city whose safety and sanctity are in God alone (vv 6-13).

The Fourth Vision (Chapter 3:1-10)
The Justification of the High Priest

How can a holy and righteous God promise such blessings to such a sinful and unworthy people? The Lord gives the answer in the fourth vision.

Joshua, as the high priest in this vision and in reality, represents the people of Israel; his filthy garments, the sins of the nation. Satan accuses Joshua before the Lord, but God in His mercy removes the sin and clothes him in righteousness. The Lord then admonishes him, as the high priest and representative of the people, to walk in his ways; for then and only

276

then will he have charge of the courts of the Lord, and free access to the throne of grace.

Joshua may also be said to be a type of Christ.[38] Just as Jesus was later charged with the people's sins, Joshua now stands charged and Satan challenges the right of Joshua to stand before the Lord, since he is a sinner. Satan is rebuffed before he can speak a word. "The Lord rebuke thee," are the words of the Angel of the Lord. And then commands the filthy garments of Joshua to be removed, signifying that with this act, there is full absolution of all guilt. Joshua will receive new garments of beauty and glory.

Zechariah is eager to see Joshua fully robed and cries out: "Let them set a fair mitre upon his head." The head-gear did not symbolize what God's people received, but rather what they were to strive for — the needed sanctification. All are to receive the forgiveness that God gives with a penitent heart.

The crowning is to show that he is an intercessor for the people. In the priesthood of Joshua there were things that were prophetic of the future. On these all are to fix their attention. Laetsch interprets this: "We must not overlook the fact that the high priest represented the entire sinful nation. His absolution and reacceptance includes that of the nation as the kingdom of priests and a holy nation."[39] Joshua and his fellow priests were only a type of the coming Messiah who would do the work of priest perfectly.

The Lord exhorts Joshua to "walk in his ways." This can mean only that if they keep his commandments, follow the examples which Yahweh had given them in the prophets and patriarchs that they will be rewarded. He promises them that if they should do this they will be watched over by "those who stand by," meaning His angels.

The Lord then directed attention away from Joshua as God promises to send the Jews, "His Servant the Branch . . ." "Including Zechariah's prophecies, we find the Savior Jesus Christ foretold as the Branch or Shoot in four different places in the Old Testament."[40] In Jeremiah 23:5-6 and 33:15-16, the Messiah is described as a branch who as King will reign and rule in righteousness. In Isaiah 11:1 the Messiah is depicted as a shoot coming out of the slump of the tree of Jesse's house while in Zechariah 3:8 and 6:12 Jesus is depicted as "the Branch."

The Angel of the Lord further told Zechariah: "For behold, upon the stone which I have set before Joshua, upon a single stone with seven facets, I will remove the guilt of this land in a single day" (RSV). The Berkely version renders this verse as follows: "See the stone which I have set before Joshua, upon one stone seven eyes."[41] Unger and Luther see the stone as symbolic of Christ.[42] Leupold, on the other hand, contends that the stone is symbolic of the church of God. The stone spoken of here cannot be the cornerstone of the temple, for this was already in existence. Laetsch claims the stone does not symbolize the Messiah, for he was still to come, while the stone was placed before Joshua. Joshua was told that he was to judge the house of the Lord and keep his courts (vs. 7).

Now he is given another honorable charge. He is to be not only the caretaker and ruler of the visible Temple, but of the invisible, spiritual temple, the church represented by the stone which is the object of God's loving attention.[43] The seven eyes are those of the Holy Spirit directed upon the Messiah's Church. Finally the angel of the Lord tells Zechariah that in that day, "every one of you will invite his neighbor under his vine and under his fig tree." In that day, the New Testament era, the justified members of God's Church, enjoying peace with God, will share the joy of their fellow believers and urge one another to rejoice and sing with them, to taste and see how good the Lord is.

Vision Five (4:1-14) The Temple Rebuilt by the Spirit Alone or The Sacred Candlestick and the Two Olive Trees

How beautifully these visions supplement one another and progress. The fifth vision carries forward the reader from the last vision, for after the moral obstacles (filthy garments) were removed, then Israel is prepared for God's original purpose as the bearer of light and truth. Though the vision occupies itself with Zerubbabel, Israel is certainly in view.

When Zechariah is awakened again, he sees a golden candelabrum and its seven lamps connected by pipes supplied with oil from two olive trees. The candlestick plainly represents the "Church, God's people." This is based on the assumption that in Rev. 1:20 the lampstand with seven lamps represents the chosen people of God. What keeps the lamps burning? The oil supplied by a reservoir above the lampstand. What gives God's people power to function? The Holy Spirit.

The Lord is directing this vision to Zerubbabel specifically, and to Israel generally. Zerubbabel is the representative of the people as Joshua was in the last vision.

To Zerubbabel and to the people Yahweh declares: "You cannot get things done by your own might or strength, but by the power of My Spirit. You may say that you have a mountain of trouble and difficulty standing in the way. Well, it will be flattened before you. You shall put the top stone of the temple in its place. The final act of construction will be a reality. With Zerubbabel you have laid the foundation of My house, with him you shall complete it. Those of you who view the small, insignificant appearance of it all with contempt shall be glad, for you shall see Zerubbabel with tools of construction in his hand. What was begun shall be finished. I am watching over everything."

The two olive branches are representative of the offices of the high priest and the king, or more specifically relate to Joshua and Zerubbabel. It is difficult to determine whether oil is pouring out of the trees or out of the two pipes which are apparently connected to the lampstand in some way. However, in Rev. 11:3,4 two olive trees can be interpreted as symbolic of the two witnesses who are to prophesy. If a comparison can be drawn, then it is quite possible that the trees in this vision are supplying oil to the lamps; for anointed servants of the Lord must be filled with the Holy Spirit. As they witness by the Spirit to the people, the Spirit then works in the hearts of the people who receive their witness.

Vision Six (5:1-4) The Flying Roll

How would God deal with sinners and ungodly people? The vision of the Flying Scroll is the Lord's answer.

The scroll Zechariah sees is about thirty feet long and fifteen feet wide, obviously too large to be an ordinary scroll. Since these are the approximate dimensions of the Holy Place in the Tabernacle, Ellison and others conclude this scroll is representative of the Law.[44] The earliest Scriptures were written on materials made of the skins of animals or ancient paper. The roll was wrapped around two sticks, so that when it was read, it could be readily rerolled again. The scroll that Zechariah saw was not sealed, but open. Not only Palestine, but all the Israelites throughout the earth are included. In a broad sense, the curse points to the Law of Moses against anyone who did not continue in the commands of the Law. Specifically, it covers the infraction of the two commandments singled out on the scroll, namely, theft and lying. Everyone breaking the Seventh Commandment, as well as everyone transgressing against the Second Commandment is to be removed, cut off, and swept away. God's curse will not be forgotten, but will consume the wicked and their house, even the very timber and stones. This curse will not only be temporal, but also eternal.

The Seventh Vision (5:5-10) The Flying Ephah

The seventh vision carries much the same thought as the sixth and shows that the punishment on sinners is not all, but that sin also must be removed, not only from the land, but from its very source.

The angel who had retired from the scene returns and says, "Lift up thine eyes, and see what is this that goeth forth . . ." Had the prophet absorbed all that was expected of him that he asks, "What is it?" Or did he readily recognize the ephah and its significance? At any rate he saw a cover of lead lift up and a woman sitting in the ephah. Then two more women came and lifted the ephah up between earth and heaven.

Laetsch is of the opinion that the ephah, which is about a bushel in our measure, signifies that the Lord demands honesty and full measure in all transactions.[45] The Lord sees this beginning to disappear in the spirit of selfishness and greed and which had already begun in pre-exilic times when merchants were concerned with only personal profit. The prophet is to warn his fellow Jews of this root evil of their hearts.

Pusey had a somewhat different view. He says that the Lord administers things in weights and measures, and that God will punish individual sinners as well as the whole nation.[46] "The measure then, which was seen, pointed to the filling up of the measure of transgression of the people against Himself . . . think the Lord alluded to the words of the prophet as though he would say, 'fill up the measure of sins' which your fathers began of old as it is in Zechariah, ye will soon fill it; for ye so hate to do evil, that ye will soon fill it to the utmost." The cover of lead, Pusey compares to the punishment of sin, as lead is by nature heavy.[47] Laetsch says the woman symbolizes wickedness because of the deceptive, captivating power of sin.[48]

The imprisonment of the woman is not the end of the vision. Two more women with wings appear and fly away, carrying an ephah and the first woman between earth and heaven. It may be that evil spirits are symbolized as snatching away the souls of the damned, who by serving them have become like they are.

The number of the women carrying the ephah is understandable, if the measuring vessel is full it would necessitate two women to carry it. The wings of the bearers suggests celerity of motion. Why women are selected is not clear.

The removal of the ephah by the women prompted the prophet Zechariah to ask as to its destination. The ephah was to be borne away, says the interpreting angel to the land of Shinar. But where is the land of Shinar? Gordon and Henshaw find the answer in the geographical Babylon.[49] Unger, with his extended telescope looks far beyond to the Babylon of Rev. 17 and 18.[50] Leupold, on the other hand, more correctly looks back to Gen. 10 and 11, and the Tower of Babel for an explanation.[51] Shinar was the first place, where man attempted to build a world empire against God. Such a warning against wickedness was necessary in Zechariah's day. Evil was showing its ugly head in the Holy Land. A lack for zeal has caused the stoppage of building the temple for fifteen years. Rebellion and wickedness must be removed from God's church. This is a lesson which the Jews needed in the fifth century B.C. and is one still needed today.

Vision Eight (Chapter 6:1-8) The Four War Chariots

The first and the eighth visions have certain features in common. In the first vision there is what seems to be a delay in God's promise to carry out His judgment against the enemies of Israel. The vision of the Four Chariots does not answer the question "How long?," but it does reassure the people that God will indeed keep His promises, and that His "justice shall prevail."

Zechariah lifted up his eyes, and looked, and behold, there came four chariots out from between the two mountains; and the mountains were mountains of brass or copper (Heb. nechosheth). Commentators differ as to what the mountains mean or represent.

In Rev. 1:15 Christ is described as having feet of brass. Brass seems to suggest strength and justice. Mountains composed of this material could then be symbolic of the tremendous power and crushing judgment of the Lord.

Some of the commentators have identified the two mountains with Zion and Olivet. The mountains must be symbolic because they are made of brass or copper. Leupold will not identify the mountains with any known mountain or hill, for none are of bronze. The mountains in the text form the gate towers that guard the palace entrance to the ruler of the universe. Laetsch[52] and Leupold[53] agree that the mountains represent the gates of the enclosure that held the chariots and argue that the bronze mountains represent the strong agencies that God must employ for His work. Another view is that they are two forms of divine appointment represented by Zion and Moriah, later by Jerubbabel and Joshua, and by Church and state. Calvin believed that the mountains are agencies for concealing God's secret promises,[54] and Luther interpreted the bronze mountains as "the Law and the Prophets."[55]

The Prophet Zechariah saw four chariots, each having a team of horses. There are four colors mentioned: red, white, black and dappled. As in the first vision, the red horses could represent war and bloodshed, the white ones victory, the black death, and the dappled ones a mixture of death and victory.

At first glance the number four would seem to suggest the whole earth in all four directions; but with a second look one becomes aware of the fact that only three teams go out, and they only go north and south. As in the first vision where the red horse is set apart as special by its rider, so also the red team in this vision is unusual in that it alone is not sent anywhere.

"Death" and "Victory" are sent north to Babylon. The dappled team is sent south to Egypt, another long standing enemy of Israel.

The horse chariots represent four spirits, four angelic ministers. The horses portray the judgments: the chariots the angelic executors, administering justice to dispossess wicked earth squatters for possession by "the Lord of the whole earth." The message concludes with a note of hope for the prophet's own day. One judgment has been carried out, God Himself declares: "My Spirit is at rest in the north country." The anger of the Lord has ceased.

Some scholars believe that the eighth vision is an expansion of the thought and vision of Horns and Smiths (1:18-21). The purpose of this vision is to show that issuing from the presence of the Lord of all the earth, and teaching God's protecting providence will be over his people and their sanctuary, even though the city's walls need a Nehemiah to repair them. Kline interprets it as follows: "Under the symbolism of our chariots of judgment which go to the several points of the compass and appease the wrath of God there is depicted the final judgment of the Serpent's seed."[56]

The Climax of the Night Visions

The eight nocturnal visions reach a climax in the second half of chapter 6:9-15, where Yahweh requires Zechariah to make a crown of silver and gold offered by returned exiles and with it to crown the high priest Joshua as king. Thus by means of this striking symbolism the Messianic figure of the Branch is shown to combine in one person the offices of both Joshua and Zerubbabel.

The "Branch" (3:8-9) was the name of the coming Messiah of David's family, to be called the "Nazarene" (Is. 4:2; 11:1-10; Jer. 23:5-6; 33:15-17; Rev. 5:5; 22:16), and Joshua, the Priest, is crowned, and is represented as the "Branch." Here is a symbolic prediction that Jesus Christ would be both priest and king in one person.

II.
Permanent Lessons for Our Time as Reflected
In the Eight Nocturnal Visions

1. In the book of Zechariah the reader finds how the drooping faith of a community may be revived through the preaching of a sincere prophet, inspired by God. The present day church has the prophetic Scriptures of the Old and New Testaments to inspire and guide it and will be blessed to the extent that its members "read, study and inwardly digest" and live according to the Word of the Triune God.
2. God states that He is in control of world affairs and can and will protect his church. Christ's promise is, that "the gates shall not prevail against her."
3. The Jews were told that the true religion would someday become worldwide (2:11; 6:15 also 8:13; 14:16). In the last two centuries the world has witnessed the fulfillment of these remarkable prophecies, which should strengthen Christians' confidence in the reliability of God's prophetic word.
4. The rebuilding of God's House was an indispensable condition for a better era (1:16). Zechariah speaks five times in the first part (1:16; 3:7; 4:9; 7:3; 8:9) concerning the need to rebuild the temple. There can be no permanent blessings without the maintenance of the church, the assembling together of those committed to Christ and as center for the spread of His kingdom.
5. Satan was the great enemy of the Israel of Zechariah's time. In every century of the church's existence Satan has been the chief assailant of the church. Satan employs all manner of means to hinder the work of Christ and the spread of His kingdom in our day.
6. Success in the work of the church, whether in Zechariah's day or the twentieth century cannot be achieved "by might, nor by power, but by my Spirit, saith the Lord of hosts."
7. The Church will always be surrounded by enemies, which in the end will be judged by Christ. In the end the church will be victorious.
8. The Old Testament envisioned the coming of the world's Redeemer, who would in New Testament times exercise the offices of prophet, priest and king. A book like Zechariah emphasizes the preparatory character of Old Testament revelation, to prepare the world for the coming of Christ and the establishment of His kingdom.
9. The origin of our salvation and the ground of our hope are in the love and grace of God and not in our own in worthiness.
10. The history of the world is all arranged and conducted in reference to the destinies of the Church, and the agencies that control that history go forth from the seat of the Church's great head.
11. Every individual, and every nation, has a measure of sin; and until that measure is filled up, God's longsuffering will wait for repentance and reformation.
12. God often uses instruments to chastise his people, which, when he has done with them, he breaks and casts into the fire.

13. The Church is externally a humble and lowly thing, neglected and often despised in the world; a grove of myrtles, rather than cedars of Lebanon.

14. Delay of punishment is no proof of immunity. God, while not acting immediately, has a time table when His heralds will go out and call upon the earth to be silent before Him.

15. Men are saved by the imputed righteousness of Christ.

16. A gratuitous justification does not excuse sin and inaction, but should lead to obedience.

Footnotes

1. Robert William Rogers, *A History of Ancient Persia* (New York and London: Charles Scribner's Sons, 1929), p. 63.

2. John Bright, *A History of Israel*, Second Edition (Philadelphia: The Westminster Press, 1969.) pp. 363-364.

3. Rogers, **op. cit.**, p. 71.

4. Louis Fuerbringer, "Sacharja, der Prophet der Hoffnung," *Synodal-Bericht Verhandlungen der Evangelischen Lutherischen Synodevon Missouri, Ohio und andersen Staaten*, Nord-Wisconsin-Distrikts, 1918 (St Louis: Concordia Publishing House, 1918) pp. 8-9.

5. Lic. Wilhelm Moller, *Grundriss fur altestamentliche Einleitung* (Berlin: Evangelische Verlag, 1958), pp. 257-258.

6. Fuerbringer, **op. cit.**, p. 9.

7. P. R. Ackroyd, "Zechariah," *Peake's Commentary on the Bible*, ed. by Matthew Black and H. H. Rowley, (New York, London, Edinburgh, Toronto, 1962), p. 647.

8. G. Campbell Morgan, *The Minor Prophets* (Westwood, New Jersey: Fleming H. Revell Company, 1949), p. 135.

9. Claus Westermann, *Handbook to the Old Testament* (Minneapolis: Augsburg Publishing Company, 1967), pp. 201-203; James H. Gailey Jr., *Micah, Nahum, Habakkuk, Zephaniah, Haggai, Zechariah, Malachi* (Richmond: John Knox Press, 1902), pp. 101-102; "Zechariah," Gaalyahu, Corfeld, Pictorial Biblical Encyclopedia (New York: The Macmillan Company, 1964). p. 711. W. Neill, "Zechariah, Book of," *The Interpreter's Dictionary of the Bible* (Nashville and New York: Abingdon Press, 1962), p. 944-945. J. Winton Thomas, "Zechariah, Exegesis of," *The Interpreter's Bible* (Nashville and New York: Abingdon Press, 1956), VI, pp, 1053-1054.

10. Gailey, **op. cit.**, p. 97.

11. George L. Robinson, *The Twelve Minor Prophets* (New York: George H. Doran Company, 1926), pp. 150-151; Kyle M. Yates, *Preaching From the Prophets* (New York; Harper & Brothers, 1942). pp. 208-209; John R. Sampey, *The Heart of the Old Testament* (Garden City, New York: Doubleday, Doran and Company, 1922), p. 205.

12. H. L. Ellison, *Men Spake From God* (Grand Rapids: Wm. B. Eerdmans Publishing Company, 1958), p. 126.

13. H. C. Leupold, *Exposition of Zechariah* (Columbus: The Wartburg Press, 1956). p. 28.

14. **Ibid.**, p. 28.

15. Lic. Wilhelm Moller und Lie. Hans Moller, *Biblische Theologie des Alten Testaments in heilsgeschichtlicher Entwickelung* (Zwickau) Sachsen: Verlag un Druck von Herrmann, 1938), pp. 401-402.

16. P. E. Kretzmann, *Popular Commentary of the Bible* (St Louis: Concordia Publishing House, 1924), II. pp. 702-708.

17. *Luther's Works - Minor Prophets III*, Zechariah St. Louis: Concordia Publishing House, 1973), p. 13.

18. Meredith Kline, "Zechariah, Bible Book of the Month," *Christianity Today*, April 14, 1958. p. 23.
19. Merrill F. Unger, *Unger's Bible Commentary, Zechariah* (Grand Rapids: Zondervan Publishing Company, 1963), p. 1-99; Charles L. Feinberg, *God Remembers* (Wheaton, Illinois: Van Kempen Press), pp. 4-6; A. C. Gaebelein, *The Annotated Bible* (New York: Publication Office "Our Hope," no date) pp. 268-282; G. Coleman Luck, *Zechariah* (Chicago: Moody Press, 1971), pp. 14-67.
20. Gailey, **op. cit.**, p. 97.
21. Unger, **op. cit.**, p. 27.
22. **Ibid.**
23. Leupold, **op. cit.**, pp. 34 and 38.
24. Fuerbringer. **op. cit.**, p. 11; Laetsch, *Bible Commentary -The Minor Prophets* (St. Louis: Concordia Publishing Company. 1956), p. 413.
25. Leupold, **op. cit.**, p. 38.
26. Unger, **op. cit.**, p 28: Leupold, **op. cit.**, p 38.
27. Leupold. **op. cit.**, p. 33.
28. Unger, **op. cit.**, p. 28.
29. Ellison, **op. cit.**, p. 127.
30. Alex R. Gordon, *The Prophets of the Old Testament* (New York: George H. Doran Company, 1916), p. 276.
31. Unger, **op. cit.**, p. 25.
32. **Ibid.**, p. 37
33. Leupold, **op. cit.**, p. 45.
34. Fuerbringer, **op. cit.**, p. 17.
35. D.O. Pusey, *The Minor Prophets* (Grand Rapids: Baker Book House, 1950). p. 348. Kretzmann, **op. cit.**, p. 704; Laetsch, **op. cit.**, p. 418.
36. Laetsch, **op. cit.**, p. 418.
37. Pusey, **op. cit.**, p 348.
38. R. E . Higginson, "Zechariah," D, Guthrie, J. A. Motyer, A. M. Stibbs, D. J. Wiseman, *The New Bible Commentary*, Revised (Grand Rapids: Wm. B. Eerdmans Publishing Company. 1970), p. 790. J. Wash Watts. *A Survey of Old Testament Teaching* (Nashville: Broadman Press, 1947), II, pp. 284-285.
39. Laetsch, **op. cit.**, p. 424.
40. Benjamin Davies and E.C. Mitchell, *A Compendious and Complete Hebrew and Chaldee Lexicon to the Old Testament* (Grand Rapids: Zondervan Publishing Company, 1880; 1950 reissue), p. 541.
41. *The Holy Bible - The New Berkeley Version in Modern English.* Gerrit Verkuye, editor-in-chief (Grand Rapids; Zondervan Publishing House, 1969), p 933.
42. Unger, **op. cit.**, p. 66; *Luther's Work on Zechariah*, **op. cit.**, p. 40.
43. Laetsch, **op. cit.**, p. 426.
44. Ellison, **op. cit.**, p. 129.
45. Laetsch, **op. cit.**, p. 432.
46. Pusey, **op. cit.**, p. 367.
47. **Ibid.**, p 367.
48. Laetsch, **op. cit.**, p. 434.
49. Gordon, **op. cit.**, p. 290. T. Henshaw, *The Latter Prophets* (New York: The Macmillan Company, 1958), p. 250.
50. Unger, **op. cit.**, p. 99.
51. Leupold, **op. cit.**, p. 108.
52. Laetsch, **op. cit.**, p. 436.
53. Leupold, **op. cit.**, p. 113.
54. John Calvin, *Commentaries on the Twelve Minor Prophets.* Translated from Latin by Rev. John Owen (Grand Rapids: Wm. B. Eerdmans Publishing Company, 1950), V. p 146.
55. *Luther's Works. Minor Prophets III.* Zechariah, **op. cit.**, p 248
56. Kline, **op. cit.**, p 24.

Questions

1. Cyrus was king of ____.
2. Haggai reminded the people that they were not blessed because ____.
3. Luther said that Zechariah was one of the most ____.
4. The visions deal with ____.
5. Zechariah repeats that what he proclaims is ____.
6. Most conservative scholars regard the man of the Red Horse as ____.
7. In Scripture the horn is a symbol of ____.
8. The man with the measuring line is ____.
9. Joshua may also be said to be a type of ____.
10. In Zechariah 3:8 and 6:12 Jesus is depicted as ____.
11. The earliest Scripture were written on ____.
12. Luther interpreted the bronze mountains as ____.
13. The horse chariots represent ____.
14. The "Branch" was the name of ____.
15. The present day church will be blessed to the extent that ____.
16. In every century ___ is the chief assailant of the church.
17. Who will be victorious in the end? ____
18. The Old Testament envisions the ____.
19. Men are saved by ____.

The Fourfold Biblical Evidences for the Messianicity of the Old Testament

Christian News, December 23, 1991

I. Old Testament Prophecies in New Testament

Jesus Christ is heart and center of God's revelation to mankind, set forth in the Old and New Testament Scriptures.[1] The New Testament clearly and unequivocally shows how by means of predictive statements, by types, by Christophanies and other ways Christ was foretold and fore-shadowed in the Old Testament. The Old Testament received its complete fulfillment in the life, ministry and saving work of Christ.

Liberal Jewish and liberal Christian scholars deny the fact that Christ is found described in many different ways in the Old Testament.[2] Jesus told the scribes and Pharisees: "Search the scriptures (i.e. the Old Testament) for in them you think that you have eternal life and they are they which testify of me (John 5:39)." On Easter afternoon and Easter evening Jesus very clearly told His followers that the entire Old Testament predicted important events about His life and ministry. To the two Emmaus disciples Jesus said: "O fools and slow of heart to believe all that the prophets have spoken: ought not Christ to have suffered these things and come to His glory? (Luke 24:25-27)."

On Easter evening Jesus declared to the eleven, the Emmaus disciples and others: "These are my words which I spoke to you while I was still present with you that everything written about me in the Law of Moses, and the prophets and the psalms must be fulfilled." Then he opened their minds to understand the Scripture, and said to them: "Thus it is written, that the Christ should suffer and on the third day rise from the dead, and that repentance and remission of sins be preached in his name among all nations, beginning from Jerusalem."

Paul stated that the purpose of the Old Testament Scriptures was to "make people wise unto salvation by faith in Christ Jesus," such was the purpose of the Old Testament, told Timothy (2 Timothy 3:15-17). In Romans Paul informed the Roman congregation that to the Jews "belong the glory, the covenants, the giving of the law, and the promises," by the latter are probably meant the promises about the coming Messiah.[3] Luke reported in Acts 18:24, 28 that "a certain Jew named Apollos, born in Alexandria, and an eloquent man, mighty in the Scriptures came to Ephesus, for he mightily convinced the Jews in publicly showing from the Scriptures that Jesus was the Christ."

Peter in his Pentecost Gentile sermon told Cornelius and his household how Jesus had been crucified and that God had raised Him from the dead, who after His resurrection had given His disciples the charge to testify that this was He whom God ordained to be the judge of the living and dead. "To him all, the prophets bear witness, testifying that through this name everyone that believed on him will receive remission of sins (Acts 10:40,43)."

In a synagogue in Antioch in Pisidia, Paul told his hearers: "For those who dwell in Jerusalem and their rulers, because they knew him not the utterances of the prophets which are read every Sabbath, fulfilled them by condemning him (Acts 13:27)." Luke, Paul's friend and sometimes travel companion, reports that Paul regularly visited synagogues. In Thessalonica Paul stayed for three Sabbaths and reasoned with them out of the Scriptures, explaining and quoting passages to prove that Jesus of Nazareth was the promised Messiah (Acts 17:3) who had to suffer and to rise again from the dead[4] (Acts 17:1-8).

In Caesarea, in his defense before King Agrippa, Paul stated: "But having obtained the help that cometh from God, I stand even to this day witnessing both to small and great, saying nothing except what the prophets and Moses send should come, how that the Christ must suffer, and how he should be the first to rise from the dead, and should bring a message of light to the Jewish people and to the Gentiles" (Centenary Translation, Acts 26:22).[4] To the Jews during his first Roman captivity in A.D. 60, Paul expounded the matter to them, testifying to the kingdom of God, and persuading them about Jesus, from morning to evening, both from the law and the prophets (Acts 28:23, Centenary Translation). In his first letter to the Corinthians Paul assured his Corinthian readers: "For I delivered to you as of first importance, what I also received, that Christ died according to the scripture, that he was buried and the third day was raised from the dead in accordance with the scripture (I Corinthians 15:1-2)."

The Importance of I Peter 1:10-12 for
Old Testament Interpretation

The apostle Peter in chapter 1:10-12, taught the following about the true nature of the Old Testament. 1. Christ sent His Spirit, to dwell in the Old Testament prophets; 2. The Old Testament prophets foretold the sufferings of Christ and His subsequent glorification; 3. The prophets predicted important facts about the New Testament era; 4. The prophets did not always understand what they were being made the recipients of by the Holy Spirit; and 5. Peter's remarkable passage, following immediately after his introductory prayer of thanksgiving, assumes the unity and continuity of the time before Christ's coming with that after His appearance on earth.

Revelation 19:10 asserts: "The witness of Jesus is the spirit of prophecy." "The Apostle John had been beholding the marvels of the Divine operation among men and the guidance" (Rev. 17:1). So overwhelmed was he with the wonder and glory of it, that he fell down in worship before the angel. But the angel said: "See then, thou do it not, I am a fellow-servant with thee, and with thy brethren that have the testimony of Jesus, worship God; for the testimony of Jesus is the spirit of prophecy."[4]

Gospel Known Already in Old Testament Times

In the opening verses of his great theological epistle Paul declared: "Paul, a servant of Jesus Christ, called to be an apostle, set apart for the

Gospel of God, which he promised beforehand through his prophets in the holy scriptures, the Gospel concerning His Son, who was descended from David according to the flesh and designated Son of God in power according to the Spirit of holiness by his resurrection from the dead" (1:1-4). In this passage Paul sets forth clearly the unity of the two dispensations. The Gospel, the good news that men have forgiveness through Jesus Christ, was foretold in the Old Testament Scriptures. This means that the Old Testament believers had a knowledge of the coming of the Messiah and what He was to accomplish for mankind.

Galatians 3 and Justification by Faith

In Galatians 3:6-9 Paul, by inspiration of the Holy Spirit, declared that Abraham was justified by faith. Can any Biblical truth be stated more clearly as when Paul wrote: "Thus Abraham 'believed God, and it was reckoned to him as righteousness.' So you see it is men of faith who are the sons of Abraham. And the scripture, foreseeing that God would justify the Gentiles by faith, preached the Gospel beforehand to Abraham saying 'in you all the nations of the earth will be blessed.' So then, those who are men of faith are blessed with Abraham by faith."

The Gospel of salvation was known in the Old Testament, for as Jesus asserted: "Abraham rejoiced to see my day, and he saw it, and was glad." Here Jesus agrees with Paul, both claiming that Abraham had knowledge of Jesus Christ. Again the continuity of the two dispensations is affirmed. The Old Testament cannot be understood apart from the New Testament, and the New Testament cannot be interpreted apart from the Old. The prophet Isaiah saw Christ in his remarkable vision in Isaiah chapter 6. Speaking about the Jews' unbelief, John wrote: "Therefore they could not believe as Isaiah said: 'He hath blinded their eyes and hardened their hearts, lest they would see with their eyes and perceive with their heart, and turn for me to heal them.' Isaiah said this because he saw his glory (i.e. Christ's) and spoke of him" (John 12:39-40).

Other New Testament passages could be cited supporting the contention that Christ was known from the time of Adam and Eve, as is also evident from Hebrew 11:1-12.

II. Prophecies in Old Testament about the Messiah

The main proof for the coming of Christ in the Old Testament, are the prophecies which predict various aspects of Christ's life and ministry.[5] Beginning with Genesis 3:15 and ending with Malachi 3:1-2 and 4:5-7 there are hundreds of prophecies that foretold many facts about the life, vocation, death, resurrection of the Messiah, the Christ, identified in the New Testament scriptures with Jesus of Nazareth.[6]

The Prophecy of the Seed of the Woman

The Messianic stream, which flows throughout the three major divisions of the Hebrew Old Testament canon, as well as giving unity to the content of the Old Testament, begins with Genesis 3:15. After the fall of mankind's first parents, brought about by the Serpent, God said to the

Serpent: "And I will put enmity between you and the woman and between your descendants and her Descendant. He will crush your head, and you will bruise his heel."[7] Here is the Bible's first promise of a coming Redeemer. This was a very general prophecy, which as time went on would be made more specific and clearer. In Genesis 9:25-27 the Biblical reader is informed that it would be Shem, who would know the true God, Yahweh, and that ultimately the descendants of Japheth and Ham would live in the tents of Shem.[8]

The Abrahamic Messianic Covenant

Abraham, the son of Terah, a Shemite, was chosen by God to be the father of that people, the Hebrew nation from whom the Messiah would come. At Haran in northern Mesopotamia, God made a covenant with Abram (later called Abraham).[9] The most important aspect of the Abrahamic covenant was the promise: "And in you all the people of the world will be blessed."[10] A number of modern translations render the Hebrew verb (nibrekhua) as shall bless themselves.[11] The New English Bible translation promotes the erroneous idea that nations can save themselves (work righteousness) instead of something being done for them.[12] Paul in Galatians tells believers: "Now the promises were made to Abraham and to his Descendant. He does not say," and by the descendants, in the plural, but in the singular: "by your Descendant, which is Christ."[13] This promise was repeated to Isaac and to Jacob.

When Jacob was about to die he blessed his sons and under Divine inspiration informed the world that the Messiah was to come from Judah's family by asserting: "The Scepter will not pass from Judah or a ruler from between his feet till SHILOH (Man of Rest) comes."[14] This is the first prophecy to announce that the Messiah would be a ruler or king. Modern translations endeavor to reject any Messianic interpretation, by rendering Genesis 49:10, like this: "The scepter shall not pass from Judah nor the staff from his descendants, so long as tribute is brought to him the obedience and the nations is his." (New English Bible of 1970).[15] The University of Chicago's The Bible, An American Translation renders: "The scepter shall never depart from Judah nor the staff from between his feet, until his ruler comes to whom the people shall be obedient."[16] The Jewish 1917 rendering of Genesis 49:10 has this translation: "The Scepter shall not depart from Judah nor the ruler's staff from between his feet, as long as men come to Shiloh."[17] In Jacob's blessing the Messiah is described as a Lion. In the Book of Revelation it is said that the Lion of the tribe of Judah has triumphed (5:5).

When Balaam, the seer of the Gentiles, whose eyes the God of Israel opened, saw Him who was to come, and viewed from afar, he pointed to Jacob, to Israel, from whom should originate the great Ruler of the future; "There shall come forth a Star out of Jacob, and a Scepter shall rise out Israel (Numbers 24:17)."[18] God similarly emphasized this fact when He said to Moses concerning the great prophet of the future: "I will raise up a prophet from your brethren (Deut. 18:18)."[19] From the Hebrew people God would awaken Him whose mouth would speak the Word of God.

During the reign of David, after the latter had achieved great power, Yahweh established with David a covenant and said: "The LORD also tells you He will build a house for you. When your time is up and you lie down with your ancestors, I will give you a Descendant who will come from you, and I will establish His kingdom. He will build a temple in My name, and I will make the throne of His Kingdom stand forever. I will be His Father, and He will be My Son"[20] (2 Sam. 7:13). The Lord was not speaking of Solomon or any other king of Israel. David himself acknowledges that the Lord had spoken concerning Him who was to come in the distant future (2 Samuel 7:19).[21] The future Ruler should be a descendant of David and in the New Testament Jesus is repeatedly referred to as "The Son of David." Thus King David in a number of his psalms praises the greater King of the future and He was the Dayspring from on high, to whom God had promised that His throne should remain to all eternity. Read Psalm 89:4,5,36,37.[22] Later Biblical writers refer to Jesus of Nazareth as "the Son of David."

The Messianic Psalms of David

Halley noted that "the Book of Psalms is replete with predictions about many facts about the life of Christ."[23] In fact, the Book of Psalms contains probably more predictions about the future Messiah, than the rest of the Old Testament, except Isaiah.[24] The New Testament quotes the book of Psalms, often, of whom David wrote seventy-five times.[25]

Psalm 2 and the Messiah the Lord's Anointed

Psalm 2, quoted at least six times in the New Testament, and interpreted as speaking about Jesus Christ.[26] Psalm 2 is a psalm which does not speak about David or any other king, but solely of Jesus Christ.[27] The Messiah is denominated as the Lord's anointed. Yahweh says to the Messiah: "Thou art My son, today I have begotten you."[28] God further declared: "I have set my King upon My holy hill;" again God says to the Messiah: "I will give thee the nations for an inheritance." The nations are told: "Kiss the Son" (v. 12). The believers are promised: "Blessed are they who put their trust in thee."

Christ's Resurrection Foretold

Psalm 16 is quoted by Peter as a prediction of Christ's resurrection.[29] When David wrote: "Thou wilt not suffer thy Holy One to see corruption," Acts 2:27,31 is cited as proof that it was foreknown that the Messiah would not permanently die but be raised from the dead.

Psalm 22 and Christ's Suffering and Crucifixion

The first half of Psalm 22:1-21, beginning with "My God, My God why hast thou forsaken me," (v.i.) was uttered by Jesus as His first word from the cross (Matt. 27:46). "All that see Me laugh Me to scorn. He trusted in God, let God deliver Him" (vv. 7,8). The sneer of Christ's enemies is given in words from Psalm 22 (Matthew 27:43). "They pierced My hands and my feet (v. 16)" and thus predicted the manner of Christ crucifixion (John

20:20,21). "They parted My garments and cast lots upon My vesture (v. 18)." This was fulfilled in Matthew 27:35.[30]

David Predicts the Messiah's Betrayal

Psalm 41 announced nearly a thousand years before it happened the betrayal of Jesus.[31] "My own familiar friend whom I trusted, who did eat my bread, lifted up his heel against me," thus David described what Judas committed in the Garden of Gethsemane, when he betrayed the Son of Man with a kiss. Both John 13:18-21 and Luke 22:47,48 quoted Psalm 41:9 as fulfilled by Judas' treacherous action.

Psalm 45 Announces Before Hand the Nature of Messiah's Reign

Psalm 45 announced at least ten centuries in advance the glorious reign of the Messiah, bearing the name of God. "Your throne is forever and ever, your rule as a King with a righteous scepter. You love righteousness and hate wickedness, that is why God, Your God has anointed you above your companions."[32] The author of Hebrews quoted Psalm 45:6,7 as speaking absolutely about Jesus Christ.[33]

Psalm 69:21, A Prediction that Jesus Would Be Given Vinegar on the Cross

Matthew 27:34,48 states that the fact that the Savior would be given vinegar while in great agony on the cross had been foretold in Psalm 69:21.[34]

Psalm 110, the Messiah as King and Judge of His Enemies

This psalm is the most frequently cited in the New Testament as a description of the Messiah's kingship and victory over His enemies. Jesus quoted Psalm 110 as speaking about the Son of God and not about David (Matthew 22:42-44). The truth that Jesus was not an Aaronic priest, but after the order of Melchizedek is the basis for the comparison of Jesus and Melchizedek, to whom Abraham paid tithes. Psalm 110 has nothing to do with any king of Judah or of Israel but applies only to Jesus Christ.[35]

Psalm 72 and Christ's Universal Rule Over the World

Psalm 72 and 127 are the two psalms that Solomon authored. The beautiful 72nd psalm gives a depiction of the flourishing kingdom over which Christ will rule. No earthly king can be matched with the assertions and Claims made about the Messiah in Psalm 72.[36]

The Many Messianic Prophecies Found in Isaiah

Of all the prophets of the Old Testament who describe the life and ministry of the Messiah none has more Messianic predictions and foreshadowing of the Lord Christ than Isaiah.[37] Fittingly Isaiah has been called the fifth evangelist of the Old Testament. In chapter 2:1-4 the prophet has given a magnificent prevision of the Messianic age.[38] In chapter 7:14

Isaiah predicted the Virgin Conception and Virgin Birth of Christ. God's prophet announced that the virgin's child would be called Immanuel.[39] Somewhat later Isaiah described the birth of Immanuel as a wonder child who would be called, the Miracle, Counselor, the mighty God, everlasting Father and prince of peace, whose rule would bring about endless peace.[40]

The Servant Passages

Outstanding and significant are Isaiah's prophecies relative to the suffering servant[41] (42:1-9, 49:1-7; 50:4-9 and 52:13-53:12). Three of the four are quoted in the New Testament and are said to speak about Christ. Isaiah 52:13-53:12 has been called "The Holy of the Holies of the Old Testament." The fourth servant passage is cited a number of times in the New Testament. Christ's prophetic priestly offices are clearly enunciated seven hundred years before the Son of God exercised these offices. No more vivid portrayal of Jesus suffering, death and resurrection are found in the whole Old Testament.[42]

The Prophets From 800 B.C. to 400 B.C.

A number of prophecies set forth in the last four hundred years of Old Testament history have unique Messianic facts about Christ. Thus Micah 5:2 informed Biblical readers that the Messiah was to be born in Bethlehem of Judea.[43] The prophet Jeremiah in the seventh or sixth Centuries B.C. has this remarkable announcement about the Messiah: "The days are Coming, that I will raise up unto David a righteous Branch. . . This is His name whereby He shall be called: THE LORD OUR RIGHTEOUSNESS."[44] As Isaiah, Chapters 4 and 11 speaks of the Coming King as a BRANCH out of the family of David, so here Jeremiah repeats the same name and asserts His deity.[45] The swallowing of Jonah by a fish was intended to be a prediction of Christ's death and resurrection (Matthew 12:39-41; 16:4; Luke 11:29-32).[46]

In Hosea 1:10 Hosea says: "In the place where it was said, Ye are not my people, it shall be said unto them. You are sons of the living God." Here Hosea repeats what had been previously been asserted that the Messianic Kingdom will include all nations. In Chapter 11:1 the same prophet wrote: "Out of Egypt have I Called my Son," and thereby declared that a part of the childhood of Jesus would be spent in Egypt.[47]

The prophet Ezekiel in 34:22-24 announced in the sixth Century B.C.: "My servant David. . .shall be a Shepherd. . . of my flock. He shall be a Prince forever.[48] The prophet statesman Daniel announced in Babylon the fact that the Messianic kingdom would supplant the Roman (2:40,44).[49] Two outstanding Messianic prophecies are found in Daniel 7:13-14 (basis of San of Man for Christ and Chapter 9:25-27.)"[48a] Zechariah in the fifth century B.C. announced the entry of Christ on a donkey (Matthew 21:1-9). In chapter 9-14 a number of events connected with Christ's last days were foretold.[50] The prophet Haggai in 2:6-7 foresaw the coming of Christ to the temple, when he wrote: "Yet a little while . . . and the Desire of all nations shall come . . . and fill this house with glory." In Malachi one finds the last Messianic prophecy, where in Chapter 4:5 the waypreparer will come, a prophecy fulfilled in the ministry of John the Baptist.[52]

III. Messianic Teachings by Means of Symbols

Besides direct predictions the Old Testament sets forth Messianic teachings by means of types. Types in the Old Testament are of various kinds. Persons, actions, cultic arrangements may serve as types.[53] The study of Old Testament typology is based mainly upon the teachings of the New Testament. Theodore Graebner has defined "a type in the Bible like a printer's type. It is a sign that makes an impression of something yet to come. The sign is called the type and the 'real something' is called the antitype."[54] The type may be obscured and hard to read but when the antitype appears the meaning is clear and plain.

God has made his plan of Salvation not only known in words, but also in facts. "The word explains the fact," averred Berkhof, "and the facts give Concrete embodiment to the words."[55] Further, the same writer claimed that a perfect synthesis of the two is found in Christ, "for in Him the Word was made flesh."[56] The various lines of revelation converge toward it. It is only in their binding center Jesus Christ that the narratives of Scripture find their explanation. The interpreter will truly understand them only insofar as he discerns this connection with its great central fact of Sacred History.

As already stated, a type may be a person as Adam who is a type of Christ in that by one man sin entered into the world and death by sin, so by one man life and salvation have been made possible. Melchizedek is portrayed by the writer of Hebrews as a type of the priesthood of Jesus, not according to the Aaronic. In addition Christ was a King as was Melchizedek.[57]

A type may also be a cultic event as the killing of the Passover lamb, for Paul declared: "Christ our Passover lamb has been sacrificed for us" (I Cor. 5:7). Once a year on the day of the atonement two goats were killed. One was killed as a sin-offering. The high Priest laid hands on the other, called the Scapegoat. Confessing over the latter the people's sins, it was led away in the wilderness, there to die. The killing of the goat foreshadowed the death of Christ for mankind's sins. On the way to the land of promise Israel sinned grievously. Serpents appeared that bit the people so that they were marked for death. At God's command Moses erected a brazen serpent in the camp of Israel. Those who looked at it in faith, did not die from the poison circulating through their veins. In John 3:16 Jesus took this to be a picture of Himself being lifted on the Cross (John 3:14). All mankind could look to Him and escape eternal death.[58]

The tabernacle with its structure and organization and all its appurtenances can be interpreted as type of some aspect of Christ and His salvatory work on behalf of mankind. The Veil of the Temple is (Heb. 10:20) a type of the human body of Christ.[59]

Relative to 1 Corinthians 10:11, Graebner wrote: "In I Cor. 10:11 the authorized version says 'ensample,' the margin says 'types.' So we understand that the events (clustered around the exodus and the wilderness journey are to be considered as types of our journey through life."[60]

The much discussed Pauline passage of Galatians 4:22-31 can best be explained as striking types of two different ways of salvation, represented by Hagar and Sarah, with their two sons of Ishmael and Isaac. A valid interpretation of Galatians 4:22-31 would be: Ishmael as the son of the bondwoman, is a type of the Old Covenant given from Mount Sinai, while Isaac, as the son of promise, is a type off the new Jerusalem from which comes the covenant of grace. Paul further draws out the comparison by referring to the persecution inflicted by Ishmael upon Isaac, as a type of the persecution now being borne by the true children of God at the hands of those who are carnal and under the law.[61]

For the exact meaning the Old Testament types conveyed the people of God, the interpreter will have to turn to the New Testament and from the New Testament obtain real insight into the truth in a veiled form.[62] It is patent that the types present the Christological truths in a less clear form as compared with the Old Testament rectilinear prophecies. The New Testament dispels the shadows of the Old Testament revelation and make them stand forth in undimmed lustre. Since Old Testament types are an aspect of Old Testament prophecy, the former can only be understood in their fulfillment. The Old Testament cannot adequately be explained without the interpretation of the New Testament. Let the reader observe the additional light given by Hebrews on the truths embraced in the tabernacle.

Direct Messianic prophecies and Messianic types as explained by the new Epistle of Hebrews. New Testament demonstrates the Messianicity of the Old Testament.

IV. The Appearance of God in Human Form
The Maleakh Yahweh (LORD) Supports
Old Testament Messianicity

The Maleakh Yahweh, "the Angel of the LORD," mentioned a number of times in the Old Testament and for the doctrine of the Trinity.[63] The 1927 *Concordia Cyclopedia*[64] and its revision; renamed *The Lutheran Cyclopedia*,[65] both have an article on "the Angel of the Lord." Both encyclopedias took the stance that in numerous passages "the Angel of the Lord" was none other than Jesus Christ, who temporarily assumed human form before permanently assuming flesh and blood. However, the 1975 edition of the Concordia Cyclopedia abandoned the understanding of "the Angel of the Lord" set forth in its two previous editions.[67] Professor Walter Wegner of the Old Testament St. Louis Exegetical Department that walked out in 1974, is the author of this article. He lists the usual explanations which have been offered by scholars committed to the historical-critical method. He claimed that the designation "Angel of the LORD," used more than forty times, is not to be identified with Christ, and was no pre-Bethlehem appearance of Christ as held by Christian theologians since the post-apostolic period. Wegner concluded his discussion of the "Angel of the Lord" presentation like this: Examination of passages cited above reveals that the angel of the Lord speaks for the Lord, in some instances appears in both roles interchangeably. Old Testament Scriptures themselves offer no basis for definitive explanation of the precise nature of the relationship between "the Angel of the Lord" and the LORD himself. Such N.T. occurrences of the angel of the Lord as Matthew 1:24 and Luke 2:9 suggest that the N.T. writers did not relate this title to Christ.[67a]

Wegner also claimed that Luther never identified the Angel of the Lord with Christ.[68] This is not true for Plass in his *What Luther Says*, quotes from a sermon delivered on the festival of the Holy Trinity: "The Patriarch Jacob distinguishes the Persons of the Holy Trinity (Gen. 48.15f), He calls the Lord Christ an Angel."[69]

An Examination of Major "Angel of the LORD" Passages in the Old Testament

The appearances of "the Maleakh Yahweh" are pre-Bethlehem appearances of Christ and are known as "christophanies."[70]

Walter C. Kaiser, in his foreword to James Borland's Christ in the Old Testament, contended that the issue of Christophanies given in the Old Testament is of great importance for the doctrine of the person and work of Christ. William McDonald in his article "The Angel of the Lord" has claimed to hold that Christ appeared at times in human flesh would threaten the incarnation of Christ and put in doubt its uniqueness and historicity.[72] How can a theologian who accepts the reliability of John 1:18 and I Timothy 1:17 claim that believers in the Old Testament saw God but not His Son, especially when Jesus claimed that He and the Father were one? Jesus taught His followers: "He that hath seen me hath seen the Father" (John 12:45; 14:8-11).

Passages That Identify the Maleakh Yahweh and God as Identical

The first occurrence of the Maleakh Yahweh or Angel of the LORD in the Old Testament is found in Genesis 16:7-14. The expression Maleakh Yahweh means not merely an Angel of the LORD but the Angel of the LORD, it means one specific angel and not merely one of the millions of angels who glorify and serve God. Kauffeld correctly has noted that the Hebrew word **maleakh** can mean an angel as messenger of Yahweh, but the combination Maleakh Yahweh, is a construct construction, and refers to just one, namely, Jesus Christ, the Second Person of the Trinity.[73]

As God's specific Angel he was God in human form. To distinguish between men and angels is not very difficult, but, however to distinguish between a created angel and the **Uncreated Angel** of Yahweh has caused confusion among exegetes and systematicians throughout the centuries. The true identity and role of the divine Maleakh has often been obscured or denied.[74]

J. T. Mueller claimed that the term "Angel," by which the Bible designates the angels who were created by God prior to the six days of creation (Genesis 1:1-2:3) are finite beings and invisible beings does not describe their essence but their office and means "one who is sent," or a "messenger." Angels are depicted by the name "Spirit." An angel is described as

295

a Spiritual being having a mind and will and no body. Passages like Malachi 2:7 and Matthew 11:10 show that that was the purpose of angels in Old Testament and New Testament times. On occasion angels took temporary human form.[75]

The Son of God, the Messiah or Jesus Christ, is portrayed as an "uncreated angel," as the unique Messenger of God. In Malachi 3:1, the last of the prophets to prophesy in the Old Testament dispensation, declared: "Behold, I am sending my messenger and he shall prepare the way before me, and the Lord whom you seek shall suddenly come to His temple, even the Angel of the Covenant, in whom you delight, Behold, He comes says Jehovah of hosts." The prophet Isaiah wrote about this uncreated angel: "In all their affliction. He was not a foe, and the Angel of His face saved them. And His love and in His pity He redeemed them, and He bore them and carried them all the days of old (Isaiah 63:6)."[76]

When Jacob blessed Joseph, he said to him: "God before whom my father Abraham and Isaac walked, God who has been my Shepherd all my life till now, the angel who delivered me from all evil, bless the young men. Let them be called by my name and the name of my fathers, Abraham and Isaac" (Genesis 48:15).[77]

Genesis 16:7-14 and The Appearance of the Angel of the Lord to Hagar

The first reference to the Maleakh Yahweh in which the Angel is identified with God is in the days of Abraham.

The Maleakh Yahweh and Hagar

After Hagar had become pregnant and despised her mistress Sarah, who had given Hagar to Abraham for the purposes of raising a son for her mistress and Hagar then despised Sarah; then Sarah mistreated Hagar, so that she fled. Moses informs his readers that the LORD'S Angel found Hagar in the desert. The ANGEL of the LORD told Hagar to return and be submissive to Sarah. The outcome of the appearance of the Maleakh Yahweh was that Hagar gave the LORD who talked with her the name El-roi, because She said: "Have here I really seen the back of Him who cares for me?" Reported the author of Genesis: "This is why the well is called Beer-lahai-roi (i.e. Well-of-the-Living One-Who-Cares for me)." It should be noted that in this Hagar episode that the names of Yahweh and the divine name Elohim are used interchangeably.[78]

The Maleakh Yahweh and the Sacrifice of Abraham (Genesis 22)

The second appearance of the Angel of the LORD occurs in connection with Abraham's attempted sacrifice of his Son Isaac on Mount Moriah. In obedience to the commander of Yahweh to sacrifice his only son, Abraham was about to kill his son when God intervened. Just as Abraham was raising the knife to kill his son, Abraham heard a voice from heaven, saying: "Do not lay your hand on the boy or do anything to him." Then Yahweh caused Abraham to see a ram which he took and sacrificed for his son. In concluding this account, Moses wrote: "And the Maleakh Yahweh called out of heaven a second time: And I have sworn by Myself, Says Yahweh, because you have done this thing, and have not withheld your only son . . . I will multiply your seed like the stars of the sky, etc." In Chapter 22:15 the clear identification of Yahweh with the Maleakh Yahweh is made.[79]

The Maleakh Yahweh and God's First Appearance to Moses

In Exodus chapter 3:1-14 the Maleakh Yahweh appeared to Moses in a burning bush, in the wilderness near Horeb. When Moses saw this remarkable event of a bush burning and not being consumed, and proceeded to examine it, he heard a voice which said: "I am the God (Elohim) of your fathers, the God of Abraham, the God of Isaac, and the God of Jacob" (v. 4). A careful explanation of Exodus 3:1-14 shows clearly that the Maleakh Yahweh is called both Yahweh (LORD) and God (Elohim).[80] So here God appeared in visible form. The only person of the Trinity to appear in visible form and speak like a human being was the Second Person of the Trinity, namely, Jesus of Nazareth, who by His Incarnation assumed human form forever. The fact is that Christ was with the Hebrew people in Egypt and in the course of their wilderness wanderings. It was this Maleakh Yahweh who led the Israelites through the waters of the Red Sea. For forty years the pillar of Cloud by day and pillar of fire was none other than the Son of God. That Christ was with the Hebrews during their wilderness wanderings is unequivocally asserted by Paul in his first epistle to the Corinthians.[81] Beck translated the opening verse of chapter 10:1: "I want you to know fellow Christians, our fathers were all under the cloud and all went through the sea, and by baptism in the cloud and the sea all were united with Moses, all ate the same food of the Spirit, and all drank the same water of the Spirit because they drank from the spiritual Rock that went with them, and that Rock was Christ."[82]

The Maleakh Yahweh As Israel's
Guide Through the Wilderness

In Exodus 23:20-22 God Said: "Behold, I am about to send an Angel before you, to guard you in the way and bring you to the place which I have prepared. Be careful before Him, and listen to His voice, do not be rebellious against Him, for He will not forgive your transgression in Him." This passage clearly identifies the Maleakh Yahweh and the God of Israel as the same person Yahweh Himself testifies to the fact that the power of judgment for sins rests in Him, in the Maleakh Yahweh. In Numbers 20:16 Moses in writing a letter to Edom speaks of the fact that the Maleakh Yahweh was the Person to bring Israel out of Egypt.

The Appearance of the Maleakh Yahweh to Joshua

Like Moses, his successor Joshua met the ANGEL of the LORD in the beginning of his career as leader of the Israelites. As Joshua was about to lead the children of Israel through the Jordan, he met a man Standing opposite to him with a drawn sword. Joshua inquired of this man whether he was for or against Israel, The Man responded: "NO, I am come as the Captain of the army of Yahweh," Joshua fell to the ground and worshipped Him. In reply to the question whether he had a message for Joshua, the Captain of the army of the LORD, replied: "Take your shoes from off your feet, for the place on which you are standing is holy," and Joshua did so. In the dialogue which ensued with Joshua and Captain of the army of Yahweh, the latter informed Israel's leader how to take the city. Only God has such power so that here again one may assume that only Jesus Christ could do what Joshua was instructed to do. It would seem that the Captain of the army of Yahweh was the uncreated Angel spoken previously so that the Maleakh Yahweh and the Captain of the army of the LORD were one and the same.[84]

The Maleakh Yahweh Appears to Gideon

After Israel had lived in the Promised Land, a number of years, and Israel had elapsed into idolatry against, which Moses in his farewell addresses had warned his countrymen against, the author of Judges relates that the Maleakh Yahweh appeared to Gideon at Bochim and rebuked the Israelites and reminded them that they had broken the covenant made at Shechem with the result that God had sent the Midianites to oppress them. The result was that Yahweh was going to give the Israelites another opportunity. It was the Maleakh Yahweh who had spoken to them and the result was that the people lifted up their voices and wept. So they named the place Bochim and worshipped Yahweh there (Judges 3:1-5).[84a]

The period of the Judges was a sad period in Israel, for there were at least seven defections from Yahweh. When Israel worshipped other gods, even Baal, the Canaanite fertility God, Yahweh punished them as he had done in the days of Othniel, Ehud and Deborah. Chapter 6 of Judges report shows how the Maleakh Yahweh enabled Gideon and his three hundred men to defeat the Midianites. At Gideon's request the Maleakh Yahweh performed two miracles that would show that Yahweh would help in defeating the Midianites.

The Appearance of the Maleakh Yahweh in Judges

The last major defection of Israel in the days of the Judges is reported in connection with the life and activity of Samson. Samson was the son of Manoah of the tribe of Dan who resided at Zorah. In Judges 13:2-23 the account is given of the appearance of the Maleakh Yahweh, who announced to Manoah the birth of a son, Samson, who would judge Israel for twenty years and inflict a great disaster upon the Philistines. As Kauffeld phrased it: "It is interesting to note that when Menoah knew that the messenger whom God had sent to them was the Maleakh he thought he would die because he had seen God. It is quite evident Manoah and his wife believed in the existence of the Maleakh and knew he was divine."[85] They found comfort not only in the message they had received but that the Lord had accepted an offering from them.

Later Old Testament References To The Maleakh Yahweh

In the eighth century B.C. Isaiah recalled past Christophanies. In chapter 63:9 Isaiah wrote: "In all their distress he too was distressed, the angel of his presence saved them. In his love and mercy he redeemed them; he lifted them up and carried them all the days of old."[86] Thus toward the end of his prophetic book, Isaiah declared that the Maleakh Yahweh was with the people's sufferings and saved them.

V. Christ Depicted as the Wisdom of God

A fourth type of evidence for the Messianicity of the Old Testament is to be found the term "wisdom."[87] The Hebrew word "Chochman," "wisdom," exhibits considerable development in meaning, from ordinary skillfulness in applied knowledge, through morality to the fullness of reverence and faith (Job 28:25). Wisdom in certain passages appears to be more than an attribute and to become actually objective for God. In Proverbs, especially there is a persistent personification of wisdom that is unique in Scripture.

In Proverbs 1:20-33 and 8:22-36 and 9:1-9 Chochman passes the limits of even personification and is actually hypostatized by Solomon.[88]

Especially 8:22-31 describes Chochman as existing before creation. P. E. Kretzmann held the view that in 8:23-36 the world had a passage that described the part played by Christ in creation.[89] Louis Fuerbringer wrote a series of three articles entitled "Die personliche Weisheit Gottes" in which he shows that Chochman of 8:23-36 was none other than Christ.[90]

Chochman (Wisdom) is descriptive of the Messiah and found its fulfillment centuries later in the person of Christ, the Wisdom of God (I Cor. 1:14). This personalized Wisdom proclaims the truth (8:7-9; cf. John 1:17; 8:14-19,31,32,45-47 Heb. 2:3). This personalized Wisdom calls upon mankind to seek first God's kingdom before comfort or wealth (w. 10, 11-19:9:10, cf. Matt. 6:33) and at the same time fills all needs (vv. 18, 20, 21; Cf. Rom. 8:32; Phil. 4:19).

The hypostatized Wisdom of God of Proverbs 8:23-36 is the LOGOS of John 1:1-3; and is preexistent (w. 22-26; John 8:58; 17:24; Eph. 1:4). The personized Wisdom of proverbs 8 and 9 is vitally associated with the world's creation (8:27-31; cf John 1:1-3,10; I Cor. 8:6; Col. 1:16). Wisdom, Christ, is the life of men (v. 35), repeated in the New Testament as a truth in John 1:4; 8:12; 10:10; 11:25; 14:6. Christ as Wisdom is the source of life (I Cor. 1:30), and through none other may eternal life be received (Acts 4:12; I Cor. 3:11).

Footnotes

1. *D. Martin Luthers Werke.* Kritische Gesanmtausgabe (Weimar: 1883-46, 28).
2. **Ibid.**, 54, 67.
3. C. M. Zorn, *Der Brief an die Roemer* (Zwickau, Germany; Johann Herman, no date), p. 118.
4. Helen Barrett Montgomery, *The New Testament in Modern English* (Philadelphia; Judson Press, 1924), p. 386.
5. Henry M. Halley, *Halley's Bible Handbook* (Grand Rapids: Zondervan Publishing House, 1965), pp. 388-401.

6. Frank Charles Thompson, *The New Chain Reference Bible*. Third Improved Edition (Indianapolis; B. A. Kirkbrick Bible Co., 1934), pp. 246-249 of the Appendix.

7. Edward Mack, *The Christ of the Old Testament* (Richmond: The Presbyterian, Committee of Publication, 1926), pp. 41-42. Franz Delitzsch, *Messianic Prophecy in Historical Succession* (New York; Charles Scribner's Sons, 18910), pp. 43-46.

8. Delitzsch, **op. cit.**, pp. 43-46.

9. Aaron Judah Kligerman, *Messianic Prophecy in the Old Testament* (Grand Rapids: Zondervan Publishing House, 1931), pp. 16-17.

10. Genesis 12:3 in the *Authorized Version* of 1611.

11. Genesis 3:15 in the *Revised Standard Version*, 1952.

12. *The New English Bible with the Apocrypha* (Oxford and Cambridge University Presses, 1970), p. 12.

13. William Beck, *The Holy Bible* (New Haven, Missouri: Leader Publishing Company, 1976), *New Testament*, p. 237.

14. **Ibid.**, Old Testament, p. 49.

15. New English Bible of 1970, p. 58.

16. Theophile Meek, in *The Bible - An American Translation* (Chicago: The University of Chicago Press, 1931), p. 87.

17. *The Holy Scriptures According to the Masoretic Text - A New Translation* (Philadelphia: The Jewish Publication Society of America, 1877-1917), p. 63.

18. George Stoeckhardt, *Christ in the Old Testament*. Translated by Erwin Koehlinger (Fort Wayne: Concordia Print Shop, no date), pp. 21-23.

19. **Ibid.**, pp. 5-6; Kligerman, **op. cit.**, pp. 21-23.

20. Beck, **op. cit,**. Old Testament, p. 357.

21. Stoeckhardt-Koehlinger, **op. cit.**, p. 6.

22. **Ibid.**

23. Halley, **op. cit.**, p. 192.

24. G. T. Manley, *The New Bible Handbook* (Chicago: Inter-Varsity Christian, 1947), p. 274.

25. G. Stoeckhardt, *Adventspredigten, Auslegung vornehmsten Weisagungen des Alten Testaments* (St. Louis: Lutherischer Concordia Verlag, 1887), pp. 61-68.

26. Francis Pieper, *Christian Dogmatics* (St. Louis; Concordia Publishing House, 1954), 1, 214; Harold E. Monser, *Cross Reference Bible* (Chicago: Cross Reference Bible Company, no date), pp. 82-90.

27. Stoeckhardt, **op. cit.**, p. 62.

28. Pieper, **op. cit.**, 1, p. 394.

29. Leslie S. M'Caw, "The Psalms," in F. Davidson, A. M. Stibbs and E. F. Kevan, *The New Bible Commentary* (Grand Rapids: Wm. B. Eerdmans Publishing Company, no date), p. 427.

30. Kligerman, **op. cit.**, pp. 40-41.

31. Halley, **op. cit.**, p. 193.

32. Pieper, *Christian Dogmatics*, **op. cit.**, I, p. 502.

33. Stoeckhardts, Adventspredigten, **op. cit.**, pp. 101-107.

34. P. E. Kretzmann, *Popular Commentary of the Bible* (St. Louis; Concordia Publishing House, 1921), Old Testament, Vol. I, p. 32 and New Testament, II, p. 460.

35. Stoeckhardt, Adventspredigten, **op. cit.**, pp. 108-115.

36. **Ibid.**, pp. 101-107.

37. Kligerman, **op. cit.**, p. 69.

38. L. W. Slotki, *Isaiah, Soncino Books of the Bible* (London: Sonccaco Press, 1949), p. 20.

39. Halley, **op. cit.**, p. 395.

40. Paul Heinisch, *Christ in Prophecy*, Translated by W. C. Heidt (Collegeville: Minnesota; The Order of St. Benedict, 1956), pp. 80-87.

41. W. Fitch, "Isaiah," *The New Bible Commentary*, **op cit.**, pp. 146-175, p. 596; George L. Robinson, The Book of Isaiah, *In Fifteen Studies* (Grand Rapids: Baker Book House, 1954), pp. 141-149.

42. Frederick Aston, *The Challenge of the Ages* (New York: Research Press, 1969), p. 18.

43. Heinisch-Heidt, **op. cit.,** 109-111.

44. Theo Laetsch, *Bible Commentary, Jeremiah* (St. Louis: Concordia Publishing House, 1952), pp. 188-193.

45. L. R. Elliott, "Psalms," in C. F. Pfeiffer, H. V. Vos and J. Rea, *Wycliffe Bible Encyclopedia* (Chicago: Moody Press, 1975), 1, p. 272.

46. Kretzmann, *Popular Commentary, New Testament*, I, p. 70.

47. Pieper, **op. cit.,** I, p. 248.

48. Mack, **op. cit.,** p. 112.

48a. Edward Young, *The Messianic Prophecies of Daniel* (Grand Rapids; Wm. B. Eerdmans, 1954), pp. 43-48; 55-60.

49. H. C. Leupold, *Exposition of Daniel* (Columbus: The Wartburg Press, 1949), pp. 123-1266.

50. Halley, **op. cit.,** pp. 383, 400.

51. (missing)

52. Burton Goddard, "Malachi," in C. F. Henry, Consulting Editor, *The Biblical Expositor* (Philadelphia: A. J. Holman Company, 1960).

53. Bernard Ramm, *Protestant Biblical Interpretation* (Grand Rapids: Baker Book House, 1970), pp. 231-232.

54. Theodore Graebner, *A Dictionary of Bible Topics* (Grand Rapids: Baker Book House, 1950), p. 95.

55. L. Berkhof, *Principles of Biblical Interpretation* (Grand Rapids: Baker Book House, 1950), p. 142.

56. **Ibid.**

57. A. Berkely Michelson, *Interpreting the Bible* (Grand Rapids: Wm. B. Eerdmans Publishing Company, 1963), pp. 249-250.

58. Numbers 21:1-9; Halley, **op. cit.,** p. 390.

59. Theodore H. Epp, *Portraits of Christ* (Lincoln, Nebraska: Back to the Bible, 1976), p. 9.

60. Graebner, **op. cit.,** p. 96.

61. Kretzmann, *Popular Commentary, New Testament*, **op. cit.,** II, pp. 248-268.

62. Berkhof, **op. cit.,** p. 146.

63. James R. Batterfield, *An Exegetical Study of the Maleakh Yahweh in the Old Testament.* Postgraduate Study at Grace Theological Seminary, January 5, 1970.

64. L. Fuerbringer, Th. Engelder and Paul E. Kretzmann, *The Concordia Cyclopedia* (St. Louis: Concordia Publishing House, 1927), pp. 22.

65. Erwin L. Lueker, *Lutheran Cyclopedia* (St. Louis: Concordia Publishing House, 1954), pp. 31-32.

66. Erwin L. Lueker, *Lutheran Cyclopedia* (St. Concordia Publishing House, 1975), p. 32.

67. **Ibid.,** p. 32b.

67a. **Ibid.**

68. **Ibid.**

69. Ewald Plass, *What Luther Says* (St. Louis: Concordia Publishing House, 1959), No. 434.

70. James A. Garland, *Christ in the Old Testament* (Chicago; Moody Press, 1978), pp. 1-12.

71. **Ibid.,** p. VIII (Foreword).

72. **Ibid.,** p. VIII.

73. Eugene P. Kauffeld, *Divine Footprint - Christ In The Old Testament* (Milwaukee: Northwestern Publishing House, 1983), pp. 93-94.

74. Pieper, **op. cit.,** I, p. 390.

75. John Theodore Mueller, *Christian Dogmatics* (St. Louis; Concordia Publishing House, 1934), pp. 196-197.

76. **Ibid.,** pp. 159-160.

77. D. Martin Luther's *Saemtliche Werke, Gesamtausgage* (Weimar, 1883), 52, p. 339.

78. G. Stoeckhardt, *Die Riblische Geschichte des Alteh Testaments* (St. Louis; Concordia Publishing House, 1906), p. 21.

79. **Ibid.**, p. 30.

80. Kauffeld, **op. cit.**, pp. 105-106; Merril F. Unger "Exodus," in Henry, *The Biblical Expositor*, **op. cit.**, I, pp. 97-98.

81. Chapter 10:1-10.

82. Beck, **op. cit.**, *New Testament*, pp. 215-216.

83. Kauffeld, **op. cit.**, pp. 107-108.

84. **Ibid.**, pp. 103-104.

84a. Kauffeld, **op. cit.**, pp. 11-112.

85. "Angel of the Lord," in *Concordia Cyclopedia*, 1927 Edition.

86. Kauffeld, **op. cit.**, p. 116.

87. J. Barton Payne, *The Theology of the Older Testament* (Grand Rapids; Zondervan Publishing House, 1962), p. 170.

88. **Ibid.**, p. 171.

89. Kretzmann, *Popular Commentary, Old Testament*, **op. cit.**, II, 224.

90. Louis Fuerbringer, "Die persoenliche Weissagung Gottes," *Concordia Theological Monthly*, 4:241-243; 321-324; 401-407, April, May and June, 1932.

91. Based on and adapted from Kenneth A. Kitchen, "Proverbs," *The Biblical Expositor*, II, p. 78.

Questions

1. Who is at the heart and center of God's revelation to mankind? ____
2. What did Paul say about Moses and the prophets? ____
3. What did Peter teach about the Old Testament? ____
4. The Old Testament believers had a knowledge of ____.
5. The Bible's first promise of a coming Messiah is ____.
6. The New English Bible translation promotes the idea that ____.
7. Modern Bible translations render Genesis 49:10 with ____.
8. 2 Samuel 7:13 refers to ____.
9. Psalm 2 speaks about ____.
10. Psalm 16 is a prediction of ____.
11. Psalm 22 predicted ____.
12. Psalm 41 announced ____.
13. The author of Hebrews quoted Psalm 45:6,7 as referring to ____.
14. Psalm 69:21 foretold ____.
15. Psalm 110 applies only to ____.
16. Isaiah has been called ____.
17. Isaiah 7:14 predicted the ____.
18. Isaiah 52:13-53-53:12 has been called ____.
19. The swallowing of Jonah by a fish was intended to be ____.
20. The "Angel of the Lord" is none other than ____.
21. The 1975 edition of the *Concordia Cyclopedia* abandoned ____.
22. Who was Walter Wegner? ____
23. What are "christophanies?" ____
24. An angel is described as ____.
25. The Maleack Yahweh is called both ____ and ____.
26. The pillar of ____ by day and the pillar of ___ by night was ____.
27. Christ is depicted as the ____ of God.
28. The Chochman (wisdom) of Proverbs 8:23-36 is none other than ____.

The CTCR vs. The LCMS

The History of Messianic Prophecy in the Lutheran Church-Missouri Synod From 1847 Till the Issuing of the CTCR's "Prophecy and Typology" in 1996

Christian News, September 30, 1996

The Lutheran Church-Missouri Synod has founded its belief that Christ is the center and heart of Holy Scriptures on New Testament assertions. To the Jews Jesus declared "You search the Scriptures, because you think that in them you have eternal life; and it is these that bear witness of Me" (John 5:39, NASB).

On Easter afternoon Christ explained to Cleophas and his friend that the happenings of Good Friday and the following Sunday morning had been predicted centuries before and asserted: "And beginning with Moses and the prophets, he interpreted to them in all the scriptures the things concerning himself" (Luke 24:27, RSV). In the same chapter, on Easter evening Jesus claimed that the three divisions of the Old Testament Scriptures; the Law, the Prophets and the Psalms spoke of Him, reminded the disciples and others on that memorable Easter evening. This is what I told you while I was still with you: "Everything must be fulfilled that is written about me in the Law of Moses, the Prophets and Psalms" (Luke 24:44). After opening their minds, He further said: "This is what is written: 'The Christ will suffer and rise from the dead on the third day'" (Luke 24:46, NIV).

The Apostle Peter in his sermons, reported in Acts, and in his epistles stressed the truth that the whole Old Testament pointed to Christ. Relative to Christ's suffering and death, he told his compatriots: "But the things which God announced beforehand by the mouth of all the prophets that His Christ should suffer. He has thus fulfilled" (Acts 3:18, NASB). To the same audience, Peter declared: "Likewise, all the prophets who have spoken, from Samuel and his successors onward also announced these days" (Acts 3:24, NASB). In his sermon before the Roman centurion Cornelius, Peter, the Rock Man, uttered these significant words: "And he commended us to preach to the people, and to testify that he is the one ordained of God to be judge of the living and the dead. To him all the prophets bear witness that everyone who believes in him receives forgiveness of sins through his name" (Acts 10:42, RSV). One of the most informative passages about Christ as found in the Old Testament is Peter's instruction as contained in I Peter 1:10-12, which reads: "As to this salvation the prophets who prophesied of the grace that would come to you made careful search and inquiry, seeking to know what person or time the Spirit of Christ within them was so indicated as he predicted the sufferings of Christ and the glories to follow. It was revealed to them that they were not serving themselves, but you, in these things which now have been announced to you who preach the Gospel to you by the Holy Spirit sent from heaven things into which angels long to look"

(NASB).

According to St. Paul the purpose of Holy Writ is designed to make people wise unto salvation through faith in Christ Jesus. The same Holy Scriptures will through reproof, correction and teaching make the man of God completely equipped for every good work (2 Timothy 3:15-16). Halley has correctly written: "The Old Testament was written to create an anticipation of, and pave the way for, the Coming of Christ. It is the story of the Hebrew nation, dealing largely with events and exigencies of its own times. But all through the story there runs, unceasing Expectancy and Prevision of the coming of One, Majestic Person, who will Rule and Bless the Whole World. This Person, long before He arrived, came to be known as The Messiah."[1]

Luther and the Christocentricity of the Old Testament

Plass contended that Luther's theology is Christology.[2] The Reformer made Christ the Redeemer the center of his writing as he found Him to be the center of Scripture. Without understanding who and what Christ is, neither Luther nor Scripture can be properly appreciated. That Scripture and Christianity are foreign ground to all who do not recognize Christ the Redeemer, Luther stated in his sermonic exposition of John 16:3.[3] In the introduction of the Exposition of the Prophet Habakkuk (1526) Luther gave a summarization of the writings of the prophets. In this introduction the Doctor claimed that all prophets directed their predictions chiefly to Christ. Thus St. Peter shows (Acts 3:24) that all prophets have spoken of the time of the New Testament; for the entire Old Testament is nothing else than a preparation of the New Testament and an introduction to it.[4]

In a sermon preached on the festival of the Holy Trinity in 1535, with the Gospel for that Sunday as his text (John 3:1-15), Luther expressed his conviction that the pre-incarnated Christ figured largely in Old Testament history, as "The Angel of the Lord."[5] Luther identifies Christ with the God of the Old Testament.[6] In fact, all revelations of God gave there necessarily came through Christ. According to the Reformer, this includes the giving of the Ten Commandments.[6a] Here is Plass's translation: "Yes, Jesus of Nazareth who died on the cross, is the God who says, in the First Commandment: 'I am the Lord, thy God.' If the Jews and the Mohammedans were to hear this, how they would rage! Yet it is true and must remain true forever; and he who does not believe it is destined to tremble and burn forever for this unbelief."[7]

Luther, in a Pentecost sermon of 1532 on John 3:16-21, claimed that it seemed that the Holy Spirit in Scriptures could only speak about Christ. In his *Bondage of the Will*, Luther told Erasmus that there were obscurities in Holy Writ, but these were peripheral, for Christ and His redemption—and these for all practical purposes may be found there by all.[8]

Bornkamm, Luther and the Old Testament asserted: "The direct application of the Old Testament to Jesus Christ, His words and deeds and resurrection. His church and His work in the believer was by far the strongest and commonest comprehensive theme in Luther's interpretation of the Old Testament. In fact, countless events and sayings in the Old Testament became much clearer to him as he applied them to Christ and His work."[9]

In numerous writings Luther declares that the heart of the Scriptures is Christ and this would be the correct mode to interpret the prophecies of the Old Testament.[10] The Reformer once listed the Messianic prophecies in the Books of Moses (WA 24, 1:1ff.),[11] namely, the Proto-evangelium, the blessing on Abraham's seed (Gen. 22:18) Cf. Sermon on Genesis, 1523-1514,[12] WA 14, 223:18, and the promise of a prophet like Moses whom God will send (Deut. 18:15 and Luther, The Deuteronomy of Moses with notes) (525,[13] WA 765:11f; 680:1ff LW 9:176ff; 171-172). At other points Luther added to the direct prophecies Eve's cry (Gen. 4:1) which after several attempts he translated: "I have the man the Lord" and so offered this as proof of divine human nature of Christ and the Messianic prophecy about Judah (Gen. 49:10), about which he often quarreled with the Jewish interpretation (In Sermons on Genesis, 1523-1524, WA 14,481).

Moreover, there were many passages on Moses which were not messianic prophecies but which nevertheless contained Christological promises. The interpretations of Exodus 33 and 34 in the writing On the Last Words of David are particularly clear examples of this interpretation.

The following are the major works of Luther treating of Messianic Prophecy: 1523 Das Jesus Christus ein geborne, Jude Sei; St. Louis Edition, XX, 792-1821. 1542 Von den Juden und ihren Luegen, St. L. XX, 1860-2029, Weimar, 53, 412-552. 1543 Von Schem Hamphoras und von Deschlect Christi, Walch Edition, XX, 2028-2109. 1543 Von den letzten Worten Davids, Weimar, 54 16-100. Weimar 53, 573-648.

I. The History of the Interpretation of Messianic Prophecy from 1847 to 1947

Carl Ferdinand Walther and Rectilinear Prophecy

Walther was a great admirer of Martin Luther and followed him in his Biblical interpretation. The early leaders of The Lutheran Church-Missouri Synod were greatly influenced by Ferdinand Walther. In one of his major theological works, namely. The Lutheran Church, the True visible Church of God on Earth,[14] he elucidated on the principles of Biblical interpretation. Theses XIII till XXI set forth fundamental principles of sound interpretation Thesis XVI D reads: "The Ev. Lutheran Church holds the literal sense as a true sense. XVI E stated: The Ev. Lutheran Church, in interpreting, is guided by the context and the intention. Otherwise the Scripture is garbled."[15] Thesis XVIII A avers: "It makes the teaching concerning Christ or justification, the foundation of all teaching." Relative to the literal sense of the Biblical text, thesis XVI D declares: "The Ev. Lutheran Church holds that the literal sense has but one sense."[16]

In his many publications Walther, called "The American Luther" followed the interpretation of Luther, The Lutheran Confessions and of the Post Reformation theologians and exegetes relative to rectilinear Messianic prophecies.[17] It can be safely said that the interpretation of Messianic prophecy in The Lutheran Church-Missouri Synod was determined by Walther for a century, till 1947. There followed in his footsteps a number of theologians who were convinced of Walther's theological positions as well as his interpretation of the passages which the New Testament claimed predicted Christ's life and suffering, death and resurrection.

It was especially at Concordia Seminary, St. Louis, both on Jefferson Avenue, St. Louis and 801 DeMunn, Clayton, Missouri, that there were outstanding theologians like Stoeckhardt, Pardiek, F. Pieper, L. Fuerbringer, J.T. Mueller, O. Graebner, P.E. Kretzmann, W. A. Maier, Sr., Engelder, Laetsch and others that followed Luther's views on Old Testament predictive Messianic prophecy. The theologians at Concordia Theological Seminary, Springfield, also followed the thinking of their fellow professors in St. Louis-Clayton relative to rectilinear Messianic prophecy.

George Stoeckhardt (1842-1913)

Stoeckardt replaced Walther on the faculty of Concordia Seminary in 1887; he was primarily professor of hermeneutics and of Biblical exegesis. In two major series of articles in *Lehre und Wehre* dealt with the Old Testament passages that were interpreted as being Messianic.[18] The first series selected passages that set forth various facts and events about Jesus Christ, explained as having been predictive of Christ's life and work of salvation according to Matthew. In another series, also appearing in *Lehre und Wehre*, Stoeckhardt organized various passages that were Christological under the caption: "Christus im Alten Testament."[18a] In all his writings he never interpreted what he called direct and clear passages in a typological manner as was later done by St. Louis professors in the years since the 1940's. In 1887, Concordia Publishing House published Stoeckhardt's *Adventspredigten* which contained an exposition of the most prominent Prophecies of the Old Testament. He explained the following texts: Genesis 3:15; Genesis 12:1-3; Genesis 49:8-12; Numbers 24:17; Deuteronomy 18:15; 2 Samuel 7:12-14; Psalm 2, 8, 16, 40, 45, 72, 110; Hosea 1:19-20; Amos 9:11-12;Micah 5:1-5; Isaiah 11:1-10; Jeremiah 23:5-6; Ezekiel 34:11-17,23-24; Daniel 7:13-14; Haggai 2:7-10; Zechariah 9:9-11; Isaiah 9:2-7; Isaiah 60; Malachi 3:1-6; Isaiah 7:10-15; Joel 3:1-5; Isaiah 40:15.[19] In his *Commentary on Isaiah* and *Selected Psalms* Stoeckhardt deals with Old Testament passages identified as Messianic by Christ and the New Testament writers.[20] In the preface to his *Adventspredigten*[21], Stoeckhardt told his readers: "Es ist das Eigenthum altestamentlicher prophetie, dass sie zumeist als in kurzer Summa den ganzen Rath Gottes von unser Seligkeit darlegt, dass sie in grossen Zeugen das Heil, das in Christovorhanden, beschreibt. Alle Propheten haben von der Gnade Jesu Christi, die uns zu Theil geworden is, geweissagt" (p. iv).[21a]

The Christology of Augustus Lawrence Graebner (1849-1904)

A contemporary of Stoeckhardt was A. L. Graebner, who joined the St.

Louis Concordia Seminary faculty in 1887. He follows Walther and Stoeckhardt's hermeneutics. In his *Doctrinal Outlines*, in the section dealing with the person and work of Christ, he cited Old Testament passages that were predictive of Christ. Thus Genesis 3:15, Isaiah 7:14; Isaiah 9:6; Daniel 9:24; Micah 5:2; Psalm 31:10-12; Psalm 40:13; Psalm 69:2-4; Isaiah 53:8; Isaiah 53:4; 53:12; 8-9, Psalm 16:10; Psalm 110:7; Psalm 8:6-7; Psalm 47:5; Psalm 110:4; Isaiah 53:4-7; 5-6; 12,5-7; Isaiah 53:5; Hosea 13:14; Deut. 18:18; Proverbs 8:12,22,31; Isaiah 11:1-2; Hosea 1:10; Isaiah 61:1; Psalm 8:6-7; Daniel 7:14; Jeremiah 23:5-6; Isaiah 40:11; Ezekiel 34:16; Isaiah 9:7; Psalm 23; Isaiah 9:7 A study of Graebner's *Outlines of Theology*[22] will reveal that in his understanding of Old Testament Christological passages he followed Luther, Walther and Stoeckhardt and perpetuated the emphasis upon rectilinear prophecy which characterized the exegetical endeavors of Luther, the post-Reformation period, and the first one hundred years of the LCMS history.

Francis August Otto Pieper (1852-1931)

Probably next to C.F.W. Walther, Francis Pieper is considered the second outstanding theologian in the first hundred years of the LCMS history. His outstanding theological contributions were in the field of dogmatics. Lueker judged of Pieper: "True to his convictions the person who himself clearly understands a doctrine should present it clearly, Pieper always strove to present Biblical doctrine clearly. His scholarly treatment of textual criticism, exegesis, history, etc., may be seen in the footnotes of his *Christian Dogmatics*, first published in German, Concordia Publishing House, 1920-1924."[23]

Pieper's three-volume work quotes many Bible passages from both the Old and New Testaments. Like his great predecessors Walther, Stoeckhardt, A. L. Graebner, he cited passages from the Old Testament that speak of Christ and the redemption he was going to effect. In connection with a discussion on the prophetic office of Christ, Pieper wrote: "Christ and the Apostles (Acts 10:43) taught that the entire Scripture of the Old Testament named Christ as the Giver of Life".[24] In volume 2. He also wrote: "It should be noted that the Son of God, even before His incarnation, in the days of the Old Testament, was that Person of the Trinity, Who spoke to men and acted as intermediary for the Trinity in its intercourse with men." The Holy Scripture testifies (a) that the "Spirit of Christ" spoke through the prophets (1 Pet. 1:11), and (b) that it was the Son of God who communicated with men, Isaiah 6 (cp. John 12:41) and dealt with Israel in the desert, 1 Cor. 10:4 (2,341).[25]

John Theodore Mueller and
Old Testament Rectilinear Messianic Prophecy

J.T. Mueller was a one-volume condensation of Pieper's three volume *Christian Dogmatics*, in which Luther's views on rectilinear prophecy were forcefully set forth. Cf. page 99, where Mueller gives evidence of his views relative to Old Testament Messianic prophecy.

307

Carl Manthey Zorn (1846-1928)

Originally Zorn was a missionary to India and then was a pastor of the LCMS at Milwaukee and later was pastor at Zion Lutheran Church, Cleveland, Ohio. He wrote a host of popular commentaries on various New Testament books, of which the most scholarly was *Der Apostolische Brief and die Colosser.*[26] In the area of Old Testament interpretation his greatest work is *Die Psalmen* (751 pages). In his interpretation of the 150 psalms, he, on the strength of the New Testament, believed that a number of them predicted facts about Christ's life and ministry. In his interpretative efforts he followed Luther and the hermeneutical principles of the Lutheran Confessions. Thus Psalm 2 he entitled "Christi Reich und seine Feinde." Psalm 2 spoke about Christ and not about David. The New Testament cites this psalm at least four times and teaches various theological facts about Jesus Christ, Whom the Father eternally begets, who is the ruler of the world and who will judge all His enemies. Psalm 8, which all critical and some conservative scholars believe speaks about the greatness of man, Zorn on the strength of the New Testament, holds to be Jesus Christ. Psalm 8 is cited in Hebrews 1:5 as having spoken, about the eternal begetting of Christ by His Father. Psalm 16 contains a prediction that the dead body of Jesus would not see decay. Psalm 22 depicts the suffering, death and resurrection of Christ. Zorn followed Luther's interpretation of the rectilinear psalms, as did Stoeckhardt in his *Ausgewaelte Psalmen.* In the introduction to his *Die Psalmen,* Zorn wrote: "And the Lord Jesus Christ expresses clearly, that in the Psalms there were predictions about Him. Luke 24:44. So also do the Apostles, i.e., Acts 2:25-35. So clear, direct and in the amount of psalms about Christ, so that one could construct the entire history about Christ, and that one could construct the entire saving teaching about Christ and the Apostles. 2 Timothy 3:15-17." In fact Zorn contends that there were foretold facts about the life of Christ not revealed in the New Testament. The Cleveland pastor said it was a lie when scholars claimed that the direct, primary and rectilinear prophecies were merely types, and that truths about Christ clearly foretold, dealt with other matters and people and not specifically with Christ.[27]

Zorn's best known and beloved book was his *Der Heiland,* published by Northwestern Publishing House, 1909, and went through four editions. This literary production was a harmony of the life of Christ, 403 pages. Part I, pages 3-12, set forth Zorn's views on rectilinear Messianic prophecies and their fulfillment in the New Testament.

Theodore Laetsch (1877-1962) and Messianic Prophecy

Theodore Laetsch was professor of Old Testament interpretation at Concordia Seminary, St. Louis from 1927-1947. He was editor of the two volumes of *The Abiding Word* (1946-1947),[28] the author of *The Minor Prophets,*[29] and *The Commentary on Jeremiah,*[30] many sermon studies, and various essays in *The Concordia Theological Monthly.* An analysis of Laetsch's writings will show that he followed the views on Messianic prophecy set forth by Walther, Pieper, Stoeckhardt, P. Kretzmann, L.

Fuerbringer, and Walter A. Maier, Sr.

In contrast to P. Kretzmann, Laetsch understood Jeremiah 33:11[30] and Hosea 11:1[31] as being direct rectilinear prophecies and not as typological in character.[32] In his *Jeremiah Commentary* he claims that both Jeremiah 23:5-6 and 33:15-6 were rectilinear prophecies,[33] which spoke of Christ and identified the Messiah with Yahweh: "This is the name by which He (i.e. the Messiah) shall be called 'Yahweh is our righteousness.'"

In his commentary on the *Minor Prophets* Laetsch found a number of predictive Messianic prophecies in Hosea, Amos, Micah, Zechariah and Malachi.

Ludwig Fuerbringer (1864-1947) and Messianic Prophecy

Fuerbringer was professor at Concordia Seminary, St. Louis from 1893-1947 and was one of the outstanding theologians of the early twentieth-century. He gave evidence of scholarship across a broad front. He was famous for his opposition to higher criticism and his repudiation of Pentateuchal criticism. He was a great exponent of rectilinear Messianic prophecy. He produced a heremeneutical manual in which he showed the influence of Luther's views and the hermeneutics and exegesis of the Lutheran Confessions.[34] One of the popular courses taught by Fuerbringer was a course entitled: "Exegesis of Messianic Prophecies."[35] These lectures were made available to students by The Concordia Seminary Mimeograph Company. In this work Fuerbringer discussed twenty-three passages and introduced his discussions with "The Picture of the Messiah in the Psalms," and "The Picture of the Messiah in Isaiah." The work begins with four pages of generalities about the Messianic concept in the Old Testament.[36] Here are some of his views about Old Testament Messianic prophecy: "Messianic prophecies are in such places in the Old Testament which treat of the promised Messiah, the Redeemer of Israel, and the Savior of the world (p. 2)." "The Messiah is the chief content of the Old Testament. So says Christ Himself, John 5:39." Cf. Luther III, 747; VII, 1673; *Lehre und Wehre* 28, p. 58.[37]

Walter A. Maier, Sr. and Messianic Prophecy

Walter A. Maier Sr. (1893-1950) followed the views on Messianic prophecy held by Luther, Walther, Stoeckhardt, L. Fuerbringer, Laetsch and other contemporaries. In his *Notes on the Genesis Seminary Course*[38] and in his *Noten of Selected Psalms*[39] he defended rectilinear prophecy and was opposed to the substitution of typological prophecy in place of rectilinear. In opposition to many scholars of his day he accepted Psalm 8 as a rectilinear prophecy dealing with Christ and not having as its purpose the praise of the greatness of man as God's creature. He vigorously defended the Christo-centricity of the Old Testament. In a published Christmas sermon he claimed that there were over three hundred Messianic prophecies in the Old Testament.[40] Maier relied upon the clear statements of the New Testament for the establishment of numerous Old Testament predictions about Christ's life and work. L. Fuerbringer and Th. Laetsch were two other contemporary exegetes who agreed with Maier about rectilinear prophecy.

P. E. Kretzmann (1883-1965) and Messianic Prophecy

P. E. Kretzmann, the author of *The Popular Commentary* (4-volumes) gives much evidence that he believed in rectilinear Messianic prophecy. Kretzmann was a great devotee of Luther and his writings, and consequently would interpret many Old Testament verses as predictive rectilinear prophecies. He found Christ as predicted in Genesis 3:15,12:3; 18:18; 22:18; 26:4 of Jacob's blessing, he asserted, regarding 49:10: "This is one of the most remarkable and inspiring Messianic promises in the entire Old Testament . . . The government, the princely power, was to remain in the hands of Judah, culminating finally in the reign of Shiloh, the Messiah, the Author and Source of true rest, the Prince of Peace, through whom all mankind should have peace with God by the acceptance of the justification earned by Him, Rom. 5,1. To Him the nations, His people render obedience in faith and thus become part of all the blessings of His kingdom here in time, and hereafter in eternity."[41] The reader of *The Popular Commentary* will find that in numerous passages Kretzmann found rectilinear Messianic prophecies, and in volumes 3 and 4 (New Testament) will show how Old Testament rectilinear prophecies were literally fulfilled in Christ.

While professor of the newly founded theological seminary of The Orthodox Lutheran Church, Minneapolis, he wrote a major study dealing with the Messianic prophecies of the Old Testament and vigorously supported rectilinear Messianic prophecy.[42]

Ernst Eckhardt (1868-1938) And Messianic Prophecy

Eckhardt, a St. Louis graduate of 1891, a pastor of a number of congregations in Nebraska and later statistician from 1921-1928 of The Lutheran Church-Missouri Synod. He was the author of *Homiletisches Reallexicon, nebst index Rerum*, a multi-volume work, in which he analyzed the theology, teaching and pastoral practice of the Synod from 1847 till 1908 and gave references on many subjects and topics occurring in the LCMS's variegated literature. Based on district synodical reports, *Der Lutheraner*, and other periodicals, and in the exegetical and sermonic literature, the reader can easily ascertain what the LCMS held for its first sixty years.[43] In volumes C-F, pp. 559-562, he discussed the topic "Christus im Alten Testament," as well as "Christus" and in another article elucidated from the LCMS's writings *Lutheran Hermeneutical Principles* as they are expressed under the caption "Schriftauslegung," in volume S-T, pp. 657-688.[44] In his article "Christus im Alten Testament," the reader will find the following Old Testament texts considered as rectilinear Messianic prophecies: Gen. 3:15, Num. 24:7; Deut. 18:15; 2 Sam. 7:12f; Psalms 2, 16, 22, 40, 68, 47:6; 68:19; 11:1; Is. 7:14 (virgin Birth foretold). Is. 11:1; 42:8; 53:12-53:12.

William F. Beck and Rectilinear Messianic Prophecies

William Beck, at one time visiting instructor at Concordia Seminary, Clayton, was an accomplished Biblical scholar, well-versed in the three Biblical languages found in Holy Writ. He gave a course on Messianic prophecy at the Saint Louis, Clayton Seminary. He wrote a very incisive article on Isaiah 7:14 and defended the rectilinear nature of the Isaianic oracle. This was available in the bookstore of Concordia Theological Seminary, Springfield, and was used by the Old Testament professors, Drs. Naumann and Surburg. He also issued a study of the rectilinear Prophecy found in Deuteronomy, 18-15-18 reproduced in this writer's *Exegetical Essays and Materials Dealing With Messianic Prophecy* (Concordia Seminary Press, no date), pp. 104-112.

Beck translated the entire Bible into twentieth-century American English and was known as **The Holy Bible, An American Translation** (New Haven: Leader Publishing Company, 1978). In this version Beck took special note of Old Testament Messianic prophecies and in the translation Beck indicated those passages that were messianic by capital letters, where the Messiah was mentioned and in the margin next to the translation listed the New Testament passages where verses of the Old Testament were alluded to and fulfilled in the New Testament.

Mennicke on Bible Interpretation

In 1947 The Lutheran Church-Missouri Synod celebrated the centennial of its founding in 1847. A series of essays was delivered at various synodical district conventions setting forth the official position of the Synod on its doctrines and church practices. One essay dealt with the matter of "Bible interpretation," written and delivered by the father of the former vice-President of the LCMS.[45] In this article the reader will find in summary form the essentials of Biblical and Lutheran interpretation. Mennicke wrote: "The first and foremost principle of Bible interpretation is that the Scripture interprets itself" (*Synodal Bericht, Noerdlicher Distrikt*, 1876, pp. 9-20).[46] As one of a number of examples Mennicke cited Acts 16:10, where Peter showed from the context and attending circumstances that the words of Ps. 16:10 do not apply to David but to Christ. In the same manner the Christian Church still lets Scripture interpret itself.[47]

Another principle stressed by Mennicke as central in Lutheran hermeneutics concerning which he wrote: "The foremost help in Bible interpretation is the knowledge that the central thought of Scripture is to present Christ as Savior of the world" (*Lehre und Wehre*, 1882), pp. 57ff). He quoted John 1:45, John 5:46.47 used also by Luther to the effect: "All prophets preached of the Christ who was to come" (St. L XII, 335). "That alone in the true Gospel which presents Christ to us and teaches what good things we should expect from Him... In the Gospel nothing else should count than only this person of Christ, Jesus. Whoever knows that may thank God (St. L XI: 1835f). Thus the entire Holy Scriptures and especially the Prophets and psalms, say that He (Jesus) was sent to take upon himself the woe of the entire human race (St. L XI: I, 526f)."[48]

Averred Mennicke: "Taking those passages which clearly tell us of Christ and letting these illumine all that the Bible tells us about our life on earth and the gaining of life everlasting."[49]

Another principle enunciated by Mennicke was this one: "Each passage of Scripture has only one Spirit intended meaning" (Synodal Bericht, Noerdlicher Distrikt). According to Mennicke "every passage of the Bible is to be understood only in that sense which the Holy Spirit intended to convey when He inspired it.[50] Only in this sense is the true, the real, the actual sense." If Isaiah 7:14 refers to a natural birth and not a supernatural birth as the New Testament teaches, to hold that Isaiah is not specifically announcing the virginal conception and virgin Birth would mean the Isaianic text has one meaning in the Old Testament and a different one in the N.T.

Frederick Wenger (1923-1956)

Frederick Wenger (1878-1956) was professor of heremeneutics and Biblical exegesis from, 1923-1956 at Concordia Seminary, Springfield, Illinois. He was the author of *Biblical Heremeneutics*,[51] in which he claimed that there was no multiple sense prophecy. In paragraph 113, chapter 15, he wrote: "But there is no double or manifold sense of one and the same text, else Scripture would not possess the quality clearness" (p. 42). Again Wenger declared in paragraph 113: "It causes confusion here if the doctrine of types and antitypes is so understood as, if also the report of the type, that is the language itself, were thereby to have a double sense. The type is not in the language but in the reported matter. The language merely relates the event, names and describes the person which is typical. For instance, the 2 Psalm cannot treat of David and Christ. It treats either of Christ or David. Lutheran exegetes usually support the former reference, namely, that it treats of Christ directly."[52]

Reinhold Pieper (1850-1920)

Reinhold Pieper was the brother of F.A.O. Pieper. He was professor and also president of Concordia Seminary, Springfield 1891-1914. He delivered a series of sermons on the Old Testament, under the title, *Predigten ueber Altestamentliche Text* (1915) which he claimed were the foremost texts setting forth the Messiah in predictive prophecy.[53] In his introduction Reinhold quotes Luther's view on Old Testament Messianic prophecy. Clearly he asserted: "The prophecies concerning the Messiah draw themselves as a golden threat through Moses and the prophets shine in them as a bright star. One prophecy follows upon another and like previous one enlarges and explains and one book the other, thus declares the Scriptures of the New Testament that of the Old Testament. The New Testament is contained in the Old Testament, the Old is fulfilled and explained by the new."[54]

Robert Preus, President of Concordia Theological Seminary, Springfield-Ft. Wayne, 1973-1994

He was in harmony with Stoeckhardt's Biblical exegesis and encouraged Erwin W. Koehlinger to translate a number of Stoeckhardt's books dealing with Messianic prophecy. On November 1-2, 1973 he delivered three lectures on "How is the Lutheran Church to Interpret and Use the Old and New Testaments?" In his second lecture he asserts, with the reformers, "Christ as Savior was the object of Old Testament prophecy, they were not saved by some implicit faith in the power or goodness of God." Preus agreed with Luther by asserting "Adam was a Christian long before the birth of Christ for he had the same faith in Christ that we have." So pivotal was Genesis 3:15 that Preus treated it as the equivalent of John 3:16.

II. The History of Messianic Prophecy from 1947 to 1996

The Promotion of the Typological Messianic Interpretation of the Old Testament

The typological interpretation of Messianic Old Testament prophecy was developed by von Hofman, the foremost Lutheran proponent of the **heils-geschichte** approach to the Old Testament and Biblical history. This was the objection of a writer in *Lehre und Wehre*, who simply signed himself as H.F. In an article entitled "Ueber Messianische Weissagung," *Lehre und Wehre*. H.F. wrote: "Delitzsch proves by his example only that one who denies the direct prophecy of the Messiah and accepts only typical prophecy, which is realized by the means of heilsgeschichte development, most of necessity give up to the pure Messianic doctrine of the Old Testament."[55]

The **heilsgeschichte** school of Biblical interpretation contended that certain themes recurred in the Old Testament.[56] Especially prominent among the themes was that of redemption; the first great example was the freeing of the Children of Israel from the Egyptian bondage. The theme of bondage-deliverance occurs a number of times in the Old Testament. The same motif is found in the prophecies that deal with historical situations. According to this position prophecy is nothing but developmental history. The history of Israel is typological throughout. According to this stance history automatically progresses toward God's predetermined goal. The proponents of the heilgeschichte view claimed that since through all periods the same similar events occur, and that which follows is interpreted by what went before, step-by-step prophecy is changed into fulfillment, and every fulfillment is again a prophecy which will experience a future fulfillment (Stoeckhardt, *Lehre und Wehre*, Vol. 30, pp. 46-47).[57] Thus the prophecy of Israel's deliverance was first fulfilled with Joshua and Zerubbabel led the Jews back to Judea from the Babylonian captivity; it was further later fulfilled by the redemption achieved by Jesus Christ; and in the third fulfillment will consist in the conversion of Israel when Jesus returns at the (end of the age to judge all mankind. In this interpretation of New Testament history, history is only a continuation of the history of the Old Testament. Every Old Testament prophecy has accordingly a multitude of messages. This would make Old Testament prophecy complex in character. One might add that there is not too much difference between this hermeneutical approach end the use of allegory, a method which also permits giving a text at least four different meanings as was the case at Luther's time.

William Arndt (1880-1959) and Typological Prophecy

William F. Arndt was professor at the St. Louis Seminary from 1923-1957. He published an essay in *Lehre und Wehre*, "Typische Messianische

Weissagungen," in which he espoused a different stance on a number of prophecies once held to be rectilinear by previous professors of Concordia Seminary; in fact that were regarded as rectilinear by a number of his contemporaries. In his presentation Arndt suggested the following hermeneutical principles of interpretation:

1. The entire Old Testament has a typical character; 2. Where Scripture itself indicates that a type exists, the reader possesses the correct interpretation; 3. When the New Testament points out that there are types in the Old Testament, the Bible student must search them out; 4. The rule that one cannot go beyond making those passages which are so indicated is to go too far; 5. It is not proper to claim a typical meaning where the text, context and the New Testament indicates a verbal prophecy. Psalm 22, the Great Good Friday Psalm, is wrongly interpreted when it is treated typologically; 6. The interpreter should observe with exactitude how Christ and the Apostles call attention to Old Testament types and then follow these principles in the practice of exegesis; and 7. However, for a typological interpretation not expressly stated in the Bible, the exegete cannot demand unconditional acceptance. Under these circumstances the typological can only be advanced as a possible interpretation.[58]

Alfred von Rohr Sauer (1948-1974) and Messianic Prophecy

Sauer was professor of Old Testament interpretation, from 1948-1974. He published an essay, entitled "Problems of Messianic Interpretation," in which he discussed Old Testament Messianic materials and the manner they were understood by New Testament writers. He distinguished three types of Messianic materials. According to von Sauer these were: 1. direct Messianic predictions; 2. typological prophecies; and 3. applications of Old Testament materials.[59] This threefold classification was proposed earlier by the 19th century German scholar, Tholuck. The reader of von Rohr Sauer will find that prophecies formerly understood in Missouri as rectilinear are placed in the category of typological. In a sermon study of Isaiah 40:1-8 Sauer did not accept Matthew's statement that the preaching of John the Baptist had been foretold in Isaiah 40:1-6.[60] Psalm 8, Hosea 1; Jer. 31:15 Psalms 69:4; 35:19 and other texts before his time considered as rectilinear were simply understood as applications by New Testament writers.[61] Texts the New Testaments cited as being direct predictions about Christ were reinterpreted as applications, their Old Testament bases in no way were intended to be direct Messianic prophecies. By 1964 von Rohr Sauer had undergone a theological conversion involving the adoption of higher criticism and thus he was interested in challenging his past theological and isagogical stances and this involved the reduction of rectilinear Messianic prophecy.

Von Rohr Sauer suggested the following hermeneutical guidelines for the understanding of Old Testament texts used in some manner Messianically in the New Testament. Here are some of his proposals. He asked: "How do I know I am dealing with a direct atypical prophecy, or only a New Testament application?" The answer according to Sauer is this: "The answer is that the original text and its context must determine what the text meant at the time originally spoken or given. If the literal sense of the passage clearly refers to an ideal deliverer of the future and not to any contemporary figure, then a prophecy may be involved. If the literal sense permits and identification of the deliverer with a leader of that day as with the ideal figure of the prophecy; if the literal sense bas to do with an incident or circumstance which is relevant for the people of that day and nothing is about predictive prophecy or prophetic but which is Messianically in the New Testament, then the interpreter may regard this as the application of and Old Testament situation."[62]

Already in 1945 the winds of theological change were blowing through the LCMS, as maybe seen from the publication of the Forty-Four in 1945, entitled *Speaking the Truth in Love*.[63] In this book a number of traditional LCMS teaching's which were not conducive to church fellowship and church union, were attacked. Dr. Repp, Academic Dean of Concordia Seminary, St. Louis claimed that the historical-critical movement which surfaced at the St. Louis Seminary after 1945 to 1975, had its inception with the document of the Forty-Four, which is now being revived again by those more liberal-minded in the LCMS. By 1950 the historical-critical method had been adopted by many members of Exegetical Department and was also advocated and practiced in the other three departments of Synod's most influential seminary. A hallmark of critical Biblical theology as relating to the Old Testament was that a passage, first of all must have meaning for the first time it was spoken in. **The report of the Synodical President of the Lutheran Church-Missouri Synod, in Compliance with resolution 2-28 of the 49th Regular Convention of the Synod held at Milwaukee, Wisconsin, July 9-16**, shows how Old Testament professors denied the rectilinear Messianic prophecies of the Old Testament. The following professors were shown to have jettisoned rectilinear Messianic prophecies: Ehlen, Kalin, von Rohr Sauer, Wengert, Graesser, Habel, Jones, F. Danker, W. Bartling and as did also professors of other departments.

While Roehrs believed that there was a number of passages that directly predicted data about the Messiah's life, still he embarked on a campaign to enlarge the typological meaning of a number of texts that formerly were understood as rectilinear prophecies. An analysis of his course is mimeographed material given to students, entitled "The Typological Interpretation of the Old Testament in the New."[64] In this course Roehrs listed a series of books by critical scholars who wrote articles against rectilinear prophecy and proposed some views that promulgated a typological interpretation which were formerly considered rectilinear.[65]

Roehrs refers to articles by W. Eichrodt, G.W.H. Lampe and K.J. Woolcombe, R. Dentam: J.C.K. Hofmann, Hebert, Martin Noth, Gerhard von Rad, W. Zimmerli, Hans W. Wolff,[66] all of whom have written essays, articles and books rejecting rectilinear prophecy, departing from the historical Lutheran stance as in seen in that he does not refer to one book or piece of literature presenting the position of Luther, Walther, Stoeckhardt, Fuerbringer or Maier. The relationship between the two testaments is that purely of typology. Roehrs was a member of the hermeneutics committee which met from 1965-1969. For this committee he wrote: "the Typological Use of the Old Testament in the New Testament."[67] This contribution appeared in *A Project in Biblical Hermeneutics*, and in it be discussed 1 Cor. 10:1-13; Romans 5:12-19 and Romans Chapter 4. His typological views appear in *Concordia Self-Study Commentary*[68] and in certain sections of the *Concordia Self-Study Bible*.[69]

During the period between 1950-1975, Roehrs was under great pressure by members of The Exegetical Department, for he steadfastly resisted the higher-criticism adopted by most members of his Department. Whether this was the reason that he caved in before the pressure of other Old Testament professors of St. Louis and why he denied the rectilinear character or primary meaning of a number of Christological Old Testament verses which the New Testament clearly stated had been spoken about Christ, he alone knows, (now deceased) nor do we accuse him of making a change for that reason. But the fact remains that Roehrs in making the "**Almah**" spoken of in Isaiah 7:14 as a young girl of Ahab's time and that this "**Almah**" was a type of the Virgin birth contradicts God's Word clearly. Here he was supporting the higher criticism's denial of predictive prophecy.[70]

While Roehrs believes that there are a number of passages in the Old Testament that are predictive rectilinearly prophecies of Christ, still he embarked on a well-intentioned campaign to enlarge the typological meaning of a number of texts that traditionally and historically were understood by Luther, the post-Reformation theologians, the exegetes of the early history of the LCMS as rectilinear prophecies.

Roehrs does recognize as rectilinearly Messianic Genesis 3:15; Jeremiah 23:5-6; Daniel 7:13-14; Amos 9:11-14, still he made Genesis 49:10; Numbers 24:17; Deuteronomy 18:15; and 2 Samuel 7:12-17 and many psalms (2, 8, 16, 40, 45, 69, 89) as typological prophecies. In the passages just cited as being typological, Roehrs makes David a type of Christ, who is depicted as the Antitype. This substitution of David for Christ is especially prominent in the Psalms, which according to the New Testament is replete with rectilinear prophecies about Christ. This raises the interesting question: How did the Old Testament believers, who could only be saved by faith in Christ and who were justified by faith, know about Christ as their Redeemer, if these truths were not **directly** made known to Adam, Noah, Abel, Abram, Isaac, Jacob, Moses and the congregation of Israel while in Egypt; then how could Jesus say "Abraham rejoiced to see my day?" Benjamin Warfield in the last century declared: "The Messianic hope was aboriginal in Israel, and formed indeed, in all ages the heart of the Israelitish religion ... It is an essential element in the eschatological system of the Old Testament and is inseparably imbedded in the hope of God to His kingdom."[71]

The Importance of Typology in the Hermeneutical and Exegetical Scheme

The use of typology Roehrs claimed was one of the great issues of Biblical hermeneutics. According to him typology involves a number of basic hermeneutical questions, namely, 1. The meaning of Old Testament references in their Old Testament context. 2. The historicity of Old Testament accounts. 3. The meaning of **heilsgeschichte**. 4. The historical framework of New Testament apocalyptical references. 5. The validity of New Testament use of the Old Testament.[72]

Typology according to Roehrs proceeds from basic presuppositions: 1. Faith is the only hope of salvation; 2. The God of the Old Testament is the Father of Jesus Christ. 3. In Jesus Christ the promises of God in the Old Testament receive their YEA and AMEN; 4. Faith in Christ appropriated is a present possession but also a faith in the final consummation of salvation (already yet not). Typology is one way in which the New Testament links itself with the Old Testament. Others are designated: 1. Scripture proof (Schriftbeweis), the quotation of words of Old Testament passages; 2. Allegory (?) Cf. the exposition of Galatians 4.[73]

Roehrs has examined the structure and thought pattern of typology as derived from 1. Cor. 10:1-13; Rom. 5:12-19 and Romans 4. On the basis of this study on observations and conclusions drawn from these Pauline pericopes, he also examined 1 Cor. 15:20-22; 44-49; Colossians 2:16-17 and Galatians 4:21-30. There is no doubt about the fact that some of these passages, in which the word **typos** occurs, are typological. However, there are New Testament scholars who do not agree with Roehrs when he makes Romans 4:21-30 typological, he himself admits that the word **typos** is not employed in Romans 4.[74]

It is interesting to see how Roehrs tries to circumvent the fact that Paul does not employ the word **typos** to describe the fact of the relationship between Abraham's faith and justifying faith in Christ. Thus he wrote: "The absence of the term type in Romans 4 furthermore gives additional support to the observation that typology is not strictly speaking, the application of a hermeneutical canon of interpretation. Actually no linguistic heuristic technique is involved. Paul again simply sets forth his conviction that in Jesus Christ God has in fact done what he set out to do in order to reconcile the world to Himself. The coming of Jesus Christ is the YEA and AMEN to God's promises, the validation of Abraham's faith in a merciful God."[75]

Von Hofmann's Influence on Roehrs

Von Hofmann's Interpreting the Bible has views on typology which Roehrs and others have adopted. Thus the German scholar wrote: "The typology of the Old Testament is not confined, as was formerly held, only to those instances which happen to be referred to in the New Testament. Taken by themselves and in isolation it is not feasible to interpret the facts of the Old Testament history in a typological way. It is necessary always to interpret a single fact as part of a whole history of the Old Testament. By proceeding in that manner there is no danger that we should arbitrarily single out certain facts. Rather we scrutinize the whole history of the Old Testament for those basic elements which are typical. There is no danger either with this method's individual features that an Old Testament event should be given a wrong interpretation as a result of

317

isolating them. This method resembles the interpretation of a parable. What matters above all is that the specific significance of the total story should be recognized. By doing so its individual features will be given a typological interpretation merely in as much as they are related to the story as a whole. No individual feature will be interpreted in isolation."[76]

Scriptural Types and Their Interpretation

Moorehead warned: "Inadequate and erroneous views alike are entertained on the subject of Typology." "Some find types everywhere in the Old Testament, especially in the Pentateuch, others next to none."[77] That the Old Testament contains types is clear from the New Testament. However, Moorehead averred: "Let this two-fold caution guide people when searching for types: 1) Do not seek types everywhere; 2) never press the typical teaching to such an extent as to imperil the historical character of the Bible."[78]

The Meaning of Type In the New Testament

The word **type** is derived from the Greek term **tupos**, which occurs sixteen times in the New Testament.[78] It is variously translated, e.g., twice print (John 10:25), twice **figure** Acts. 7:14; Rome. 5:14); once fashion, Acts. 7:43; once **manner** Acts 23:25; once form, Rom. 6:17; twice pattern, Titus 2:7, Heb. 8:5; and seven times **example** 1 Cor. 10:6,11; Phil. 3:17,1; Thess. 1:7; 2 Thess. 3:9; 1 Tim. 4:12; 1 Pet. 5:3. Moorehead claimed that "it is clear that the inspired writers use the word type with some degree of latitude of application."[79] However, one general idea is common to all of them, viz. **likeness** the one matches the other in some essential particulars; the one matches the other in some prominent feature. The Old Testament type must have a correspondence in the New Testament and the latter is called anti-type.[79a]

The Distinctive Characteristics of Biblical Types

A type to be so-called 1) must be a true picture it represents or typifies; 2) the type must be by divine appointment. The type is designed in its original institution to resemble the anti-type; 3) a type always prefigures something future.[80] In all Scripture there is prophecy. Type which may be classified under three heads. 1. Personal type, by which are meant those personages of Scripture that illustrate some truth or principle of redemption. Such are Adam, Melchizedek, Moses, Jonah. 2. Historical: In which are included great historical events that under the guidance of God become foreshadowing of good things to come, i.e., the deliverance from Egypt, wilderness journey, conflict for Canaan. 3. Ritual: Such as the altar, the sacrifices, priesthood and tabernacle. There are typical persons, places, times, and actions in the Old Testament Scriptures. Professor Stuart expressed the following view on how much of the Old Testament is typical: "Just so much of the Old Testament is to be accounted typical as the New Testament affirms."[81]

Was King David A Type of Christ?

LCMS typologists make David a type of Christ. Many rectilinear prophecies are said by Roehrs to be fulfilled in David and in his reign and he makes David a type of Christ. This substitution of David for Christ in Old Testament Messianic prophecies is especially prominent in his interpretation of various psalms, such as 2, 8, 16, 40, 45, 89. However, what are the facts? There is no suggestion that David is a type and Christ the antitype in the New Testament. The majority of David references allude to Christ's kingly lineage, Christ ultimately being descended from David. The expression "Son of David" was a term, for the Messiah and it is in this latter sense that this designation is employed of Jesus Christ in the New Testament.

Horace Hummel's Typological Interpretation of the Old Testament

Hummel, in his voluminous introduction to the Old Testament, called *The Word Becoming Flesh*,[83] presents a defense of a form of typological interpretation of Messianic prophecies, which appears to have been influenced by L. Goppelt, *Typos: die typologische Deutung des Alten Testament*.[84] The typological approach dominates Hummel's *magnum opus*. He has devoted a number of pages in the early part of his book to his concept of typology. Hummel distinguished between "'vertical typology," said by him to be advocated by scholars who derive salvation primarily from history, a position Hummel rejects. The other kind, "horizontal typology" he claims is the Bible's kind of typology, one which Hummel sees as going toward the future (salvation incarnationally through history), and thus for Hummel all typology is both eschatologically and Christologically oriented.[85]

In describing the relationship of the vertical and the horizontal Hummel wrote as follows: "Nevertheless, the differences may be overdone as liberalism generally does. It is more a matter of accent than of mutual exclusiveness. Thus the earthly tabernacle/temple is also a type of the heavenly temple, its 'reflection' or miniature. The holy war of Biblical history is fought both and often simultaneously in heaven and earth. God chose to come down to deal with man, as Christ did climatically. Only eschatologically, at the end of our sinful time, will both the vertical and the horizontal types be totally fulfilled or consummated in the new heavens and a new earth in which righteousness dwells" (2 Peter 3:13).[86]

Hummel avers that both liberals (positivists, historicists) as well as conservatives have attacked typology. The author of *The Word Becoming Flesh* admits that conservatives have been correct in their criticism that unlike allegory, typological correspondences must be real, and must be rooted in real and genuine history.[87] But, asserts Hummel, the matter cannot stop there. It is Hummel's contention that typology, as we understand it, implies much more than mere correspondence, analogy or symbol. Lutherans especially have no or little difficulty with the use of the word "sacrament" in this connection. The external history (or elements) must be real enough, but "in, with, and under" it lies the ultimate meaning. There is an integral connection between type and anti-type.[88]

It is Hummel's further contention that it is wrong to distinguish or place in opposition to each other typology and "prophecy-fulfillment." No, so argues the St. Louis professor, they are two sides of the same coin, and thus ultimately are asserting the same thing. In describing the relationship of prophecy to fulfillment to type-antitype, Hummel has advanced the following proposition:

"Prophecy-fulfillment is to type antitype as Word is to Sacrament. Neither part of the proportion is complete without its mate. Prophecy and preaching would be only words about words, great ideas and ideals, if the 'visible Word' did not accompany it. Similarly, more history or sacramental elements are mute without the inspired word to explain and apply."[89]

Hummel conceives of Old Testament history as being our history via Christ. The history of the Old Testament was also accomplished for us and for our salvation, and into it we too were baptized. According to Hummel, Christ is Israel reduced to one; furthermore since Israel's inner history was all recapitulated and consummated in Christ, "the new Israel," "the church," expressed its identity and mission in terms of promise given the Old Israel. The relationship to the Old Testament and the new is not theological at all, but basically only that the first Israel was both "church" and state, while in the age of the antitype or fulfillment the political (and accompanying ceremonial) scaffolding fell away.[90]

Critique of Hummel's Typology

Hummel's views on typology are **sui generis**. They are unique. Besides where he sets forth his unique typological views, he interprets and applies his unique views at fifty-two places in *The Word Becoming Flesh*. His inter-penetration of typology and prophecy is overdone. He practically wipes out the difference between prophecy and fulfillment. He denies predictive prophecy, even though he claims he does not. His view of predictive prophecy slides into immanentistic directions. The essayist does not see the viability of the distinction between vertical and horizontal typology. Hummel and all those who make direct predictive Messianic prophecies typological violate the hermeneutical principle that a text has only one intended sense and does not have multiple meanings. Lieber in his *Legal and Political Hermeneutics* asserted:

> No sentence or form of words can have more than one true sense, and this is only the one we have to inquire for. This is the very basis or all interpretation. Interpretation without it has no meaning. Every man or body of persons making use of words does so in order to convey a certain meaning, and to find this precise meaning in the object of interpretation. To have two meanings in view is equivalent to having no meaning. The interpretation of two meanings implies absurdity.[91]

Luther wrote: "We should not say that Scripture, or God's Word, has more than one sense."

In his discussion of the Book of Isaiah, Hummel refers to the three passages that occur in the Immanuel segments of chapters 7-12; namely, 7:14; 9:1-7; and 11. Thus this scholar wrote:

"The distinction between Messianism and the more general eschatology is ultimately artificially as we noted earlier, but at the moment we pinpoint the former. The atomistic critics and well-meaning conserva-

tives are often guilty of isolating these oracles from the total Isaianic con-
test. Involved are not only some of the best-known prophecies in the Old
Testament (Is. 7,9,11), but others that are not so well known (e.g. chapters 32 and 33). It is especially nugatory to try to distinguish historical
and eschatological content of these pericopies."[92] On page 203 he discussed three major Isaianic passages and stated that in chapters 7,9,11
a member of the house of David is meant, possibly Hezekiah. He claims
that these three passages formerly always considered to be rectilinear
predictions are simply passages about a Judean king.

Relative to 7:14 and its **almah** word, he asserts that **almah** techni-
cally means "a young woman" of marriageable age, who may or may not
be a virgin. While Hummel prefers the translation "virgin," he avers that
it would not be wrong for those conservatives to understand **almah** as
referring to Isaiah's (future) wife and son.[93] Thus he allows the text to
have a multiple meaning! What does such an interpretation, which
pleases two different schools of interpretation, do to the Lutheran belief
of the perspicuity of Holy Writ?

Relative to Isaiah 7:14 Hummel stated on page 203: "What is that
'sign?'" The Matthean citation (1:23) makes clear the Messianic import
beyond all cavil, but the *fides quaerens intellectum* still explores the empirical dimensions of the miraculous prediction. Both context and the
analogy of prophecy indicates that here too we should avoid any false pre-
diction-typology antithesis. Both "house of David" in Is. 7:13 and the
apostrophe to Immanuel in 8:8 confirm a royal-Messianic import. It
would seem likely that, as in the contiguous prophecies of Is. 9 and 11,
the prophet points to a Davidic or Daviddes of the near future
(Hezekiah?) as a type and illustration accompanying his prediction of the
further fulfillment in Immanuel incarnate. If the total Biblical context is
not critically truncated, there is no reason why Ahaz too should not have
fully perceived that eschatological-Messianic import. Particularly in Isaiah, the prayer "'Thy kingdom come' (which Isaiah commends to Ahaz) is
unthinkable apart from the King."[94]

Relative to the Christmas prophecy of Jesus' birth in Isaiah 9:5-6,
Hummel has this interpretation:

The pericope in Isaiah 9:5-6 has Messianic import. Further he claims
that the New Testament linkage helps readers to realize that the
prophecy had contemporary, historical as well as eschatological-Messianic import (the latter by itself easily distoricized and treated spiritu-
ally). He claimed that his interpretation would also support the position
held by recent critics who regard the oracle as genuine over against the
consensus of most classical liberals who judge the oracles as necessarily
late inauthentic.[95]

Hummel averred that the oracle of Isaiah 9:5-6 concentrates on the
Messianic king as much as on the kingdom. The St. Louis professor
claimed that liberals are not totally wrong in seeing some reference to
the historical bearers of the Davidic promise but are wrong in limiting
its original meaning to that. The epithets did apply to the heirs of David
in a lesser, metaphorical sense "sons" of God by election not adoption-not

radically different from the sense in which all true Israelites, then and now are "sons of God."[96]

Hummel and the Messianic Psalms

Hummel has worked through the Psalms in *The Concordia Self-Study Bible*, pages 780-941. Psalms which professors of Concordia Seminary St. Louis, as Pieper, Stoeckhardt, L. Graebner, Walter A. Maier, Sr., P. Kretzmann, Engelder, J. T. Mueller Theo. Laetsch, Pardiek, William Beck considered Messianic rectilinearly are interpreted according to the liberal scholar, Herman Gunkel, the "father of form criticism." With the latter Psalm 2 is alleged to be "a royal psalm."[97] Wrote Hummel: "A royal psalm, it was originally composed for the coronation of Davidic kings, in the light of the covenant with David" (2 Sa. 7). He admits Psalm 2 is quoted in the New Testament where various writers apply words of Psalm 2 to Jesus. Although the New Testament ascribes Psalm 2 to David, Hummel states that the Jews ascribed the Psalm 2 to David,[98] Peter asserts in Acts 4:25 that the Holy Spirit spoke by the mouth of David. Psalm 8 is not a predictive Messianic Psalms but the New Testament applies verses from this Psalm to Jesus. Psalm 16 is not purely a Davidic Psalm and Verses 10-11 are said by Peter to predict Christ's not seeing corruption, as again applied by New Testament writers to Jesus, but this does not mean that the Old Testament had predicted these happenings.

Psalm 22, which Arndt considered a Predictive Messianic psalm, Hummel considers to be the anguished prayer of David and statements in Psalm 22 pointed to facts about Christ's suffering and death. Verses 22-31 do not refer to Christ's resurrection. The Hummel interpretation is the best of liberal tradition.[99]

Psalm 45 which Luther considered speaking about Christ and Christendom was for the Reformer Messianic. By contrast Hummel follows Gunkel, namely, that Psalm 45 was a song in praise of the king on his wedding day.[100] Psalm 69 cited in the New Testament as speaking about Christ was for Hummel only a Davidic psalm, Psalm 110 has the marks of a coronation Psalm, composed for the use of the coronation of a new Davidic king.

Eventually the Jew a viewed this psalm as Messianic and so it was viewed in the New Testament.

According to Hummel, to obtain the right understanding of the Messianic Psalms, it would be advisable to read Mowinckel's *The Psalms in Israelite Worship*.[101] His interpretations are totally different from those advocated by Stoeckhardt, Walter A. Maier, Sr., P. Kretzmann, Fuerbringer, Laetsch, L. Graebner, Pardiek and others.

The historical overview here presented, shows that there were radical differences between Old Testament professors and theologians of the Old Concordia Seminary, St. Louis, 1847-1947 and the New Concordia Seminary (1947-1996).

The CTCR's Opinion on Prophecy and Typology

In August, 1996 the Commission on Theology and Church Relations of the LCMS issued an opinion on **"Prophecy and Typology."**[102] This was made in response to the Missouri District's request on the subjects of prophecy and typology. The study deals with how to identify prophecy. How does one identify a type? What hermeneutical rules guide the interpretation of prophecy? How are these rules established?[103] *(Ed. The entire CTCR statement was photographed in the September 30, 1996 Christian News. The CTCR in its "The Creator's Tapestry" disagrees with Luther and says Psalm 8 refers to a human and not Jesus Christ. Christian News, April 26, 2010).*

Who the author or authors of this document are, are not indicated. One thing can be said for sure, it is written in the best tradition of Roehrs and Hummel. The document has pulled out all stops for the typological approach to Messianic prophecy. It contains a composite of those in the thinking of the Synod, especially at our two theological seminaries who have been gathering argumentations for the typological understanding of Messianic prophecy for years. The study relies heavily upon Walter R. Roehrs revised version of "Typological Use of the Old Testament in the New Testament." Added to the 1969 version were five addenda.[104]

"Prophecy and Typology" claims that typology expresses the unity of the Scriptures and the consistency of God's character. The books on apologetics that this writer has read argue that predictive prophecy and their fulfillment argue for the unity of Scriptures and that Old and New Testament together are the Word of God.

The CTCR document endeavors to show that Post-Reformation Lutheranism agrees with LCMS's typologists, Glassius, Gerhardt, Hollaz and Michael Walther are adduced as supporting the document's position on typology.

In rebuttal to the CTCR's use of the Post-Reformation theologians, Robert Preus specialist in Post-Reformation Lutheran theology, wrote this: "And therefore there is not a prior reason for insisting that every Old Testament prophecy must somehow refer to the people who would first hear or read it. The Old Testament abounds in rectilinear prophecies that refer only to Christ; in such a way these prophecies are understood by the New Testament, and in the same way they were to be understood when first delivered in the Old Testament."[105]

Preus claims: "The New Testament, then, is the key to understanding these Old Testament prophecies; it is the inspired interpretation of the prophecies in the light of fulfillment."[106] Then Brochmand is cited, who wrote: "Hebrews 1 interprets many Old Testament prophecies as pointing to Christ and to no one else." To the writer of Hebrews Ps. 102:25 in itself "demonstrates ... that the Son is not some sort of creature but the very Creator Himself."[107] Psalm 8:5 refers directly and only to the humiliation and exaltation of Christ. And Ps. 45:6 points to Christ's throne and in no sense to Solomon's, as the Jews contended. Admittedly, according to such exegesis, the New Testament interpretation will settle the meaning of an Old Testament passage. This fact, however, does not imply that the Lutheran exegetes pay no consideration to the context of the Old Testament prophecies. On the contrary, they repeatedly attempt to show the Messianic character of such prophecies by the Old Testament context. Brochmand goes to a great length in order to show from Old Testament text alone that Ps. 45 can refer only to the coming King Christ."

The Socinians and Arminians accused the old Lutherans of not reading the New Testament into their Old Testament context, to which they responded "that the New Testament understands perfectly and takes into account the Old Testament context; and furthermore the fulfillment of prophecy in the New Testament belongs to the wider context of the prophecies themselves."[108]

Robert Preus on the Distinction
Between Prophecy and Typology

In an article, entitled "The Unity of Scripture" Preus insisted in every possible way that there was an important difference between prophecy and typology. Thus he wrote: "In the case of predictive prophecy we have a rectilinear correspondence between the Old Testament descriptive and cognitive prediction and a thing, person, or event described in the New Testament. In typology there is also a straight correspondence, or event in the New Testament. In the case of predictive prophecy the words of the Old Testament predict; in the case of typology **reference** to the words predict. The correspondence of unity between type and antitype in the case of biblical typology it is only a unity of two references, type from the Old and antitype from the New Testament. Except in cases where the New Testament itself clearly marked out an Old Testament type, the practice of typological exegesis can become open-ended and precariously arbitrary as a hermeneutical principle, since it is an application not of the unity of Scripture, but unity of the references of Scripture. It is thus no more based on the explicative meaning of the biblical narrative than the application of the unitary principles of Semler and his followers who believed that there was no unity in Scripture except that which was applicatively derived" (pp. 7-8).[108a]

The Commission on Theology and Church Relations points out the fact that The Wisconsin Synod, in contrast to the interpretation of the LCMS for about a hundred years, understood passages typologically.[109] However, the Wisconsinites embraced a view about Church and Ministry, with which the LCMS has disagreed, a view with which the typologists of LCMS would not agree.

Differences Between the Stance of 1847-1947 as
Compared with the Position of 1947-1996

Since the effects of higher criticism in the LCMS on the Old Testament and on Christological views in the fifth to eighth decades of the twentieth century, there has resulted a reduction of the clear Old Testament texts about The Messiah and the elimination of Old Testament **sedes doctrinae** dealing with various truths about Christ's ministry.

There Are Significant Differences
Between the Two Time Periods

These two periods differ: 1) in their understanding of what is meant by the Lutheran principle that a text has only one intended meaning; 2) They differ in their understanding when and where typology is to be found; 3) they differ in their understanding when types are fulfilled ; 4) They differ in their understanding what is meant by the hermeneutical principle "that Scripture interprets Scripture;"

5) They differ in their understanding how Old Testament believers comprehended how Old Testament texts were rectilinear and how they are to be understood typologically; 5) They differ in their understanding of the New Testament, when it asserts that certain Old Testament texts were fulfilled in events connected with Christ's life and ministry; and 6) They differ in their interpretation of the word "fulfill."

Conservative Protestants Advocating Rectilinear Messianic Prophecies

A number of conservative Protestant hermeneuticists and exegetes are in agreement with Luther and early scholars of the LCMS relative to rectilinear prophecy. Here are scholars that find rectilinear Messianic prophecies in the Old Testament. D. Duncan, *Hermeneutics, A Textbook*, pp. 395-399 and listed 60 passages as Messianic Henry H. Halley, *Halley's Bible Handbook*, pp. 387-401.[110]

J. Barton Payne, *The Theology of the Older Testament*, pp. 257-284.[111]

Howard A. Hanke, *Christ and the Church in the Old Testament. A Survey of Redemptive Unity in the Testaments.*[112]

Norman Geisler, *Christ: The Theme of the Bible*, pp. 7-23. Contains both rectilinear and typological materials.[113]

Hebert Lockyer, *All the Messianic Prophecies of the Bible*, pp. 23-211.[114]

John Ankerberg, John Weldon and Walter C. Kaiser, Jr. The Case for Jesus the Messiah (Eugene, Oregon: Harvest House Publishers, Inc., 1989).155 pp.

Eugene P. Kauffeld, "Jesus Christ, the Promised Messiah," in Vernon H. Harley, *Jesus Christ Fact or Fiction*, pp. 102-133.[115]

Benjamin Breckinridge Warfield, in *Biblical and Theological Studies*, edited by Samuel G. Craig, "The Divine Messiah in the Old Testament," pp. 79-126.[116]

Frank Charles Thompson, *The New Chain-Reference Bible*, Third Improved Edition, 1934, Appendix, no. 4221 "The Messianic Stars," p. 182.[117]

Addendum

Ideas and concepts in this essay are partly found in the following contributions of the writer:

Raymond F. Surburg, "The Interpretation of Isaiah 7:14," *The Springfielder*, XXXVIII, 110-118.

"The Proper Interpretation of Old Testament Messianic Prophecy", *The Lutheran Synod Quarterly*, XX, No. 4, pp. 6-36.

"Currents Trends in the Old Testament Hermeneutics," *The Lutheran Synod Quarterly*, XXI, No. 2, pp. 7-37, June 1981.

The Principles of Biblical Interpretation (Fort Wayne: Concordia Seminary Press, 1980), pp. 123-131.

Luther and the Christology of the Old Testament, The 1982 Reformation Lectures, October 28-29; 1982, three lectures.

"The Messianic Prophecies of Zechariah With Special Reference to His Prediction of Holy Week," *Christian News Encyclopedia*, V, 2669-2670.

"The Relationship of Genesis 3:15 to the Incarnation of God's Son," *Christian News Encyclopedia*, IV, pp. 2673-2674.

"Additions to the 1974 Article, 'The Interpretation of Isaiah 7:14,'" *Christian News Encyclopedia*, IV, p. 2676.

Exegetical Essays and Materials Dealing With Messianic Prophecy, Fort Wayne: Concordia Seminary Press, 1985), pp. 1-142.

"Messianic Prophecy and Messianism," *The Springfielder*, 37 (June 1973), 17-34).

Footnotes

1. Henry H. Halley, *Halley's Bible Handbook* (Grand Rapids: Zondervon Publishing House, 1965, 24th edition), p. 387.
2. Ewald M. Plass, *What Luther Says - An Anthology* (St. Louis: Concordia Publishing House, 1959), I, p. 145b.
3. **Ibid.**, p. 145; Weimar 46, 28; St. L. 8, 638.
4. *D. Martin Luthers Werke, kritische Gasamtaugabe* (Weimar: 1888). Hereafter referred to as W or Weimar, 69, 351; St. L. 14, 1417.
5. Martin Luther's *Saemmtliche Schriften*, 23 volumes in 25, edited by Johann Walsh in modern German (St. Louis: Concordia Publishing House, 1880-1910, 13, 670f.; Hereafter referred to as St. L; St. 13a. 670f.; W 59,67.
5a. Weimar, 45, 295.
6. Weimar 54, 67; St. L. 1931.
6a. Weimer 54, 67; St. L. 3, 1931.
7. Weimer 64,67.
8. St. L. 18, 1681.
9. Heinrich Bornkmamm, *Luther and the Old Testament* translated by Eric W. and Ruth C. Gritsch (Philadelphia: Fortress Press, 1969), p. 191.
10. St. L. 2, 1820; Weimar 4, 163.
11. Weimar 24:1ff.
12. Weimar 14, 223.
13. Weimer, 14, 223:18.
14. William Dallmann, W. H. Dau, and Th. Engelder, *Walther and the Church* (St. Louis: Concordia Publishing House, 1938) pp. 122-127.
15. **Ibid.**, p. 125.
16. **Ibid.**, p. 125. Walther cites 1 Cor. 3:11; 2:2; Rev. 10:10, *Augsburg Confession* XXIV 4, Cf. Robert C. Schultz, "The Distinction Between Law and Gospel," *Concordia Theological Monthly*, 32:59 1-597, October 1961.
17. Raymond F. Surburg, "Walther's Hermeneuti cs," in A. Drevlow, C.F.W.'s Walther, *The American Luther* (Mankato: The Walther Press, 1987). pp. 95-114.
18. G. Stoeckhardt, Weissagung und Erfuellung, *Lehre und Wehre*, 30:42-49 (1884), 95-114; 161-170; 193-200; 252-259; 335-344; 375-380; 31:220-232 (1886), 265-275.
18a. G. Stoeckhardt, "Christus in der Alttesstamentlichen Weissagung," *Lehre und Wehre*, 36 (1890), 209-217; 278-286; 317-325; 354-360; (1890) 209-217; 278-286:317-325;354-360; 37 (1891), 5-12; 37-45; 97-107; 137-145; 295-303; 328-332; 365-372; 38 (1892). 7-15; 70.79; 132-142; 161-172.
19. G. Stoeckhardt, Advent spredigten. Auslegung der vornemsten Weissagungen des Alten Testaments (St. Louis: Lutherischer Concordia Verlag, 1887), 246 pp.
20. G. Stoeckhardt, *Der Prophet Jesaja* (St. Louis: Concordia Publishing House, 1902), pp. 83-90.
21. G. Stoeckhardt, *Lectures on Select Psalms*. Translated by H. W. Degner (Lake Mills, Iowa: Graphic Publishing Co., 1965), 172 pp.
21a. Stoeckhardt, Advent-spredigten, **op. cit.**, p. iv. 22. A. L. Graebner. *Outlines of*

Theology (St. Louis: Concordia Publishing House, 1910), as is evident in his use of the Testament passages, claiming they speak about Christ, pp. 100, 106, 108; 113; 115, 116, 112, 119; 120; 121, 122, 124, 130, 133.

23. Lueker, *The Lutheran Cyclopedia.* p. 8117. cf. especially, *The Christian Dogmatics* (3 vols.) V. 4 as an Index of the contents of the three-volume opus.

24. F. Pieper, *Christian Dogmatics* (St. Louis: Concordia Publishing House, 1950) II. p. 337.

25. **Ibid.**, p. 341.

26. Carl Manthey Zorn, *Der apostoliche Brief an die Kolosser* (St. Louis: Concordia Publishing House, 1915), 545 pp.

27. Carl Manthey Zorn, *Die Psalmen* (Zwickau (in Saxen) Verlag des Schriftvereins (E. Klaemer), 1921), Worwort, iii. In Die Psalme please consult Psalms 8, 16, 22 to see how Zorn followed Luther Walther, Stoeckhardt.

28. Theodore Laetsch, *The Abiding Word* (St. Louis: Concordia Publishing House, 1947), two volumes.

29. Theo. Laetsch, *Bible Commentary - The Minor Prophets* (St. Louis: Concordia Publishing House, 1956), cf. especially pages 257-28; 425-430; 457-458ff.

30. Theo. Laetsch, *Bible Commentary, Jeremiah* (St. Louis: Concordia Publishing House, 1952).

31. Laetsch, Jeremiah, **op. cit.**, p. 270.

32. Laetsch, The Minor Prophet, **op. cit.**, pp. 87-93.

33. Laetsch, Jeremiah, **op. cit.**, pp. 194ff.; 270ff.

34. L. Fuerbringer, *Theological Hermeneutics* (St. Louis: Concordia Publishing House, 1924), 24 pp.

35. L. Fuerbringer, *Exegesis of Messianic Prophecies* (St. Louis: Concordia Mimeograph Company, 1933), 95 pp.

36. **Ibid.**, pp. 1-4.

37. **Ibid.**

38. W. A. Maier, *Notes on the Book of Genesis* (St. Louis: Concordia Mimeograph Company, 1930).

39. *Exegetical Notes on the Psalms* (St. Louis: Concordia Seminary Mimeograph Company, 1930), cf. especially his arguments for rectilinear prophecy and rejection of typological prophecy in Pa. 2, 8, 16.

40. Walter A. Maier, Sr., *The Radio for Christ* (St. Louis: Concordia Publishing House, 1939), p. 50 in a sermon for Christmas on Isaiah 9:6-7.

41. P. E. Kretzmann *Popular Commentary - Old Testament* (St. Louis: Concordia in Publishing House, I, p. 108.

42. P. E. Kretzmann, *The Messianic Predictions in The Old Testament* (Minneapolis: 1960), 350 pp. McLaughlin in *The Conservative Defender* published many of Kretzmann's Messiannic prophecies studies.

43. E. Eckhardt, *Homiletisches Reallexikon, nebst Index Rerum* (St. Louis: The Banner Press 1912) "Christus im Alten Testament," in vol. C.F. pp. 559-562.

44. **Ibid.**

45. Victor Mennicke, "Bible Interpretation," *The Abiding Word* (St. Louis: Concordia Publishing House, 1947), II, pp. 35-58.

46. **Ibid.**, p. 38.

47. **Ibid.**

48. **Ibid.**, p. 50.

49. **Ibid.**

50. **Ibid.**

51. Frederick S. Wenger, *Biblical Hermeneutics* (Springfield, Illinois: Concordia Seminary Print Shop, 1964), 67 pp.

52. **Ibid.**, p. 41; cf. especially p. 42.

52a. **Ibid.**, p. 41.

53. R. Pieper, *Predigten ueber Alttestamentilche Texte* (St. Louis: Concordia Publishing House, 1915) 448 pp. R. Pieper discusses 33 Old Testament texts.

54. **Ibid.**, p. v.
55. H.F., "Ueber Messianische Weissagung," *Lehre und Wehre,* 25; 197, 1879.
56. J.C.K. von Hofmann, *Interpreting the Bible* (Minneapolis: Augsburg Press, 1959. Translated by Ch. Preus. Cf. also Raymond F. Surburg "Hofmann Redivivus,"Twentieth Century, attempts to revive "Hermeneutics and Theology of Von Hoffmann," *Christian News*, vol. 9, April 26, 1976, pp. 8-12.
57. Stoeckhart, *Lehre und Wehre*, 30:46-47.
58. W. Arndt, "Typisch Messianische Weissagungen", *Lehre und Wehre*, 67:366-367.
59. Alfred von Rohr Sauer, "Problems of Messianic Interpretation," *Concordia Theological Monthly,* 35:566-574, 1964.
60. Alfred von Rohr Sauer, "Sermon Study on Isaiah 40:1-8," *Concordia Theological Monthly*, 21:850, 1964.
61. **Ibid.**, p. 574.
62. **Ibid.**, p. 574.
63. *Speaking the Truth in Love - Essays Related to A Statement*, Chicago, Nineteen forty-five (Chicago: The Willow Press, 1945), 80 pp.
64. The writer has the course material in his possession obtained from a graduate pastor who took Roehr's course.
65. G. W. H. Lampe and K. J. Woolcomb, *Essays in Typology* (Naperville: Illinois: Alec R. Allenson, 1956), 75 pp.
66. Claus Westermann, *Essays on Biblical Hermeneutics* (Richmond: John Knox Press, 19 Cf. pp. 7-30; 50-75; 76-88; 89-123; 160-190; 221-245.
67. Walter Roehrs, "The Typological Use of the Old Testament," in *A Project in Biblical Hermeneutics* (St. Louis: The Commission on Theology and Church Relations of the Missouri Synod, 1969), pp. 39-53.
68. Walter R. Roehrs and Martin Franzmann, *Concordia Self-Study Commentary* (St. Louis: Concordia Publishing House, 1971), pp. 1-587.
69. Roebrt G. Hoerber, H. D. Hummel, Walter Roehrs and Dean Wenthe, *Concordia Self-Study Bible* (St. Louis: Concordia Publishing House, 1986), by Roehrs, "The Pentateuch", pp. 1-256; "The Minor Prophets," pp. 1016-1326.
70. Roehrs, *Self-Explanatory Commentary*, op. city., 1029.
71. Benjamin Warfield, "The Divine Messiah in the Old Testament," in *Biblical and Theological Studies* (Philadelphia: The Presbyterian and Reformed Publishing Company, 1952), p. 115.
72. Roehrs, "The Typological Use of the Old Testament," **op. cit.**, p. 39.
73. **Ibid.**, p. 39.
74. Ibid, p. 46.
75. **Ibid.**, p. 46.
76. Von Hofmann, *Interpreting the Bible*, **op. cit.**, p. 145.
77. W. G. Moorehead, *Outline Studies in the Books of the Old Testament* (New York Fleming Revell Co., 1874), p. 12.
78. **Ibid.**, p. 12.
79. **Ibid.**, p. 13
79a. **Ibid.**, p. 13
80. **Ibid.**, p. 14.
81. Stuart as cited by Moorehead, **op. cit.**, p. 17.
82. Robert Young, *Analytical Concordance to the Bible*. Twentieth American Edition by Wm. B. Stevenson (New York: Funk and Wagnalls Company, no date, p. 227).
83. Horace Hummel, *The Word Becoming Flesh* (St. Louis: Concordia Publishing House, 1979), cf. especially pp. 16-18.
84. Leonard Goeppelt, *Typos, Die Tuepologische Deuetung des Alten Testaments* (Guertersloh: Verlag von C. Bertelmann, 1939), 255 pp.
85. Hummel, *The Word Becoming Flesh*, **op. cit.**, p. 16.
86. **Ibid.**, p. 16.
87. **Ibid.**
88. **Ibid.**, p. 18.

89. **Ibid.**, p. 18.
90. **Ibid.**, p. 16.
91. Lieber, *Legal and Political Hermeneutics*, 3ʳᵈ edition, p. 74 as cited by Mennicke, *The Abiding Word*, **op. cit.**, II, p. 55.
92. Hummel, *The Word Becoming Flesh*, **op. cit.**, p. 16.
93. **Ibid.**, p. 203.
94. **Ibid.**, p. 203.
95. **Ibid.**, pp. 204·205.
96. **Ibid.**, pp. 204·205.
97. Sigmund Mowinckel, *The Psalms in Israel's Worship*. Translated by D. R. Ap-Thomas (New York: Abingdon Press 1962), I 42-45; 106-139.
98. Hummel, *Concordia Self-Study Bible*, **op. cit.**, p. 787.
99. Hummel, **Ibid.**, p. 05.
100. **Ibid.**, p. 831.
101. **Ibid.**, p. 906.
102. This study document was issued in August, 1996. 17 pages.
103. "Prophecy and Typology," Document of the Commission and Theology and Church Relations, p. 1.
104. Walter R. Roehrs, "Rectilinear or Typological interpretation of Messianic Prophecy?", *Concordia Theological Monthly*, 38:155-167, (1965).
105. Robert D. Preus, *The Theology of Post-Reformation Lutheranism* (St. Louis: Concordia Publishing House, 1970), II, p. 334.
106. **Ibid.**, R. D. Preus, "The Unity of Scripture," *Concordia Theological Quarterly*, 54, 1 (January 1990), pp. 7-8.
107. Brochmand, *Commmentarius in Epistorlarum and Hebracis*, p. 53.
108. As cited by Preus, **op. cit.**, II, p. 335.
108a. **Ibid.**
109. William J. Hassold, "Rectilinear or Typological Interpretation of Messianic Prophecy," *Concordia Theological Monthly*, 37:162, March, 1967.
110. Published by (Grand Rapids: Zondervan Publishing Company, 1965).
111. Published by (Grand Rapids: Zondervan Publishing Company, 1962).
112. Published by (Grand Rapids: Zondervan Publishing Company, 1957).
113. Published by (Chicago: The Moody Press, 1968).
114. Published by (Grand Rapids: Zondervan Publishing Company, 1973).
115. Published by (Milwaukee: Northwestern Publishing House, 1969).
116. Published originally by The Oxford University Press, New York; the work cited from was published by The Presbyterian and Reformed Publishing Company of Philadelphia, 1952.
117. Published by B. B. Kirkbride Bible Co., Indianapolis, Indiana, 1934.

Questions

1. The Lutheran Church – Missouri Synod was found on the belief that _____.
2. Plass contended that Luther's theology is _____.
3. Luther identifies Christ with the _____.
4. How did Luther translate Genesis 4:1? _____
5. Walther followed _____ in his Biblical interpretation.
6. Walther is called the American _____.
7. Who in the LCMS followed Luther's position on predictive prophecy? _____
8. Who replaced Walther on the faculty of Concordia Seminary, St. Louis? _____
9. A.L. Graebner in his *Doctrinal Outlines* perpetuated _____.

10. Next to Walther who is considered the LCMS's outstanding theologian? _____
11. J.T. Mueller's condensed Pieper's _____.
12. Who was Carl Manthy Zorn? _____
13. Zorn said the Psalm 2 speaks about _____ and not _____.
14. What did Zorn teach about Psalm 8 _____.
15. According to Zorn, Psalm 16 contains a prediction the _____.
16. Zorn's best known and beloved book is _____.
17. What did Theodore Laetsch write about Messianic Prophecy? _____
18. Ludwig Furbringer was famous for _____.
19. Walter A. Maier Sr. followed the views on Messianic prophecy? _____
20. Maier accepted Psalm 8 as _____.
21. Maier claimed that there were over _____ Messianic prophecies in the Old Testament.
22. Who is the author of the 4 volume *The Popular Commentary*? _____
23. Ernst Eckhardt is the author of _____.
24. William Beck was an accomplished _____.
25. How did Beck in his An American Translation of the Bible take note of Messianic prophecies? _____
26. Robert Preus agreed with Luther by asserting that Adam was _____.
27. Who developed typological interpretation of Old Testament prophecy? _____
28. What happened to Alfred von Rohr Sauer in 1964? _____
29. When did the historical-critical method surface at Concordia Seminary, St. Louis? _____
30. Who were the St. Louis seminary professors who jettisoned rectilinear Messianic prophecies? _____
31. The typological views of Walter Roehrs appeared in _____.
32. What did Roehrs teach about almah and the virgin birth? _____
33. How were the Old Testament believers saved? _____
34. Horace Hummel in his *The Word Becoming Flesh* presents _____.
35. Surburg claims Hummel denied _____.
36. Hummel avers that it would not be wrong to understand that almah in Isaiah 7:14 refers to _____.
37. What does the *Concordia Self-Study Bible* teach about Psalms? _____
38. What did Peter in Acts 4:25 assert about Psalm 2?____
39. The Hummel interpretation is the best of _____.
40. Hummel's interpretations are totally different from _____.
41. The CTCR's opinion on "Prophecy was made in response to _____."
42. The CTCR's opinion is written in the tradition of _____.
43. In rebuttal to the CTCR opinion Robert Preus wrote _____.
44. Preus maintained that Psalm 8:5 referred to only _____.
45. What did the CTCR say about the position of the Wisconsin Synod? _____
46. What happened in the LCMS in the fifth to eighth decade of the twentieth century? _____
47. Who are some conservative Protestants who find rectilinear prophecy in the Old Testament? _____

Dr. Raymond Surburg, Concordia Seminary, Ft. Wayne: "The Typologists Have Won"
New CTCR Statement Takes Issue With LCMS On Messianic Prophecy

By Herman Otten
Christian News, September 30, 1996

A new statement adopted by The Lutheran Church-Missouri Synod's Commission on Theology and Church Relations on "Prophecy and Typology" takes issue with the position on messianic prophecy long held in The Lutheran Church-Missouri Synod. The 1995 convention of the LCMS reaffirmed the scriptural position of the LCMS on direct rectilinear messianic prophecy with which the LCMS's CTCR now disagrees. In the LCMS, a convention resolution is above any statement its CTCR may adopt.

Dr. Raymond Surburg, retired Old Testament professor at Concordia Seminary, Fort Wayne, told *CN* that the new CTCR statement shows that "the typologists have won." Surburg has written many articles on messianic prophecy. He contends that when the New Testament says that a certain passage in the Old Testament directly refers to Jesus Christ and no one else then a confessional church body must insist that that Old Testament passage refers directly to Jesus Christ and not also someone living at the time the prophet wrote the passage. Surburg says that when the prophet Isaiah says in Isaiah 7:14 that the **Almah** ("virgin") will conceive and have a child and that this child will be called Immanuel, then the LCMS must insist that the child of this virgin is only Jesus Christ and not some child born at the time of Isaiah who lived some seven centuries before Christ. LCMS theologians who insist along with St. Matthew (1:23) and Luther that **Almah** must be translated "virgin," observe that in all history there has only been one virgin birth.

The new CTCR statement takes issue with what the Apostle Peter taught about an Old Testament passage referring directly to Jesus Christ rather than first to King David.

The new CTCR statement defends the position taken in Concordia Publishing House's Self-Study Bible (NIV) in its comments on Psalm 16:9-11.The Concordia Self Study Bible claims that "David speaks here, as in the rest of his psalms, first of all of himself . . ." Peter said that David is not here speaking about himself but only about Jesus Christ (Acts 2:25-36).

Surburg writes in his article on the new CTCR statement: "St. Peter shows (Acts 3:24) that all prophets have spoken of the time of the New Testament; for the entire Old Testament is nothing else than a preparation of the New Testament and an introduction to it."

According to Surburg, "In numerous writings Luther declares that the heart of the Scriptures is Christ and this would be the correct mode to interpret the prophecies of the Old Testament."

Surburg shows that Dr. C. F. W. Walther insisted upon rectilinear prophecy which the CTCR statement now rejects. Surburg writes: "It was especially at Concordia Seminary, St. Louis, both on Jefferson Avenue, St. Louis and 801 De Mun, Clayton, Missouri, that there were outstanding theologians like Stoeckhardt, Pardiek, F. Pieper, L. Fuerbringer, O. Graebner, P. E. Kretzmann, W. A . Maier, Sr., Engelder, Laetsch and others that followed Luther's view on Old Testament predictive Messianic prophecy. The theologians at Concordia Theological Seminary, Springfield, also followed the thinking of their fellow professors in St. Louis-Clayton relative to rectilinear Messianic prophecy."

In an article titled "If someone says 'Otten is slandering'" (*Christian News Encyclopedia*, p. 456) Dr. William Beck, author of An American Translation of the Bible, who taught part-time in the graduate school at Concordia Seminary, St. Louis, wrote: "Over five years ago the exegetical department of our seminary faculty approved by a special resolution the elimination of 'virgin' in Isaiah 7:14 in the RSV. For months I worked on this and finally succeeded in presenting to our faculty men the evidence on the 'virgin.' Then I pleaded with them to print the total evidence, everything they had for their stand and mine, in the *Concordia Theological Monthly*. Nothing was ever printed. From the time the RSV first came out I offered the *CTM* solid evidence on the many doctrinal errors in the RSV. I was twice told: 'we don't care about your evidence: we want to show people how to use the RSV.'"

After the *Concordia Self-Study Bible*, edited by various professors at Concordia Seminary, St. Louis, and Concordia Seminary, Ft. Wayne, rejected the position the LCMS had long held on direct messianic prophecy and Isaiah 7:14, *Christian News* wrote to the faculty of Concordia Seminary, St. Louis, on November 14, 1986: "Beck was greatly concerned that even some of the 'conservative' members on the faculty maintained that when Isaiah first wrote 7:14 he was not referring to the virgin Mary who came 700 years later but rather to some woman living at the time he was writing. He insisted, along with Luther, Stoeckhardt, Walter Maier and other orthodox Lutherans, that Isaiah 7:14 was a direct rectilinear messianic prophecy and not typological.

"What is the position of your faculty today? Have you repudiated the resolution adopted by the exegetical department mentioned by Beck? Does the entire faculty today insist that **almah** must be translated as 'virgin' in Isaiah 7:14 and that **almah** here is a direct reference to the Virgin Mary and can refer to no one else since in all history there has been only one virgin birth?"

Concordia Seminary responded: ". . . it is improper for you to address your letter of November 1, 1986, to the faculty or to write about the matter in *Christian News*.

"The faculty does not feel obliged to respond to your request or to any future requests from you which go beyond your call and which are contrary to the established synodical procedure."

(Editor's Note: When *Surburg's Works* went to press in October of 2017 the faculty of Concordia Seminary had still not repudiated the resolution of its exegetical department that Isaiah 7:14 does not refer to the virgin Mary.)

Surburg writes: "Beck translated the entire Bible into twentieth-century American English which was known as the Holy Bible An American Translation: (New Haven: Leader Publishing Company, 1978). In this version Beck took special note of Old Testament Messianic prophecies and in the translation, Beck indicated those passages that were Messianic by capital letters, where the Messiah was mentioned and in the margin next to the translation listed the New Testament passages where verses of the Old Testament were alluded to and fulfilled in the New Testament."

Christian News turned over the editing and publishing of An American Translation to God's Word To the Nations Bible Society when *CN* was told that large grants would be available as soon as an uncertified editor was no longer primarily responsible for the translation project. GWNBS's God's Word translation eliminated all of Beck's notations pointing out the messianic prophecies.

Surburg observes: "If Isaiah 7:14 refers to a natural birth and not a supernatural birth as the New Testament teaches, to hold that Isaiah is not specifically announcing the virginal conception and Virgin Birth would mean the Isaianic text has one meaning in the Old Testament and a different one in the New Testament."

According to Surburg, Dr. Alfred von Rohr Sauer of Concordia Seminary, St. Louis, was one of the first at Concordia Seminary to challenge the LCMS's traditional view of rectilinear messianic prophecy. He notes: "By 1964 von Rohr Sauer had undergone a theological conversion involving the adoption of higher criticism and thus he was interested in challenging his past theological and isagogical stances, and this involved the reduction of rectilinear Messianic prophecy." Sauer left Concordia and helped form Seminex. One of his students, Dr. Henry Rowold, received his Th.D. at Seminex, defended Sauer's position, and is now teaching at Concordia Seminary, St. Louis. *CN* asked Rowold if he has retracted his defense of Sauer and Seminex. Rowold did not respond.

In a section on "Horace Hummel's Typological Interpretation of the Old Testament," Surburg writes: "Hummel, in his voluminous introduction to the Old Testament, called *The Word Becoming Flesh*, presents a defense of a form of typological interpretation of Messianic prophecies, which appears to have been influenced by L. Goppelt, Typos: die typologische Deutung dies Alten Testaments." Surburg says that Hummel "practically wipes out the difference between prophecy and fulfillment. He denies predictive prophecy, even though he claims he does not. His view of predictive prophecy slides into imanentalistic directions. The essayist does not see the viability of the distinction between vertical and horizontal typology. Hummel and all those who make direct predictive Messianic prophecies typological violate the hermeneutical principle that a text has only one intended sense and does not have multiple meanings." "While Hummel prefers the translation 'virgin,' he avers that it would not be wrong for those conservatives to understand **almah** as referring to Isaiah's (future) wife and son. Thus he allows the text to have a multiple meaning! What does such an interpretation, which pleases two different schools of interpretation, due to the Lutheran belief of the perspicuity of Holy Writ?"

Commenting on the CTCR's statement on "Prophecy and Typology," Surburg writes: "The document has pulled out all the stops for the typological approach to Messianic prophecy. It contains a composite of those in the Synod, especially at our two theological seminaries, who have been gathering argumentations for the typological understanding of Messianic prophecy for years."

Surburg adds: "In rebuttal to the CTCR's use of the Post-Reformation theologians, Robert Preus specialist in Post-Reformation Lutheran theology, wrote this: 'And therefore there is not a prior reason for insisting that every Old Testament prophecy must somehow refer to the people who first heard or read it. The Old Testament abounds in rectilinear prophecies that refer only to Christ; in such a way these prophecies are understood by the New Testament, and in the same way they were to be understood when first delivered in the Old Testament."

The CTCR statement on typology and prophecy adopted on May 21, 1996, says: "We do not believe that a specific exegesis of given prophetic passages (as requested in the overture) can be legislated." A CTCR executive told *Christian News* that the overture was unanimously adopted by the CTCR. When the CTCR adopts a statement on which it has spent so many years, it is generally sent to the congregations of the LCMS with a letter from the LCMS president commending the statement. Since the CTCR statement on prophecy and typology has not yet been sent to the congregations of the LCMS, *CN* will publish the document.

CN has previously noted that the 1996 Convention of the LCMS adopted a resolution which affirmed a resolution on messianic prophecy which an overture presented to the 1988 Missouri District wanted the LCMS to affirm. The Washington Circuit Forum brought the matter to the Missouri District. The new position of the CTCR is not in accord with the position formerly taken by the LCMS and reaffirmed at the LCMS's 1995 convention.

The 1995 convention of the LCMS reaffirmed this position: "When the New Testament teaches that an Old Testament passage (e.g., Is. 7:14 and Matt. 1:23; Ps. and Acts 2:25-28,30,31) is a direct prophecy of Jesus Christ, then this messianic passage must be accepted as a direct rectilinear prophecy of Jesus Christ." *Christian News*, July 24, 1995.

The new statement of the LCMS's CTCR defends the position taken by the Concordia Self-Study Bible and not Peter. Dr. Harvey Lange, formerly a professor at Concordia Teachers College, Seward, Nebraska, argued in a Th.D. thesis for Concordia Seminary, St. Louis, that when Psalm 22 was first written it did not refer to Jesus Christ. Concordia Seminary considered Lange's position acceptable.

David wrote in Psalm 22 "My God, My God, why did You Forsake Me?" "They divide My clothes among themselves and throw lots for My garment." The New Testament says these words refer to Christ and no one else (Matthew 27:35; Mark 15:24; Luke 23:34; John 19:24). The position now taken by the LCMS's CTCR allows for a denial of what the New Testament teaches (*Christian News Encyclopedia*, pp. 661 ff.; 254,257, 546).

The Overture which the CTCR found unacceptable wanted the LCMS to reaffirm what Martin Luther and orthodox Lutheran theologians taught and what the LCMS taught until recent years:

1) "Christ's and the New Testament's interpretation of Old Testament Messianic prophecies is doctrinally binding upon all pastors and professors in the Lutheran Church-Missouri Synod."
2) "The Hebrew word '**almah**' in Isaiah 7:14 must be translated 'virgin' and can only refer to the virgin Mary and no other woman."
3) "Psalm 16,22, and 110 are direct-rectilinear prophecies of the Messiah, Jesus Christ, and did not first refer to David, Solomon, etc."

Those responsible for the overture recognize typology in the Old Testament but insist that when Jesus Christ and the writers of the New Testament say a passage in the Old Testament is a direct reference to Jesus Christ then Christians must accept what Jesus Christ and the Word of God says. The CTCR statement says that "it is clear that a simplistic, surface reading of the New Testament evidence about the fulfillment of specific prophecies may lead one astray." According to the CTCR, "on the surface Scripture negates statements or ideas that are clearly true."

The August 5, 1996, *Christian News* included the overture mentioned in the CTCR report. It is in a report published in the November 23,1987, *CN* titled: "**Almah** Must Be Translated 'virgin'-Psalm 16,22,110 Are Direct Rectilinear Prophecies of Christ—LCMS DISTRICT ASKED TO REAFFIRM ORTHODOX POSITION ON MESSIANIC PROPHECIES." The August 5, 1996, issue of *CN* also included "Why All the Secrecy About the Messianic Prophecy?"; "Both Rectilinear Messianic Prophecy and Typology in The Old Testament—CHRIST IN THE OLD TESTAMENT," "Why Is *CN* So Dangerous for Students?", "Is Peter or the CPH NIV Study Bible Correct?," and some correspondence the editor of *Christian News* had with the faculty of Concordia Seminary, St. Louis, on this matter. The letters are titled "Where Does Concordia Seminary Stand Today on Isaiah 7:14—**Almah**—Messianic Prophecy," "Beyond Your Call," and "Please Answer."

The *Christian News Encyclopedia* has articles on **Almah**, Isaiah 7:14, Hosea 11, Psalm 22, and Messianic Prophecies which defend the position taken by the New Testament and Luther and takes issue with the position of the latest statement from the LCMS's CTCR.

Questions
1. The LCMS's CTCR took issue with ____.
2. Surburg's insisted that **almah** in Isaiah 7:14 must be translated ____ and only referred to ____.
3. The CTCR statement defended what the Concordia Publishing

335

House's Self Study Bible (NIV) says about ____.

4. Dr. C.F.W. Walther insisted upon ____.

5. What did William Beck write about the exegetical department of Concordia Seminary, St. Louis? ____

6. How did the faculty of Concordia Seminary, St. Louis respond in 1986? ____

7. What did Surburg write about Beck and messianic prophecy? ____

8. Concordia Seminary, St. Louis Professor Henry Rowold received his Th.D. from ____.

9. What did Surburg write about *The Word Become Flesh* by Horace Hummel? ____

10. What was the position of Robert Preus on Messianic prophecy? ____

11. What did the Washington Circuit Forum bring to the Missouri District? ____

12. What did the LCMS's 1995 convention resolve about direct rectilinear prophecy? ____

13. Harvey Lange of Concordia Teachers College, Seward, Nebraska argued in his Th.D. thesis for Concordia Seminary, St. Louis ____.

The Christ of the Old Testament
A Knowledge of the Christ of the Old Testament as Set Forth by the New Testament, An Excellent Preparation for the Celebration of the Birth of Christ

Christian News, December 23, 1996

The Protestant European Biblical scholar Vischer reasoned that the hallmark of Christian theology is that it is Christology, a theology can affirm nothing of God except and through Jesus Christ. It is clear that all knowledge of God which resides in the Old Testament is mediated through Christ Jesus. Consequently the theological exposition of these writings within the Church can be nothing other than Christology.[1] Vischer began his volume, *Das Christuszeugnis des Alten Testaments* with the words of Christ: "Search the Scriptures; for in them you think that you have eternal life and they are they which testify of me" (John 5:39).[2]

Vischer in the twentieth century was enunciating the same views as the one the Protestant reformers did. The Luther scholar Ewald Plass claimed that Luther also found Christ everywhere in the Old Testament. The Wittenberg Reformer already in his first Psalm lectures (1513-1516) refers to the suffering of Christ in Ps. 102:5. Luther identified Christ with the God of the Old Testament. All revelations God gave the Old Testament believers necessarily came through Christ, and this included the Ten Commandments.[3] The Wittenberg professor contended that in 2 Samuel 23:1-7 that it was Christ who spoke to Moses the words of the Decalogue.[4] In this Messianic prophecy, of which Christ is the subject and not Solomon, the Old Testament must be explained in the light of the New Testament's teachings. In his book, *The Bondage of the Will,* Luther informed the scholar, Erasmus, that there are obscurities in Scripture, yet these were peripheral. Christ and His salvation was central to the whole Scriptures.[5] To omit the centrality of Christ for the Scriptures which existed before Christ's birth was to do an injustice to the interpretation and proper understanding of the larger part of the Holy Writ, found in the 39 books of the Old Testament. In one of his writings Luther argued "what matter of more importance can be hidden in Scriptures now that the seals are broken, the stone is rolled away from the sepulcher, and the greatest of all mysteries is brought to light, Christ, the Son of God made God-man Triune God and yet One, Christ: who suffered for us and will rule eternally? Take Christ out of the Scriptures and what else will you find in them?"[6]

Luther's Christological understanding of the Old Testament was drawn from the New Testament and based on various indications found in the Old Testament itself.[7] Luther was simply asserting what Jesus Christ Himself claimed. To the Jews the Savior declared: "You are searching the Scriptures because you suppose that in them you have eternal life, and though these are they that bear witness concerning me, you will not come to me that you may have life" (John 5:39-40).

337

On Easter afternoon Christ explained to Cleophas and his friend that the happenings of Good Friday and the following Sunday morning had been predicted centuries before and asserted: "And beginning with Moses and the prophets, He interpreted to them in all the Scriptures the things concerning himself" (Luke 24:27, RSV). In the same chapter, on Easter evening, Jesus claimed that the three divisions of the Old Testament: The Law, the Prophets and the Psalms spoke of Him and also reminded the disciple on that memorable evening: "This is what I told you: Everything must be fulfilled that was written about men, the Law of Moses, the Prophets, and Psalms" (Luke 24:44). After opening their minds, He further said: "This is what is written: The Christ will suffer and rise from the dead on the third day" (Luke 24:46, NIV).

Paul, called by Jesus on the Damascene Road, told his spiritual son Timothy, that he had been brought to faith in Christ Jesus by the Old Testament Scriptures (2 Timothy 3:15-16). There are numerous statements in the Pauline preaching and writings to the effect that the Old Testament clearly spoke of many happenings that occurred in Christ's life. The Corinthian congregation was told that Paul delivered to them the ABC of Christianity, namely that Jesus died and rose again according to the Scriptures (1 Corinthians 15:2). Luke, the great church historian, told in his volume acts dealing with the growth and expansion of Christianity, how Paul in Rome had a meeting with a Jewish contingent. "He expounded the matter to them testifying to the kingdom of God and persuading them about Jesus from morning till evening from the Law of Moses and from the Prophets" (Acts 28:23).

Peter, upon whose confession that Christ was the Son of God the church was built, shared the same attitude about the Old Testament's teaching about the Messiah. The Rock Man in his sermons in Acts, and in his epistles stressed the truth that the whole Old Testament pointed to Christ, both to Christ's suffering and death, he told his compatriots. "But the thing which God announced beforehand by the mouth of all the prophet that His Christ should suffer, he was thus fulfilled (Acts 3:18 NASB)." To the same audience Peter declared: "Likewise all the prophets who have spoken, from Samuel and his successors onward also announced these days (Acts 3:24, NASB)." Before the Roman centurion and his gathering Peter uttered these significant words: "And he commanded us to preach to the people, and to testify that he is the one ordained of God to be judge of the living and the dead. To him all prophets bear witness that everyone who believes in him receives forgiveness of sins through his name" (Acts 10:42; RSV).

One of the most informative passages about Christ as found in the Old Testament is Peter's instruction as contained in the latter part of chapter 1 of his first letter to the congregations of Asia Minor (I Peter 1:10-12), which reads: "As to this salvation the prophets who prophesied of the grace that would come to you made careful search and inquiry seeking to know what person or time the Spirit of Christ within them was indicated as he predicted the sufferings of Christ and the glories to follow. It was revealed to them that they were not serving themselves, but you, in these things which now have been announced to you by the Holy Spirit sent from heaven—things into which angels long to look (NASB)." Other writers who found Christ predicted in the Old Testament were John, the author of the Epistle to the Hebrews and the four evangelists.

It is the belief of New Testament writers that the Christian Church was a continuation of the Old Testament Church, which believed that apart from Christ there was no salvation. Yes, Jesus, born in Bethlehem and who spent most of his life in Nazareth is the center and heart of the whole Bible, of which the Old Testament is the foundation. What the sun is to the world that Christ is to the Scriptures. The many Messianic prophecies in the Old Testament testify to the importance of Jesus in the true scheme of Christian theology. It is certainly appropriate at Christmas that the Christians should constantly bear in mind the redemptive work of Jesus Christ and the work of justification by faith as the core of revealed Biblical religion. Only when the Christological character of the Old Testament is remembered can Christmas be adequately celebrated.

I. The Person of Christ
1. Christ's Deity Taught in the Old Testament[8]

Only God's Son could destroy the Devil and his program and work (Gen. 3:15; Rom. 16:20). Jesus informed the Jews that "before Abraham was I Am" thus teaching that Christ existed before Abraham and his times who lived in the third millennium before Christ. According to the message given Abraham all nations were to be blessed through Abraham's SEED (Cf. Gal. 3:13). Only God could accomplish the salvation of the nations. Because of His deity, all nations would seek after the LION OF THE TRIBE OF JUDAH (Gen. 49:1). Because Jesus possessed deity, Yahweh did say to His Son: "You are My Son, today I have begotten you" (Psalm 2:7; Heb. 1:5). Jesus assured His followers that the Messiah to whom God spoke the words in Psalm 110:11 "was the LORD" of whom David spoke (Cf. Matt. 22:43-44; Mark 12:36; Luke 20:42-43). God is described as having anointed Jesus of Nazareth with the Holy Spirit beyond measure (Acts 10:38). The prophet Isaiah predicted that the virgin-born Son would be called Immanuel, i.e., "God with us." This means that Christ, although a man, at the same time, was God, beginning His humanity in the womb of the Virgin Mary. In the beginning of the second half of Isaiah 40-66, Israel is told about the Messiah: "Behold! Your God." In the seventh century B.C. the prophet Jeremiah, in a Messianic prophecy, in speaking about the future Messiah said that He would be "Yahweh our righteousness" (23:5-6).

Solomon in Proverbs 9:23-31 speaks about the Messiah as the wisdom of God, who was Creator with the Father and the Holy Spirit.[9] In certain passages in Proverbs Christ, as the wisdom of God, is described as Creator with the Father and present before anything that was created (Cf. John 1:1-3). In one of the most remarkable Messianic prophecies Isaiah declared this: "For unto us a Child is born unto us a Son is given, and the government will be upon His shoulder and His name will be called Wonderful, counselor, Mighty God, Everlasting Father, Prince of Peace, of the increase of His government and peace there will be no end" (8:6-7). The deity of the Messiah, the Christ, is clearly taught in the Old Testament Scriptures, just as it is put forth in various passages in the Scriptures of the New Covenant.

The **Maleakh Yahweh** (the Angel of the LORD), which occurs a number of times in Genesis and other Old Testament books, describes the Angel of the LORD as different from the Father.[10] In certain passages the Angel of the LORD, a separate person from the Father is depicted as God. There are a number of passages that distinguish between YAHWEH, the Messiah and the Spirit of God, three persons in one divine essence.

2. Christ's Humanity

In God's first Messianic prophecy the SEED of the woman who will destroy Satan is said to be a descendant of Eve, the mother of all living humans. The humanity of the Messiah is found as an integral part of all Messianic prophecies, of which there are many scattered throughout the three major divisions of the Old Testament, i.e., the Law, the Prophets and the Writings.

The patriarchs, Abraham, Isaac, and Jacob, were told of the SEED who would redeem the nations. In the SEED all the nations shall be blessed. In Galatians, Paul identified the promise given to Abram and Isaac as Christ (3:16). In Numbers 24:17, Moses records the prophecy that there would come a star out of Jacob indicating that the future Redeemer would be of kingly stature, that is a man. In his farewell to the people whom he had guided for forty years, Moses announced the coming of a great Prophet, to whom the people would listen (Deut. 18:15-18). The prophet Isaiah describes the coming of the Messiah as being a humble one, "for there shall come forth a Rod from the stem of Jesse, and a Branch shall grow out of his roots" (11:1). The prophet Jeremiah hundreds of years before Christ's birth informed his countrymen that there would come a future king, who would be descended from David. There is no lack of Old Testament texts that portray the Messiah as a human being (Jer. 23:5-6).

3. Christ's Sinlessness

Because the Messiah was going to accomplish perfectly for mankind which the latter could not achieve for itself namely fulfill God's requirements for its justification, it was essential that the Messiah should be sinless.[11] Christ beginning as a human person in womb of the Virgin Mary, His conception was effected by the Holy Spirit thus the Messiah was protected from the taint of sin, for the angel Gabriel informed Mary that that Holy Life which was found in her was none other than Emmanuel i.e., "God with us" (Luke 1:35): Isaiah in his Fourth Servant Song (52:13-53:12) described the Messiah as "the Righteous One." In the same song the Messiah is portrayed as a lamb led to the slaughter, was held up before Israel as One who had not done any wrong, that there was no deceit in His mouth (53:9).

4. The Works of Christ

Christ participated in the creation of this universe. Thus the Psalmist David in Psalm 33:6 wrote under inspiration of the Holy Spirit: "By the Word of the Lord were heavens made and by the breath of His mouth all their hosts." David's son Solomon in Proverbs 8:22-30 gives a description of Christ as the Personal Wisdom of God. In a creation passage Solomon said of the Messiah, the Second Person of the Godhead: "When he prepared the heavens I was there, when he drew a circle on the face when he established the cloud's above, when he strengthened the foundations of the earth, then I was beside him as a master craftsman" (8:29-29). This interpretation agrees with John 1:1-3; Colossians 1:16; and Hebrews 1:2. Outstanding in Christ's ministry. The climax of Christ's ministry was the work of redemption achieved on Mt. Calvary.

II. Christ's State of Humiliation

On the basis of the Apostles' Creed Christian theologians have discussed Christ's state of humiliation and proposed the following steps: 1. Manner of conception; 2. Manner and circumstances of Birth; 3. The Circumcision; 4. Life in Nazareth; 5. Public Life and Ministry; 6. Passion; 7. Death; and 8. Burial.[12] Isaiah 7:14 predicted both the conception and virgin-born birth fulfilled in Mary's giving birth to Jesus who will save His people from their sins. Although the Messiah was the Creator and Sustainer of the universe Isaiah portrays Christ as a root coming out of dry ground (11:1). He had no comeliness which would cause mankind to recognize Him for Who He was. The eight-century prophet Micah predicted that the Messiah would be born in Bethlehem of Judea (5:2; Matthew 2:6).

The Old Testament has a number of prophecies that foretold a number of happenings of Jesus thirty-three year life. Hosea the prophet (11:1) [Ed. Numbers 24:8] predicted that the Holy Family would flee to Egypt (Matt. 2:15). Jeremiah announced hundreds of years in advance the killing of innocent infants by jealous Herod (Matt. 2:16-18), Matthew indicated that Jesus would be taken to Nazareth by His parents after Herod's demise (Matt. 2:23) and called a Nazarene. Matthew had probably Isaiah 11:1 in mind where Messiah's lowly birth is described. The Hebrew text reads: "weyatza hoter mitzerah Jishai," "and there shall come forth a shoot from the stock of Jesse," and a **nezer** shall grow out of his roots. The Hebrew word **nezer** suggested the concept of Christ being called a "Nazarene."[13] When all infants two years and under were slaughtered, there was great wailing in Bethlehem, an event Jeremiah had predicted in chapter 31:15 and fulfilled in Matthew 2:18.

Both Isaiah and Malachi foretold the coming of John the Baptist (Is. 40:1-5; Mal. 4:5-6). Matthew (3:3), Mark (1:3) and John 1:25 cite Malachi 3:1, Is. 40:3 as the way preparer for Jesus in the Judean wilderness. Mark 1:2, Luke 7:27 cite Mal. 3:1 and Is. 40:3 as predicting John as the forerunner. David in Psalm 69:9 announces the first cleansing of the Temple, so John reports in his account of the Judean ministry of Christ (2:17). The beginning of the Galilean ministry of our Lord was depicted centuries before in chapter 9:1-2; thus Matthew reported in his account of Phase 1 of the Galilean ministry (Matthew 4:14-16). This also included Jesus return to Capernaum. Peter in his speech in Acts 3:22-23 and Stephen in his defense of his life and ministry spoke of Christ's work as a prophet and cited Deuteronomy 18:15,16,19. Both Luke and Matthew quote from the second part of Isaiah (i.e., 40-66; 42:1-4) and 61:1-2 to support Christ's ministry of compassion and 53:4 as predictive of Christ's healing work (Matthew 8:17). The writer of the Hebrews Letter adduces Psalm 110:4 for the historical occurrence that in Christ's ministry he exercised besides the Prophetic and Kingly offices also the High Priestly.

1. The Suffering and Passion of Christ

The Old Testament has outstanding prophecies announcing Christ's suffering, passion and death, a part of His Priestly office. Psalm 22 and the fourth Servant Song (Is. 52:13-53:12) announced centuries before their occurrence various aspects of the passive obedience of Christ. Liberal scholarship as well as conservative savants do not recognize the true Messianic character of Psalm 22.[14] On the strength of past and present Biblical scholarship, this writer considers Psalm 22 as "The Psalm of the Cross and of Resurrection Victory." Its opening words were used by Christ in the darkest moment of His life (cf. Matt. 27:46; Mark 15:34). Jesus ascribed His exceeding sorrow to God and His treatment of Him as Surety and as the substitute of mankind, including the Jews.

David in Psalm 22 stated that Christ would suffer at the hands for righteousness sake. This side of Christ's Passion is fully dwelt upon. The Psalmist ascribed the Messiah's suffering to God. The vicarious atonement is clearly taught in Psalm 22. Christ was to suffer at the hands of evil men. This side of Christ's suffering is completely emphasized. With amazing force and accuracy the rage and fury of His foes are depicted. They rush upon Him like ferocious beasts. They roared about Him like the savage bulls of Basham. He stands among them as though surrounded by baying dogs. He is innocent and guileless like the hunted hind.[15] In Psalm 40, a Messianic psalm, the Messiah exclaimed: "Be pleased, O Lord, to deliver me, make haste, O Lord, to help me. Let those be turned back and dishonored who delight in my hurt" (40:13-15).

The Gospel records show that Jesus' contemporaries generally hardened their hearts against God's Messiah (Isaiah 6:9-10). Isaiah 53:1 and Psalm 118:22-23 and Isaiah 8:14 predicted the rejection of the Christ by the Jews. Psalms 35:19 and 69:4 indicated centuries before Christ's public ministry that the Messiah would be hated by many Jewish people.

A number of the events that the Gospels record that occurred during Holy Week relative to Christ's suffering and death were foretold by the postexilic prophet Zechariah.[16] In 9:9 Christ's triumphal entrance into Jerusalem is foretold (Cf. Matthew 21:5; John 12:14-15). The second part of Zechariah (9-14) listed a number of events of Christ's Passion. There are thus found predictions about the Messiah's betrayal, seizure, capture and abandonment. In chapter 13:7 Haggai's contemporary stated that the Messiah would experience the cowardice of His disciples while in

Psalm 41:9 that Judas would betray Him. The disciple Judas's end is depicted prophetically in Zechariah 11:12-13. David in Psalm 2 announced a thousand years beforehand that the mighty would conspire against the Lord and His Messiah (Acts 4:25-26). The great Old Testament Passion Psalm, 22, predicted that Christ would thirst (John 19:28). The Old Testament writers had prophecies as to what would happen to Christ's body on the cross. Psalm 34:20 announced that the Lord's bones would not be broken. Zechariah predicted a half century before the death of the Messiah, that His side would be pierced a fact that John has recorded in chapter 19:37.

2. The Death and Burial of the Messiah, Jesus Christ

In the Fourth Servant passage the eighth-century son of Amoz announced: "He was taken from prison and from judgment and who will declare His generation? He was cut off from the land of the living and who will declare his generation?" (v. 8). In verse 13 God's spokesman ended his great song "For he bore the sins of many and made intercession for the transgressors." The same prophet has this about the burial of Jesus: "He was assigned a grave with the wicked and with the rich in his death though he had done no violence nor was deceit in his mouth." Before Christ died Psalm 22:18 foretold that his garments were to be divided, a fact that John in 19:24 reports.

III. The State of Exaltation
1. Christ's Resurrection

Paul informed the Corinthians that he had brought them the very essence of Christianity, namely, that Christ died and rose again according to the Old Testament Scriptures. Nathan in 2 Samuel 7:12-13 predicted Christ's resurrection. Some scholars believe that Hosea 6:2 may also possibly announce the Savior's resurrection. Isaiah indicated that God would lengthen the Messiah's days (53:10).

2. Christ's Ascension

In his Ephesian Letter Paul discusses Christ's ascending on high and the Son's return to the glory that had been His before assuming life in the body of Mary. Thus Paul asserted: "Thou hast ascended on high, Thou has led captivity captive and gave gifts to men" (Psalm 68:18, Ephesians 4:8). Peter on the day of Pentecost declared: "For David did not ascend into heaven: But he himself said: 'The Lord said to my Lord, sit thou on my right hand until I make thine enemies a footstool under thy feet'" Acts 2:34).

3. The Exaltation of Christ at the Right Hand

There are a number of passages that set forth Christ's exaltation after His Passion. In addition to Peter's assertion in Acts 2:34-35, the session at the right hand of God was the direct result of the Ascension. The writer of the Hebrews Letter asked: "To which of the angels has he ever said: Sit at my right hand, till I make thy foes a footstool for thy feet" (1:13).

The Session of Christ at God's right hand was predicted by David, in one of the important Old Testament Messianic Psalms. Christ in controversy with the Pharisees, quoted the opening verse of Psalm 110: "The Lord said unto my Lord, sit thou on my right hand, until I put thine enemies beneath thy feet?" as proof that David was not speaking of himself but of the Messiah.

Between the Resurrection and the Ascension's forty days, the New Testament refers to the matter of Judas' replacement. Peter, in the Upper Room, stated that it had been foreordained that Judas had to be replaced in the apostolic group of Twelve, and cited Psalm 109: "Let his days be few, and let another take his office" (v. 8) and Peter also quoted Psalm 69:25.

4. Christ's Promise to Send the Paraclete

In his farewell address Christ promised His disciples the gift of the Holy Spirit whom He would send from the Father, a promise fulfilled on the Day of Pentecost. This remarkable event was announced by the prophet Joel in chapter 2:28-32 (English text) and in the Hebrew 3:1-5, the New Testament used the Septuagint's translation.

IV. The Redemptive Work of Christ

The Old Testament expressed on different occasions the truth that Yahweh would redeem Israel.

Thus David prayed at the end of Psalm 25: "Redeem Israel, O God, out of all troubles." How God effected man' redemption is adequately described by Isaiah in his Fourth Servant song. Thus God's prophet asserted: "Surely he took our infirmities and carried our sorrow, yet we considered him stricken by God, smitten by him and afflicted. But he was pierced for our transgression, he was crushed for our iniquities; but the punishment that brought us peace was upon him and by his wounds we are healed" (vv. 4-5). Again: "For he was cut off from the land of the living: For the transgression of my people he was stricken" (v. 8).

Toward the end of the Fourth Song Isaiah is made to predict: "by his knowledge my righteous servant will justify many and bear their iniquities" (v. 11). The last verse of Isaiah 53 states: "For he bore the sin of many, and made intercession for the transgressors." There are no less than eighteen verses of Isaiah 53 in the New Testament that interpret Isaiah as describing Christ's suffering, innocent suffering, his vicarious atonement, the justifying work as affecting repentant sinners, His resurrection and ultimate victory. However there are New Testament passages which cite and use the Fourth Servant Song (Matthew 8:17; 1 Peter 2:24; Acts 8:32; Revelation 5:, 12; 13:8; 14:5; 1 John 3:5; Romans 5:19; 4:25; Philippians 2:7-9; Ephesians 5:2, 25; Mark 15:28; Luke 22:37; Hebrews 9:28; Galatians 4:27.

1. The Universal Expansion of the Gospel

Already to the Three Patriarchs God announced that the nations of the earth would be blessed by Abraham's Seed. Various Old Testament passages proclaimed the truth that the salvation given originally to the Jews should become available to non-Jews. Isaiah called on people outside of Israel: "Listen to me, you islands, hear this you distant nations, before I was born the LORD called from my birth, he has made mention of my name" (49:1). Other Old Testament passages proclaiming the universal expansion of the Gospel would be: Amos 9:11-12; Hosea 2:23; 1:10; Deut. 32:43; 2 Sam. 22:50; Psalm 18:49; 117:1, Isaiah 11:10 the New Testament fulfillments are found in assertions in Luke 24:47; Acts 13:47; Acts 15:14-18; Romans 9:25-26; Romans 15:9-12; Galatians 3:8; and 4:27.

2. The Hardening of the Jews Against the Gospel
Isaiah 6:9-10; Deut. 29:4; Psalm 35:8; 69:22-23 (Isaiah 29:10), Isaiah 10:22-23 (Hos. 1:10), originating in various periods of Old Testament history predicted the hardening of heart by Jews against the Gospel. In the New Testament it becomes clear from Acts 28:26-27; Romans 9:27,33 and 11:8-10 that hardening of many Jews had set in as their own prophets has announced centuries before.

3. The Persecutions of Christians
St. Paul in Romans 8 warned Christians among dangers facing their faith was "persecution," and as proof cited Psalm 44:22.

4. Christ's Viewing of Believers as His Brethren
The Hebrew Letter's author in chapter 2:12-13 announced that believers were Christ's brothers, a truth Psalm 22:22; Isaiah 8:17 (Septuagint and 8:18) has foretold.

5. The Blessings of the New Covenant
The Bible, in both testaments described two different covenants, which would characterize God's revelation to humanity. In the Old Testament Exodus 29:45; Lev. 26:12; Ezek. 37:27 (Is. 52:11); Jeremiah 32:38 (Ezek. 20:34), describe the nature of the covenant God gave his people. Jeremiah 32:13-34; 33-34 compare the Old Covenant with a future one, of which the New Testament speaks. The prophecy of Jeremiah 31:31-35 was fulfilled in the New Testament, this is the contention of Paul in 2 Corinthians 6:6-18; and also that of the writer of Hebrews, as he does in 8:8-12; 10:16-17.

6. The Appropriation of Christ's Salvation
The acquisition of the blessings of salvation are made available through preaching. The preaching brings about faith and conversion. Isaiah 53:11 says that the Righteous Servant will declare many justified. In Psalm 22, in part 2, the resurrection portion, the Messiah declared that He would proclaim God's name. In Isaiah 49:1 Zion is called upon to listen to God's salvatory message. In Psalm 22 the Messiah asserted: "In all parts of the world people will remember and come back to the LORD, all the families of the nations will worship you, because the LORD is King and rules all nation (22:23)." Men and women may have food and do not

need to pay for it (Is. 55:1). The grace of God makes salvation freely available to all men.

7. The Gathering of the Church
Jacob announced that unto Shiloh would be gathering of the nations (Genesis 49:10), future generations would render the Messiah their obedience. In Psalm 117:1 the Psalmist calls upon the nations to praise Yahweh and that all peoples should extol the LORD, whose love is great toward them. In New Testament times this could only be the true believers who constitute the Church. The Book of Acts and the subsequent history of the Church show how these invitations applying to the future were fulfilled.

8. The Realization of Salvation
The Old Testament believed in a life after death and a happy existence with the Triune God. David in Psalm 17 believed that he and others would see God's faith in righteousness, when David and fellow believers will "be satisfied with seeing your likeness" (v. 15). Job in chapter 19:25-27 expressed the hope that with his own eyes, in his resurrected body he would see Christ. The New Testament shows how these wishes and predictions were fulfilled by Christ who rose from the dead and became the first fruits of those whom Christ will bring back to life. The New Testament has many more comforting passages about the afterlife and heaven, and about the enjoyment of the beatific vision.

Footnotes
1. Wilhelm Vischer, *Das Cristuszeugnis des Alten Testaments* (Zollikon-Zuerich: Evangelisher Verlag, 1943), Erster Teil, Das Gesetz, pp. 7-46
2. **Ibid.**, p. 5.
3. Weimar Edition of *Luther's Works*, as cited by Ewald Plass. *What Luther Says* (St. Louis: Concordia Publishing House, 1959), No. 440, I, p. 148.
4. Weimar 54, 62 as cited by Plass, **op. cit.**, I, No. 435. p. 147.
5. Weimar, 18606, Plass, **op. cit.**, No. 437, I, p. 148.
6. Weimar Edition of *Luther's Works*, 18, 606.
7. Cf. H. Wayne House, *Chronological and Background Charts of the New Testament* (Grand Rapids: Zondervan Publishing House, 1981), pp. 98-101; O. M. Norlie, *The Open Bible* (Minneapolis: Augsburg Publishing House, 1918), pp. 644-646. Henry H. Halley, *Halley's Bible Handbook* (Grand Rapids: Zondervan Publishing House, 1965), pp. 387-401.
8. J.T. Mueller, *Christian Dogmatics* (St. Louis: Concordia Publishing House, 1955), pp. 256-257.
9. Louis Fuerbringer, "Persoenliche Weisheit Gottes," *Concordia Theological Monthly*, 4:241-248; 321-329; 401-407. April, May, June, 1933.
10. "Angel of the Lord," in Erwin L. Lueker, *Lutheran Cyclopedia* (St. Louis: Concordia Publishing House. 1954), pp. 31-32.
11. Francis Pieper, *Christian Dogmatics* (St. Louis: Concordia Publishing House, 1951), II, pp. 73-74.
12. Joseph Stump. *The Christian Faith - A System of Christian Dogmatics* (New York: The Macmillan Company, 1932), pp. 167-169.
13. "Nazarene," Henry Snyder Gehman, *The New Westminster Dictionary of the Bible* (Philadelphia: The Westminster Press, 1970), p. 653.
14. Cf. Psalm 22 in *Concordia Self-Study Bible* (St. Louis: Concordia Publishing

House, 1986), p. 805-06.

15. George Stoeckhardt, *Lectures on Select Psalms*. Presented in English by H.W. Degner (Lake Mills, Iowa, 1965), pp. 65-83.
16. Stump, **op. cit.**, pp. 170-180.
17. L. Fuerbringer, "Sacharja, der Prophet der Hoffnung," Synodal=Bericht, North Wiscon=districks, (St. Louis, Concordia Publishing House, 1919), p. 9; Halley **op. cit.**, p. 383.

Questions

1. The hallmark of Christian theology is that it is ____.
2. All knowledge of God in the Old Testament is mediated through ____.
3. Luther found Christ everywhere in the ____.
4. Who is the center and heart of the entire Bible? ____
5. Solomon in Proverbs 9 speaks about the Messiah as ___.
6. Did Christ participate in the creation of the universe? ____
7. What did Isaiah 7:14 predict? ____
8. The author considers Psalm 22 as ____.
9. Psalm 35:19 and 69:4 indicated that the Messiah would be hated by ____.
10. What did Psalm 22 predict would happen to the garments of the Messiah? ____
11. David was not speaking of himself but of ____.
12. There are no less than eighteen verses in Isaiah 53 that predict ____.
13. Job in chapter 19:25-27 expressed the hope that ____.

www.ingramcontent.com/pod-product-compliance
Lightning Source LLC
Chambersburg PA
CBHW021958090426
42811CB00001B/81